W9-BEB-410

THE TREASURER'S HANDBOOK OF FINANCIAL MANAGEMENT

Applying the Theories, Concepts and Quantitative Methods of Corporate Finance

TREASURY MANAGEMENT ASSOCIATION

PROBUS PUBLISHING

Chicago, Illinois
Cambridge, England

© 1995, Treasury Management Association

ALL RIGHTS RESERVED. No part of this publication may be reproduced, stored in a retrieval system, or transmitted, in any form or by any means, electronic, mechanical, photocopying, recording, or otherwise, without the prior written permission of the publisher and the author.

This publication is designed to provide accurate and authoritative information in regard to the subject matter covered. It is sold with the understanding that the author and the publisher are not engaged in rendering legal, accounting, or other professional service.

Authorization to photocopy items for internal or personal use, or the internal or personal use of specific clients, is granted by PROBUS PUBLISHING COMPANY, provided that the U.S. $7.00 per page fee is paid directly to Copyright Clearance Center, 222 Rosewood Drive, Danvers, MA 01923, USA; Phone: 1-508-750-8400. For those organizations that have been granted a photocopy license by CCC, a separate system of payment has been arranged. The fee code for users of the Transactional Reporting Service is 1-55738-884-9/95/$00.00 + $7.00.

ISBN 1-55738-884-9

Printed in the United States of America

BB

1 2 3 4 5 6 7 8 9 0

CB

Probus books are available at quantity discounts when purchased for business, educational, or sales promotional use. For more information, please call the Director, Corporate/Institutional Sales at (800) 998-4644, or write:

Director, Corporate/Institutional Sales
Probus Publishing Company
1925 N. Clybourn Avenue
Chicago, IL 60614
PHONE (800) 998-4644   FAX (312) 868-6250

The Treasurer's Handbook of Financial Management

About the Author

Dubos J. Masson, Ph.D., CCM, is the author of The Treasurer's Handbook of Financial Management and a principal of The Resource Alliance, a Colorado-based, independent consulting firm specializing in management education, executive consulting, process redesign and treasury operation audits. Masson was the editor of the Treasury Management Guide—A Practitioner's Handbook.

About the Editors

John G. Oros, CCM, was the editor of the project. Mr. Oros is the assistant treasurer for Welbilt Corporation in Stamford, Connecticut, where he is responsible for treasury operations, liquidity, working capital management, bank relations, exposure management, foreign exchange, interest and risk management.

Michael J. Flagg, an associate editor, is the vice president - finance for Alliance Capital in New York. His experience includes treasury, tax, strategic planning, mergers, acquisitions, divestitures and restructuring in investment management, manufacturing, distribution, telecommunications and banking industries.

Basil P. Mavrovitis, CCM, CCE, an associate editor, is the senior vice president and chief financial officer for Eastern Cable Network in Stamford, Connecticut. He has more than 17 years experience in working capital management, treasury and credit management with four Fortune 100 companies.

About Treasury Management Association

The Treasury Management Association is the principal organization representing private sector treasury professionals. The TMA supports the treasury management profession through continuing education, professional certification, publications, industry standards and government relations. Today, the Treasury Management Association represents more than 7,500 treasury professionals who work for 3,000 corporations and other organizations. These organizations are drawn generally from the Fortune 1,000 and the largest of the middle-market companies. Contact the TMA at 301-907-2862.

Table of Contents

9   Managing and Financing Inventories   239

10   Fiancial Analysis   251

11   Financial Planning and Control   287

Preface and Acknowledgments

The planning and writing of this text has been a long but rewarding process, and there have been many individuals who contributed their efforts to ensure its completion. This project would not have been possible without the funding and support of the Treasury Management Association (TMA), headed by Donald Manger, President and Chief Executive Officer. In particular, I would like to thank Jacqueline Callahan, TMA's Director of Professional Development, who was the driving force behind the many meetings and revisions required to create this text. The excellent task force volunteers also made the writing and the editing of the material both an educational and rewarding experience.

The chair of the task force, John Oros, was responsible for making the editorial meetings both productive and efficient. In addition, his incisive comments helped to provide consistency in the structure and format of this text, especially in the financial analysis and capital budgeting chapters. Michael Flagg was extremely helpful in providing information and comments on the long-term finance and capital markets chapters, while Basil Mavrovitis kept things in line for the working capital management chapters. The entire task force pitched in to make sure the chapters on specialty treasury management topics were up-to-date and accurate.

I would like to thank my research assistants in Colorado, Ann Philpot and John Mann, for their efforts to track down a myriad of miscellaneous facts and information needed for the final completion of many of the checklists, calculations, and tables. Ruth Andersen of EDI Partners provided helpful reviews of several of the earlier versions of financial planning and capital budgeting chapters. Also, my thanks go to my business partner, David Wikoff, who provided many useful editorial comments and carried a heavier share of our business responsibilities while I completed the final stages of the text.

In the final stages of publishing the text, I would like to thank Margaret Yao Pursell, TMA's Director of Communications, for her hard work and good humor during this tedious (but very necessary) stage of the project, as well as Robert Bowen, who copyedited the entire text and made many useful corrections and improvements.

I would like to thank both the authors and the editors of the *Treasury Management Guide,* the predecessor to this text. The authors of the *Guide* include Professor Mac Clouse of the University of Denver, David Cox of the University of Denver, Alan Cunningham of Cash Forecasting Associates, Dr. George Head of the Insurance Institute of America, Professor

Ned Hill of Brigham Young University, and Professor Bill Sartoris of Indiana University. The Associate Editor of the Guide was Ken Emens of Rhode-Poulenc Rorer, Inc. and the Assistant Editors included Alan Cunningham of Cash Management Associates, Jim Grenfell of BellSouth Company, and Homer Sessions of Public Company of Colorado.

I would like to thank my parents for their understanding and support, especially when this project kept me too busy to visit. Finally, and most importantly, my thanks go to my wife Betsy for her patience, support, and understanding while I was spending many days (and nights) working on this publication.

Dubos J. Masson

1 Introduction and Overview

I. General Introduction

The primary purpose of this text is to provide the treasury professional with a guide to the theories, quantitative methodologies, and step-by-step application of these concepts to the area of treasury management. In essence, it is a how-to book for treasurers, and can be used as either a reference or as a study guide. The topics covered in this text are:

- Capital Structure
  - Capital Market Relations
  - Mergers and Acquisitions
  - Costs of Capital
- Working Capital Management
  - Inventory Management
- Financial Planning and Analysis and Capital Budgeting
- Specialty Topics
  - Electronic Data Interchange
  - Insurance and Risk Management
  - Employee Pension Fund and Benefit Management
  - Tax, Legal, Audit, and Ethical Issues

II. How to Use This Book

Practicing treasurers and senior financial executives can utilize this book as a reference for financial topics or as a guide to assist in expanding their financial knowledge base. It is useful to anyone interested in learning more about the duties and responsibilities of treasurers. Since this text details the activities of treasurers in their various areas of responsibility, it can be used to help benchmark practices in a specific firm against common treasury management practices. References to additional readings or source materials are provided throughout the text where appropriate.[1]

III. General Overview of Topics

A. What Is Treasury Management?

In general, treasury management concerns all the actions and responsibilities related to the assets of the firm. Treasurers have overall financial responsibility for the assets of the firm, including their purchase, financing and disposal. In the broadest sense, treasury management responsibility flows from the chief financial officer (or the equivalent) and encompasses both long-term and short-term financial responsibilities of the firm.

The *Treasurer's Handbook of Financial Management* covers four basic topic areas:

1. **Long-Term Corporate Finance:** This area includes corporate finance topics such as: capital structure, capital market relations, cost of capital, and mergers and acquisitions.

2. **Working Capital Management:** This area focuses primarily on the short-term aspects of financial management, including: working capital policy, short-term investment and borrowing, and the management of receivables, payables and inventory.

3. **Other Corporate Finance Areas:** This area includes the topics of: financial analysis and planning, capital budgeting and leasing.

4. **Specialty Topics in Treasury Management:** This area includes the topics of: electronic data interchange; insurance and risk management; employee pension fund and benefits management; and tax, legal, audit, and ethical issues.

B. Corporate Finance

The discipline of corporate finance covers a wide variety of topics of interest to the treasurer. Treasury management, working capital management and cash management are all just subsets of corporate finance. For our purposes, the term corporate finance will refer primarily to the long-term side of treasury management (more than 1 year); the term working capital management will refer to the short-term side (less than 1 year). Specifically, in the corporate finance area we will cover the following material:

1. **Overview of Capital Markets and Capital Market Relations:** (Chapters 2 and 3) This portion of the material includes the external relations of the treasurer with respect to the long-term capital activities of the firm. As the treasurer is often the primary contact between the firm and the capital markets, this is a critical part of treasury management. The topics covered include debt and equity capital markets, hybrid, synthetic and derivative securities markets, initial public offerings, the investment banking process, regulatory and due diligence issues, responsibilities of the board of directors, and bankruptcy.

2. **Capital Structure and Dividend Policy:** (Chapters 4 and 5) This portion of the text covers the specific impact of the capital structure and dividend policies on the value of the firm, as well as the impact on both debt and stock holders. This material includes topics from the following areas: valuation of the firm's securities (debt and equity), risk and rates of return, cost of capital, capital structure of the firm and dividend policy.

3. **Mergers and Acquisitions:** (Chapter 6) A merger, acquisition, or divestiture is a critical time in the life of a firm, and the treasurer usually is involved in the process.

This material covers the reasons for and implications of corporate mergers. Specifically, the topics presented are: rationale for mergers, types of mergers, issues in mergers, merger analysis, role of investment bankers, leveraged buyouts and divestitures.

4. **Financial Analysis and Planning:** (Chapters 10 and 11) This material concerns the review, analysis and interpretation of financial statements and reports, and is useful for measuring the performance of one firm against another or to see if financial managers are meeting ongoing goals of the firm. A topic closely related to the analysis of financial statements is the preparation of *pro forma* statements for planning and control purposes. Proper financial planning will help to provide accurate forecasts of the long-term financial condition of the firm and enhance management's ability to better control the firm at the highest levels.

5. **Capital Budgeting and Leasing:** (Chapter 12) This material first covers capital budgeting, which includes the basics of capital budgeting, estimation of cash flows and adjusting for the risk of the capital project. The material concludes with a discussion of the evaluation of leasing from the viewpoints of both lessee and lessor.

C. Working Capital Management

This portion of the **Handbook** presents the short-term financial topics and strategies essential to treasury management. These areas relate to the management of working capital of the firm and how these current assets are financed with current liabilities. The specific areas included are:

1. **Working Capital Strategies:** (Chapter 7) This section of the text covers the general topic of working capital policy, or how the level of current assets and how they are financed, affect the overall operational and financial goals of the firm. More specifically, the topics include an overview of working capital management, current asset investment and financing approaches, and the costs and risks of different debt maturities.

2. **Short-Term Financial Management:** (Chapter 8) This section of the text explores the general areas of short-term (money-market) investment management and short-term sources of funds. It expands upon the basics of short-term investment and borrowing management and focuses on the interaction of these two areas and their impact on the financial welfare of the firm. Included in this section is the management of accounts receivable and accounts payable. It contains an introduction to credit and collections, followed by a discussion of managing credit policy and accounts receivable and management of accounts payable and accruals.

3. **Managing and Financing Inventories:** (Chapter 9) This section discusses the basics of inventory management, including basic inventory policy, economic order quantity (EOQ) models, just-in-time (JIT) models, and their impact on working capital management.

D. Other Treasury Management Areas

The final portion of the *Treasurer's Handbook of Financial Management* covers specialty areas of treasury management such as:

1. **Electronic Commerce and Electronic Data Interchange (EDI):** (Chapter 13) EDI is defined as the movement of business information, in a standardized format, from one firm's computer to another firm's computer. This can include financial and treasury information. The specific topics covered are the basics of EDI, costs and benefits, EDI standards, value-added networks (VANs) and the impact of EDI on credit terms. In addition, this section discusses the ability of EDI to reduce lead-times, cycle times, error rates and overall levels of working capital. Finally, this section covers the use of electronic commerce to re-engineer the business processes of a firm.

2. **Insurance and Risk Management:** (Chapter 14) As insurance costs increase and firms begin to bear more of the risk themselves (or otherwise finance the risk), insurance and risk management has become an important subject for treasurers. The specific topics in this section include: the different types of insurance and their funding, identification of risks, measurement of potential loss and financial impact, risk management techniques, negotiating insurance programs, captive insurance companies, types of insurance and risk management services.

3. **Employee Pension Fund and Benefit Management:** (Chapter 15) This section covers the management of employee pension funds. Often treasurers utilize internal or external authorities in this area. The specific topics covered include the Employee Retirement Income Security Act (ERISA), types of pension plans, funding of the pension plan, setting investment objectives, managing the fund, insured plans, deferred compensation, non-qualified plans and employee benefits.

4. **Tax, Legal, Audit and Ethical Issues in Treasury Management:** (Chapter 16) This section encompasses a variety of topics that all have some impact on the treasury management of the firm, including tax, legal, audit and ethical concerns for treasurers.

IV. Prerequisites

This text assumes a basic understanding of financial management and corporate finance topics,[2] including the following:

1. **General Overview of Financial Management:** Because almost every managerial decision of the firm has financial implications, it is important to apply proper financial principles to such decisions. As will be discussed later, the two primary concepts in financial management are the time value of money and the risk/return tradeoff. These concepts can be applied to almost any financial decision.

2. **Financial Statements, Taxes and Cash Flows:** The *Handbook* treats in detail the various types of financial statements that are available to the financial manager and the methods that can be used to analyze them. Basically, the reader should be familiar with income statements, balance sheets, statements of cash flow (sources and uses of funds) and statements of retained earnings. Another important consideration is taxes and their impact on the cash flows of the firm. In any type of financial decision-making, the effect of taxes must be taken into account, because the relevant cash flows associated with a given investment/project are the after-tax cash flows associated with that investment.

Finally, the treasurer must be aware of the differences between accounting (accrual) profits and cash flows. Cash flows relate to the actual inflow or outflow of cash from the firm. In the short term, these may bear very little relation to the accounting-based profit figures that are derived from accrual accounting rules. In the long-run, however, accrual-based profits track more closely to cash flows and will be used later in this section to analyze financial statements. When analyzing financial decisions, the manager should be certain that the actual after-tax cash flows are determined and used in the decision.

3. **Financial Markets, Institutions and Interest Rates:** The treasurer must be familiar with the various financial markets and the institutions that operate in those markets. In Chapter 3 of the *Handbook*, the markets and institutions that are important to the treasurer will be discussed in detail. Generally, the important markets are the money market, the stock and bond markets and the various international financial markets. The primary institutions with which treasurers deal are commercial banks and, on the long-term side, investment banks. In addition, insurance brokers and underwriters, pension fund managers, rating agencies, regulatory agencies, government (in general), accountants, auditors, and outside legal counsel are important advisors to the treasurer.

    The forces driving investing in the financial markets are the required rates of return (interest rates) associated with various types of financial assets. These interest rates will vary with the risk, maturity and liquidity of the investment, the collateral associated with the investment, the currency denomination of the investment, the supply and demand for the investment and the general level of interest rates in the economy.

4. **Valuation Framework:** One of the most basic concepts in the general area of finance, valuation framework holds that given a rate of return, the present value of any stream of cash flows can be determined. The value of any investment (whether a single project or an entire firm) can be determined as the sum of the present values of all the future cash flows. In addition, the concept of a risk/return tradeoff is critical to the understanding of any financial topic. That concept maintains that any project has some level of expected return as well as some uncertainty (risk) in that return. For any rational investor (or manager), taking on additional risk would require additional expected return.

V. Role of the Treasurer in the Firm

In an extensive survey of treasury professionals, the Treasury Management Association (TMA) has determined that the role of the treasury professional typically encompasses all of the tasks traditionally related to the financial management of a firm.[3] However, the definition of financial management has been expanded in recent years to include more of the short-term aspects that were previously segregated in the area of cash management. Therefore, in the broadest sense, treasurers may essentially have under their control all of the financial management responsibilities and tasks detailed in the sections that follow.

Some treasury professionals will have responsibility for more of the areas outlined in this text than others because the scope of those responsibilities will vary from firm to firm. It is also true that treasurers, like other professionals, find that their areas of responsibility are expanding as firms downsize and consolidate operations. Treasurers in all types of firms are being asked to do more with less and to do it better than ever before. Finally, many firms are beginning to outsource many of the traditional treasury functions to banks and other third-party providers, forcing the treasurer to manage additional service-provider relationships.

VI. Endnotes

1. In order to maintain a consistent framework for definitions of terms, Barron's Business and Financial Guides were used as a source for many definitions in this text. The following were used: *Dictionary of Business Terms,* 1987; *Dictionary of Finance and Investment Terms, 3rd Edition,* 1991; *Dictionary of Banking Terms, 2nd Edition,* 1993; *Dictionary of Accounting Terms,* 1987; and *Dictionary of Insurance Terms, 2nd Edition,* 1991.

2. See the current editions of the following textbooks: *Financial Management, Theory and Practice,* by E.F. Brigham and L.C. Gapenski, Dryden Publishers; *Introduction to Financial Management, by L.D. Schall and C.W. Haley, McGraw-Hill Book Company; Principles of Corporate Finance,* by R.A. Brealey and S.C. Meyers, McGraw-Hill Book Company; and *Fundamentals of Corporate Finance,* by S.A. Ross, R.W. Westerfield and B.D. Jordan.

3   See: "Becoming a World-Class Treasurer," *Journal of Cash Management,* Jeffrey S. Rosengard, November/December 1993, pp. 4–14.

2 Overview of Capital Markets

I. Outline of the Chapter

A. Role of the Treasurer in Determining and Managing Costs of Capital
1. Raising Capital
2. Managing Outstanding Capital
3. Shareholder and Bondholder Relations
4. Factors in Costs of Capital

B. Debt Capital Markets
1. Short-Term Sources of Capital (Money Markets)
   a. Bank Loans and Letters of Credit
   b. Trade Credit and Financing
   c. Master Notes
   d. Commercial Paper
2. Long-Term Debt Capital
   a. Term Loans
   b. Medium- or Intermediate-Term Notes and Bonds
   c. Bonds
   d. Other Forms of Debt Capital
   e. Debt Contract Provisions
   f. Issues in Secured Lending
   g. Bond Ratings
3. Other Factors Influencing Long-Term Debt Decisions
   a. Capital Structure Considerations
   b. Maturity Matching
   c. Effects of Interest Rate Levels and Forecasts
   d. Amount of Financing Required
   e. Availability of Collateral

2. International Capital Markets
   a. International Debt Markets
   b. International Equity Markets
3. Venture Capital
4. Bankruptcy

Chapter Checklists

A. Characteristics and Rights of Stakeholders in a Corporation
B. Listing of Required SEC Reports
C. Listing of Typical Restrictive Covenants
D. Listing of Foreign Security Market Regulations
E. Listing of Futures and Options Markets (Global)

Chapter Calculations

A. Calculations in Sinking Fund Arrangements
B. Calculations Involved in Bond Refunding Operations
C. Calculations and Mechanics Involved in Forwards and Futures
D. Calculations Involved in Swaps
E. Calculations Involved in Options (Single and Multi-Period)

II. Introduction

This chapter provides an overview of the sources of capital available to the typical firm in the United States, as well as a discussion of the primary markets for this capital. Although foreign capital markets will be briefly discussed, it will be only as they relate to capital raised by U.S.-based firms. The markets for all forms of capital are changing rapidly as new capital formats are developed, and this text is not designed to be the definitive work on all forms of capital and capital markets.

This chapter provides a background for financial managers on the sources and markets for capital. In later chapters, the cost of these various sources will be covered as well as the general theory and practice of capital structure, dividend policy, and mergers and acquisitions.

III. Coverage of the Chapter Material

A. Role of the Treasurer in Determining and Managing Costs of Capital

The treasurer of a firm plays a very important role in both the determination and the management of the firm's cost of capital. The treasurer is often responsible (along with the CFO and board of directors) for determining the type and amount of various forms of capital that will be raised. In addition, the treasury area of a firm is often responsible for the management of the firm's securities once they are issued. Finally, the mix of different types of securities, the timing of the issues, and perceptions of the firm by analysts and investors, will ultimately determine the overall availability and costs of capital for the firm. Each of these topics will be discussed in detail below.

1. Raising Capital: For any firm, the ability to raise capital at a reasonable price is often one of the primary determinants of long-term success. This capital may be raised in the "private" or public markets.

Many firms sell debt instruments, preferred and common stock in the private market rather than to the general public. The purchaser in a private sale is usually an institutional investor such as a pension fund, insurance company, bank or trust. Some reasons for this type of private placement may include: size of the issue, need for speed in issuance, complexity of the securities, a desire for minimal public disclosure, speed of being able to place the debt, or pricing of the issue.

There are advantages and disadvantages to raising capital through public offerings. On the plus side, access to capital markets offers the potential to raise large amounts of capital at prevailing rates. The negative side, however, is that there is significant overhead involved in managing the reporting and disclosure requirements for public security issues.

Initial public offerings (covered later) require significant disclosure of firm's ownership, business activities and financial statements. In addition, publicly held firms are required by the Securities and Exchange Commission (SEC) to file a wide variety of forms and reports on a regular basis. These reports are summarized in a checklist at the end of this chapter.

In addition, the price of capital for a firm may fluctuate widely due to factors over which the firm has no control. These factors include: the general economic environment, new technologies, government regulations, public perceptions of the firm and its prospects, etc.

In both the raising and management of capital, the treasurer must deal with a wide variety of different parties, including: investment bankers, corporate bankers, regulatory agencies, analysts, rating agencies, auditors, shareholders and bondholders. Each of these parties requires different types and amounts of information and has a different perspective of the corporation. In order to successfully raise the needed capital for the firm, the treasurer must be able to provide the required information to each of these parties.

2. Managing Outstanding Capital: Once the firm has issued stocks, bonds or other securities, the treasurer must manage the information and payment requirements for each of those entities. The treasurer may have to manage trustee relationships and responsibilities relative to the firm's securities as well as act as disbursing agent for related payments. Some of the more important obligations include:

- Bondholders must receive their interest payments
- Sinking fund obligations on bond issues must be met

- Covenants on bond issues must be met
- Shareholders must receive dividends as declared
- Financial reports must be completed and sent to interested parties in a timely manner
- Various reports must be prepared and sent to regulatory agencies (i.e., SEC Filings)
- Planning for the future retirement of maturing issues
- Management of bank relationships (relative to lines of credit and liquidity)

3. Shareholder and Bondholder Relations: In addition to the trustee and disbursing responsibilities outlined above, the treasurer is often required to maintain shareholder and bondholder relations. These responsibilities include: maintaining shareholder lists, sending out reports, communication with shareholders and bondholders, and dealing with their questions and issues.

4. Factors in Costs of Capital: The overall cost of capital for a firm is a function of the mix of capital components used and the individual costs of those components.

- In the simplest model of corporate long-term capital, there is a mix of debt (bonds) and equity (common stock) as the primary sources of capital. Debt is usually less expensive due to the lower rate of return required by investors and the tax-deductibility of interest payments on the debt. Chapter 4 provides a detailed discussion of the use of debt and equity capital and the impact of the costs and mix of these capital components on the capital structure of the firm, as well as how this mix is determined and who is responsible for the capital structure.
- The other primary source of long-term capital for a firm is the ability of the firm to generate profits and retain those profits for reinvestment in the firm.
- The dividend policy of the firm has a major impact on the firm's ability to retain capital in the firm, as opposed to paying all earnings out to shareholders.
- As will be discussed in later chapters, the ultimate mix of debt and equity (and other forms of capital) for a particular firm is primarily a function of the firm's ability to generate earnings and its acquisition and dividend policy.

B. Debt Capital Markets

Firms can raise debt capital in either short-term money markets or long-term capital markets. In either case, debt capital typically imposes a fixed payment requirement on the part of the firm. The interest portion of these payments is usually tax deductible and must be paid prior to any payments to equity holders. In addition, debt holders have priority claims on the firm's assets in the event of financial distress. Finally, given the fixed nature and tax deductibility of debt payments, the use of debt provides financial leverage for the firm. Some important observations concerning the use of debt are:

- In order to properly utilize debt in the firm's capital structure, the treasurer must understand the basic concept of debt, the lender's perspective and the credit process. In addition, the treasurer must be aware of the advantages and disadvantages of using both short- and long-term debt in the firm.

- Under most conditions, the use of debt by the firm will result in a lower overall cost of capital and in increased cash flows (and higher value) per dollar of equity. This advantage results from the generally lower cost of debt (versus equity), the tax deductibility of interest payments and the fixed nature of the debt payment.

- If a firm is profitable, then debt represents an attractive source of funds, as the payments are limited to principal and interest, and the profits after the related principal and interest expense can be either retained for investment purposes or distributed to the firm's owners as dividends.

- Debt use carries the risk that the firm's cash flows may not always be sufficient to service the debt, causing the firm to possibly borrow additional funds to service the debt, or in extreme cases, raising the possibility of default or bankruptcy.

- Another consideration in utilizing debt is the intended use of the funds. A very common and important reason for the use of debt is to pay expenses that are due when other funds are not available or to finance working capital needs. It may be a timing problem with receipts and disbursements or the seasonal needs of the business. If the funds are used to purchase an asset or to buy a security, then the major justification for the borrowing should be that the asset or other investment will help generate funds for repayment of the loan.

- It is important to consider the maturities of assets versus those of the liabilities funding those assets. Although matching the duration of the assets to the liabilities is a common practice, there are other approaches used by treasurers. This topic is discussed in greater detail in later chapters on Working Capital Policies and Management.

- The relationship between the borrower (company using debt) and the lender (supplier of funds) is intended to be mutually beneficial to both parties. The borrower receives needed funds, while the lender realizes a return on investment in the form of fees, interest, and sometimes other considerations such as warrants allowing the purchase of the firm's stock at a predetermined price. To the lender, the loan is an investment, with an expected return in the form of interest, fees, and sometimes other considerations. To the borrower, the loan allows immediate access to needed funds that can be repaid in the future, and the interest paid is the cost of using the funds. The lender wants to be certain that both the principal of the loan and the interest can be repaid by the borrower as agreed. In the credit process, the borrower usually develops a business plan that demonstrates the firm's ability to repay the loan according to the terms of the loan agreement. The business plan is usually part of a more comprehensive strategic plan for the future of the company. It will generally include extensive financial statements, both historical and projected, which may be used to justify the need for the loan and the likelihood of its repayment.

- A general rule for successful use of debt is that management must understand the nature of its business. Businesses with stable cash flows and large amounts of assets generally will not significantly increase their overall riskiness with the use of debt. On the other hand, firms with high fluctuations in operating cash flows or high operating risk may find that the use of debt will magnify that risk.

- Since the use of debt may have an impact on the risk profile of the firm, treasurers must consider how this debt use will affect the purchase of their company's stock. Investors generally gravitate toward stocks that provide a cash flow stream and risk/return profile that fit their needs. This is called the "clientele effect." The use of debt will potentially impact the amount and timing of dividends as well as the overall riskiness of the firm, thus possibly changing the mix of investors in the firm's stock and price investors are willing to pay for the stock.

1. Short-Term Sources of Capital (Money Markets): Short-term borrowing is an important source of financing for many firms for several reasons.

- Because short-term borrowing is more flexible and easier to initiate in small increments than longer-term financing, it is used in increasing amounts until refinancing for a longer term is economically justified.

- Short-term borrowing is used to provide a temporary source of financing to support a temporary need for funds, such as a seasonal peak in accounts receivable or inventory.

- In addition, short-term borrowing generally carries a lower interest rate than long-term financing and is often used on a continuing basis to provide a layer of lower-cost debt. However, its availability may evaporate or the cost significantly increase in times of distress. This distress could be caused by any of the following:
  - deterioration of the borrowing firm's financial condition
  - credit rationing on the part of the lenders
  - change in bank lending practices or regulatory agency policies
  - general reduction in the availability of credit in the economy
  - increases in general short-term interest rates

- Another important consideration is the use of maturity matching for the firm's short-term debt. In general, this entails matching the maturity of the debt to specific financing needs of the firm. An example would be a firm that borrows to purchase inventory then pays off the loan as the inventory is sold.

- Short-term borrowing can carry either a fixed or variable interest rate. The choice between a fixed or variable rate loan is affected by the spread between the fixed and variable rates, expected future changes in interest rates and the effect of potential changes in interest rates on the firm's cash flows.

- Short-term borrowing is an important part of the overall strategic plan. Failure to incorporate short-term borrowing plans into the long-range strategic plan may result in inappropriate levels or types of borrowing.

- The use of short-term sources of funds will often be determined by the firm's type of business as well as its strategic objectives. Factors such as seasonality of sales, timing of collections and disbursements and economic conditions and trends can affect both use and cost of short-term borrowing. In addition, many firms and state and local governments use short-term borrowing as a temporary source of funds until they can roll over these short-term obligations into a long-term bond, term loan or another form of long-term debt or equity.

a. Bank Loans and Letters of Credit: Although the dominance of commercial banks has declined over the last two decades, they still represent the largest single source of financing for short-term corporate needs. This situation is changing, however, as the commercial paper market grows in size. Between 1980 and 1990, commercial paper issued by non-financial corporations increased almost 500%, from $35 billion in 1980 to $160 billion in 1990. During this period, the ratio of commercial and industrial loans at commercial banks fell from being 2.3 times the amount of commercial paper outstanding in 1980 to 1.2 in 1990.[1]

Commercial banks continue to provide a variety of loans and credit enhancement products for many types of firms, such as trade letters of credit and stand-by letters of credit.

- For many small- to medium-size firms, banks may represent the only feasible source of short-term credit available. Traditionally, banks have viewed lending as a part of the overall banking relationship with a client.

- Treasurers must be concerned with any problems relating to the capital adequacy of banks with which they deal. Capital adequacy is a regulatory issue related to leverage that deals with the level of equity that a bank must have relative to its loan and deposit base, and the rules in this area are constantly changing. Banks with capital adequacy problems may be restricted by the Federal Reserve or other regulatory agencies in the types and amounts of loans they can grant due to a lack of sufficient capital to support the activity. This can make credit difficult to obtain when a company is a customer of such a bank.

- Commercial banks make a wide variety of loans, from working capital loans for small restaurants with inventory and/or equipment as collateral to unsecured bridge loans to support tender offers for acquisitions. Regardless of the purpose of the loan, commercial banks generally make loans based on an analysis of the borrower's overall financial condition. Because banks offer a wide variety of loan products, a lending arrangement tailored to the borrower's needs usually can be negotiated.

- Typical bank loans include: single payment loans, lines of credit, revolving credit agreements, receivables lending, equipment loans, and term loans. Some of these products such as revolving credit agreements and equipment or term loans are technically longer term credit arrangements as per Generally Accepted Accounting Principals (GAAP), but are really a part of the short-term debt of the firm. These are typically offered at floating rates using the Prime Rate, London Interbank Offered Rate (LIBOR) or other base lending rates (FED Funds rate, T-Bill rate, etc.) as the basis for the rate computation.

- Banks offer various forms of trade letters of credit. The most typical use of letters of credit is for the financing and management of international or domestic trade. These letters of credit are tied to specific transactions and help to reduce the risk of non-completion of the transaction, and may provide needed financing for the deal.

- Banks are significant issuers in the standby letters of credit market. Stand-by LCs are often used in conjunction with commercial paper issues, but recently firms have been using them for other purposes, such as backup to worker's compensation plans, health and benefit plans, or other insurance plans.
- Finally, banks act as facilitators and brokers for private placements, matching large investors to large borrowers.

b. Trade Credit and Financing: Banks and other financial institutions provide firms with sources of financing for trade transactions. These arrangements help firms to finance accounts receivable and inventories, as well as international trade. In addition, many firms receive trade credit from their suppliers in the form of deferred payment for goods or services received. For most smaller firms, their accounts payable is the primary source of short-term financing received.

c. Master Notes: Master notes are a form of borrowing available to some larger firms through the trust departments of commercial banks. In essence, a master note is a direct placement of a short-term loan with the bank trust department, rather than through a lending department. It is similar to a direct placement of commercial paper. These types of direct-placement notes are generally issued at a lower rate due to the top quality of the borrower and the low issuance cost involved, but may have significant restrictive covenants attached to them.

d. Commercial Paper: This is a firm's unsecured note (usually 30 day–270 day maturity) issued directly to the supplier of funds. While it originally was issued only by large, top quality firms, the expansion of the market has increased its use among smaller companies. Commercial paper is a discount loan with its interest rate dependent upon the market and the credit rating assigned by the rating agencies. Virtually all commercial paper programs have a backup credit arrangement (committed backup line of credit or stand-by LC), either partial or full, to pay off the paper if it cannot be rolled over or otherwise paid off at maturity. The paper may be sold directly to the investor or through dealers. Specialty commercial paper, such as paper backed by specific receivables, has been developed in recent years.

2. Long-Term Debt Capital

a. Term Loans: This is a loan with a fixed maturity, usually greater than one year, which can be repaid either in installments or in a single payment (bullet form). Frequently a term loan is issued for a specific financing need such as the purchase of a new plant or equipment or for general expansion. Interest is usually paid at periodic intervals and may be fixed or variable. A term loan is usually secured by the asset being financed and the maturity is related to the useful life of the asset. For many firms, leasing of equipment is an alternative to term loans, especially where the seller/manufacturer of the equipment provides specialized leasing arrangements.

b. Medium- or Intermediate-Term Notes and Bonds: These are notes or bonds issued by firms or municipalities with terms in the 2 to 10 year range. In most cases they are coupon bearing and very similar to long-term bonds except for their initial shorter maturity.

c. Bonds: Bonds represent a major source of long-term debt financing for many firms and are available in a wide variety of formats. The calculations involved in determining the cost or rate of return on various types of bonds will be covered in detail in Chapter 4.

- **General Terms:** Bonds are a long-term contract where the issuer of the bond (the borrower) agrees to make specific payments of interest (usually semi-annually) and principal (at maturity) to the holders (lenders/investors) of the bonds. Bonds are typically issued for periods of 10–30 years and are usually sold to the general public through investment banks. The priority of claims for these securities in the event of bankruptcy is discussed in Chapter 3 of this text.

- **Mortgage Bonds:** These bonds are used to finance specific assets, which are pledged as security against the issue. They usually include substantial covenants (or indenture agreements) which outline the assets involved, the ability of the firm to issue additional bonds, the use of second or junior mortgages, sinking fund requirements (covered later in this chapter), reporting requirements and restrictions involving key financial ratios. These indenture agreements serve to protect the interests of the bondholders by restricting the actions of managers, which may reduce the value of the bonds.

- **Debentures:** These are unsecured bonds which represent general claims against the assets of a firm and may carry a higher cost than secured bonds. Large, financially secure firms can easily issue debentures based on their reputation in the marketplace. Debentures may be used by firms which do not have easily mortgaged assets, and thus must utilize unsecured borrowing. The claim of debentures on the assets of the firm is generally junior to that of bonds, but senior to equity. Debentures may be issued on a subordinated basis, indicating that their claim on assets is subordinate to (after) designated notes payable, bank loans or other specified debt.

- **Convertible Bonds:** These are securities that are convertible into shares of common or preferred stock, at a fixed price at the option of the holder or sometimes the issuer. These bonds provide the holder with a potential for capital growth in return for a lower interest rate. Bonds issued with warrants are similar in nature to convertible bonds. Warrants are options to buy stock at a stated price for a stated period of time, thus allowing the holder to receive potential capital gains. This allows the investor to participate in the upside gain as a firm grows and prospers, while being protected to some extent on the downside by receiving interest and principal repayment.

- **Income Bonds:** These bonds will pay interest only if the firm has profits, thus reducing some of the risk of issuing debt from the firm's viewpoint.

- **Collateral Trust Bonds:** These bonds are backed by securities such as other companies' stocks and bonds held by the issuing company.

- **Equipment Trust Certificates:** These are loans secured by movable equipment, such as a fleet of trucks or railroad equipment.

- **Other Types of Bonds and Long-Term Debt:** There are many other types of bonds used for special purposes or related to specific types of assets. These include: indexed bonds (interest rates are tied to some economic index) used in high-inflation countries, industrial development bonds, special tax-exempt bonds, receivable loans, and loans related to asset sales. This area is changing rapidly and new types of bonds are being continually developed to meet special needs.

d. Other Forms of Debt Capital: There are many types of debt-like instruments which can be utilized in raising capital. The listing below provides a sample of some of the current products available:

- **Zero (or Low) Coupon Bonds:** These types of bonds typically pay no or very low interest payments during the life of the bond, but rather pay just the face value (par value) at maturity. As a result, they are issued at a substantial discount from the par value. For the issuer there are several advantages: there is no cash outflow until maturity, and the firm receives an annual tax deduction until maturity. But there are several disadvantages: (1) the bond is not callable or refundable, (2) the firm does face a large outflow to redeem the bonds at maturity, and (3) current tax codes make them unattractive to most investors except for pension funds and some institutional investors. Current tax codes require non-institutional investors to pay taxes on the estimated interest earnings each year, even though the interest is not received until maturity. Thus, for institutional investors, there is a negative cash flow stream (tax outflows) during the life of the bond.

- **Floating (Adjustable) Rate Debt:** These bonds are especially attractive to investors during periods of rising interest rates. Some investors may like floating rate debt because it has a stable market value and matches current interest rates. Borrowers like floating rate debt because they can take advantage of falling interest rates, yet still match the maturity of their debt to that of their assets.

- **High-Yield Bonds:**[2] These have also been referred to as "junk bonds" or "below investment grade" and usually come from one of two sources. The first are bonds that were originally sound, but which become high-risk when the firm issuing them got into financial trouble. These bonds are also referred to as "fallen angels," and though they have reasonable coupon payments, the riskiness of the firm's financial position causes them to sell at a deep discount (thus providing a high yield-to-maturity). The other types of high-yield bonds are those which originally sold as high-risk instruments. These bonds are often sold by firms to either finance a leveraged buyout (covered in Chapter 3), or to bail themselves out of deep financial trouble. Although there was a brief slump in this market during the early 90s, it has begun to re-emerge as a useful source of financing.

- **Payment-in-Kind Bonds:** These bonds are often used in leveraged or management buyouts and make bond payments in the form of stocks, warrants or other securities rather than in cash. They provide the firm with the ability to raise capital, without tying it to a long-term obligation to pay cash out of the firm.

- **Project Financing:**[3] This type of financing applies to large projects, usually related to energy explorations, refineries, utility power plants, etc. The typical project financing arrangement is very complex, involving several firms (sponsors) forming a separate legal entity to operate the project. The lenders are paid from the project cash flows and generally do not have recourse to the individual sponsors or owners of the project.

- **Securitization:** In recent years, many types of debt instruments have been securitized in order to increase their liquidity, thus lowering the cost of capital to borrowers. At one level, securitization of debt instruments has occurred simply because certain financial institutions have been willing to "make a market" in these instruments. This has been the case for commercial paper and for high-yield bonds in particular. The other type of securitization is called asset securitization or asset-backed securities. The primary example of this type of securitization is in the home mortgage market where many different entities, e.g., Federal National Mortgage Association (FNMA), Government National Mortgage Association (GNMA), Federal Home Loan Mortgage Corporation (FHLMC), Collateralized Mortgage Obligations (CMOs), etc. bundle together pools of mortgages into securities and sell the securities to investors. This arrangement adds a significant amount of liquidity to the mortgage market and benefits both borrowers and lenders. The primary corporate applications of securitization are in the areas of accounts receivable and inventory where they are bundled together to back securities, making them more liquid due to the specific security behind them, and therefore, more saleable.

- **Off-Balance Sheet Financing:** This type of financing is typically used by firms having high current levels of debt or those which have very restrictive covenants on the use of additional debt. These sources of financing typically do not appear on the firm's balance sheet and usually entail the use of some type of leasing arrangements or sale of receivables. There are significant restrictions on the use of this type of financing and they are outlined in FASB statement #13 issued by the Financial Accounting Standards Board. This requires that firms entering into certain types of leases must "capitalize the lease," restating their balance sheets to report leased assets as a fixed asset and the present value of the future lease payments as a liability (covered in Chapter 13).

- **Swaps and Derivatives:**[4] These products will be covered in detail later in this chapter, but basically include: currency swaps (i.e., one currency versus another), interest rate swaps (i.e., fixed versus variable), basis rate swaps (i.e., prime rate versus LIBOR), timing swaps (i.e., short-term versus long-term) and synthetic securities (i.e., derivatives). Though these arrangements are not technically sources of capital, they do provide an important means for treasurers to adjust the risk profile of their capital structure. One of the more recent innovations in this market has been in the development of standardized contracts for most kinds of swaps. This provides two benefits in the use of swaps: (1) lower transaction costs, and (2) the emergence of a secondary market, resulting in increased liquidity and efficiency. Many multinational banks now make markets in swaps and offer quotes on standard types of swaps.

e. Debt Contract Provisions: Although debt will generally result in lower costs of capital for the firm, it does require that managers accept some restrictions on their action in return for the debt. The only way that debtholders can effectively protect their interests is to establish, at the time of the initial debt contract, certain provisions (i.e., representations, warrants, and covenants) which prevent the managers or equity holders from reducing the value of the bonds and give them additional rights under certain deteriorating conditions. In addition, treasurers may make provisions for early retirement of the debt, repayment of the principal or possible refinancing of the issue.

- **Bond Indentures and Covenants:** An indenture is a legal document that outlines the rights of both the borrower (bond issuer) and the lender (bondholder). These indentures may be quite lengthy and will include various restrictive covenants (a typical listing appears at the end of this chapter) which impose constraints on the actions of the firm's management. The purpose of this document is to protect the bondholders from actions by the firm's management which would increase the value of the equity holders or other stakeholders at the expense of the bondholders. Violation of an indenture agreement is usually sufficient grounds for the bondholders to make the debt immediately due and payable, and possibly to force the firm into bankruptcy. In addition, the SEC approves indenture agreements in public offerings and ensures that all indenture provisions are met before allowing a company to sell new securities to the general public.

- **Call Provisions:** These provisions give the issuing firm the right to call in a bond or other issue for redemption prior to the original maturity. As a compensation to the investors for early redemption, a call premium is paid if the bond is called. The call premium is usually set on a sliding scale, with larger premiums above par required the earlier an issue is called. The call privilege is very valuable to the firm because it allows it to redeem a bond issue if interest rates fall or if excess cash becomes available and refinancing becomes an attractive option. As a result, bonds with call provisions attached typically require a higher coupon rate than non-callable bonds of similar size, duration, and quality in order to attract investors. The primary danger to the investor is that the bond will be called if interest rates fall, and the investor will be forced to reinvest the call proceeds at a lower rate.

- **Sinking Funds:** The usual format for bond issues is for the firm to pay interest only (coupon payments) for the life of the bond and then to repay the principal (par or face value) at maturity. This means that a treasurer must plan on how this large lump sum payment will be made at the issue's maturity. Typically, sinking fund provisions in the indenture require firms either to call or repurchase on the open market a portion of the outstanding bond issue each year, in essence amortizing the issue over its life. An example of this type of calculation is provided at the end of this chapter. Other types of sinking funds require the firm to make payments into a trust account, which either repurchases bonds on the open market or amasses a lump sum for retirement of the bonds at maturity. The existence of some type of sinking fund arrangement (specified in the bond indenture) generally increases the safety of the bonds, thus lowering the required interest rate.

- **Refinancing Operations:** These refunding operations are often used following periods of high interest rates. During the high interest rate periods many firms which must issue bonds will attach call provisions which allow them to redeem the bonds prior to maturity. When interest rates fall, these firms will then issue new bonds at a lower interest rate and use the proceeds to call in the older, higher-interest bonds.[5] The primary purpose of these operations is to take advantage of falling interest rates and reduce the overall cost of debt (and weighted average cost of capital) for the firm.

- **Defeasance of Debt:** This is a method for removing debt from a firm's balance sheet, without actually retiring the debt issue. In this arrangement, a firm places sufficient funds in escrow, usually in U.S. Government securities, to pay for interest and principal on the debt issue in question. Because payment and retirement of the debt issue is now guaranteed, this debt (and the related securities) can be removed from the balance sheet, as well as any restrictive covenants related to the debt.

f. Issues in Secured Lending: For any long-term debt using some type of asset(s) as security, there are several issues which must be addressed:

- **Collateral:** The assets which are to be used as security are called collateral for the loan. They could be physical assets (plant, equipment, inventory, etc.) or financial assets (receivables, marketable securities, etc.). The condition of the assets must be monitored, and in the case of physical assets, insurance is also a requirement.

- **Liens:** In most types of secured lending the lender has a lien, or legal claim, on the assets used as collateral. This may be in the form of a mortgage for larger assets, or a blanket lien against inventory or receivables. In the event the borrower defaults on the loan or bond issue, the lender can seize the assets in lieu of repayment. In order to ensure this process, the lender will file a UCC-1 under Article 9 of the Uniform Commercial Code with the Secretary of State in each of the states in which the company does business. This filing becomes a matter of public record and establishes the order of priority of secured claims on the firm's assets. In addition to the UCC-1 filing, the creditor executes a security agreement outlining the nature of the assets pledged on the loan. These items will "perfect" the lien and make the security interest enforceable in courts of law. Also, lenders will often perform a lien search on a potential borrower to determine if the assets being pledged are already pledged to some other creditor.

- **Guarantee:** When a subsidiary of a larger company is borrowing funds or floating a bond issue, the lenders may require that the parent corporation (or sister subsidiary, supplier, customer or other entity) provide a guarantee of principal for the arrangement. This allows the lender to go back to the parent to get their payment in the event the subsidiary is unable to make payment. There are several levels of guarantees which the parent corporation can make, and these are listed in the order of protection for the lender:

1) Full Guarantee: The parent fully guarantees any borrowing arrangement by the subsidiary and agrees to take over the loan if the subsidiary fails to make timely payments.

2) Specific Project Guarantee: The parent guarantees only loans relating to specific projects of the subsidiary, not all loans.

3) Guarantee of Payment or Collection: The parent guarantees to make payment on the loan, or to collect payment from the subsidiary, only if the subsidiary formally defaults on the loan. This usually requires the lender to initiate default proceedings on the subsidiary and make efforts at collection before the parent will become involved.

4) Comfort Letter: This type of guarantee is generally just a letter from another party stating actions they will (or will not) take on behalf of the party taking out the loan. This agreement usually is not legally enforceable and is considered a "gentlemen's agreement."

- **Performance Guarantees:** In some cases the lender may ask for specific performance guarantees relative to the assets being financed.

1) Full Guarantee: The parent fully guarantees performance by the subsidiary.

2) Best Efforts Guarantee: In this case the parent will make "best efforts" to make the subsidiary perform, but does not guarantee subsidiary performance.

g. Bond Ratings: Bond issues are assigned quality ratings that reflect the probability of the firm issuing the bonds defaulting on the issue in question. Each bond issue, short or long term, is independently rated. The three major rating agencies are Standard and Poor's Corporation, Duff and Phelps, and Moody's Investors Service. The basic bond rating scales are provided in the table below:

Typical Bond Ratings			
General Quality Level	Standard and Poor's	Duff and Phelps	Moody's Investors Service
High Quality	AAA and AA	AAA and AA	Aaa and Aa
Investment Grade	A and BBB	A and BBB	A and Baa
Substandard	BB and B	BB and B	Ba and B
Speculative	CCC to D	CCC to C	Caa to C

There are also several other considerations relative to bond ratings:

- **Bond Rating Criteria:** Ratings are generally based on both qualitative and quantitative factors, but do tend to be somewhat subjective. Given the complexity of most large firms, there is no precise mathematical formula that analysts can use to determine the rating; many factors must be taken into account.

- **Importance of Bond Ratings:** Ratings are important to both investors and firm management. Many institutional investors are restricted to buying investment grade bonds or better by their charters, and these investors make up the bulk of the bond market. Also, a firm's bond rating is a direct measure of the riskiness of the firm, and this will have an impact on the firm's cost of capital (i.e., the rating sets the pricing). Additional detail on the process of bond ratings and the information required by the bond rating agencies is provided at the end of Chapter 4: Cost of Capital and Capital Structure.

- **Changes in Bond Ratings:** Rating agencies review outstanding bonds on a periodic basis and may upgrade or downgrade an issue based on changes in either the firm or in the general economic environment. Firms or municipalities whose bonds are downgraded will find they have a more difficult time raising additional capital in the market and will have to pay a higher price to get it.

3. Other Factors Influencing Long-Term Debt Decisions: There are a variety of other factors which will influence a firm's decisions regarding its long-term debt issues. These are outlined below.

a. Capital Structure Considerations: Most treasurers and CFOs have some target capital structure in mind for their firm. As will be discussed in later chapters, the target capital structure is a function of a variety of factors: the type of company, its financial history, the industry, general economic conditions, operating risk of the firm, and the type of investors holding the firm's securities. The availability and choice of debt issues obviously will have a major impact on the ultimate capital structure for a firm. Since debt issues can usually be planned, many firms will be able to steer their capital structure in the general direction of their target over time.

b. Maturity Matching: Maturity matching involves matching the life of the debt issue to the life of the assets it is financing. Generally, firms do try to match maturities of debt issues and assets wherever possible in order to reduce the overall riskiness of the firm.

c. Effects of Interest Rate Levels and Forecasts: The general level of interest rates and economic activity will have an impact on both the use and cost of debt for firms. A treasurer's forecast of future interest rates will have an impact on the type of capital raised by a firm, and the provisions that may be attached to these capital issues. Treasurers must consider the issue of "flight to quality" whenever financial market conditions decline. In these times, investors move toward safe or quality investments and the spread between high- and low-risk investments typically increases significantly. In good financial markets, however, the spread between high-

and low-risk investments may be much smaller and a high-risk borrower may get relatively good rates.

d. Amount of Financing Required: Smaller amounts of debt are usually raised through bank loans or short-term financing, whereas larger amounts may be raised through a public bond issue.

e. Availability of Collateral: Firms such as power utilities, which have large available assets that can be used as collateral, will typically be able to borrow at lower rates than firms of the same credit quality and rating which do not have such collateral. Firms with a lower risk profile will have the financial strength to borrow on an unsecured basis and obtain funds at lower rates than those firms which are more prone to default and therefore must resort to secured borrowing in order to obtain funds.

C. Equity (Stock) Markets

1. Common Stock: Common stock represents the ownership of the firm, and the management of the firm acts as the agent for the shareholders and must protect their interest. Common equity usually represents a significant portion of the firm's capital base, and has the following characteristics:

a. Balance Sheet Accounts and Definitions: There are several terms relating to common stock of which treasurers must be aware: (1) par value, (2) retained earnings and (3) paid-in capital. The total amount of stockholders' equity is the sum of these accounts. It is important to realize that these accounts only represent the historical accounting value of the equity, not the current market value.

- **Par Value:** An arbitrary amount (usually stated in the corporate charter) that indicates the minimum amount that stockholders have put up (or must put up) in the event of bankruptcy. For many publicly traded firms this is $1.00 or $0 (no par value).

- **Retained Earnings:** This balance sheet account represents the accumulated net earnings of a corporation since its inception, less dividends paid to shareholders. This is part of the stockholders' equity and is an accounting of the money re-invested in the firm in lieu of dividends being paid out. It is important to realize that retained earnings are simply an accounting concept and are not a pool of money just sitting in the firm.

- **Paid-in Capital:** This account reflects the difference at the time of the issue between the par value and the issuance price (less underwriting costs) of any new stock that is sold by the firm. For example, if a firm were to sell a new issue of stock with a par value of $1, and the firm nets $25 per share, then a $1 per share increase would be shown in the par value account and a $24 increase in the additional paid-in capital account per share.

- **Book Value per Share:** This is defined as total common stockholders' equity divided by the number of shares outstanding.

- **Market Value per Share:** This is defined as the current price at which a share of the stock is traded. Though this is not technically part of the accounting statements, it is often included in reports issued by various financial reporting services and the company.

b. Legal Rights and Privileges of Common Stockholders:

A brief listing of the rights and privileges of common stockholders is provided below. Additional information on this topic is provided in Chapter 3 of this text.

- **Control of Firm:** As owners of the firm, stockholders have the right to elect the firm's directors who, in turn, select the officers who manage the business. There are many state and federal regulations concerning the election of directors and the specific management of the process.

- **Cumulative Voting:** Typically, corporate bylaws allow one vote per share of stock, and in some cases allow for cumulative voting. If, for example, a firm had five directors, cumulative voting would allow each share of stock to have five votes, and, if the shareholder wished, all five of these votes could be made for one director. This is especially attractive to minority shareholders, as it may allow them to get at least one or more seats on the board by pooling their votes for one or two candidates.

- **Proxy:** The right to vote at the annual meeting can be assigned to another individual through a proxy, and, for most firms with satisfied stockholders, the proxies are routinely assigned back to the firm. If, however, a group of stockholders are dissatisfied with the management of the firm, or other parties try to take control of the firm, a proxy battle may occur as each side attempts to accumulate more proxies (votes) than the other side.

- **Staggered Election of Directors:** Another recent practice for maintaining control is the staggered election of directors to multi-year terms, so that only a non-majority portion of the board is elected each year. This prevents a rapid change of directors in the event of an attempted takeover.

- **Pre-emptive Right:** This is the right that certain or all shareholders have to first rights of purchase, on a *pro-rata* basis, of any new shares of stock issued by the firm. This is usually done through a rights offering or "subscription" to any new stock issued by the firm. The current shareholders may either purchase additional shares on a *pro-rata* basis or sell their rights to other parties. Although not a requirement in all states, most corporations include this right in their charters. It offers the stockholder protection against dilution of value and protects the power of control for the existing shareholders.

c. Types of Common Stock:
While most firms have only one class of common stock, more and more firms are beginning to issue multiple levels of stock to different types of investors.

- Classified stocks are typically referred to as Class A or Class B, but these terms have no standard meaning; rather, they are specific to each firm.

- Generally, the different classes of stock may limit voting privileges, dividends and/or resale. The use of multiple classes is true for some preferred stock. The general purpose is to raise capital through the issue of new equity, while still maintaining control of the firm.

- Different classes of stock may be issued to differentiate returns for various pieces (divisions) of a large, diversified company. This is often done by large multinational corporations to offer non-diversified investments to certain classes of stockholders.

d. Convertibles:[6] These securities were introduced in the section on long-term debt because they are a combination of debt and equity components.

- Convertible securities are usually bonds or preferred stock which may be exchangeable at the holder's or issuer's option for a firm's common stock under certain terms and conditions at a prestated price. The conversion does not provide any new capital for the firm. It simply converts existing debt or preferred stock into common equity.

- The conversion ratio states the number of shares of stock that one bond could be converted to if the owner chooses. The maturity value of the bond and the conversion ratio determine the conversion price of the issue. For example, a $1,000 par value bond with a conversion ratio of 20 (20 shares of common stock per bond) implies a stock conversion price of $50.

- Most convertibles contain clauses which protect against the dilution of value due to stock splits, stock dividends, or depressed stock prices. The typical provision states that if new common stock is sold at a price below the conversion price, then the conversion ratio must be raised (and thus the conversion price lowered) to the issue price of the new stock.

- Convertibles have an important advantage for the issuer in that they offer the firm a chance to sell debt with lower interest rates and less restrictive covenants in exchange for a chance for the investor to participate in potential capital gains as the value of the firm, and therefore the equity, rises.

- Convertibles have some significant disadvantages for the issuer:

  1. If the firm's stock price increases significantly during the convertible's life, the firm might have been better off issuing regular debt, and then refunding the debt with a new stock issue.

  2. If the convertible issue has a low coupon rate, this will be lost if the holders convert the bonds into stock.

  3. If stock prices do not rise, the firm may be stuck with the debt issue, although it will typically be at a lower coupon rate than regular debt.

e. Warrants:[7] These securities were introduced in the section on long-term debt because they are often combined with long-term bond issues to make the purchase of the bonds more attractive to investors.

- Warrants are options issued by a company which give the warrant's owner the right to buy a stated number of shares of the company's stock at a specified price for a specified period of time. They are often listed on an exchange and traded like options.

- Unlike convertibles, warrants issued with bonds do represent additional equity capital for the issuing firm. Most warrants are "detachable," meaning they can be traded separately from the bond. When these warrants are exercised, the low-coupon bond issue remains outstanding, so the warrants bring additional funds into the firm while keeping its debt costs low.

- Warrants have been used extensively by small, rapidly growing firms as "sweeteners" when they were selling either debt or preferred stock.

- A bond with warrants has some of the characteristics of debt and some characteristics of equity, thus creating a hybrid security (sometimes called a bond with an "equity kicker") that provides the firm with the ability to expand its mix of securities and to appeal to a broader group of investors.

- Warrants may have the effect of diluting the value of the current stockholders' equity as well as the earnings per share (EPS). Some firms report a fully-diluted EPS figure which assumes that all outstanding warrants have been exercised. The SEC requires that disclosure of EPS should include information on the capital structure, explanation of the computation of EPS, identification of common stock equivalents (including convertibles, rights and warrants), number of shares converted, and assumptions made.

2. Preferred Stock: Although preferred stock is considered equity, it is very different from common stock both in terms of stockholder rights and payment stream. In terms of cash flows, it is more like debt than equity because of the fixed nature of its return. Unlike the case with debt, however, the firm will not risk bankruptcy by missing a preferred stock dividend.

a. Major Provisions of Preferred Stock Issues:

- **Priority in Assets and Earnings:** Preferred stockholders have priority in both earnings and assets. That is, they are paid their share of the earnings before the common shareholders. In the event of bankruptcy, their claims on the firm's assets are senior to those of the common shareholders but still behind those of the creditors.

- **Par Value:** Preferred stock always has a par value, which is usually used as the basis for setting dividends as a percentage or rate of return based on the par value.

- **Cumulative Dividends:** In the event that a firm is not able to pay required preferred dividends, these dividends become "in arrears." In most cases, preferred stock dividends are cumulative, which means that all arrears dividends owed must be paid in full before any common stock dividends can be paid. Therefore, a firm will not be able to pay any common stock dividends until all of the past-due (arrears) preferred dividends are paid. Many issues of preferred stock have provisions that if dividends are in arrears for a certain number of periods, the preferred stockholders may be granted voting rights and/or board memberships in order to protect their interests.

- **Convertibility:** Many preferred stock issues are convertible into either common stock or debt under certain conditions. Either of these features offers more flexibility to the issuer of the preferred stock, as well as a unique investment opportunity to the purchasers.

- **Other Provisions:** In recent years, many new provisions have been offered to help make preferred stock more attractive to investors. These include voting rights, participation in earnings, sinking funds, maturity dates, retirement dates, and exchange and call provisions.

b. Evaluation of Preferred Stock:

- **Issuer's Viewpoint:** The main advantage is that the firm can fix its financing costs and potentially leverage up the return to the common shareholders. With preferred stock, it can accomplish this without increasing the firm's default risk. Also, a large portion of preferred stock issues are private issues to institutional investors, which usually means substantially lower flotation costs and less stringent disclosure requirements for the issue. The major disadvantage is that preferred stock does not have the tax deductibility feature that debt does; therefore, its real cost is generally much higher than that of a similar debt issue.

- **Investor's Viewpoint:** Preferred stock provides investors with a steadier and more assured income than common stock does. Also, for most corporate holders of preferred stock, 70% of the dividends may be excluded from federal income tax. This makes preferred stocks especially attractive to institutional investors.

c. Recent Trends: Many firms have found the unique features of preferred stock to be advantageous to raising capital in certain circumstances.

- Utilities and financial institutions have been heavy users of preferred stock, and money markets have seen the development of adjustable rate preferred stocks (ARPS), which take advantage of the tax exclusion on dividends to offer higher returns to money market investors.

- As previously mentioned, there has been a movement toward offering convertible preferred. This has been the case in recent mergers, where convertible preferred was used to finalize the last bit of financing needed for the deals.

- Another recent development has been the introduction of adjustable rate preferred stock as a money market investment. This type of preferred stock is discussed in greater detail in Chapter 8, Short-Term Financial Management.

D. Hybrid, Synthetic and Derivative Security Markets

An increasing number of treasurers and CFOs are making extensive use of new types of securities to raise capital for their firms. Many of these securities are specially created to meet certain characteristics needed or desired by firms in the formation of their capital structure. These financial products include hybrid securities, hedges, swaps, options, synthetics, and derivatives, and their use is called "financial engineering."[8]

The first step in using hybrid and related securities is to perform a risk analysis of the firm's financing options. The purpose of this process is to: (1) identify business and financial risks,

(2) measure the risks, and (3) determine the kinds of outcomes the firm's management would like to achieve. After completing the analysis, a new financial structure for the firm can be developed using a variety of existing products such as swaps, futures, and forwards.

The basic types of securities, such as debt-related bonds and loans and equity-related common and preferred stock, were discussed earlier in this chapter. Some of the older forms of hybrid securities, such as convertible bonds and bonds issued with equity warrants, have been covered. The remainder of this section of the chapter will discuss some of the newer financial engineering tools, such as hybrids, hedges, swaps, options, and synthetic securities.

1. Hybrid Securities: Hybrid securities can be defined as securities which combine products from two or more different elemental markets to create a new security with unique risk/return characteristics. Typically, the primary elemental markets are: (1) interest rate (debt) markets, (2) foreign exchange (FOREX) markets, (3) equities markets, and (4) commodities markets. Several common market combinations are discussed below:

a. Interest-Rate/FOREX: A typical example of this type of security is the dual currency bond. In its simplest form, a dual currency bond is a fixed rate bond with interest payments denominated in one currency and principal payments (typically at maturity, but sometimes during the term) denominated in another currency. This type of arrangement would allow a multinational firm to raise capital in one currency (dollars, for example) to build a foreign plant but make the interest payments in a foreign currency. Examples of this type of security include Indexed Currency Option Notes (ICONS), Principal Exchange Rate-Linked Securities (PERLS), and Reverse Dual Currency Bonds.

b. Interest-Rate/Equity: The most common examples of this type of hybrid are equity-linked bonds, such as convertibles or bonds sold with stock warrants attached. These types of securities provide a return stream that is composed of both fixed interest payments and an equity component. A more recent innovation in this area would be bonds issued with a maturity value tied to some equity index. These instruments pay a regular fixed interest stream during their life, and at maturity the value of the principal repayment is linked to a major equity market index (MMI, S&P 500, NYSE Index, Nikkei 225, etc.). By offering an equity kicker, the bonds may be more attractive to certain investors, or the firm may be able to get a lower interest rate on the bonds.

c. Currency/Commodity: These securities combine a currency-based return with one that is commodity-based. For many of these securities, the underlying commodity is oil. One example of this type of security would be and oil/yen-linked issue which pays a fixed coupon in U.S. dollars over its life, but whose maturity value is linked to the differential between the yen-based price of a barrel of oil at the time of issuance versus the yen-based price of the barrel of oil at the security's maturity. The ultimate return on this type of instrument would be a function of both the commodity market for oil and the foreign exchange market for dollars versus yen.

These types of securities may be used by firms that deal in oil products and generate significant revenues in foreign markets.

2. Hedges, Swaps and Options: The different financial products and processes described in this section form the basic tool kit for the financial engineer.

a. Forwards and Futures:[9] Forwards and futures are contracts between two parties that require some specific action at a later date. Many firms use these types of products in the currency, financial, and commodity markets to provide hedges against risk by allowing the user to lock in a future price or rate on a financial asset, currency, or commodity item. In most cases, forwards and futures involve the contractual obligation of delivery of some underlying asset.

For currency futures and forwards, foreign currencies are the underlying assets; for financial futures and forwards, government securities are the underlying assets; and for the commodity markets, a wide variety of standard agricultural and resource commodities (gold, pork bellies, lumber, oil, etc.) serve as the underlying assets. Each of these products is discussed below, and the calculations involved in these types of contracts are provided at the end of this chapter.

- **Forwards:** Forward contracts are typically negotiated for specific transactions between two parties, and usually result in delivery of the underlying assets.
  - The advantage of forwards is that they can usually be created for almost any asset over any period of time.
  - The disadvantages are that (1) the cost of negotiating the contracts usually means they are only available for relatively large values, and (2) the market is very "thin" in the long-term (beyond 3–5 years).
  - The most active of the forward markets are the foreign exchange (currency) and money markets (short-term government securities).
  - The typical example of the forward market is a forward currency exchange. In this market a firm could contract to exchange one currency for another at a specified rate of exchange on a specified date. This allows the firm to hedge the transaction-based risk of foreign exchange exposure.

- **Futures:** Futures are similar to forwards in concept and their ability to provide risk management and hedging. There are, however, several important differences:
  - Futures are based on standardized contracts, with standard underlying assets, denomination amounts, delivery dates and terms. This may mean that a treasurer may not be able to hedge exactly an exposure in the futures market.
  - Futures are normally bought and traded on organized exchanges and require both margin accounts and constant adjustment of the value of the future to market. The primary futures markets in the U.S. are the Chicago Board of Trade, the Chicago Mercantile Exchange, the New York Mercantile Exchange, and the Commodity Exchange (New York). A more complete listing of these markets appears at the end of this chapter.

– The existence of margin accounts on futures allows investors in the market to benefit from leverage on their holding of futures. Margin requirements vary with the underlying asset and the riskiness of the market and specify the percentage of the total position that must be put up, in cash, in the margin account. For high risk markets and speculative positions, the required margin could be as high as 5–7%. For hedging positions, the typical margin would be in the 2–4% range, and for a spread position (long and short in the same commodity) the margin could be as little as 1–3%.

– In order to protect all of the participants in the market, contracts are "marked to the market" continuously throughout the trading day. The gains or losses are posted to the contract account, and a margin call is issued if the value of a future drops below a specified level. The holder of the contract is required to either put additional funds into the margin account, or close out his/her position. Similarly, if the contract increases in value, the excess above the required margin may be removed from the account and used elsewhere.

– Futures are only occasionally settled by actual delivery of the underlying asset, but rather are closed out prior to their maturity. The profit or loss from the futures position provides the required hedge for the holder of the futures contract. A listing of typical futures contract sizes and types is provided at the end of this chapter, as well as examples of futures contracts.

– Futures provide a true vehicle for both speculation and hedging by allowing smaller players in the market as compared to the forward market.

– The primary futures exchange in the United States is the Chicago Board of Trade (CBOT), which provides futures in agricultural commodities, financial instruments, currencies futures, and stock-market index futures.

– The primary market for currency futures is the International Monetary Exchange (IMM), which is part of the Chicago Mercantile Exchange. Active futures markets in a variety of commodities, currencies, and financial instruments also exist in New York, London, continental Europe, and Tokyo.

b. Swaps:[10] These very flexible instruments have shown rapid growth in recent years[11] and are now an important tool in financial risk management. In its simplest form, a swap is nothing more than two parties agreeing to exchange some underlying asset (or the stream of cash flows associated with an asset) for a specified period of time. It is very difficult, however, for two parties to a potential swap opportunity to find each other without some kind of intermediary. For many currency and interest rate swaps, this party is usually a financial intermediary (multinational bank) who acts as a counter-party or swap dealer. These swap dealers usually maintain "swap books" in which they try to balance out their overall exposure by arranging different swaps or hedges with other swap dealers and other clients throughout the world. In addition, these swap dealers make use of short-term money and currency markets to hedge their positions. Examples of swaps and the calculations involved appear at the end of this chapter.

The most common swaps include:

1) **Interest Rate Swaps:**[12] These arrangements are used to convert fixed-rate obligations to floating-rate obligations and vice-versa.

- The primary reason for these types of swaps is to change the type of risk and reduce the cost of financing.

- Typically, two parties want to borrow (or have borrowed) in two different markets. At least one of the borrowers can obtain better pricing than the other in one of the markets. The two markets are typically fixed-rate and floating-rate.

- By entering into a swap agreement (either directly or more likely through a swap dealer), both parties can obtain the kind of financing they prefer, while simultaneously taking full advantage of their relative borrowing efficiencies.

- For financial reporting purposes, the swap agreement in itself is not reflected on the balance sheet of either party. Each party records only the original transaction through which it funds the swap. The net interest differential paid or received under the swap agreement is booked as an adjustment to interest expense. Potential withholding taxes can be a consideration in an interest rate swap with a foreign counterparty.

- There is credit risk exposure for a firm entering into interest rate swap arrangements, but it can be minimized through selection of strong financial intermediaries or counterparties if it is a direct arrangement. The risk is also reduced because it does not involve repayment of principal, but only exchange of interest payments.

- Swap transactions are, however, potentially expensive to unwind and consequently may limit management's flexibility.

- The typical swap dealer in these kinds of transactions is a large financial intermediary that stands willing to make a market in interest rate swaps and takes the credit risk. Therefore, the user of swaps should also carefully check the credit condition of the dealer used in a swap arrangement. This will help to reduce further the riskiness of the transaction.

- A typical interest rate swap arrangement is outlined in Figure 2.1. In this arrangement the corporate client has an outstanding 5-year floating-rate note at LIBOR +0.75%, but would prefer to make fixed-rate payments. Through the commercial bank, the firm is able to arrange a swap by which the firm pays the bank fixed-rate payment (at 9.5%) on the underlying principal amount of the debt (called the notional amount). The bank "swaps" payments with the firm, paying them LIBOR + 0.75%, which is passed on to the holders of the note. The bank will generally offset their payments either internally (against other swap agreements) or externally as is shown in Figure 2-1. In this example, the bank is able to receive payments on floating-rate funds of LIBOR +0.875, while paying out fixed-rate interest of 9.0%.

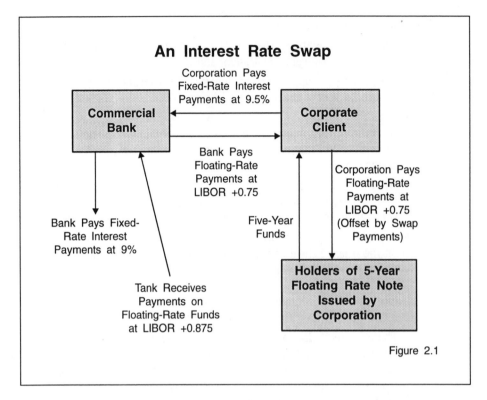

Figure 2.1

- The benefit of this type of arrangement to the firm is that they are able to convert a stream of variable-rate interest payments into a stream of fixed-rate interest payments. The bank benefits by earning a spread of 50 basis points in the fixed-rate portion of the transaction and 12.5 basis points on the floating-rate portion, for a total spread of 62.5 basis points or 0.625%.

2) **Currency Swaps:** These arrangements are used to convert an obligation in one currency to an obligation in another currency.

- Currency swaps are similar to interest rate swaps, but involve different currencies rather than different types of interest payments.

- Currency swaps may be combined with interest rate swaps in an arrangement known as a CIRCUS (covered in Chapter 8).

- A currency swap is viable whenever one party to the transaction has relatively less expensive access to one currency than it does to another. Typically, each party would have good access to financing in its own currency markets.

- A typical transaction involves one party that has access to dollar-based financing, but would prefer financing in another currency—Swiss francs, for example. Another party may have excellent access to Swiss franc financing or have large inflows from operations in Swiss francs, but would prefer dollar-based financing. These two parties may both benefit from a swap arrangement.

- The primary basis for the currency swap is that the two parties can borrow the currencies they need more efficiently (less expensively) through the swap than they can through directly accessing the foreign currency and money markets.

3) Commodity Swaps: These arrangements are used to convert a floating price for a commodity into a fixed price for that commodity.

- These types of swaps are often used in the oil market by both producers and manufacturers.

- A typical transaction involves one party that wants to fix the price it receives for selling a commodity and a second party that wants to fix the price it pays for the same commodity.

- Commodity swaps can be approximated by using commodity futures and options to lock in prices of commodities.

- The swap dealers in this market do typically bear some risk, but may be able to offset some of the risk in futures or forward markets for the underlying commodity.

4) Basis Swap: These arrangements (also known as a rate-basis swap) are used to convert a borrowing agreement from one rate basis to another. For example, one firm may have a variable-rate liability based on the prime rate, while another firm may have similar liability based on LIBOR. The companies may be inclined to swap liabilities if they feel that the other's rate index would save interest dollar expenses over the near term. This has been referred to as a "floating swap" and may involve compensation from one party to the other to make it an even transaction.

c. Single-Period Options:[13] Options are typically broken out by whether they exist over a single time period or over multiple time periods. This section covers the features and characteristics of single-period options. Examples of options pricing and calculations are included at the end of this chapter.

- An option is a contract between two parties in which one of the parties (the purchaser of the option) has the right, but not the obligation, to buy or sell some underlying asset at specified price during some future time period.

- An option to buy the underlying asset is a call option, while an option to sell the underlying assets is a put option.

- In return for this right, the purchaser of the option pays the seller a flat, up-front fee called a premium.

- The seller of the option (usually called the writer of the option) keeps the premium whether the purchaser exercises the option or not. The writer, however, has the obligation to fulfill the contract (buy or sell the underlying asset) if the buyer of the option chooses to exercise it.

- The typical use of an option is to provide the purchaser of the option with either a floor price for selling the underlying asset, or a ceiling price for buying the underlying asset. This provides protection against harmful price movements, but allows unlimited potential for gain. This is a very different concept from futures and forwards, which simply lock in a known price for some exchange in the future.

- Options exist for a wide variety of underlying assets, including: stocks, currencies, market indices, futures, and commodities.

- Most options traded in the U.S. are American Options, which allow the option to be exercised at any time during its effective life. This is in contrast to the European Option, which can only be exercised on the expiration date or during the five-day period prior to that date.

- Many options are listed and traded on organized exchanges such as the CBOE (Chicago Board of Options Exchange). Most options in the United States are cleared through the Option Clearing Corporation (OCC) located in Chicago.

- Since option writers have an open-ended commitment, they must maintain margin accounts with the exchanges. Purchasers of options have no commitment, therefore margin accounts are not required for them.

- As an alternative to the over-the-counter options market, many multinational banks are active in the options market, providing specialized currency options for their customers. While a sophisticated options user may be able to manage the creation of complex options (where several over-the-counter options must be combined to achieve a desired result), it is often easier for less sophisticated users to purchase this kind of option from a bank.

d. Multi-Period Options:[14] These types of instruments are similar to the single-period options covered above, but are designed to exist over multiple periods or to have multi-period assets as the underlying commodity. The most common of these instruments are caps, floors, and collars on interest rates. Examples of the calculations involved are provided at the end of this chapter.

- **Interest Rate Caps:** Caps provide borrowers (buyers of funds) with a maximum rate (ceiling) on their loan interest over the period of the loan or credit agreement. This protects the borrower on a variable-rate credit arrangement from rising interest rates, but allows them to take advantage of possible decreasing interest rates.

- **Interest Rate Floors:** Floors provide investors (sellers of funds) with a minimum rate (floor) on their investment earnings over the period of the investment. This protects the investors from falling interest rates, but allows them the potential to benefit if interest rates increase. Debt issuers may also be able to get a lower rate if they agree to an interest rate floor on variable rate borrowings.

- **Interest Rate Collars:** These arrangements provide a simultaneous cap and floor that lock the interest rate either paid or earned within a predetermined range. Due to the limited potential for loss on the part of the option writer, collars are often less expensive to obtain than either caps or floors. Collars generally are priced in a variety of ways, depending on the size of the range. They may be obtained for little or no fee by choosing one side of the collar and allowing the other party to choose the opposite side of the collar.

e. Forward Rate Agreements (FRA):[15] This is a contract by which two parties agree on the interest rate to be paid at a future settlement date. The contract period is quoted as, for example, six against nine months, and the interest rate for a three-month period commencing in six-months time. The principal amounts are agreed, but never exchanged, and the contracts are settled in cash; exposure is limited to the difference in interest rates between the agreed and actual rates at settlement. The majority of FRAs are based on Eurodollar rates, although others are available.

3. Arbitrage and Synthetics:[16] Arbitrage typically involves two or more simultaneous transactions, usually in different markets, to take advantage of relative inefficiencies or price discrepancies between these markets.

- Many of the arbitrage arrangements utilize synthetic securities in order to manage the arbitrage process. The key reason for their development is to create securities that either do not currently exist or exist in very short supply.

- Synthetic instruments or securities are not really securities, but rather a combination or decomposition of cash flow streams from certain instruments or financial arrangements, which replicate or synthesize cash flow streams from real assets. Almost anything can be created for a price and with a willing counterparty.

- One of the early developments of synthetic securities was the synthetic zero (zero-coupon) bond. A real zero coupon bond has no coupon payments, only a single payment at maturity. At one point, these bonds were very popular investments and the demand far outweighed the supply. Banks and other financial institutions created synthetic zeros by taking regular coupon bonds, stripping off the coupons, and selling this payment stream to investors looking for regular income (like pension funds). They then took the remaining principal payment and sold that as a zero-coupon synthetic. The synthetic in this case was created by stripping the cash flows into two separate streams.

There is a wide variety of synthetic instruments available today in the financial markets. The more important of these are discussed in the following section:

a. Cash-and-Carry Synthetic: This transaction involves the purchase of a long-term instrument and the simultaneous sale of a futures contract against the instrument to create a synthetic short-term instrument. These are created in order to earn low-risk, higher short-term rates, and are often referred to as synthetic T-Bills. Due to arbitrage differentials between the money markets and the futures markets, there are times when synthetic T-Bills provide superior returns to the actual purchase of a T-Bill.

b. Synthetic Long-Term Bonds: In this case, several short-term T-Bills are strung together with T-Bond futures to create a synthetic long-term instrument. As in the case above, depending on market conditions, there are sometimes arbitrage differentials that make the synthetic superior to the real T-Bond. The incentive for this type of contract is to get a better long-term rate than would be available from using conventional instruments.

c. Using Swaps to Synthesize Positions: When swaps are properly structured and combined with appropriate cash positions, it is possible to create the cash flow stream associated with almost any financial instrument. Some of the possible securities which can be replicated though the synthesis of swaps are dual currency bonds and foreign currency zero-coupon bonds. As above, the advantages of using these types of synthetics would be a cash flow stream superior to a similar conventional instrument, and their availability versus the conventional instrument.

d. Synthetic Equity: These instruments are similar to equity options and index futures currently sold on many exchanges but are available in larger denominations and for longer terms. The primary advantages to these types of instruments are that they trade on an over-the-counter basis rather than on exchanges, and can therefore be tailored more easily to fit the needs of individual clients (i.e., flexible amounts and maturity dates rather than those fixed by the exchange).

e. Differences between Synthetic and Real Securities: While the cash flow streams between real and synthetic securities may be quantitatively the same or very similar, there may be significant qualitative differences between the two cash flow streams. Qualitative features include:

- The likelihood that a cash flow pattern may change on one instrument but not another.
- The jurisdiction for litigating an instrument in the event of default or bankruptcy.
- The difficulty in tracking returns from the instrument.
- The amount and type of documentation needed to fully effect and to enforce a transaction.
- Any lags involved in the receipt of payments.
- The length of time it takes to put a deal together.
- Any variation margins that might be required in synthetics involving futures or the writing of options.
- Whether a position is on- or off-balance financing.

f. Risks in Using Synthetic Financing: Based on the discussion above, it is obvious that the use of synthetics changes the risk profile of the firm. Whether this causes an increase or a decrease in the overall risk is very much dependent on the exact mix of financing instruments used by the firm. It is important to consider the overall risk placed on the financial markets by the increased use of those instruments (systemic risk). The basic recommendation is that both the quantitative and qualitative differences between the real and synthetic instruments must be considered at the outset or the firm may run the risk of unpleasant surprises later. The financial condition of both the dealer and counterparty to the transaction should be carefully considered.

E. Other Issues and Markets

1. Market for Private Placements: Private placements of debt and equity securities are becoming more and more popular as a source of funds for firms. In these arrangements, securities are typically sold to one, or a small group, of institutional investors. The primary advantages are lower flotation costs and a faster issuance process due to the lack of SEC registration requirements.

a. Debt Private Placements: Debt issues are often placed privately with either institutional investors (pension funds, insurance companies, etc.) or with bank trust departments. The advantages for the firm are generally less restrictive covenants on the debt, lower flotation costs on the issue and speedier access to funds. Additional considerations are less stringent disclosure requirements and the associated work and costs of disclosure.

b. Equity Private Placements: Most equity private placements are preferred stock to institutional investors. As in the case of debt, private placement usually results in less restrictive covenants, lower flotation costs, and faster issuance. The potential disadvantage in the equity arena is that large institutional investors are increasingly asking for representation on the firm's board of directors as a condition of the placement. Firms may use private equity placements to get stock (common or voting preferred) into "friendly hands" to avoid a potential takeover or to provide quick access to capital without formal registration procedures, as long as no pre-emptive rights covenants are violated in the process.

2. International Capital Markets:[17] From the perspective of a U.S. firm, foreign capital markets are a potential source of additional capital, especially for their international operations. Though the bulk of the activity in these markets is debt-related, there are more and more U.S. firms issuing equity in foreign markets. For securities of U.S. firms listed outside the U.S., security regulations of the foreign markets will apply. A partial listing of the regulations by major market is provided in a checklist at the end of this chapter.

a. International Debt Markets: Any bond which is sold outside of the U.S. is referred to as an international bond, but there are actually two basic types of these bonds:

- **Foreign Bonds:** For a U.S.-based firm, foreign bonds are those which are issued in foreign countries and are denominated in the currency of that country. For example, if a U.S.-based firm were to issue French franc denominated bonds in France, they would be called foreign bonds.

- **Eurobonds:** This second type of international bond represents bonds which are sold by international syndicates and are denominated in currencies other than that of the country of issue. For example, if a U.S.-based firm were to sell U.S. dollar denominated bonds in France, they would be referred to as Eurobonds. They are attractive to both issuers and investors. For issuers, the disclosure requirements are reduced and government regulations are significantly relaxed. For the investor, these bonds are issued in bearer form (rather than registered form), which provides for investor privacy.

b. International Equity Markets: The primary international equity markets outside of the United States are located in London, Europe (continental) and Tokyo. The primary benefits of international equity issues are:

1. They enable a firm to gain access to alternative capital markets and to diversify its funding sources.

2. The distribution of the firm's stock is widened to include international investors and a broader, more liquid market for the equity.

3. The firm has increased recognition and visibility in global capital markets, which makes it easier to raise capital in the future.

There are several forms which the equity issues in foreign capital markets can take:

- **Euroequity Offerings:** These are international offerings of common stock, typically underwritten by an international syndicate of investment banks. The stock is issued on European capital markets, but will also trade on the international over-the-counter market, on the issuer's domestic stock exchange, and on any foreign exchange where the firm's shares may be listed.

- **Multi-market or Foreign Offerings:** These are offerings of shares which are issued and registered simultaneously in more than one national market. Such issues are usually underwritten and distributed separately in each major national market, and typically are listed and traded on each market's stock exchange.

- **International Private Placements:** These are private sales of shares to major institutional investors abroad. These issues are usually in the form of venture capital financing, and are not generally traded or sold outside of the institutional investor community until the issuer goes public.

- **Euroconvertible Market:** There is a market for equity-linked bonds and convertibles in the foreign capital markets, just as there is in the U.S. These issues are typically referred to as: equity-linked Eurobonds, convertible Eurobonds, Euroconvertibles or Eurobonds with Equity Warrants. This market may be especially attractive for U.S. issuers for several reasons:

  - European investors may regard bonds issued by a well-known U.S. corporation as particularly desirable due to tax considerations and different investment criteria.

  - A U.S. issuer has much more timing flexibility in issuing a Euroconvertible than a domestic issue because the foreign issue does not have to be filed with the SEC as long as it is not sold in the U.S. The existence of such financing, however, must be disclosed to U.S. investors in SEC reports filed by the firm.

  - Selling securities in a foreign market will have less of an impact on the price of the firm's securities than selling the same amount in the firm's primary domestic market.

  - A convertible Eurobond will help to establish the issuer's presence in both the bond and equity sectors of the Euromarket, creating additional interest among non-U.S. dollar-based investors.

3. Venture Capital:[18] The venture capital market is a large, diverse market that provides financing and management expertise for many types of firms. Venture capital financing is typically directed toward firms with high risk, but yielding high-potential returns.

- A distinguishing characteristic of most venture capital investments is that the venture capitalists take an active rather than a passive role in their investments. For the firms they are involved in, they often serve on the board of directors and are likely to stipulate specific performance objectives as part of a financing deal through management covenants.

- The venture capital market provides both capital and managerial expertise to small companies that are at their first stage of real growth (i.e., businesses that need additional capital to initiate or expand commercial manufacturing and sales).

- The venture capitalists in this market also provide capital and expertise to expand second-stage companies, which are already producing a product and/or making sales, and need additional capital for expansion.

- Finally, venture capital often plays a significant role in management of leveraged buyouts by providing the final portion of the required financing.

There are several types of venture capital firms or arrangements which provide capital and expertise to emerging firms:

- The typical provider of venture capital is a private venture capital firm. These companies are usually run as limited partnerships, in which the venture capitalist acts as a general partner and typically raises from $5 million to $100 million or more from pension funds, insurance companies, and large investors. The general partner seeks companies which are likely candidates for venture capital funding, and will usually retain 20% of any profits from the investment after the original investment and management fees are returned. The typical venture capital provider requires a payback and investment horizon of no more than 3–5 years, as well as required after-tax returns of 30–50% per year on the investment.

- Another type of capital venture firm is the Small Business Investment Companies (SBIC) which are supported by the federal government and work in conjunction with the Small Business Administration (SBA) to make investments in smaller U.S.-based companies.

- The final type of venture capital firm is the corporate venture capital firm, which is typically a subsidiary of a large corporation. These subsidiaries provide the large corporation with a window on new technologies, new markets and products, a partnership to eliminate a potential competitor, potential acquisition candidates, and a vehicle for acquiring entrepreneurial talent for the corporation's other divisions.

4. Bankruptcy:[19] For a firm in financial distress, bankruptcy may be the only option to save the firm. Bankruptcy will be covered in greater detail in Chapter 3, but relative to the topics in this chapter, the following observations can be made:

- Bankruptcies may be classified as either operational or financial. In operational bankruptcy, the firm is not able to generate profits, even before its debt obligations. The primary options in this case are either restructuring the firm's business, closing some part of the business, or complete liquidation of the firm's assets. Firms may be in financial bankruptcy, where the firm makes money on an operational basis but cannot make its required debt payments. In this case, reorganization may be used to reduce, eliminate, or restructure the timing of the debt.

- In essence, a firm is a potential candidate for bankruptcy if it cannot meet its current or upcoming financial obligations. Firms may consider bankruptcy if large potential or contingent liabilities (i.e., from a lawsuit) far outweigh the firm's' ability to meet those liabilities. The threat of bankruptcy, or even liquidation, may be used to force the current bondholders of a firm to accept equity in exchange for their bonds.

- Bankruptcy proceedings may be either formal or informal and can result in either a reorganization of the company (Chapter 11—worth more alive than dead) or in liquidation (Chapter 7—worth more dead than alive).

IV. Chapter Checklists

A. Characteristics and Rights of Stakeholders in a Corporation

Stakeholders may be creditors, employees, customers, suppliers, or even citizens in towns with production plants. Stakeholders may not necessarily have a contractual relationship with the firm, but all stakeholders have an interest in the firm's solvency.

Bondholders:

- Hold debt security, generally medium- to long-term.
- Receive interest and principal payments at contractual time frames.
- May be subordinated to senior debt.

Equityholders:

- Residual owners of the firm.
- Can have preference in payment of dividends, i.e., "preferred" equity versus no preference, as in the case of holders of common shares.
- General pre-emptive right to anything of value distributed by the firm.
- Ultimate control of the firm's affairs through the right to vote on appointment of the Board of Directors.

Creditors:

- May be entities or individuals to whom debt is owed in a hierarchy of claims (see section on bankruptcy for priority of claims).
- Hold negotiated contract with defined terms and conditions.
- May hold a security interest in assets of the firm.

- May request guarantees of shareholders, principals, or business partners.
- Hold a contractual agreement outlining repayment of principal and interest at set intervals.

B. Listing of Required SEC Reports

Types of companies and relevant sections of the 1934 Act under which firms must report to the SEC include:

- Companies whose securities are listed on the national securities exchanges [Section 12(b)].
- Companies whose securities are traded over the counter, if those companies have total assets in excess of $3 million and 500 or more stockholders [Section 12(g)].
- Companies whose securities are traded over the counter, which do not meet the asset and stockholder tests above, but which have elected to voluntarily comply with the 1934 Act reporting requirements [Section 15(g)].
- Companies with over 500 stockholders of a class of securities that are registered under the 1934 Act [Section 15(d)].

Categories of Report Forms:

- Forms for registration of national securities exchanges.
- Forms for reports to be filed by officers, directors, and security holders.
- Forms for registration of securities on national securities exchanges.
- Forms for annual and other reports of issuers.
- Forms for amendments to registration statements and reports to issuers.
- Forms for registration of brokers and dealers on over-the-counter markets.
- Forms for reports by certain exchange members, brokers, and dealers.
- Forms for reports concerning stabilization.
- Forms for registration and reporting by national securities associations and affiliates.
- Forms for reports by market makers and certain other registered broker-dealers in securities traded on national securities exchanges.

SEC Report Forms:

8-A	For registration of certain classes of securities
8-B	For registration of securities of certain issuers
10	For registration of a class of securities for which no other form is specified
18	For registration of securities of foreign governments or political subdivisions
19	For permanent registration of American certificates issued against securities of certain other foreign issuers
20-F	For registration of certain foreign issuers
BD	General registration form for all brokers and dealers

8-K   Current report required to be filed within 15 days after the occurrence of a "material" event

10-K   Annual report for which no other form is prescribed and which must be filed within 90 days of the end of each fiscal year

11-K   Annual report for employee stock purchase or similar plans

18-K   Annual reports of foreign governments or political subdivisions

19-K   Annual report form for issuers of American certificates

20-K   Annual report form for foreign private issuers

7-Q   Quarterly reports of real estate investment trusts or of companies whose major business is holding real estate

10-Q   Quarterly reports containing specified financial information filed for each of the first three quarters of a company's fiscal year and which must be filed within 30 days of the end of each fiscal quarter

SEC Schedules:

I.   Marketable securities—other investments

II.   Amounts receivable from related parties and underwriters, promoters, and employees other than related parties

III.   Condensed financial information of registrant

IV.   Indebtedness of and to related parties

V.   Property, plant, and equipment

VI.   Accumulated depreciation, depletion, and amortization of property, plant, and equipment

VII.   Guarantees of securities of other issues

VIII.   Valuation and qualifying accounts

IX.   Short-term borrowings

X.   Supplemental income statement information

XI.   Real estate and accumulated depreciation

XII.   Mortgage loans on real estate

XIII.   Other investments

C. Listing of Typical Restrictive Covenants

Typical Restrictive Covenants:

- Restriction on new debt issues
- Restriction on dividend payments
- Restriction on mergers, acquisitions, or divestitures
- Cross-default clauses

Other Covenants:

- Minimum levels of working capital
- Minimum levels of net worth
- Interest coverage ratios
- Operating ratios
- Maintenance of qualified management
- Material Adverse Changes (MAC) clauses
- Ownership change restrictions

D. Listing of Foreign Security Market Regulations

The following are basic requirements for U.S. companies to be listed on various foreign exchanges. The requirements for listing on the primary U.S. exchanges are presented at the end of Chapter 3.

1. Australian Stock Exchange Limited (AUSTRALIA)

Listing Requirements: concerned with the constitution of the company, how the capital is raised, and disclosure of information about the company to shareholders.

2. Central Bank and the Securities Commission (BRAZIL)

Listing Requirements: past audited financial statements along with other detailed information, having a wide distribution of stock so that an adequate market will exist, and several minimum numerical standards.

3. Toronto Stock Exchange (CANADA)

Listing Requirements (two ways):

1. Net assets of C$1 million
2. Adequate working capital
3. Evidence showing an opportunity of future profitability
4. One million freely tradable shares totaling at least C$1 million in market value must be held by at least 300 public shareholders.

OR

1. C$100,000 in earnings before taxes and extraordinary items in the last fiscal year
2. Cash flow (pretax) of $400,000 in the last fiscal year
3. Adequate working capital
4. One million freely tradable shares totaling C$1,000,000 in value must be held by at least 300 public shareholders.

4. Commission des Operations de Bourse (COB) (FRANCE)

Listing Requirements: details of the company must be submitted to the COB and the *Conseil des Bourses de Valeurs*; authorization from the Ministry of Economy, Finance and Budget;

register shares with the *Societe Interprofessionnelle pour la Compensation de Valeurs Mobilieres* over a two-year period if equal to at least FF50 million; and fulfill certain publication, notice, and periodic reporting requirements.

5. Frankfurt Stock Exchange (GERMANY)

Listing Requirements: application must be made by a bank, containing financial information about the company along with a moderately detailed prospectus, and annual reports must be submitted.

6. National Commission for Companies and the Stock Exchange (CONSOB) (ITALY)

Listing Requirements: net equity greater than Lit50 billion (Lit = Italian lira) for banks and insurance companies, net equity greater than Lit10 billion for other organizations; have a net profit over the last three years; 25% of outstanding shares must be publicly owned; periodic financial statements and reports along with other public data and information must be submitted.

7. Tokyo Stock Exchange (JAPAN)

Listing Requirements: must be listed on a United States stock exchange; must have been incorporated and been in business for the last five years; good liquidity on one of the United States stock exchanges; possibility of at least 1,000 Japanese shareholders; shareholders' equity in the preceding year must have been at least 10 billion Yen; profit before taxes must be over 2 billion Yen for each of the last three years; and paid dividend over the last three years.

8. Mexican Stock Exchange (MEXICO)

Listing Requirements: prior approval from the National Securities Commission, provide annual audited financial statements, and unaudited quarterly financial statements.

9. Securities Market National Commission (SPAIN)

Listing Requirements: previous year's audited financial statements, statement of last year's profits, number of shareholders, be an incorporated company, and company statutes.

10. Swiss Stock Exchange Association (SWITZERLAND)

Listing Requirements: last five years' audited financial statements, paid-in-capital of at least SFr5 million, issue size must be at least SFr20 million or market value of at least SFr50 million, and approval from the Swiss Admission Board.

11. London Stock Exchange

Listing Requirements: market value of the new issues must be £700,000; 25% of outstanding stocks must be publicly owned; show a trading record over the last five years; assets cannot be all cash or short-dated securities; and provide immediate notification of dividends, profit, losses, capital changes, and other relevant information.

E. Listing Futures and Options Markets (Global)

1. Exchanges for Commodity Futures and Futures Options:

BIFFEX	Baltic International Freight Futures Exchange
CBT	Chicago Board of Trade
CME	Chicago Mercantile Exchange
COMEX	Commodity Exchange, New York
CSCE	Coffee, Sugar & Cocoa Exchange, New York
CTN	New York Cotton Exchange
IMM	International Monetary Market (at CME)
IPE	International Petroleum Exchange
KC	Kansas City Board of Trade
LCE	London Commodity Exchange
LGF	London Grain Futures Market
LIFFE	London International Financial Futures Exchange
LME	London Metal Exchange
LPFA	London Potato Futures Association
LSFM	London Sugar Futures Market
MCE	MidAmerica Commodity Exchange
ME	Montreal Exchange
MPLS	Minneapolis Grain Exchange
NYFE	New York Futures Exchange (unit of the NYSE)
NYMEX	New York Mercantile Exchange
PhilSE	Philadelphia Stock Exchange
SFE	Sydney Futures Exchange
WPG	Winnipeg Commodity Exchange

2. Commodity Futures

a. Agricultural/Animal

COMMODITY	MARKETS	CONTRACT SIZE	QUOTE AMOUNT
Cattle	CME, MCE	feeder—50,000 lbs. live—40,000 lbs.	cents per lb. cents per lb.
Cocoa	CSCE, LCE	10 metric tons	$ per ton
Coffee	CSCE, LCE	37,500 lbs.	cents per lb.
Corn	CBT, MCE	5,000 bu.	cents per lb.
Cotton	CTN	50,000 lbs.	cents per lb.
Hogs	CME, MCE	40,000 lbs.	cents per lb.
Oats	CBT, MCE, WPG	5,000 bu.	cents per lb.
Orange Juice	CTN	15,000 lbs.	cents per lb.
Pork Bellies	CME	40,000 lbs.	cents per lb.

COMMODITY	MARKETS	CONTRACT SIZE	QUOTE AMOUNT
Soybean Oil	CBT	60,00 lbs.	cents per lb.
Soybean Meal	CBT, MCE	100 tons	$ per ton
Soybeans	CBT, MCE	5,000 bu.	cents per lb.
Sugar	CSCE, LSFM	112,000 lbs.	cents per lb.
Wheat	CBT, KC, LGF, MCE, MPLS, WPG	50,000 bu. WPG—20 metric tons	cents per bu. Can. $ per ton

b. Metals/Natural Resources

COMMODITY	MARKETS	CONTRACT SIZE	QUOTE AMOUNT
Aluminum	COMEX, LME	40,000 lbs.	cents per lb.
Copper	COMEX, LME, MCE	25,000 lbs.	cents per lb.
Crude Oil	NYMEX	1,000 bbls.	$ per bbl.
Gas Oil	IPE	100 metric tons	$ per ton
Gold	CBT, COMEX, MCE	100 troy oz.	$ per troy oz.
Heating Oil	NYMEX	42,000 gal.	$ per gal.
Lumber	CME, ME	160,000 board ft.	$ per 1,000 board ft.
Palladium	NYMEX	100 troy oz.	$ per troy oz.
Platinum	MCE, NYMEX	50 troy oz.	$ per troy oz.
Propane	CTN	42,000 gal.	cents per lb.
Silver	CBT, COMEX, LME, MCE	1,000 troy oz. 5,000 troy oz.	cents per troy oz.

3. Financial Futures

COMMODITY	MARKETS	CONTRACT SIZE	QUOTE AMOUNT
Australian Dollar	IMM	100,000 Aust. $	cents per Aust. $
Canadian Dollar	IMM, MCE	100,000 Can. $	cents per Can $
German Deutschmark	IMM, LIFFE, MCE	125,000 marks	cents per mark
European Currency Unit (ECU)	IMM	125,000 ECU	cents per ECU
U.K. Pound Sterling (BP)	IMM, LIFFE, MCE	62,500 BP	cents per BP
Swiss Franc	IMM, LIFFE, MCE	125,000 francs	cents per franc
U.S. Dollar Index	CTN	500 times index	pts of 100%

COMMODITY	MARKETS	CONTRACT SIZE	QUOTE AMOUNT
Japanese Yen	IMM, LIFFE, MCE	12.5 million yen	cents per yen
U.S. Stock Market Indexes (S&P 500, NYSE)	CBT, IMM, KC, NYFE, PhilSE	500 times index	pts of 100%
U.S. Treasury Bills	IMM, MCE	$1 million	pts. of 100%
U.S. Treasury Notes	CBT	$100,000	pts. 32nds of 100%
U.S. Treasury Bonds	CBT, LIFFE, MCE	$100,000 or $50,000	pts. 32nds of 100%
Eurodollar Deposits	IMM, LIFFE	$1 million	pts. of 100%
U.S. Municipal Bond Index	CBT	$100,000	pts 32nds of 100%

4. Option Exchanges:

AMEX   American Stock Exchange
CBOE   Chicago Board Options Exchange
CBT   Chicago Board of Trade
CME   Chicago Mercantile Exchange
COMEX   Commodity Exchange, New York
CSCE   Coffee, Sugar & Cocoa Exchange, New York
EOE   European Options Exchange
IMM   International Monetary Market (at CME)
KC   Kansas City Board of Trade
LIFFE   London International Financial Futures Exchange
LSE   London Stock Exchange
MCE   MidAmerica Commodity Exchange
MPLS   Minneapolis Grain Exchange
ME   Montreal Exchange
NASDAQ   National Association of Securities Dealers Automated Quotations
NYCE   New York Cotton Exchange
NYFE   New York Futures Exchange (unit of the NYSE)
NYSE   New York Stock Exchange
PSE   Pacific Stock Exchange
PhilSE   Philadelphia Stock Exchange
SFE   Sydney Futures Exchange
TFE   Toronto Futures Exchange
VSE   Vancouver Stock Exchange

6. Options and Location of Trading:

COMMODITY	MARKETS	CONTRACT SIZE	QUOTE AMOUNT
U.S. Common Stocks	AMEX, CBOE, NYSE, PSE, PhilSE	100 shares	$ and 16ths of $
U.S. Stock Market Indexes	AMEX, CBOE, IMM, NASDAQ, NYFE, NYSE, PSE, PhilSE	500 times index	
U.S. Treasury Bonds and Notes	CBT	$100,000	pts. and 64ths of 100%
Eurodollar Deposits	IMM, LIFFE	$ million	pts. of 100%
Australian Dollars	SFE	$100,000 Aust. $	cents per Aust. $
Canadian Dollars	CBOE, ME, PhilSE, VSE	100,000 Can. $	cents per Can. $
German Deutschmark	CBOE, ME, EOE, LSE, CME, PhILSE	125,000 marks	cents per mark
European Currency Unit (ECU)	EOE	125,000 ECU	cents per ECU
U.K. Pound Sterling	CBOE, IMM, EOE, LIFFE, LSE, ME, PhilSE	62,500 BP	cents per BP
Swiss Franc	CBOE, IMM, ME, PhilSE	125,000 francs	cents per franc
Japanese Yen	CBOE, PhilSE	12.5 million yen	cents per 100 yen
Gold	COMEX, EOE, MCE, ME, VSE	100 troy oz.	$ per troy oz.
Silver	CBT, COMEX, EOE, TFE, VSE	5,000 troy oz.	cents per troy oz.
Gold and Silver Index	PhilSE		
Cattle	CME	feeder—50,000 lbs. live—40,000 lbs.	cents per lb.
Corn	CBT	5,000 bu.	cents per bu.
Cotton	NYCE	50,000 lbs.	cents per lb.
Hogs	CME	live—40,000 lbs.	cents per lb.
Soybeans	CBT, MCE	5,000 bu.	cents per bu.
Sugar	CSCE	112,000 lbs.	cents per lb.
Wheat	KC, MCE, MPLS	5,000 bu.	cents per bu.

V. Calculations and Examples

A. Calculations in Sinking Fund Arrangements

A firm issues 20-year bonds with annual sinking fund payments of 3 percent of principal beginning in the fifth year. This requirement calls for 15 annual sinking fund payments of 3%, leaving 55% of par value to be repaid at final maturity.

Percentage payable at maturity $= 100 - [15 \times 3\%] = 55\%$ payable at maturity

For a $100 million bond issue, sinking fund payments would be $3 million for 15 years, with $55 million due at maturity.

A bond issue with sinking fund provisions may have a call provision allowing the firm to call the bonds at random on the required sinking fund payment dates.

The firm should also investigate purchasing the bonds on the open market in order to satisfy the sinking fund arrangement. In this case, the firm would examine the current yield to maturity on the outstanding bonds, then compare the price of purchasing these bonds on the open market versus funding the sinking fund arrangement.

B. Calculations Involved in Bond Refunding Operations

Bond refunding: Use a net present value calculation to analyze whether or not to refund the issue. Discount future interest savings back to the present and compare the discounted value with the cash outlays associated with refunding. The firm should refund the issue if the present value of the savings is greater than the all-in cost.

Conditions:

- Original issue is for 25 years, $50 million issue, interest at 14%, with flotation costs of $2.5 million
- Currently have 20 years remaining to maturity
- Flotation costs are being amortized on a straight-line-basis over the 25-year original life of the issue
- Call provision allows retirement at this time by calling the bonds at a 10% premium
- Could sell a new issue of $50 million, 20-year maturity bonds, at 10%
- Flotation costs (payments to investment banks and other financial intermediaries) of the new refunding issue are $2.25 million
- Corporate tax rate is 40%
- To ensure that funds are available to pay off the old issue, structure in a one-month overlap and invest proceeds at short-term rate of 6%

1. Determine the Investment Outlay Required to Refund the Issue

a. Call Premium

Before-tax: $0.10 \times (\$50{,}000{,}000) = \$5{,}000{,}000$
After-tax: $\$5{,}000{,}000 \times (1-T) = \$5{,}000{,}000 \times (.6) = \$3{,}000{,}000$

b. Flotation Costs of New Issue

Flotation costs are $2.25 million and are amortized over the life of the bond. Annual tax deduction:

$2.25 million/20 = $112,500

The firm is in 40% tax bracket, therefore receives tax savings for 20 years of $112,500 × (.4) = $45,000.

All cash flows are discounted at the firm's after-tax cost of new debt, or .10 × (1–T) = .10 × (.6) = .60 = 6%.

Present value of tax savings, discounted at 6% = $516,146

The net after-tax cost of new flotation issue:

Gross flotation cost on new issue		$2,250,000
Minus:	Present value associated with tax savings	516,146
Equals:	Net after-tax flotation cost of new issue	$1,733,854

c. Flotation Costs of Old Issue

Unamortized flotation cost = (20/25) × ($2,500,000) = $2,000,000

If the original bonds were retired, unamortized flotation cost would be recognized immediately as an expense, therefore the after-tax savings are:

$2,000,000 × (T) = $2,000,000 × (.40) = $800,000

The firm can no longer receive a tax deduction of $100,000 a year for the next 20 years, or an after-tax benefit of $40,000

Present value of this tax savings, discounted at 6%, is $458,797

Net after-tax effect of the old flotation costs is $341,203, and is calculated as:

Tax savings from immediate write-off of old flotation costs		$800,000
Minus:	Present value of tax savings on old flotation costs had the refunding not occurred	458,797
Equals:	Net after-tax savings on the old flotation costs	$341,203

d. Additional Interest

One month "extra" interest on the old issue, after-tax, costs the firm $351,000.

Interest Cost = ($50,000,000) × (.14/12) × (1–T)
($50,000,000) × (.0117) × (.6) = $351,000

Proceeds from the new issue can be invested in short-term securities for one month. $50,000,000 invested at 6% will return $150,000

Interest Earned = ($50,000,000) × (.06/12) × (1–T)
($50,000,000)(.005)(.6) = $150,000

Net additional after-tax additional interest cost is $201,000:

Interest paid on old issue	$351,000
Minus: Interest earned on short-term securities	150,000
Equals: Net additional interest cost	$201,000

e. Total After-Tax Investment

Total investment outlay required to refund the bond issue:

Call premium	$3,000,000
Plus: New flotation costs, net of tax savings	1,733,854
Minus: Old flotation costs, net of tax savings	341,203
Plus: Additional interest	201,000
Equals: Total investment outlay	$4,593,651

2. Calculate the Present Value of Annual Interest Savings

a. Interest on Old Bond, After-Tax

Annual interest on the old bond, after-tax is:

$$(\$50,000,000) \times (.14)(0.6) = \$4,200,000$$

b. Interest on the New Bond, After-Tax

Annual interest on the new bond, after-tax is:

$$(\$50,000,000) \times (.10) \times (0.6) = \$3,000,000$$

c. Annual Savings

Annual, after-tax, savings on interest is:

Interest on the old bond	$4,200,000
Minus: Interest on the new bond	3,000,000
Equals: Annual net savings	$1,200,000

d. Present Value of Annual Interest Savings

The present value of $1,200,000 a year for 20 years is: $13,763,905.

3. Determine the Net Present Value of Refunding

Present value of benefits	$13,763,905
Minus: Present value of costs	4,593,651
Equals: Net present value of refunding	$9,170,254

Since the net present value of refunding is positive, it would be profitable for the firm to refund the old bond issue.

C. Calculations and Mechanics Involved in Forwards and Futures

1. Forward Loan Contract

A firm knows that at the end of eight months it will need a six-month loan for project purposes. The firm can lock in an interest rate on this future loan by buying a forward rate agreement from a financial institution. The bank offers to sell an eight-month forward rate agreement against a six-month LIBOR for $10 million at 5%. If, at the end of this term, the six-month LIBOR rate is greater than 5%, the bank will pay the firm the interest differential on the $10 million. If the reverse occurs, the firm must pay the bank. In this example $10 million is the notional amount for the transaction.

2. Forward Currency Hedge

A U.S. manufacturer buys 50,000 components from a Swiss firm for 10,000,000 Swiss francs. Payment is to be made in Swiss francs in 90 days, so the Swiss firm is extending trade credit for 90 days. The U.S. firm is concerned that the dollar might depreciate during this time frame, and therefore more dollars will be needed to buy the 10,000,000 Swiss francs. The U.S. firm can protect itself by purchasing 10,000,000 Swiss francs for delivery in 90 days. The 90-day rate is SFr1.4379/$, so the dollar cost is SFr10,000,000/SFr1.4379/$, or $6,954,587. When payment is due in 90 days, regardless of the currency's spot price, the U.S. firm will have the needed Swiss francs at a set cost of $6,954,587. If the purchase of the goods and the forward hedge are simultaneous, then there is no transaction exposure for the firm. If, however, there is a timing difference between when the firm contracts to buy the goods and the arrangement of the forward hedge, the firm may have some transaction exposure. If this is the case, the firm will have to recognize any gain of loss on the foreign payable if a forward hedge is later contracted. This could result in an accounting gain or loss from the transaction.

3. Futures

Assume a firm enters into a futures contract with a seller to deliver 10,000 bushels of corn in one year for a price of $2.79 per bushel. A contract is entered into with money being exchanged at the negotiated contract price for a delivery date in one year. One year from now, the seller will deliver the corn at a price of $2.79 per bushel and the buyer will receive the corn and will pay $27,900.

4. Treasury Bond Futures

Treasury bond futures are quoted per $100 of par value in 32nds of a dollar. The quote is a percentage of the par value of a $100,000 contract. For example, if the quotation is 110-19, then the dollar amount is 110,000 + 19/32 of $1,000, which is 593.75. The value is, therefore, $110, 593.75.

5. Stock Index Futures

For a future on the S&P 500 index, dollar amounts involved are futures quoted multiplied by $500. For example, if the futures contract is quoted at 471.65, the dollar amount is 471.65 × ($500) or $235,825.

6. Other Examples

Assume a manufacturer finances a project with short-term bank debt and has an interest rate that adjusts quarterly. The firm runs the risk that interest rates may increase during the quarter. In order to protect itself and its profit margins, the firm could short Treasury Bill futures. In essence, this means the firm promises to deliver some quantity of Treasury Bills for a specified price at a future date. If short-term interest rates go up, the profits on this short futures contract should largely (although not perfectly) offset the additional interest charges incurred from the short-term bank debt. These profits occur because the cost to purchase the T-Bills will go down with higher interest rates, but the price received by the firm on the contract remains constant.

A bank has T-Bills maturing in 30 days and feels that interest rates will decline during this period. The bank is faced with the risk that at the end of 30 days, it will have to reinvest in lower-yielding securities. To lock in the existing higher rates, the bank can go long in T-bill futures. This involves agreeing to purchase T-Bills in 30 days at a price set today. By entering into this contract, the bank continues to invest in T-bills at the end of 30 days but at an interest rate that is currently known.

The investor needing to purchase corn in July will profit from price increases. The long (purchasing) position is entered into by buying a contract at the futures price of 290¼ cents per bushel on March 21st. In July, the actual price of corn is 296 cents per bushel. The purchaser who entered into the contract at the futures price of 290¼ cents on March 21st would pay the agreed-upon $2.9025 per bushel to receive corn that at contract maturity is worth $2.96 per bushel in the market. Since each contract is for delivery of 5,000 bushels, ignoring fees, the profit to the purchaser is:

$$5,000 \times (2.9600 - 2.9025) \text{ or } \$287.50.$$

D. Calculations Involved in Swaps

1. Interest Rate Swap

A credit union may have short-term variable rate deposits and long-term fixed-rate mortgages. This institution will suffer losses if interest rates rise. Alternatively, a firm may have issued long-term noncallable fixed-rate bonds and invested in short-term or variable-rate assets. The firm will incur losses if interest rates fall. Therefore, the institution would agree to make fixed-rate payments to the firm based on a principal amount (called the notional amount in swaps) and a fixed interest rate. For example, with a fixed rate of 8%, and notional amount of $15 million, the institution would pay $1.2 million per year for the period of the swap. On the other side, the firm pays an agreed upon short-term interest rate multiplied by the notional amount to the institution. If the three-month LIBOR rate is 4%, and the firm must pay LIBOR plus .5%, then the firm will pay 4.5% of the notional amount, or $675,000 per year to the credit union. As LIBOR changes, so do the payments required of the firm.

2. Currency Swap

A U.S. firm wants to incur a dollar-denominated liability. It first borrows Swiss francs through a public bond issue or a private placement in Switzerland. An acceptable counterparty wants to borrow Swiss francs. It first borrows dollars through a public offering in the Eurodollar bond market. The U.S. dollar offering will occur simultaneously with the Swiss franc offering by the U.S. firm. Both issues will have identical maturity and redemption provisions. On the pricing date of its Swiss franc issue, the U.S. corporation will arrange a standard forward contract with a bank intermediary to sell the net proceeds of the issue for U.S. dollars on the closing date of the offering. It also will enter into a series of forward contracts imputed by the swap to sell dollars and buy Swiss francs on each future interest payment date to meet its Swiss franc obligation. The counterparty likewise sells the net proceeds of its U.S. dollar issue for Swiss francs and enters into a series of forward contracts to sell Swiss francs and buy dollars. The net effect of the transaction is that the U.S. firm obtains U.S. dollars at a fixed cost and incurs a dollar liability for financial reporting purposes. The counterparty, therefore, receives a locked-in cost of Swiss francs.

E. Calculations Involved in Options (Single and Multi-Period)

1. Single Period Option Example

A firm's stock is selling for $126 a share today and it has the following two-month option prices for 100 shares of the stock.

Strike	Call Price	Put Price
$120	$9\frac{1}{4}$	$1\frac{3}{16}$
$130	$3\frac{1}{8}$	$5\frac{1}{4}$

a. Assume that on some day in the future (on or before the exercise day) the stock price is $132, and you purchased the call option ($9\frac{1}{4}$) with a $120 strike price:

The call option would be in the money because the purchaser of the call option could buy the stock at a lower price ($120) from the writer of the option than the prevailing stock price of $132.

Prevailing stock price($132) – (Strike)Exercise Price($120) = $12 Gain

Total Gain = $12 – Cost of Call Option($9.25) = $2.75 per share

Since options are generally for 100 shares of stock, the total gain would thus be $275.

b. Assume that on some day in the future (on or before the exercise day) the stock price is $132, and you purchased the put option ($1\frac{3}{16}$) with a $120 strike price:

The put option would be out of the money since the purchaser of the put option could sell the same stock at a higher price.

Exercise Price($120) – Prevailing stock price($132) = a value less than zero.

c. Assume that on some day in the future (on or before the exercise day) the stock price is $121, and you purchased the put option (5¼) with a strike price of $130:

The put option (5¼) would be in the money because the purchaser of the put option could sell the stock at a higher price to the writer of the put ($130) than the current stock price of $121.

Exercise Price($130) – Prevailing stock price($121) = $9 Gain

Total Gain = $9 – Cost of Put Option($5.25) = $3.75

For a typical option for 100 shares of stock the total gain would be $375.

d. Assume that on some day in the future (on or before the exercise day) the stock price is $121, and you purchased the call option (3⅛) with a strike price of $130:

The call option (3⅛) would be out of money because the purchaser of the call option could buy the stock at a lower price than the $130 strike price.

Current Stock Price($121) – Exercise Price($130) = a value less than zero.

2. Multi-Period Option Example: Interest Rate Cap

A company buys an interest rate cap (ceiling) based on the six-month LIBOR (London Interbank Offered Rate). The cap has a ceiling rate of 8% with a principal or notional amount value of $25 million with settlement dates on January 20 and July 20 for two years. The firm pays an up-front fee and the following rates and values occur:

	LIBOR	Length of Pmt Period	Value
First Year:			
July 20	7.6%	181/360	0
January 20	7.3%	184/360	0
Second Year:			
July 20	8.5%	181/360 = .5028	$62,850
January 20	8.3%	184/360 = .5111	$38,333

Use the following formula:

Value = S × HIGH[LIBOR – ceiling rate, 0] × notional amount × LPP

Where: S = status of cap; either +1 if the dealer is cap seller and –1 if the dealer is cap purchaser

HIGH[LIBOR – ceiling rate,0] = The greater of LIBOR – ceiling rate or 0 (i.e., this value cannot be negative)

LPP = Length of payment period and is based on 360 days.

In the first year, the *ceiling* rate is higher than actual LIBOR, therefore the value equals zero and no payout is made to the company.

In the second year, the cap does have a value because LIBOR is above the ceiling rate. The payments to the company would be as follows:

July 20:   Value = +1 × [.085 – .08] × $25 million × .5028 = $62,850
January 20: Value = +1 × [.083 – .08] × $25 million × .5111 = $38,333

3. Multi-Period Option Example: Interest Rate Floor

Interest rate floors are similar to caps except that a firm is trying to protect from the interest rate falling. A company is able to buy an interest rate floor based on the six month T-Bill rate. The floor rate is 7% with a notional amount of $25 million and settlement dates of January 20 and July 20 for two years. The firm pays an up-front fee and the following rates and values occur:

	T-Bill	Length of Pmt Period	Value
First Year:			
July 20	7.6%	181/360	0
January 20	7.3%	184/360	0
Second Year:			
July 20	6.4%	181/360 = .5028	$75,420
January 20	6.7%	184/360 = .5111	$25,555

Use the following formula:

Value = S × HIGH[floor rate – T-Bill, 0] × notional amount × LPP

Where: S =   status of cap; either +1 if the dealer is floor seller and –1 if the dealer is floor purchaser

HIGH[floor rate – T-Bill,0] = The greater of the floor rate – T-Bill or 0, (i.e., this value cannot be negative)

LPP = Length of payment period and is based on 360 days

In first year, the *floor* rate is higher than the T-Bill; therefore the value equals zero and no money is exchanged.

In the second year, the T-Bill rate is below the floor rate and the payments to the company would be as follows:

July 20:   Value = +1 × [.07 – .064] × $25 million × .5028 = $75,420
January 20: Value = +1 × [.07 – .064] × $25 million × .5111 = $25,555

4. Multi-Period Option Example: Interest Rate Collar

An interest rate collar is structured when a cap is bought and a floor is sold simultaneously. If structured properly, this can be done on a zero-cost basis. Assume that a company has liabilities that are tied to the prime rate and wishes to protect itself against a rise in this rate. The current rate on the liabilities is 7.6% and the company purchases a cap that will insure that they will not be affected by a rise in the prime rate above 8.9%. The company also sells an interest rate floor at 6.2%, whose proceeds offset the fees paid for the interest rate cap. The purchase of ceilings and floors simultaneously means that the company's annual interest rate (on the liabilities) will be between 6.2% and 8.9%. In this case, when the prime rate is above 8.9% the counterparty to cap will pay the difference, but if the prime rate falls below the 6.2% rate the company will have to pay the difference to the counterparty on the floor. The notional amount is $25 million.

a. Assume that one year from now, the prime rate is 9.5%. In this case the counter party to the cap will pay the firm $76,665, calculated as follows:

S = +1 since the cap counterparty is the seller
LPP = 184/360 = .5111
Payment = S × HIGH[prime rate – ceiling rate, 0] × notional amount × LPP
Payment = +1 × [.095 – .089] × $25 million × .5111 = $76,665

b. Assume that 18 months from now, the prime rate has fallen to 6%. In this case the company will have to make a payment to the counterparty to the floor arrangement. This payment will be in the amount of $25,140, and is calculated as follows:

S = –1 since the seller is the company
LPP = 181/360 = .5028
Payment = S × HIGH[floor rate – prime rate, 0] × notional amount × LPP
Payment = –1 × [.062 – .06] × $25 million × .5028 = ($25,140)

VI. Endnotes

1. See: *The Troubled Money Business,* R.D. Crawford and W.W. Sihler, Harper Business Publishers, New York, 1991.

2. See: "The Growing Role of Junk Bonds in Corporate Finance," by K.J. Perry and R.A. Taggart, Jr., *Journal of Applied Corporate Finance,* Spring 1988, pp. 37–45.

3. See: "Project Finance: Raising Money the Old-Fashioned Way," by J.W. Kensinger and J.D. Martin, *Journal of Applied Corporate Finance,* Fall 1988, pp. 69–81.

4. See: *Financial Engineering: A Complete Guide to Financial Innovation,* John F. Marshall and Vipul K. Bansal, New York Institute of Finance, Allyn & Bacon Publishers, 1992.

5. See: Appendix 16B, *Financial Management: Theory and Practice, Sixth Edition,* by Brigham and Gapenski, The Dryden Press. Also, an example of the calculations involved in a refunding operation is presented at the end of this chapter.

6. See: Chapter 18, *Financial Management: Theory and Practice, Sixth Edition,* by Brigham and Gapenski, The Dryden Press.

7. Ibid.

8. The bulk of this section is derived from the work of John F. Marshall and Vipul K. Bansal. The interested reader is referred to their latest textbook, *Financial Engineering: A Complete Guide to Financial Innovation,* J.F. Marshall and V.K. Bansal, Editors, New York Institute of Finance, New York, 1992.

9. See: Chapter 12, "Futures and Forwards," by J.F. Marshall and V.K. Bansal, *Financial Engineering: A Complete Guide To Financial Innovation,* J.F. Marshall and V.K. Bansal, Editors, New York Institute of Finance, New York, 1992.

10. See: Chapter 13, "Swaps," by J.F. Marshall and V.K. Bansal, *Financial Engineering: A Complete Guide To Financial Innovation,* J.F. Marshall and V.K. Bansal, Editors, New York Institute of Finance, New York, 1992.

11. The swap market for currency and interest rates has grown from under $5 billion in 1982 to over $2.5 trillion by the end of 1990; in addition, by the end of 1989 the volume of outstanding commodity swaps was estimated at $8 billion. These data are from *Financial Engineering: A Complete Guide To Financial Innovation,* J.F. Marshall and V.K. Bansal, Editors, New York Institute of Finance, New York, 1992.

12. See: *Handbook of Modern Finance, Second Edition,* edited by Dennis E. Logue; Warren, Gorham & Lamont, New York, 1990.

13. See: Chapter 14, "Single-Period Options: Calls and Puts," by J.F. Marshall and V.K. Bansal, *Financial Engineering: A Complete Guide To Financial Innovation,* J.F. Marshall and V.K. Bansal, Editors, New York Institute of Finance, New York, 1992.

14. See: Chapter 15, "Multi-Period Options: Caps, Floors, Collars, Captions, Swaptions, and Compound Options," by J.F. Marshall and V.K. Bansal, *Financial Engineering: A Complete Guide To Financial Innovation,* J.F. Marshall and V.K. Bansal, Editors, New York Institute of Finance, New York, 1992.

15. The definition of forward rate agreements is taken from *Barron's Dictionary of Banking Terms, Second Edition,* Barron's Educational Series, 1993.

16. See: Chapter 23, "Arbitrage and Synthetic Instruments," by J.F. Marshall and V.K. Bansal, *Financial Engineering: A Complete Guide To Financial Innovation,* J.F. Marshall and V.K. Bansal, Editors, New York Institute of Finance, New York, 1992.

17. See: Chapter 42, "International Capital Markets," *Handbook of Modern Finance, Second Edition,* Dennis E. Logue, Editor, published by Warren, Gorham & Lamont, New York, 1990.

18. See: Chapter 29, "Venture Capital," William B. Gartner, *Handbook of Modern Finance, Second Edition,* Dennis E. Logue, Editor, published by Warren, Gorham & Lamont, New York, 1990.

19. See: Chapter 37, "Bankruptcy Liquidation and Reorganization," Michelle J. White, *Handbook of Modern Finance, Second Edition,* Dennis E. Logue, Editor, published by Warren, Gorham & Lamont, New York, 1990.

3 Capital Market Relations

I. Outline of the Chapter

A. Initial Public Offering (IPO)
    1. Advantages of Going Public
        a. Permits Diversification
        b. Increased Liquidity
        c. Facilitates Raising New Corporate Cash
        d. Establishes a Market Value for the Firm
        e. Strategic Advantages
        f. Spin-Off of a Subsidiary
        g. Using Stock for Acquisitions
    2. Disadvantages of Going Public
        a. Cost of Reporting
        b. Disclosure
        c. Managerial Flexibility
        d. Inactive Market/Low Price
        e. Control
        f. Rating Costs
    3. The IPO Process
        a. The Decision
        b. Selection of an Investment Banker
        c. Registration of the Issue
        d. Selling/Issuing the Stock
        e. Flips on IPOs
        f. "Quiet Period" for Registration of IPOs
B. The Decision to List the Firm's Securities

1. Advantages of Listing Securities
2. Disadvantages of Listing Securities.
3. Choice of Exchanges

C. The Decision to go Private (LBOs and MBOs)
    1. Leveraged and Management Buy Outs
    2. Advantages/Disadvantages
        a. Administrative Cost Savings
        b. Increased Management Incentives
        c. Increased Managerial Flexibility
        d. Increased Shareholder Participation
        e. Increased Financial Leverage
        f. Increased Risk

D. Procedures for Selling Additional Common Stock
    1. Rights Offerings
    2. Public Offerings
    3. Private Placements
    4. Employee Purchase Plans and ESOPs
    5. Dividend Reinvestment Plan

E. Investment Banking Process
    1. Regulation of Securities Markets
    2. Initial Decisions
        a. Dollars to Be Raised
        b. Types of Securities Issued
        c. Competitive Bid versus Negotiated Deal
        d. Selection of Investment Banker
    3. Decisions Made by the Firm and the Investment Banker
        a. Re-evaluation of Initial Decisions
        b. Best Efforts or Underwritten Issues
        c. Banker's Compensation and Other Expenses
        d. Setting the Offering Price (Valuation)
    4. Selling Procedures
    5. Shelf Registrations
    6. Due Diligence
    7. Maintenance of the Secondary Market
    8. Other Issues

Chapter Checklists

II. Introduction

Treasurers must deal with a wide variety of different entities in the capital markets, usually relating to the issuance or maintenance of their company's stocks, bonds or other security issues. These relations may involve an initial offering of stock or bonds to the public (Initial Public Offering or IPO), or may involve issuing additional securities for a firm that is already publicly traded. Other topics in this section include: the decision to go private (Leveraged or Management Buy Outs—LBOs or MBOs), the investment banking process, responsibilities of the board of directors, bankruptcy and restrictions on the actions of the firm's managers.

III. Coverage of Chapter Material

A. Initial Public Offering (IPO)

The term IPO is used to describe an issuer's first public offering of a security of any class, although the term tends to be limited to common stock. The term is also used to designate an offering of previously authorized but unissued securities.

For firms with securities (mainly equity) which are not currently available to the public, or are not listed on one of the various exchanges, the decision to go public and/or to list the firm's securities can be very important. These topics will be covered in this section and the following chapter.

Many firms have stock which is held by outside investors, but which is not carried on one of the many available exchanges for securities. For these firms, there are many considerations in the decision whether and where to list their securities. The requirements for listing on the various exchanges, as well as the fees involved, are included at the end of this chapter.

1. Advantages of Going Public: For a firm that is currently privately or closely held, the decision to take its securities public offers several advantages:

a. Permits Diversification: Owners of closely held firms usually have most of their wealth tied up in one company, and thus are not well diversified. By selling a portion of their stock to the general public, the owners are able to invest the proceeds in other areas and increase their personal diversification.

b. Increased Liquidity: For investors in closely held firms, the stock of the firm is very illiquid. It can only be sold to certain types of investors, and there is no intermediary to help in the sale. This makes it very hard for such firms to raise capital when it is needed, and their stock is an unattractive investment for most outsiders to the company. These problems are much less serious for publicly traded firms.

c. Facilitates Raising New Corporate Cash: This factor is closely related to the preceding point. By making the stock more liquid, it becomes a more attractive investment to outsiders with capital. In order to have its stock become publicly listed, a firm must meet certain levels of disclosure of information and regulatory requirements by the Securities and Exchange Commission (SEC). This disclosure and outside regulation make investors much more willing to purchase the stock of the company and greatly facilitate the firm's ability to raise new capital.

d. Establishes a Market Value for the Firm: One of the primary problems of the closely held corporation is establishing its value. By making the stock of the firm publicly available, the value will be determined by the market and disclosed as the firm's stock price.

e. Strategic Advantages: There are several other long-term advantages to going public. The first is that the firm "creates" a currency (its common stock) that can be used for future acquisitions of other companies. Another strategic advantage is that, by going public, the firm may be able to "buy out" a venture capitalist currently involved with the firm or current owners who want to sell out their interests.

f. Spin-Off of a Subsidiary: Another option is to use an IPO to spin off a portion of a wholly owned subsidiary of a public company. This enables the firm to realize the potential value of a hidden asset, thus increasing the overall market value of the parent firm.

g. Using Stock for Acquisitions: Many companies use stock rather than cash to acquire other firms. They include companies that are currently privately held, but decide to issue stock in order to finance an expansion program or acquisition of another company. Firms that are currently publicly held often use stock to finance very large acquisition programs.

2. Disadvantages of Going Public: The decision to publicly trade the stock of a firm is not without some disadvantages:

a. Cost of Reporting: Due to the increased level of disclosure and reporting, the costs of these requirements is a major consideration. For smaller firms, this may be a very costly process compared with their current level of reporting.

b. Disclosure: Owner/managers of closely held firms may not be comfortable with the level of disclosure required for publicly held corporations for several reasons:

- Competitors gain access to greater amounts of information on the company due to the public disclosure requirements.
- The compensation and net worth of the owners is now more easily determined by outside parties.

c. Managerial Flexibility: When a firm's stock is closely held, the owner/managers have great flexibility with respect to how the firm is managed. Since the owners of the firm and management are one and the same, large salaries or generous perks do not produce the kind of management-shareholder conflicts that may occur in a publicly held firm.

d. Inactive Market/Low Price: Although increased liquidity of a firm's stock may be one reason for going public, stocks of smaller firms may not actually be all that liquid. If there is a small market for the stock and/or it is not traded often, the market price may not reflect the true value of the firm. This is referred to as "not enough float in the stock."

e. Control: Owner/managers of closely held firms will surrender some control by going public, even if they retain majority ownership. In publicly held firms, minority shareholders may have significant rights with respect to the operation of the firm and representation on the board of directors. Also, there are many examples of publicly held firms being taken private by their managements in order to increase their level of control.

This is especially true if the firm is incorporated in a state where cumulative voting is allowed. This type of voting provides minority interests with a better opportunity to obtain board representation. For example, if an investor has 100 shares and there are five board seats available, that investor would gain a total of 500 votes, all of which could be allocated to one candidate. Through cumulative voting, minority shareholders (if they cooperate) could potentially ensure that one or more persons on the board would represent their interests.

f. Rating Costs: A firm going public with its debt issues may be required to have its debt rated in order to sell to the public. As was indicated in Chapter 2, the costs can be significant, especially for a smaller company first going public.

3. The IPO Process: For treasurers, the process of managing an initial public offering can be very complex. Some of the major events in the IPO issue are covered below:[1]

a. The Decision: In this stage, management must decide if the decision to go public is advantageous for the firm (see discussion of advantages and disadvantages above). The firm must decide why it wants to go public and what type of public offering it will put together.

- The duration of this stage could be from six months to several years depending on the firm and market conditions.

- Besides the firm's top management, board of directors, and CFO or Treasurer, the following parties should be involved: corporate counsel, internal and external auditors, investor relations consultants, IPO advisor or consultant, and/or potential investment bankers.

- Part of the decision process centers on when the firm will actually float the issue in the market. As the IPO market is very volatile, most firms try to plan their IPOs around certain time frames (windows). These windows for IPOs usually occur during certain periods of the year when large institutional investors have surplus cash and are prepared to buy IPO shares.

- The firm must begin to accumulate the financial and other information that will be required as part of the disclosure and due diligence process for the IPO. The firm must also determine if there are any restrictions on the issuance of new securities in existing or planned debt covenants and act accordingly to deal with them.

- There are several other options which a firm may want to consider at this stage. One is to use a simple shelf registration (discussed later in this chapter) to disseminate information to potential accredited investors. If the firm's intent is to sell securities to sophisticated investors rather than the general public, the disclosure requirements are not as stringent. This is defined in Regulation D of the SEC regulations. Due to their wealth or investment sophistication, these investors may be sold unregistered securities. Regulation D lists numerous categories of qualifications for accredited investors, most of them relating either to wealth (net worth over $1 million or annual income over $200,000), or to investment sophistication (institutional investors).

b. Selection of an Investment Banker: Since the investment banker plays a very important role in the IPO process, it is important to select the right one for the issue.

- The best procedure is to contact several bankers specializing in IPOs in the firm's area of business, and solicit proposals for managing the firm's IPO. This process is sometimes referred to as a "beauty contest." There are many types of investment bankers who specialize in different market segments, industries, etc. They are often referred to as "boutique" investment bankers. Generally, the larger the issue and/or the more attractive the firm, the more competitive the bids will be. The fees charged, however, are not the only consideration in this process. It is important to get the "right" firm (or group) to do the issue. You want an investment banker (or syndicated group) who will get the best price for the stock.

- This process usually takes one to six months and involves all of the parties listed above in the decision stage.

- The final step in this process is the execution of a letter of intent with the investment banker(s) selected.

c. Registration of the Issue: There are several steps involved in the registration of the new IPO issue, and they are generally either part of the preparation of the registration statement or of the filing of the statement. Additional information on the SEC requirements for registration of an IPO is included at the end of this chapter.

1) Preparation of the Preliminary Registration Statement

- This stage of the registration typically takes three months to one year and involves many parties at the firm, the investment banker and the SEC.

- The management of the firm selects a financial printer and transfer agent for the stock issue. The financial printer is a firm specialized in preparing and printing the required registration documents and the stock certificates. The transfer agent is generally a financial institution (usually a commercial bank), which is responsible for the transfer of the stock certificates from the issuer of the stock to the purchasers.

- The corporate counsel ensures that all of the firm's records are up to date and that the firm is in compliance with its corporate charter. If the corporate counsel does not have SEC experience, the firm may consider engaging a special counsel who has such experience, or rely on the underwriter's counsel to take the lead in this area.

- The company's outside auditors prepare the draft comfort letter for the prospective investors. The comfort letter is essentially a letter of indemnification given by the issuer of a security to the underwriter of the issue. In this letter (signed by a senior executive), the issuing company agrees to reimburse the investment banker for any realized litigation losses and expenses resulting from material omissions or misrepresentations in a registration statement, merger proposal or tender offer.

- The investment banker and the banker's counsel begin to perform the due diligence for the issue. Due diligence basically requires that a firm issuing securities to the public disclose all information relevant to the financial condition, management and operation of the firm. A sample checklist of due diligence information requirements is provided at the end of this chapter.

- The SEC is consulted to determine if there are any preliminary problems regarding the issue which need to resolved.

- The financial printer prints the preliminary registration statement.

2) File the Preliminary Registration Statement

- This stage of the registration typically takes only 1–10 days. Essentially, the formal filing of the registration statement is the culmination of the work in the previous stage.
- The company's management issues a press release concerning the upcoming issue.
- The company's outside auditors deliver the draft comfort letter prepared in the previous stage.
- The counsel for the investment banker prepares and files the required "Blue Sky" filings. Blue-Sky laws are the securities laws of individual states in the United States which regulate new securities issues and many secondary market transactions. The name comes from unrealistic promises made by some promoters of new securities.
- The financial printer prepares the package of preliminary registration filing documents to be sent to the SEC.

3) SEC Review of the Preliminary Registration

- In this final stage of the registration the SEC reviews the registration and disclosure information provided by the issuing firm.
- This review process takes place while the firm and its investment banker(s) are doing initial pre-selling of the stock.
- Any issues or comments raised by the SEC must be addressed before the final registration can take place.

d. Selling/Issuing the Stock: There are several steps in the process of selling and issuing the stock.

- The first step in selling the stock takes place when the investment banker(s) take the issue "on the road" to form the syndicate for the new issue or to court potential buyers. This process is referred to as the "road show," and it involves the top management of the firm and the underwriter in visits to many investment bankers and institutional investors (possibly both domestic and international) to convince them to buy a portion of the initial issue. This "pre-selling" helps to develop a market for the stock and is essential to ensure that the entire issue can be sold. A syndicate of investment bankers helps to ensure broad placement for the new issue, but may not be necessary for a strong IPO.
- During this stage, which may take several months, the investment banker's counsel continues due diligence and the SEC reviews the preliminary registration statement.
- The next stage in the sales process involves responding to any comments or requirements on the part of the SEC, and usually takes from 1–4 weeks. The issue may not proceed until the SEC gives its final approval of the registration statement.

- Once the final SEC approval is received, the firm can execute the final underwriting agreement with the investment banker(s). At this time, the final comfort letter is sent out by the firm's independent auditor and the final registration statement (with all amendments and changes) is filed. If the firm is using a syndicate to help place the issue, the final agreements on who will lead the process, allocation, who will control the order book, etc. will be worked out.

- The last step in the process is to close out the offering (sell the stock). The company provides the stock certificates to the investment banker(s) and receives the net proceeds from the issue.

- A very successful offering may raise additional capital for the firm (or the current owners) in the form of an over-allotment of the shares. This provision (called a "green shoe clause") in many underwriting agreements provides the underwriter or syndicate with the option to sell additional shares (usually 10–15% of the primary issue) within some limited timeframe at the same price as the original offering and with the same fees to the underwriter and some proceeds to the company.

e. Flips on IPOs:[2] "Flipping" is the action taken by a broker who is allowed to buy a "hot new issue" at an attractive price (the offering price), and then immediately resells the stock for profit.

- Flipping usually is used to compensate either members of the syndicate who prefer profits to commissions, or to reward investment bankers who are not directly part of the issuing syndicate for helping to place the issue or for other services provided to the syndicate.

- In many cases, IPO offerings are underpriced in order to encourage new shareholders to buy and investment bankers to carry the issue. In this case, a flip can occur when investment bankers who are not part of the underwriting syndicate are allowed to purchase the new shares immediately upon the opening of the market at the original issue price. If the issue is truly underpriced, or if there is a hot market for the new issue, the investment banker can resell the stock later in the day for a profit.

- The downside for the company issuing the stock is that it receives less money for the shares than it would have received had the issue been fully priced. Also, the price appreciation not achieved by the ultimate shareholders leaves them less happy than they would have been had they participated in the price rise.

f. "Quiet Period" for Registration of IPOs: This is the term used to describe the 90-day period between an issuer's IPO and the earliest time the company may make any material announcements, or its underwriters may publish and distribute original research material, about the company and its business. The purpose of this SEC rule is to enable these securities to settle into investment portfolios (as opposed to trading accounts) based on merits set forth in the prospectus. By legislating a quiet period, the SEC wants to make sure that investors are not swayed by dealers who may have a vested interest in the success of the offering and its secondary market.

B. The Decision to List the Firm's Securities

For many firms doing an IPO, the decision to go public with the firm's stock coincides with the decision to have the stock (or other securities) listed on one of the organized exchanges. Some publicly held firms do not list their stock on any exchange but rather issue and trade their stock directly with their shareholders or, as is most common, have the stock traded in the over-the-counter (OTC) market.

1. Advantages of Listing Securities:

- The primary advantage of having a firm's stock listed on one of the organized exchanges is that the marketability of the stock should increase.

- In general, listing is advantageous to both the firm and the public, as the firm's stock can be more widely traded and more investors have easy access to it.

- Listing can result in higher sales for the firm because of increased public exposure. Due to the increased level of disclosure required, listing may also lower the required rate of return on the firm's common stock, and ultimately its overall cost of capital, thereby increasing the firm's value in the market.

2. Disadvantages of Listing Securities:

- Given the additional reporting requirements and restrictions on the types of stocks that can be traded, some firms decide to remain in the over-the-counter (OTC) market rather than list their stock on an organized exchange.

- Also, in the last 10 years, liquidity in the OTC market has increased significantly, and many firms have decided to be listed through NASDAQ on the OTC market rather than apply for listing on one of the other organized exchanges. NASDAQ is the acronym for National Association of Securities Dealers Automated Quotations. It is a computerized system, owned by the National Association of Securities Dealers (NASD). It provides current quotes made by registered market makers in specific OTC securities. The service is available by subscription.

3. Choice of Exchanges: The firm must decide on which of the many exchanges it wants its stock listed.

- Public companies may have their stocks listed and traded on one of the major organized exchanges, such as the New York Stock Exchange (NYSE), the American Stock Exchange (AMEX) or one of the many regional exchanges.

- There are requirements for joining the various exchanges, and firms must abide by their rules if they want their stocks traded. A listing of the basic requirements for the New York and American Stock Exchanges, as well as the NASDAQ market, is provided at the end of the chapter.

- For companies wishing to raise capital globally, there are stock exchanges in most of the world's money centers, such as: London, Tokyo, Frankfurt, Paris, Zurich, Singapore, Taiwan and Hong Kong. Stocks of major U.S. companies may be listed and traded on stock exchanges outside the U.S., such as London, Paris and Tokyo. Similarly, stocks of large foreign multinational firms may be listed and traded in the U.S. markets.

- Institutional investors (pension funds, insurance companies and mutual funds) own about 60% of all common stock, and they trade very actively as compared with smaller investors, so they account for the bulk of the transaction volume on the exchanges. Individual brokerage firms use different criteria for determining institutional investors, but the most typical designation would be a bank, savings & loan, insurance company, registered investment company or advisor, person or mutual fund with total assets of at least $100 million.

- Foreign companies wishing to raise capital in the U.S. capital markets may do so through the use of American Depository Receipts (ADRs). These are negotiable receipts, registered in the name of the owner, for shares of a foreign corporation held in trust by a foreign branch of a U.S. bank. If the ADRs are sold in the U.S., they are subject to U.S. securities laws.

C. The Decision to go Private (LBOs and MBOs)

Due to the increasing pressure on managements of publicly held firms for short-term performance, more and more firms are opting to go private to provide management more flexibility in making longer-term decisions. Generally, in this process, the existing senior management team of the firm obtains a significant portion of the stock in the new private firm, and the firm takes on a significant amount of the debt used in financing the deal. In addition, personal guarantees of management may be required in order to complete the financing package. Another reason for taking a firm private is to increase the financial leverage of the firm and thereby increase the return to the remaining shareholders.

1. Leveraged and Management Buy Outs: The terms LBO and MBO (Leveraged and Management Buy Outs) are essentially synonymous and typically refer to the senior management team of a publicly-held corporation (or perhaps a division of a large corporation) utilizing large amounts of debt (sometimes over 90%) to purchase the firm and take it private. The term LBO is more popularly used in the United States, with MBO used more frequently in Europe.

2. Advantages/Disadvantages:

a. Administrative Cost Savings: An advantage to going private is the potential decrease in administrative costs that accompany the buyout. The firm's management no longer needs to comply with disclosure requirements, issue annual reports, file securities registrations or meet with analysts. The general impact is to cut overall administrative overhead.

b. Increased Management Incentives: Now that the managers are the owners of the firm, they have significant incentive for increasing both its profitability and long-term stability. The need to ensure that debt payments are made tends to help "focus" managers' attention on maintaining profitable operations, or at least to operate with sufficient positive cash flows to service the debt requirements.

c. Increased Managerial Flexibility: The fact that management no longer needs to consider the public's perceptions of its decisions on the firm's quarterly earnings estimates and stock price may provide additional flexibility for management to try new and innovative ideas for the company. Management has a greater degree of flexibility in determining sales of assets of the firm because it no longer has to consider the impact of the sale on a diverse group of stockholders. However, management will have to meet the demands of the primary shareholders and lenders and cope with increased debt covenants or restrictions.

d. Increased Shareholder Participation: Generally, going private replaces a large, diverse group of shareholders with a smaller, more active group (usually including management). Even the non-management investors (pension funds, investment bankers, etc.) often are now directly represented on the board of directors and have a very active role in the management of the company.

e. Increased Financial Leverage: LBOs typically require large amounts of debt (relative to equity) to be acquired by the firm. This results in a very large tax break from the interest portion of the debt payments and sets the payments to outside capital providers (the lenders) at a relative fixed level. The debt may be a combination of fixed and floating rate loans, but the floating rate portion of the debt will fluctuate with general interest rates not with the profits of the company as would equity financing and dividends. Thus, if the firm is very successful, the debt payments would be relatively fixed relative to comparable equity financing. Large debt payments provide additional incentive to streamline the management of the firm, to trim excess personnel and costs wherever possible, and to eliminate non-performing assets or businesses.

f. Increased Risk: The primary disadvantage of the LBO is a significant amount of increased risk due to the high levels of debt. Several bad quarters, or less-than-expected cashflows, may leave the firm in a severe cash crisis and may even force it into bankruptcy.

D. Procedures for Selling Additional Common Stock

Firms that are already publicly traded may, from time to time, offer additional shares of stock. These are generally classified as primary distributions of authorized, but previously unissued, common shares. Secondary distributions would involve stock that had been issued previously but is now being resold, such as the sale of treasury stock.

Treasury stock is stock that has been issued, sold to the public, and later reacquired by a corporation, usually through a stock repurchase plan. The number of shares of this stock is generally listed on the corporation's balance sheet and, while held as treasury stock, does not pay dividends and has no voting privileges. Firms repurchase treasury stock for the following reasons: (1) to provide shares for a employee stock option plan, (2) because it is a "good" on the market (i.e., undervalued), (3) to use in future acquisitions, or 4) to change the firm's capital structure and relative returns on each class of capital.

For primary distributions of new shares, there are five basic methods by which stock can be sold: (1) rights offerings to existing shareholders, (2) to the general public through investment bankers, (3) to a single buyer (or small group of buyers), (4) to the firm's employees, or (5) through a dividend reinvestment plan.

1. Rights Offerings: Most states require that their state-chartered corporations provide preemptive rights to their shareholders. This requires that existing shareholders be given the first rights to purchase any newly offered stock in the company.

- In a rights offering, each shareholder is issued an option to buy a portion of the new stock issued on a pro-rata basis to the shareholder's current percentage ownership.

- Shareholders have the option to purchase either the shares at the stated price, or sell their rights to another party who wants to purchase the stock. Most shareholders usually buy these rights in order to prevent dilution of their ownership.

- These offerings are typically handled by an investment banker, who agrees to purchase and then resell any new shares which the existing shareholders decide not to buy.

2. Public Offerings: For an IPO, or for corporations chartered in states that do not require preemptive rights, a public offering of new stock may be an option for selling the new shares. The basic public offering process has already been covered earlier in this chapter. For a firm which is already publicly traded, the process of underwriting a new stock issue is similar to that of an IPO, but greatly streamlined. Since the firm is already meeting public disclosure requirements and has been through the registration process previously, meeting the SEC requirements for the registration of the new issue is a fairly easy process. The basic investment banking process is discussed later in this chapter.

3. Private Placements: In this type of offering, the firm's securities (usually bonds or preferred stock) are sold to a single investor or a small group of investors. Due to the one-on-one nature of the private placement, the flotation costs (underwriting fees, commissions, etc.) are typically lower and the issue can be completed more quickly. The investor is typically a financial institution or pension fund and is considered to be an accredited investor by the SEC (covered earlier in this chapter). As a general rule, to qualify as a private placement, there must be fewer than 35 investors, not including any sophisticated investors (as defined in SEC Regulation D). If a sale is truly private, it is considered an exempt transaction and need not be registered with the SEC.

4. Employee Purchase Plans and ESOPs: New variations of financing continue to evolve in reaction to market and regulation changes. The evolution of Employee Stock Ownership Plans (ESOPs) from an employee benefit to a financing tool is an example.

- An ESOP, set up as a separate trust for employees, can borrow funds to purchase company stock. It is, therefore, a potential source of capital for the company.

- Company ownership by employees is viewed by Congress as good public policy, and the resulting tax exemptions granted to ESOPs encouraged their implementation.

- Dividends, which are not normally tax deductible by a company, are deductible for stock held by an ESOP. Interest income is normally taxable. However, interest income on funds lent to an ESOP established before July 10, 1989, is 50% tax excludable for the lender. This facilitates lower-cost loans to ESOPs.

- There is a downside to ESOPs. If the stock price falls, the employees may find that their jobs, their investment, and possibly their retirement funds are in danger; a classic case of "putting all their eggs in one basket." This could lead to strained relations between the company's senior management and its employees.

5. Dividend Reinvestment Plan: These plans allow current investors in a corporation to use their dividends to purchase new shares of its stock. This is generally treasury stock currently held by the firm, or may be new stock that is issued as needed if no treasury stock is available. The advantage of using treasury stock is that the firm does not need to authorize and register new shares of stock. The primary advantage to both the firm and the investor of a dividend reinvestment plan is the reduced administrative and flotation costs involved in issuing the new shares and the savings of cash dividends.

E. Investment Banking Process

Investment bankers offer many services to the firm issuing stock, bonds and other securities. The investment banking process has several levels of decision-making.

1. Regulation of Securities Markets: The sale of new common stock and the operation of the secondary markets are primarily regulated by the Securities and Exchange Commission (SEC) and, to a lesser extent, by similar agencies in each of the states. The Federal Reserve has control over the flow of credit into the securities markets through margin requirements, which specify the maximum percentage of a security's purchase price that can be borrowed. This is set forth in Federal Reserve Regulation T, which governs the amount and type of credit that a broker/dealer may extend or maintain if customers purchase, carry, or trade corporate securities. The regulation of the securities market is important to maintain stable markets and sound brokerage firms, and to prevent stock manipulation.

2. Initial Decisions: There are four basic decisions that need to made by the firm's management and board of directors at this stage:

a. Dollars to Be Raised: This stage of the decision process requires an analysis of the capital needs of the firm, tempered by the reality of how much capital can be realistically raised given the size of the firm, the state of the market, the perceived state of the business by investors, and available investment opportunities. The firm's management must consider both the total dollars to be raised and the number of shares or bonds which could be issued. There may be constraints on the type and amount of issues in existing debt or preferred stock covenants.

b. Types of Securities Issued: Should the firm issue stocks, bonds, preferred stocks or some other hybrid security? Further, if common stock, is it a new issue to the general public or a rights offering?

c. Competitive Bid versus Negotiated Deal: In a negotiated bid for the underwriting of a security, the issuer and the underwriting firm or syndicate agree upon a price for the new issue through discussion and mutual understanding. Most common stock underwritings are negotiated. In a competitive bidding process (most common in municipal bond issues), several competing underwriting syndicates propose their price to the issuer. The issue is awarded to the syndicate with the best bid, which means the highest net proceeds to the issuer.

d. Selection of Investment Banker: This can be a very important decision for a firm going public. Different investment bankers offer different services and specialize in different segments of the market. The firm must closely evaluate its investment banking needs, considering not only fees but also the ability of the underwriter to provide the best service and get the best price for the security issued.

3. Decisions Made by the Firm and the Investment Banker: These decisions are made by the firm with the advice and counsel of its investment banker:

a. Re-evaluation of Initial Decisions: This is, in essence, a reality check to make sure that the type and amount of capital to be raised are correct and that an acceptable rate (price) for the securities can be found in the market.

b. Best Efforts or Underwritten Issues: Investment bankers typically will underwrite new stock issues on either a best efforts or full underwriting basis:

- Under a best efforts agreement, the investment bank tries to get the best price possible for the securities issued, but there is no guarantee either of price or the number of shares that will be sold. The issuing company runs the risk that if the market softens for the issue, the proceeds will be less than originally projected due to a lower than expected selling price. The issuing firm may even run the risk of not selling a portion of the offering at all due to a lack of investors or acceptable price. The investment bank bears no risk in this arrangement and takes a smaller fee.

- Under a full underwriting agreement, the investment bank essentially buys the full issue from the firm at an agreed-upon price and then sells the issue to the general public (or other brokerage firms). The investment bank runs the risk that the issue's price will decline before it can be sold; or, the investment bank may be forced to hold onto the securities for a long period of time, thereby tying up its funds since it has already paid the company for the stock. The investment bank sets the spread between the expected issue price and the proceeds to the issuer, so that the bank is compensated for this risk.

- When the market is soft for a particular issue, and the underwriter is not able to sell off the entire issue within a reasonable period, the situation is called a "market overhang." In practice, the price of a soft new stock issue may have a "cap," because if somehow the price is bid up higher, the investment bank will dump more stock onto the market, thus driving the price back down.

- Most full underwriting agreements include a "market out" clause under which the investment bank can terminate its commitment to the issuer before the formal closing of the contract if certain material events occur that impair the investment quality of the securities to be offered.

c. Banker's Compensation and Other Expenses:[3] This item must be negotiated between the issuing firm and the investment bank.

- The basis for compensation is the "spread" in the price of the security, which is the difference between the price paid to the issuer and the price at which the securities are sold to the public.

- In equity offerings, the spread generally ranges from as low as 2% to a maximum of 10% of the offering price, depending on the competition and the quality of the issue.

- In debt issues, the price spread or fees typically range from a low of less than 1% to as high as 2% or more.

- If a managing underwriter deems that the normal spread or maximum allowable spread (defined in underwriting agreement) is inadequate to compensate for the risk of the issue, additional compensation to the underwriters may be provided in the form of options or warrants on the stock, or, in some instances, in direct fees for planning the offering.

- The issuing firm must consider lawyers and accountants fees, as well as the costs of printing, engraving, disclosure requirements, etc., for both itself and its advisors.

d. Setting the Offering Price (Valuation):[4] This can be a very involved process especially for a new firm going public. This is one area where the investment bank's expertise can be very helpful to the issuing firm. Even in the case of a new issue of stock by an existing firm, there are many factors to consider.

- To understand the pricing process, it is important to recognize that there are two major constituencies in an offering: 1) sellers (including the existing shareholders), who would like a high price for the offering and 2) buyers, who would like a low price for the offering to facilitate the increase in the price of the issue in the future, and thus their future profits.

- In a debt or equity issue already traded in the market, the pricing problem is significantly reduced, since investment bankers are expected to price the security near the existing market, most often the previous day's closing price.

- For securities that are being publicly offered for the first time, the pricing decision carries significant risk, as there is no objective measure of the correct price. In this case, the pricing is often based on indications of interest received by the syndicate manager for the members of the syndicate.

- To supplement indications of interest, the managing underwriter typically gathers data on similar companies in the industry to estimate the intrinsic worth on a comparative basis. Factors included in this calculation include: earnings, growth rates in earnings, capital structure, dividend history, general company visibility and reputation in the industry, and the industry outlook.

- At the time of the pricing recommendation of the underwriter, the issuer has the option of accepting or declining the final price. Should the price not be accepted by the issuer, the offering cannot proceed. Since underwriters and clients typically have a large investment in preparing for the issue, it is rare that a final offering price cannot be agreed upon by the issuance date.

4. Selling Procedures: Once all of the above items have been settled, the firm can move toward the actual selling of the issue.

- The issue must be filed with and approved by the SEC before the sale can take place.

- If this is a major initial public offering, the company's executives may visit major financial centers around the country (or the world for a globally-held company) in order to promote the new issue. As mentioned earlier, this is typically referred to as a "road show."

- In most large issues, the lead investment bank will bring in other investment banks to take pieces of the issue before it is released to the general public. This allows for wider distribution of the issue, brings more capital into play and helps to spread the underwriting risk.

5. Shelf Registrations: A large, well-known corporation that frequently issues securities may file a master registration statement with the SEC and update it with a short-form statement just prior to each of the individual offerings. This form of shelf registration allows a firm to get its issue to the market quickly to take advantage of market conditions that make rates for particular sources of funds attractive.

- This form of registration is made available under SEC Rule 415. The rule allows publicly traded companies that are already reporting on a quarterly basis to the SEC to register securities in advance of their issuance in a process called shelf registration. The registration statement is known as SEC Form S-3.

- Securities that are shelf registered may be sold at any time over a two-year period following the registration by a process resembling competitive bidding. Under the rule, a firm simply announces its intention to issue all or part of the securities registered under the shelf registration and receives offers for them from investment banks.

- Since the stock issue essentially sells at the prevailing market price, the investment bank with the smallest spread will generally receive the right to underwrite the issue.

- The effect of Rule 415 is that large corporations now usually have multiple relationships with investment banks and may use several different banks over a short period of time.

- As mentioned earlier, a simplified form of the shelf registration may be used under SEC Regulation D as an easy way to disseminate information to sophisticated investors. This is a different process than a shelf registration aimed at the general public.

6. Due Diligence: This process ensures that the financial and other statements provided by the firm are accurate and represent the true value of the firm according to current provisions of the Generally Accepted Accounting Practices (GAAP). In addition, due diligence requires the disclosure of all information that may be of interest to any potential investor in the firm's securities. It involves all areas of the firm's operations and is required of all firms issuing new securities to the general public. This process was discussed in the section on IPOs. A checklist of important factors to consider in the due diligence process is included at the end of this chapter.

7. Maintenance of the Secondary Market: A primary function of the investment bank is to keep the stock price from falling until the entire issue can be sold off. This is known as maintenance of the secondary market, and it is usually accomplished by not allowing too much of the new stock to enter the market at any one time. In the case of a fully underwritten issue, the investment banking syndicate does this to protect its investment. In the case of a best-efforts underwriting, maintaining the secondary market will help to maximize the flow of capital to the issuing firm.

8. Other Issues: There are several other issues to be considered in the issuance of new securities by a firm.

a. Emerging Trends: There have been many changes in the securities markets in the last few years, and, as deregulation of the financial sector continues, we will undoubtedly see even more change in the future.

- There has been a significant increase in the amount of competition in the securities markets, and commercial banks have been urging regulators to remove restrictions on their actions in the investment banking arena for years.

- The SEC ended the fixed commission schedule for brokerage houses; subsequently discount brokerage houses emerged, offering inexpensive trading services to investors.

- Finally, there are significant trends toward the globalization of the financial markets. All of these trends have changed and will continue to change the types of securities offered and the nature of the securities markets. More firms are using various forms of derivative and synthetic securities both to raise capital and to manage risk. Firms are increasingly looking beyond their domestic capital markets and offering their securities globally.

b. Dealing with Multiple Underwriters: In some stock issues, especially very large ones, a firm may have to deal with a team of underwriters from several investment banks. In this process, one underwriter is usually designated as the lead, but two or more could share this position as co-leads. This increases the complexity of the underwriting process, but may be necessary or desirable to float a large issue or to obtain the best price for the issuer.

c. Dealing with Securities Analysts: Because securities analysts have a significant amount of influence on investors, and thus on stock prices, most firms assure these parties good access to public information about the firm. This may include special meetings with analysts by the firm's management or additional reports to them of firm operations or decision-making.

d. Investor Relations: Most firms with publicly traded stock have an investor relations department to handle the many issues involved in dealing with shareholders. The investor relations department keeps track of stockholders of record, ensures that dividends are sent to the proper parties, sends out annual and quarterly reports, provides publicly available information to investors and potential investors, and answers their questions.

F. Responsibilities of the Board of Directors[5]

A firm's board of directors is responsible to many different parties and, in some cases, directors are finding themselves held liable if they fail to manage their responsibilities properly. This is especially true in the area of mergers and acquisitions.

1. Responsibilities to Stakeholders of the Firm: The board of directors is responsible to several different stakeholders in the corporation:

- **To the Shareholders:** The primary responsibility of a firm's board of directors to its shareholders is to ensure that the firm's management follows policies that will maximize the long-term value of the stock held by the shareholders. The primary constraints on this value maximization are the board's responsibilities to the bondholders and other creditors, and the external and internal parties discussed below.

- **To the Bondholders:** The bondholders enforce their constraints on the firm in the form of indentures or covenants which both require and prohibit certain actions on the part of the firm's management and directors. These constraints are legally binding on the actions of the management and directors and must be considered in many of the decisions by the firm, especially those with financial implications.

- **To Other External Parties:** The primary external parties to which the board of directors is responsible are (1) the various rating agencies for the firm's securities, (2) regulatory agencies (federal, state, and local), (3) communities where the firm has plants or operations, and (4) customers. Each of these parties requires attention by the board of directors in order to meet legal and other requirements.

- **To Internal Parties:** Finally, the board of directors has responsibilities relating to the management of the firm and its employees. This is especially so as more and more firms have a representative(s) of unions on their boards of directors, significant percentages of the employee retirement funds in the form of stock in the firm, and employees are more mobile in their careers.

2. Inside versus Outside Directors: It is important to distinguish between the inside and outside directors of a corporation. The inside directors are those board members serving in the senior management of the firm, while the outside directors are those not directly involved in management.

- The traditional legal model of the corporation places the board at the pinnacle of the corporate structure, grants the board authority to manage the corporation's business, and, at least implicitly, holds the board responsible for the success or failure of the corporate enterprise.

- The reality of today's corporate board on publicly held corporations is that a firm's senior management has the primary responsibility for the firm's success or failure, and the board is only expected to oversee senior management and evaluate its performance. However, this is changing as outside directors are becoming much more active in management and oversight.

3. Responsibilities of the Board in Mergers and Takeovers: When a firm becomes involved in a merger or takeover (on either side), the role of the outside directors often takes on a new level of importance.

- In almost any merger or takeover, the financial stakes are very high, and the decisions a board must make will almost always have a dramatic impact on the company involved, its managers, its shareholders, and all other parties having a stake in its operations.

- Because of the crisis atmosphere that surrounds most takeover bids, directors are likely to feel obligated to spend a significant amount of time dealing with them, despite the pressure of their other obligations.

- The courts (especially Delaware courts) have developed legal rules relating to certain aspects of takeover situations that provide directors with far more specific guidance than they usually receive.

- Before the board can authorize the use of aggressive defensive tactics (poison pills, golden parachutes, etc.—these are discussed below) to repel the takeover attempt, the outside directors are specifically required to:

  1. Establish whether or not there are reasonable grounds for believing that a takeover bid jeopardizes corporate policy or legitimate shareholder interests.

  2. Demonstrate that the measures it employs in response to the bid are reasonable in relation to the danger posed.

- Regarding the board's responsibilities to the shareholders in a takeover, the courts have ruled that once the directors have decided to sell the company, the board's primary obligation is to ensure that shareholders realize the highest possible price for their stock. Accordingly, once an auction has begun, the board cannot properly employ defensive tactics for any purpose other than advancing a fair auction.

4. Golden Parachutes: One of the classic protections that a firm's management can employ is to provide for very lucrative retirement bonuses for senior management in the event of a hostile takeover by another firm.

- The existence of these "golden parachutes" may make the firm a less attractive candidate for takeover, and serve to provide the existing management with some benefits should the firm be taken over and the management changed.

- Golden parachutes can benefit the shareholders of the firm if they are structured so that the bonuses are directly tied to the value received by the shareholders in the event of a takeover. This gives management the incentive to negotiate the maximum share price for the takeover, knowing that it, too, will benefit when the takeover actually occurs.

- An alternative view is that golden parachutes can also be used as a "bargaining chip" in takeover negotiations between the target firm's management and the parties attempting the takeover.

- Golden parachutes can be used as a means to retain good managers in a high-risk environment and may be a necessary incentive to attract and retain good managers who require compensation for the risk of a takeover and possible loss of their jobs.

5. Poison Pills: Poison pills, which are activated when a change in the firm's management takes place, are another technique for making the firm less attractive as a takeover candidate or protecting the existing management. Some poison pill tactics include:

- Borrowing on terms that require immediate repayment of all loans if the firm is acquired.

- Bond covenants that place the bond issue in default in the event of a change in the firm's management.

- Selling off the assets that originally made the firm an attractive target.

- Granting stock options or rights offerings to existing shareholders at below market prices that will cause the purchase price to the acquiring firm to increase significantly.

- Granting such large golden parachute bonuses that almost all of the firm's cash would disappear in the event of an acquisition. In addition, salaries over $1 million per year, which are not tied to operations or profits, are generally not tax deductible by the firm under the current Internal Revenue Code (IRC).

- Planning defensive mergers which would leave the firm with new assets of questionable value and a huge debt load to service.

- The use of these types of poison pills may be dangerous due to the potential for lawsuits by stockholders against the board of directors. In recent years, it has become very difficult and expensive for companies to buy insurance for their boards of directors that protects them from stockholder suits; and in many cases the insurance provided does not cover losses if the directors failed to exercise due caution and judgment.

G. Bankruptcy[6]

Bankruptcy, or "financial distress," has afflicted an increasing number of firms in the last few years. In addition to the typical financial problems that may force a firm into bankruptcy, many management teams are using the bankruptcy laws in innovative ways to protect either the firm's stakeholders or its management. The bankruptcy process is under the control of federal bankruptcy laws and generally begins when the firm is unable to meet scheduled payments on its debt. Bankruptcy may occur when a firm's projections of cash flows indicate that it will not be able to meet debt payments at some time in the near future. The management of the firm and its board of directors are the key decision makers in this process. In many cases, the major creditors may be involved in the decision concerning bankruptcy; and in some cases the creditors will force the firm into bankruptcy. Some of the critical issues which management, the board of directors and creditors need to address in bankruptcy are as follows:

- Is the firm's inability to meet scheduled debt payments a temporary cash flow problem, or is it a permanent problem caused by long-term economic and business trends?
- If the problem is temporary, a short-term restructuring arrangement may work; but the impact on the long-term value of the firm must be considered.
- The company may be worth more "dead than alive"; thus, liquidating the business and selling off the pieces may maximize its value to both the bondholders and shareholders.
- Which is the proper procedure for bankruptcy filing if it is required—formal or informal?
- Who will be in charge of the firm during the reorganization—existing management, a special bankruptcy trustee or special restructuring management?
- What type of bankruptcy is most appropriate for the organization or party in question? There are several types of bankruptcy available for corporations, municipalities and individuals. The following are the most common:
  - Chapter 7: Liquidation of a firm
  - Chapter 9: Financially distressed municipalities
  - Chapter 11: Business reorganization
  - Chapter 13: Adjustment of debts for individuals with regular income
  - Chapter 15: Establishment of bankruptcy trustees

1. Bondholder Rights: The bondholders' rights in bankruptcy are senior to those of the equityholders, especially if the bondholders have liens or mortgages on assets owned by the distressed firm. The creditors of a firm generally have the right to force a firm into bankruptcy if scheduled debt payments are not made or if the condition of the firm is such that debt payments may be in default in the near future. This is known as an "involuntary bankruptcy" and is initiated when three or more creditors of the firm petition the Bankruptcy Court to begin proceedings against the firm. This is actually quite rare in the United States as creditors who initiate unjustified involuntary bankruptcy proceedings may be held liable for damages to the firm. Voluntary bankruptcy, where the management of the firm petitions the courts for bankruptcy protection, is generally the norm. The distribution of assets under a Chapter 7 liquidation is presented in the checklist section at the end of this chapter.

2. Shareholder Rights: Generally, shareholders have limited rights in the event of financial distress for their firm. They have the lowest-priority claim on both the earnings stream and the assets of the firm. Preferred stockholders do have a higher claim on the firm's assets in liquidation than do the common shareholders. There are cases where firms under reorganization have been turned over to the creditors and all, or virtually all, of the claims of the shareholders were voided in the process.

3. Chapter 11 Reorganization:[7] Firms filing for bankruptcy have a choice between liquidation under Chapter 7 of the U.S. Bankruptcy Code and reorganization under Chapter 11 of the Code.

- The management of the firm makes the initial choice of which type of bankruptcy to file. The reorganization procedure in bankruptcy is designed to allow failing firms that are in temporary financial difficulty, but are worth saving, to continue operating while the claims of the creditors are settled using a collective procedure.

- When a firm files to reorganize under Chapter 11, the existing management typically remains in control. Creditors may petition the Bankruptcy Court to appoint a trustee, but must show grounds for suspecting that management is stealing the firm's assets or making preferential transfers to favored creditors. Incompetence of the existing management in running the business is not considered a sufficient reason for appointing a trustee.

- Firms that file under Chapter 11 must adopt a reorganization plan. There are two separate procedures for formulating such a plan: the unanimous consent procedure and the cramdown procedure.

a. The Unanimous Consent Procedure (UCP):

- Under this procedure, all classes of creditors and equityholders must consent to the reorganization plan, with a two-thirds vote of all members in each class required for consent.

- The assumption under this plan is that the firm's assets will have a higher value if it reorganizes and continues operating than if it liquidates.

- Management is in a strong bargaining position in the negotiations over the reorganization plan because, during the first four months of the filing, only management can propose a plan, and extensions of this time frame are often granted in this process. Only after all parties have voted on management's initial plan (which may take another two months), can other parties propose alternative plans.

- Managers can threaten to transfer the firm's bankruptcy filing from Chapter 11 to Chapter 7 if creditors do not agree to the plan. This threat is often most effective in prodding unsecured creditors to agree, since they may receive little or nothing in a liquidation due to their position in the liquidation hierarchy.

- Finally, management usually remains in control of the firm during this entire process. Secured creditors may fear that the market value of their lien assets will decline below the market value of their liabilities if the process drags on.

b. The Cramdown Procedure:

- This procedure is generally executed by secured creditors and comes into play when a reorganization plan fails to meet the standard for approval by all classes under the unanimous consent procedure, or when the firm is insolvent and the old equity must be eliminated.

- In a cramdown case, if at least one class of creditors has voted in favor of a plan, the court may confirm the plan (or a modified version of it) as long as each dissenting class is treated fairly and equitably. The fair and equitable standard closely reflects the Absolute Priority Rule (the APR is covered later in this chapter) in that it requires that all unsecured creditors either receive full payment on the face value of their claims, or that all lower rankings receive nothing. It also requires that secured creditors retain their pre-bankruptcy liens on assets or that they receive periodic cash payments equal to the value of their claims.

- Cramdown plans usually involve higher transaction costs than unanimous consent plans, because the bankruptcy court is likely to require appraisals by outside experts and more court hearings before approving them.

4. Formal versus Informal Bankruptcy Procedures: Bankruptcy procedures can be either formal or informal:

- In a formal bankruptcy procedure the case is filed and taken before a bankruptcy court for adjudication. The assets are distributed in accordance with the Absolute Priority Rule as outlined in Chapter 7 of the Code. The priorities of claims are outlined at the end of this chapter. There are several types of formal procedures:

  - **Freefall:** In this case a firm goes into bankruptcy (or is forced) and has no structured plan for coming out of bankruptcy.

  - **Pre-Arranged:** In this case, management has arranged a tentative deal with some of the creditors or parties, but not with all of them. Generally, these "deals" are done on an informal basis and are not legally binding.

  - **Pre-Packaged (Pre-Pac):** In this case, management has a formal plan which is filed with the SEC, and all classes of creditors have voted on and accepted the plan. Essentially, the firm goes to court with all of the details worked out and with everyone agreeing to the plan.

- It is possible to perform either a reorganization or a liquidation informally. An informal reorganization typically involves a firm which is fundamentally sound, but which is undergoing temporary financial difficulties. This is often done outside of bankruptcy in an agreed-upon writeoff of some portion of the firm's debts by its creditors.

- The firm's creditors work directly with management to establish a plan for returning the firm to a sound financial basis. These plans usually involve some restructuring of the firm's debt, with creditors agreeing either to reduce or reschedule debt payments in order to ensure the firm's continuing operation.

- Informal liquidation or assignment is an alternative to Chapter 7 liquidation procedures. In this case, title to the distressed firm's assets is transferred to a third party (called an assignee or trustee) who liquidates the assets through a sale or public auction and then distributes the proceeds to the creditors on a pro-rata basis, according to the seniority of the claims.

- The informal liquidation is usually only appropriate for smaller firms and does not automatically result in a full and legal discharge of all of the debtor's liabilities.

5. Distribution of Assets under Chapter 7 Liquidation:[8] As opposed to reorganization, which strives to preserve the firm as a going entity, liquidation is a total shutdown of the firm and the orderly liquidation of its assets.

Chapter 7 of the 1978 Bankruptcy Act is designed to accomplish three objectives:

1. Provide safeguards against the withdrawal of assets by the owners of the bankrupt firm;

2. Provide for an equitable distribution of the assets among creditors; and

3. Allow insolvent debtors to discharge all of their obligations and start over unhampered by a burden of prior debt.

The distribution of assets in a liquidation under Chapter 7 of the Bankruptcy Act is governed by the following priority of claims (also known as the Absolute Priority Rule or APR):

1. Secured creditors, who are entitled to the proceeds of the sale of specific property pledged for a lien or a mortgage. If the proceeds do not fully satisfy the secured creditors' claims, the remaining balance of such claims is treated as a general creditor claim, under item #9 below.

2. Trustee's costs to administer and operate the bankrupt firm.

3. Expenses incurred after an involuntary liquidation has begun but before a trustee is appointed.

4. Wages due workers if earned within three months prior to the filing of the bankruptcy petition. (The amount of the wages is limited to $2,000 per person.)

5. Claims for unpaid contributions to employee benefit plans that should have been paid within six months prior to filing. These claims, plus wages in item #4, may not exceed the $2,000-per-wage-earner limit.

6. Unsecured claims for customer deposits, not to exceed a maximum of $900 per individual.

7. Taxes due to federal, state, county, and any other government agency.

8. Unfunded pension plan liabilities have a claim priority over that of the general creditors for an amount up to 30% of the book value of the common and preferred equity; any remaining unfunded pension claims rank with the general creditors.

9. General, or unsecured, creditors, which include holders of trade credit, unsecured loans, the unsatisfied portion of secured loans and unfunded pension liabilities, and debenture bonds. This is the final category before equityholders. Holders of subordinated debt also fall into this category, but their claims may be junior to certain holders of senior debt.

10. Preferred stockholders can receive an amount up to the par value of the preferred stock.

11. Common stockholders receive the remaining funds, if any.

IV. Chapter Checklists

A. Requirements for Listing on Major U.S. Exchanges

1. New York Stock Exchange (NYSE) (73% of total U.S. equity trading activity):

Minimum Requirements for Companies *Currently* Trading:

1. The firm's Total Assets (excluding goodwill) minus total liabilities must be at least $18 million.
2a. Net Income for the prior year must be $2.5 million, or over $2 million for two of the three preceding years.
2b. or A Pre-Tax Income total of $6.5 million for the last three years with all years being profitable and one year of Pre-Tax Income of $4.5 million.
3. Total shares outstanding must be at least 1.1 million.
4. Market Value of the shares outstanding must be greater than $18 million.
5a. A minimum of 2,000 shareholders holding at least 100 shares.
5b. or A minimum 2,200 shareholders of publicly traded shares, and average monthly trading volume in excess of 100,000 shares for the last six months.
6. The firm must have two outside directors.
7. The firm must have an Audit Committee of directors independent from management.
8. The firm cannot list stocks that will reduce or remove the voting rights of an outstanding class of stock.
9. The firm must agree to review any related party transactions.

2. American Stock Exchange (AMEX):

Minimum Requirements for Companies *Currently* Trading (2 options):

Regular:
1. The firm must have at least $2 million in Total Assets.
2. Must have at least $1 million in Capital and Surplus
3. Market Value of the shares outstanding must be greater than $2.5 million.
4. Total shares outstanding must be at least 250,000.
5. There must be at least 300 shareholders of publicly traded shares.
6. Minimum Price per Share must be at least one dollar ($1).

Alternative:
1. The firm must have at least $2 million in Total Assets.
2. Must have at least $2 million in Capital and Surplus
3. Market Value of the shares outstanding must be greater than $2.5 million.
4. Total shares outstanding must be at least 250,000.
5. There must be at least 300 shareholders of publicly traded shares.
6. No Minimum Price per Share is required.

3. National Association of Stock Dealers Automated Quotations (NASDAQ):

Minimum Requirements for Companies *Currently* Trading:

Alternative 1:

1. The firm must be registered under Section 12(g) of the Securities Exchange Act of 1934 or equivalent.
2. The firm's Total Assets (excluding goodwill) minus total liabilities must be at least $4 million.
3. The Net Income for the prior year, or two of the last three fiscal years, must be over $400,000.
4. The Pre-Tax Income for the prior year, or two of the last three fiscal years, must be over $750,000.
5. Total shares outstanding must be at least 500,000.
6. Market Value of the shares outstanding must be greater than $3 million.
7. Minimum Price per Share must at least five dollars ($5).
8a. There must be at least 800 shareholders of publicly traded shares if the number of shares outstanding is between 0.5 and 1.0 million.
8b. or if there are more than 1 million shares outstanding and a minimum of 400 shareholders
8c. or, if the shares outstanding exceed 0.5 million and the average daily trading volume is in excess of 2,000 shares, the firm must have a minimum of 400 shareholders.
9. At least two dealers are willing to serve as Market Makers for the security.
10. No operating history required.

Alternative 2:

1. The firm must be registered under Section 12(g) of the Securities Exchange Act of 1934 or equivalent.
2. The firm's Total Assets (excluding goodwill) minus total liabilities must be at least $12 million.
3. No Net Income requirement.
4. No PreTax Income requirement.
5. Total shares outstanding must be at least 1 million.
6. Market Value of the shares outstanding must be greater than $15 million.
7. Minimum Price per Share must at least three dollars ($3).
8. There must be at least 400 shareholders of publicly traded shares if the number of shares outstanding exceeds 0.5 million.
9. There must be at least two Market Makers.
10. The firm's operating history for the past three years is required.

B. Timechart on IPO and Parties Involved[9]

IPO Timeline and Involved Parties								
Parties Involved	Serious Considera-tion	Select Investment Banker	Prepare Preliminary Registration Statement	File Preliminary Registration Statement	Selling Period "Road Shows"	Clear SEC Comments	"Go Final"	Close Offering
Company (General)	Yes	Execute letter of intent	Select financial printer and transfer agent	Issue press release	Yes	Yes	Execute underwriting agreement	Provide certificates and collect proceeds
Company Counsel	Yes	Yes	Perform "housekeep-ing" of company records	Yes	Yes	Yes	Request acceleration and file registration statement	Yes
Company CPA	Yes	Yes	Prepare draft comfort letter	Deliver draft comfort letter		Yes	Deliver final comfort letter	Deliver "bring down" comfort letter
IPO Advisor	Yes	Yes	Yes	Yes	Yes	Yes	Yes	Yes
Investment Banker	Yes	Yes	Begin due diligence process	Yes	Form syndicate and announce issue	Yes	Execute underwriting agreement	Provide net proceeds
Investment Banker's Counsel			Begin due diligence process	Prepare and file "blue sky" filings	Continue due diligence	Yes	Yes	Yes
Financial Printer			Print preliminary registration statement	Prepare SEC "filing" package			Print final registration statement	
SEC			Confer regarding any problems		Review preliminary registration statement	Issue comment letter	Declare offering effective	
Time Required	6–36 Months	1–6 Months	3–12 Months	1–10 Days	1–3 Months	1–4 Weeks	1 Day	5 Days

"Yes" indicates general involvement on the part of the personnel.

C. Due Diligence Requirements

This listing is not meant to be exhaustive, but only representative of the kinds of information which should be included in a due diligence disclosure.

A. **Material Agreements:** Listing and description of: all contracts, agreements, arrange-ments, etc., with affiliates, subsidiaries, other companies, agencies, or organizations. Also included would be: leases, licensing and royalty agreements, sales or agency contracts, rental, maintenance or service agreements, business restrictions, distribution contracts, etc. The disclosure should discuss the impact of cancellation of these agreements, impact of losing major customers or suppliers, impact of potential debt refinancings, effects of defaults on property liens.

B. **Real Property:** Listing and description of: all plants and facilities, all deeds, mortgages, notes, covenants, title insurance policies, leases on real property, pending or potential condemnation proceedings, bond financing and leases of company property to other parties.

C. **Debt Instruments and Contingent Liabilities:** Listing and description of: all debt instruments, indentures, notes, loan agreements, warrants currently outstanding, liens, mortgages, pledges, letters of credit, contingent obligations, correspondence with lenders, compliance reports, etc.

D. **Financial and Operating Data-Tax Matters:** Listing and description of: proposed bank or debt financing, materials relating to any audits or tax matters (for a minimum five year history), contested tax proceedings, budgets and future tax projections, material adverse changes, outstanding defaults, location of company records, future acquisition or divestiture plans, etc.

E. **Management and Employment Matters:** Listing and description of: pending or threatened labor controversies or strikes, written employment or consulting agreements, minutes of board of directors, board committees and shareholder meetings for last five years, key employees, management information systems, structure of management, management positions, OSHA 200 log, and state inspection reports.

F. **Benefits:** Listing and description of: bonus, stock option, incentive, pension, retirement, profit-sharing, deferred compensation and severance plans, actuarial reports, plans or trust filing statements, materials related to ERISA compliance, health and medical plans, or any other employee benefit or fringe plan. Also include actions relating to termination of pension plans, failure to contribute to pension plans, stock ownership of directors and highly compensated officers of company, and any contracts or arrangements with shareholders, dividend agreements or shareholder voting arrangements.

G. **Insurance:** Listing and description of: all insurance policies, programs and arrangements concerning assets or properties of the company; all insurance policies and self-insurance programs and all risks related to workers' compensation plans; all property and casualty insurance policies; and all company vehicles showing whether owned or leased—and information on the year, make, model, cost, garage location and state where registered.

H. **Litigation and Other Proceedings:** Listing and description of: all pending or threatened litigation or arbitration proceedings involving the firm (including all material documents); any governmental proceedings instituted or threatened involving the operations of the company; claims against the assets of the firm; any consent decrees, judgments or settlement agreements requiring or prohibiting any future activities of the firm; violation or default by the firm under any governmental regulation, court decree or law; any litigation involving an executive officer or director of the company concerning bankruptcy, crimes, securities law or business practices over the last five years.

I. **Governmental Regulations and Filings:** Listing and description of: all material requisite permits and licenses held by the firm from any governmental agency or body relating to the assets or operations of the firm, including environmental agency permits; any brokerage or investment accounts maintained by the firm, as well as any securities brokerage activities conducted by the firm; any facilities owned by the company involved in regulated industries (electric power, oil, gas, water, telecommunications, etc.); all copies of filings with any governmental agency, domestic or foreign.

J. **Environmental Matters:** Listing and description of: any claims, complaints, notices, or requests for information received by the firm with respect to alleged violations of any federal, state or local statute, regulation or ordinance relating to the environment, or any potential liability under the Comprehensive Environmental Response Compensation and Liability Act; information relating to the release of hazardous substances at any facility or property owned, leased, used or operated by the firm which may result in current or future liabilities; any reports to or correspondence with the U.S. Environmental Protection Agency or any state environmental regulatory agency; copies of any correspondence or memoranda prepared by the firm documenting complaints by citizens or employees (or labor unions) with respect to any environmental matter.

K. **Technology-Related Documents:** Listing and description of: all items and/or rights related to patents, trademarks, service marks, copyrights, and other proprietary information of the firm; any infringement of above items which might result in a material adverse change in the financial condition, operations, business, properties or prospects of the firm; any assignment of the above items; copies of all confidentiality and nondisclosure agreements of the firm executed with any other party.

L. **Sales and Marketing:** Major product line, sales and profit per product line, market share, major competitors, market trends, pricing history, inventory turnover, distributors, long-term contracts, warranties, and quality control.

M. **Transportation and Logistics:** Methods and facilities for loading and unloading, customer pickup arrangements, warehouses, safety and environmental concerns, vehicles owned or leased, and any risk of loss, damage or liabilities related to transportation.

N. **Purchasing:** Knowledge of the suppliers' industries, recycling of waste or scrap materials, monitoring of purchase activity, inventory policies.

O. **Research and Development:** Knowledge and experience of research staff, status of current projects, available resources, type of research (i.e., government or customer-sponsored), results of research projects, and how that the research will enhance the organization.

P. **Basic Corporate Information:** Listing of: name and location of party responsible for all material company records, every jurisdiction where the firm maintains property, and every state where the firm pays taxes.

Q. Public Relations: Listing and copies of: all annual reports and other reports and communications with employees, suppliers and customers; all advertising, marketing and other selling materials; customer support systems; and all recent (2–5 years) press releases and clippings.

D. Primary Elements of SEC Regulation[10]

Sales of new securities, and also sales in the secondary markets, are regulated by the Securities and Exchange Commission (SEC), and, to a lesser extent, by each of the 50 states. Here are the primary elements of SEC regulation.

1. The SEC has jurisdiction over all interstate offerings of new securities to the public in amounts of $1.5 million or more.

2. Newly issued securities must be registered with the SEC at least 20 days before they are publicly offered. The registration statement provides financial, legal, and technical information about the company to the SEC, and the prospectus summarizes this information for investors. SEC lawyers and accountants analyze both the registration statement and the prospectus; if the information is inadequate or misleading, the SEC will delay or stop the public offering.

3. After the registration has become effective, new securities may be offered, but any sales solicitation must be accompanied by the prospectus. Preliminary, or "red herring," prospectuses may be distributed to potential buyers during the 20-day waiting period, but no sales may be finalized during that time. The "red herring" prospectus contains all the key information that will appear in the final prospectus except the price, which is generally set after the market closes the day before the new securities are actually offered to the public.

4. If the registration statement or prospectus contain misrepresentations or omissions of material facts, any purchaser who suffers a loss may sue for damages. Severe penalties may be imposed on the issuer or its officers, directors, accountants, engineers, appraisers, underwriters, and all others who participated in the preparation of the registration statement or prospectus.

5. The SEC also regulates all national stock exchanges, and companies whose securities are listed on an exchange must file annual reports similar to the registration statement with both the SEC and the exchange.

6. SEC rules and regulations govern the activities of corporate insiders. An insider is typically defined as any individual who (1) controls a corporation (senior management), (2) owns 10% or more of a company's stock, or (3) has inside information. Inside information is defined as material information that (1) would influence the purchase or sale of a company's security and (2) has not been publicized in a widely used medium.

   Officers, directors, and major stockholders must file monthly reports of changes in their holdings of the stock of the corporation. They may be restricted with respect to when holdings can be changed (bought or sold) and must report these changes to the SEC via Form S-3. Any short-term profits from such transactions must be turned over to the corporation. Insider trading is punishable under the Insider Trading Sanctions

Act of 1984. Under this amendment to the SEC Act of 1934, the SEC may seek civil or criminal penalties, or both, against:[11]

a. Anyone who purchases or sells securities while in possession of material non-public information.

b. Anyone who communicates material non-public information to someone who buys or sells securities.

c. Anyone who aids and abets someone in the purchase or sale of securities while possessing material non-public information.

Any illegal profits must be forfeited and fines may be levied up to three times the amount of the illegal profit gained (or losses avoided). The law is applicable to derivative and synthetic products.

7. The SEC has the power to prohibit manipulation by such devices as pools (large amounts of money used to buy or sell stocks to artificially affect prices) or wash sales (sales between members of the same group to record artificial transaction prices).

8. The SEC has control over the form of the proxy and the way the company uses it to solicit votes.

E. SEC Guideline for Registration of Securities in an IPO[12]

To be authorized to sell securities a firm must first be registered with the SEC. This means filling out Form S-1. The components of the form are:

Form S-1:

- A company business description
- A listing of all of the company's properties
- A listing of officers and directors and the disclosure of any "material" transactions with the company in which they are involved
- A listing of competitors
- A listing of pending legal proceedings
- How the securities will be distributed
- How the proceeds will be used by the company
- Audited financial statements and other reports

Possible components that might be included:

- Reason for lack of operating history
- Reliance on key employee for the operation of the business
- Reason why the market for the securities will be small
- Any potentially unfavorable economic conditions that will affect the industry

Alternates to Form S-1:

Form SB-1 Requirements:

1. U.S. or Canadian company

2. Revenues not greater than $25 million

3. Outstanding securities not greater than $25 million

4. Cannot be an investment company

5. A subsidiary's parent must also meet the same requirements

6. Securities being offered cannot be greater than $10 million in one fiscal year

Form SB-2:

Same as above except the security amount being offered can be over $10 million and:

- The IPO can be filed at the local SEC regional office
- Not as much information needs to be included on this form as on Form S-1
- Audited financial statements for only the last two years are required

F. Key Points in Underwriting Comfort Letter[13]

The comfort letter is requested by underwriters from the firm's external auditors for financial information in the SEC registration statements not covered by the auditor's opinion and in events subsequent to the opinion date. Comfort letters are not filed with the SEC, but are required by the underwriters who have certain responsibilities under SEC regulations. Typically, comfort letters are mandated as part of the underwriting agreement. The adequacy of procedures conducted in the comfort review rests with the underwriter and not the auditor. Underwriting agreements typically provide for a closing date on which the agreement is to be consummated and a "cutoff" date shortly before the closing date. The comfort letter should specifically state that it does not cover the period between the cutoff date and the date of the letter. The contents of the comfort letter cover some or all of the following:

- Compliance with SEC rules and regulations
- Audit procedures conducted
- Unaudited financial statements and schedules
- Statistics and tables
- Changes in certain financial statement items after the latest statement contained in the filing
- Auditor independence
- An understanding regarding the limited circulation of the letter

Note that comments on unaudited statements and subsequent changes should be restricted to negative assurance since the auditor has not conducted an examination according to GAAP. Any financial statement, schedule, or other information referenced in the letter should be clearly identified together with the auditor's responsibility regarding it. The auditor should not comment on matters involving management judgment (i.e. reasons for change in income statement items). Working papers should back up statements made in comfort letters and furnish evidence of procedures carried out.

V. Endnotes

1. Sources for this section are: Gary D. Zeune, "Ducks in a row: Orchestrating the Flawless Stock Offering," *Corporate Cashflow,* February 1993, pp. 18–21; and Gary D. Zeune, *Going Public: What the CFO Needs to Know,* published by the American Institute of Certified Public Accountants.

2. See: "Beware the IPO Market," *Business Week,* April 4, 1994, pp. 84–90.

3. See: Chapter 4, Investment Banking, *Handbook of Modern Finance,* Dennis Logue, Editor, Warren, Gorham & Lamont, Publishers, 1990.

4. Ibid.

5. See: Chapter 2, *The Battle for Corporate Control: Shareholder Rights, Stakeholder Interests and Managerial Responsibilities,* Arnold W. Sametz, Editor, Salomon Brothers Center for the Study of Financial Institutions, Publisher, 1991.

6. See: Appendix 16A of *Financial Management: Theory and Practice, Sixth Edition,* by Brigham and Gapenski, The Dryden Press, 1991.

7. See: Chapter 37: Bankruptcy and Reorganization, *Handbook of Modern Finance,* Dennis E. Logue, Editor, Warren, Gorham & Lamont, Publishers, New York, 1990.

8. See: Appendix 16a of *Financial Management: Theory and Practice, Sixth Edition,* by Brigham and Gapenski, The Dryden Press, 1991.

9. Source: Gary D. Zeune, "Ducks in a Row: Orchestrating the Flawless Stock Offering," *Corporate Cashflow,* February 1993, pp. 18–21 and Gary D. Zeune, *Going Public: What the CFO Needs to Know,* published by the American Institute of Certified Public Accountants.

10. See: Chapter 15 of *Financial Management: Theory and Practice, Sixth Edition,* by Brigham and Gapenski, The Dryden Press, 1991.

11. The definition of insider trading is taken from: *The Complete Words of Wall Street,* Pessin and Ross, Business One Irwin, Publishers, 1991.

12. See: *Q&A: Small Business and the SEC,* a publication of the Office of Small Business Policy, Division of Corporation Finance, and the Office of Public Affairs of the SEC, August 1993.

13. This definition is taken from: *Dictionary of Accounting Terms,* Barron's Business Guides, 1987.

4 Capital Structure

I. Outline of the Chapter

A. Valuation of the Firm's Securities
    1. Bond Valuation
        a. Cash Flows
        b. Bond Value
        c. Yield to Maturity (YTM)
    2. Preferred Stock Valuation
        a. Cash Flows
        b. Preferred Stock Value
    3. Common Stock Valuation
        a. Cash Flows
        b. Common Stock Value

B. Risk and Rates of Return
    1. Defining and Measuring Risk
        a. Expected Rate of Return
        b. Standard Deviation (SD)
    2. Risk Aversion
    3. Portfolio Risk and Return
        a. Portfolio Expected Return
        b. Portfolio Standard Deviation
    4. Beta
    5. Relationship between Risk and Rates of Return
        a. Capital Asset Pricing Model (CAPM)
        b. Security Market Line (SML)
    6. Efficient Markets Hypothesis
        a. Weak Form Efficiency

Chapter Checklists

C.   PVIF and PVIFA Tables

Calculations and Examples

A.   Basic Valuation Model

B.   Bond Valuation Using PVIFA (Annuity)Tables

C.   Impact of Change in Interest Rates on Bond Prices

D.   Yield To Maturity (YTM) and Yield to First Call Calculations

E.   Valuation of Preferred Stock

F.   Stock Valuation Example

G.   Cost of Debt

H.   Cost of Preferred Stock

I.   Cost of Retained Earnings

J.   Cost of New Equity

K.   Determination of Marginal Cost of Capital and Breakpoints

II. Introduction

This chapter describes valuation techniques for financial assets such as bonds, preferred stock and common stock. After these techniques are presented, the relationship between risk and return is described, including measuring and adjusting for risk. Finally, the firm's (and investor's) required rate of return, called the cost of capital for the firm, is explained.

The analysis techniques in this section are critical to financial analysis in general. Starting with the valuation of securities from the investor's viewpoint makes it easier to understand the more complicated valuation techniques used in determining cost of capital. The general concept of securities valuation builds on the theories of the time value of money and the analysis of cash flows. The decision-maker must recognize the impact that valuation concepts and the investor's rate of return requirements have on the firm's value.

The key issue for corporate treasurers is to analyze the operational opportunities for the firm and obtain the required capital at the best mix and price to meet those opportunities. The question that treasurers need continually to ask is: "How do the firm's operational risks and expected returns impact the available cost and mix of capital, and what is the best combination for maximizing the firm's market capital value?"

III. Coverage of the Chapter Material

A. Valuation of the Firm's Securities

The first part of this chapter deals with the valuation by the market of the firm's securities. The securities include bonds, preferred stock and common stock. Each of these will be covered in detail.

In general, what gives a security (or any asset) its value is the cash flow stream that will be returned to the investor through the life of the security. This is true of any asset in which an investor may wish to invest. The valuation of the asset must include the opportunity cost or required return to the investor, and therefore must take the time value of money into account. For any asset, including financial assets, the value of the asset is equal to:

$$V_0 = CF_1/(1+k_i)^1 + CF_2/(1+k_i)^2 + ... + CF_n/(1+k_i)^n$$

Where: V_0 = the current value of the asset.
   CF_j = the cash flow for periods j=1 to n.
   k_i = the opportunity cost or required rate for asset type i.

This formula shows that the asset's value is equal to the discounted value (present value) of the cash flows (both positive and negative) for the asset, discounted at the required rate of return. This model works for any type of asset or stream of cash flows. The decision-maker estimates the cash flows for the asset and determines the appropriate required rate, then calculates the value of the asset. In the sections that follow, this process is described for each type of financial asset covered, and the valuation model for each is described in detail. Examples of this calculation and others in this chapter appear at the end of the chapter.

1. Bond Valuation: Bonds represent debt of the issuing firm. The contract associated with and governing the issue is known as the indenture. The indenture covers:

1   The terms of the issue, including the date the bonds mature.

2.   The payment dates for the periodic interest payments (coupons).

3.   Special provisions of the bond issue (not all bonds will have these provisions):

- **Default Provisions:** This section describes the conditions or situations under which the bonds could be declared in default and thus immediately due and payable.

- **Conversion Provisions:** This section covers any applicable conversion features of the bond issue. Generally this allows the bond to be converted to common stock under certain circumstances.

- **Sinking Fund:** Bonds will often have a provision to ensure the orderly retirement of the bond's principal. This is done through the use of a sinking fund, which either accumulates funds to retire the bonds or repurchases a portion of the bonds each year. This is similar to an amortization feature on loans.

- **Call Provision:** This section outlines the conditions under which the bond can be "called" or retired prior to maturity. Generally the holders of the bonds are given a call premium to compensate for the early retirement of their investments.

Valuation of bonds (called fixed-income securities) is very straightforward.

a. Cash Flows: The cash flows from a bond issue are easy to identify since they are outlined in the indenture described above.

- The two cash flows from bonds are the periodic coupon payment (based on the coupon rate) and the return of the principal amount borrowed.

- The periodic coupons are usually paid semiannually or annually, and the payment dates are given in the indenture.

- The decision-maker will find it easy to estimate the cash flows and the timing of those cash flows.

b. Bond Value: Following the general model above, the value of bonds can be calculated as follows:

$$V_0 = I_1/(1+k_d)^1 + I_2/(1+k_d)^2 + ... + I_n/(1+k_d)^n + M/(1+k_d)^n$$

Where: V_0 = the current value of the asset.

I = dollars of interest paid each period (or the coupon rate times the par value).

M = the par value or maturity value of the bond (typically equal to $1,000).

k_d = the appropriate required rate (opportunity cost).

n = the period that the coupon is paid, either in years or semiannual interest periods.

Recognizing that the interest payments (I) are equal, and the period between payments is the same, it is possible to treat this payment stream as an annuity in the calculation. Therefore, the computation can be reduced to:

$$V_0 = I \times (PVIFA_{kd,n}) + M \times (PVIF_{kd,n})$$

Where: V_0 = the current value of the asset.

I = dollars of interest paid each period (or the coupon rate times the par value).

$PVIFA$ = Present Value Interest Factor for Annuities, which is a precalculated value for a given interest rate (kd) and number of periods (n). When this factor is multiplied by the annual payment, the present value of the annuity can be determined. Sample annuity tables are provided at the end of this chapter.

$PVIF$ = Present Value Interest Factor for a single payment, which is a precalculated value for a given interest rate (kd) and number of periods (n). When this factor is multiplied by the single future payment, the present value of this payment can be determined.

The first step in bond valuation is determining the cost of debt (k_d). Once this has been determined, this computation makes the calculation of the bond's value a simple procedure. If the coupons are paid semiannually instead of annually, it is necessary to adjust the coupon from annual to semi-annual. The required rate must be adjusted from an annual rate to a semiannual rate and the number of periods changed from number of years to number of semiannual periods. Once these adjustments are made, calculate the value as before. It is common practice that if the adjustment is made to the rates, etc., for the coupon payments, the rates for the calculation of the present value of the maturity value are then adjusted for semiannual periods.

Several relationships are important to recognize.

- When the coupon rate (a percentage) is the same as the required rate, the price of the bond is the same as its par or maturity value.
- If the coupon rate is above the required rate, the price of the bond is above its par value (the bond is selling at a premium).
- If the coupon rate is below the required rate, the price is below the par value (the bond is selling at a discount).
- This highlights the inverse relationship that exists between the price of the bond and the level of interest rates. As interest rates rise the prices of bonds (especially long-term bonds) generally drop. As interest rates drop, the prices of bonds generally rise to restore equilibrium to the market.
- It is important to realize that k_d (the required rate or opportunity cost) is a function of:
  1. Inflation,
  2. Real economic growth,
  3. The level of risk aversion in the financial markets and
  4. The inherent risk of the debt issuer.

As any of these factors change, so does the required rate and, therefore, the value of the bond. In addition, the determination of k_d may be subjective, especially for smaller or newer firms. This could add additional uncertainty to the valuation process.

As will be discussed later in this chapter, according to the CAPM (Capital Asset Pricing Model), inflation and real economic growth determine a risk-free rate, the general level of risk in the market adds a market premium to the risk-free rate, and the individual firm risk adds an additional premium to the required rate of return.

c. Yield to Maturity (YTM): An important relationship when evaluating a bond is the concept of yield to maturity. This represents the return that the investor will receive if the bond is bought at its current price and held until it matures. In this case, the investor knows what will be paid for the bond, knows the coupon payments and knows when the bond matures. The only unknown variable is the interest rate that is being used to discount the cash flows of the bond.

For example, suppose that an investor pays \$1,368.31 for a bond with a \$1,000 par value, a 15% coupon (making the coupon \$150 per year) and 14 years remaining until the bond matures. To calculate the yield to maturity (YTM) for this bond, the decision-maker sets up the problem as follows (note that k_d is replaced by the YTM, and C represents the annual coupon payment):

$$V_0 = C/(1+YTM)^1 + C/(1+YTM)^2 + .. + C/(1+YTM)^n + M/(1+YTM)^n$$

$$\$1,368.31 = \$150/(1+YTM)^1 + \$150/(1+YTM)^2 + ..$$

$$+ \$150/(1+YTM)^n + \$1,000/(1+YTM)^n$$

- The decision-maker finds the YTM that balances the equation. Trial and error is the only effective way to find the YTM rate; however, most business calculators and computer spreadsheets have programs to calculate the YTM.
- In the above example, a YTM of 10% balances the equation.
- As a rule of thumb, if the right-hand side of the equation is too high, the estimated interest rate must be reduced. If the right-hand side is too low, the rate must be increased.

A very similar relationship is known as yield to first call, which is the yield until the company could retire the bond by calling it. A company will usually call a bond if market rates have declined sufficiently to provide an overall lower cost of debt to the firm. Investors need to take into account the likelihood that the firm will call the bond. Common practice is to assume that the company will call the bond at its first opportunity. The decision-maker performs the calculation above, substituting the call price (usually higher than the par value because of call premiums) for the maturity value and the number of periods until the bond is called for the bond's maturity.

There is a degree of callrisk that holders of callable bonds face. If the original intention of the investor was to purchase a 20-year bond, but the bond ended up being called after only five years, then the investor must reinvest the proceeds from the original bonds. If the original bonds were called, it is highly likely that interest rates had dropped significantly from their initial coupon rate, and the investor will not be able to find new bond investments with the same level of return as the called bonds. In other words, with a callable bond, the investor is only able to lock in a long-term rate of return until the first call date, not to the full maturity of the bond as in the case of a non-callable issue.

It is important to understand the relationship between the required rate of return (k_d) and the Yield to Maturity (YTM). In the valuation of bonds, the required rate of return must be determined in order to complete the valuation process. In many cases, for firms with outstanding debt, the required rate of return is equal to the current YTM on the firm's outstanding bonds of the same basic risk and maturity. As discussed above, this rate can fluctuate as a function of many economic and firm-specific factors.

2. Preferred Stock Valuation: Preferred stock has many of the features of both debt financing and equity financing. The cash flows are similar (from the investor's viewpoint) to bond cash flows, while tax treatment and other features are similar to equity. Preferred stock has preference over the common stock in the event of liquidation, and it has a prior claim on the earnings of the firm (hence the name preferred stock). Traditionally, preferred stockholders have not had voting rights for the board of directors, but this is changing. As more firms make private placements of preferred stock to large institutional investors, investors increasingly have been demanding and receiving either voting rights or, in some cases, seats on the board. In many cases, preferred shareholders are entitled to board representation if a specified number of dividends is not paid (i.e., dividends are in arrears).

Another form of preferred stock is known as adjustable rate preferred stock (ARPS) and is designed to adjust its dividend rate according to some interest rate index, and thereby maintain a more constant price level. This form of investment is attractive to many treasurers for a portion of their short-term portfolio because current tax regulations allow corporate holders of preferred stock to exclude 70% of the dividends received from federal income taxes if the stock is held for at least a 45-day period.[1] In the remainder of this section, we will deal with the traditional form of preferred stock rather than the adjustable form.

a. Cash Flows:

- The preferred stock cash flows (dividends) are normally fixed throughout the life of the preferred stock, and the stock is expected to be outstanding into perpetuity.

- This means that the cash flows are easy to estimate since they are set by contract and are the same for all periods.

- There is a liquidity preference for the investor in preferred stock compared with an investment in common stock, because the preferred share holders are paid before the common stock holders. In addition, most preferred stock dividends are "cumulative in arrears," which means that all unpaid preferred stock dividends must be paid before any common stock dividends can be paid.

- While this is the normal situation, alternative formulations of preferred stock are possible, including adjustable dividends and call features that allow the firm to retire the preferred stock. If the stock under evaluation has these alternative forms, the probability of their use must be taken into account.

b. Preferred Stock Value: Since the dividends of normal preferred stock are constant and extend into perpetuity, the appropriate valuation model for preferred stock is simply the present value model for a perpetual annuity, given as:

$$V_{ps} = D_{ps}/k_{ps}$$

Where: V_{ps} = the current value (price) of the preferred stock.
D_{ps} = the dividend for the preferred stock.
k_{ps} = the required rate for preferred stock.

If the preferred stock is not perpetual (i.e., the firm has call features attached to the issue), then the preferred stock is valued using the bond valuation model. If the dividend is allowed to adjust, then the models described for common stock may be appropriate.

3. Common Stock Valuation: Common stock valuation differs from bond and preferred stock valuation in a very important way. The common stock cash flows (dividends) are usually perpetual, but are not set by contract as is the case with preferred stock. Instead, the dividends are set by the board of directors on a period-by-period basis. This complicates the analysis because of the difficulty in estimating the dividends from period to period. An additional complication in the valuation process arises due to the fact that stock price appreciation (capital gains) is a very important consideration and must be factored into the equation.

- **a. Cash Flows:**
- The primary difficulty in valuing common stock is the estimation of cash flows. As mentioned above, the dividends are set each period by the board of directors.
- The decision-maker, theoretically, would have to estimate an infinite number of dividends, then take the present value of those dividends and project appreciation in the price of the stock.
- In order to get the cash flows into a format that allows the decision-maker to value the common stock, assumptions must be made concerning the dividends and the growth rate that those dividends will exhibit. An additional assumption is that growth in the dividend stream will be a proxy for any anticipated price appreciation (capital gains) for the stock. The general form of the common stock valuation equation is:

$$P_0 = \sum_{i-1}^{\infty} \frac{D_i}{(1 + K_s)^i}$$

Where: P_0 = the current price (value) of the common stock.
D_i = the dividend in time period i.
k_s = the required rate of return on common stock.

Note: k_s could also vary with each period of time i.

This theoretical model may not necessarily represent the reality of stock pricing. However, since common shareholders are the owners of all residual cash flows of the firm, to the extent the dividend stream captures these cash flows, the model will be valid.

The value of the stock will be very difficult to determine with both of the equation variables potentially changing with each period and the requirement of determining these values out to infinity. As discussed above, some assumptions concerning the dividends and their growth must be made.

1. The first assumption to make is that the dividends will not grow but will remain constant into the future. Technically, this assumes that there will never be any growth. Because the dividends are now known to be constant forever, they are easy to estimate. This results in a valuation model that is essentially the same as that used for preferred stock. While the calculation is simple, the assumption is not realistic because a firm's growth rate will almost always be changing over time (growing or declining) as a result of numerous factors.

2. The second assumption is that the dividends may grow at a constant rate into the foreseeable future (technically forever). This model is generally referred to as the constant growth model (also known as the Gordon Growth Model), and while this growth assumption is somewhat more realistic, it must be used judiciously because the growth rate must be reasonable. If the growth rate of

earnings and dividends is above the required rate of return on the stock, the model will not yield the proper results.

3. The third and final type of assumption is that the dividend will grow at several possible rates until, at some point, the decision-maker assumes constant growth of the remaining dividend stream. This allows the decision-maker to evaluate the impact of important events such as new product introduction, and have the company exhibit several levels of growth. The growth rate then levels off at a realistic, constant figure, and the constant growth assumption is invoked for the remaining cash flows.

4. In another situation, the growth rate is changing from period to period and, under those conditions, the decision-maker must evaluate an infinite number of dividends. Therefore, the most realistic assumption is the third, in which growth rates can be estimated for many years provided that, at some point, the decision-maker makes a constant growth assumption.

5. Since the common shareholders are the owners of all residual cash flows of the firm, an alternative approach would be to use the estimated stream of future cash flows for the entire firm (either in perpetuity or for 15-20 years, because beyond 20 years the present values of the remaining cash flows would be negligible), then discount those cash flows at an appropriate rate of return to arrive at the present value of the firm. Dividing this total firm value by the number of outstanding shares would determine the per-share stock price. In this approach, whether the value is "paid" to the shareholders as dividends or in the form of stock appreciation, is immaterial.

b. Common Stock Value: The basic model for all of the assumptions is the same, in that the models determine the discounted value of the estimated dividends. In the real world, however, investors look not only at dividends but at the entire stream of earnings available to the shareholders, including both dividends and price appreciation. The form of the calculation depends on the assumptions involved. These versions of the model are described below.

1. **Zero-Growth:** Under the zero-growth assumption, the valuation model is identical to the model for perpetual preferred stock. In this case, all of the dividends (D_i) are constant, as well as the required rate of return (k_s) and the infinite summation calculation reduces to this simple equation:

$$P_0 = D/k_s$$

Where: P_0 = the value (estimated market price) at time 0.
D = the annual dividend that will be paid.
k_s = the required rate of return on stock.

As stated above, this equation is very simple to implement, but the assumption itself is not very realistic.

2. **Constant Growth:** Another approach assumes that the dividend grows at a constant rate over time. This is known as the Gordon model, or constant growth model, and is formulated as:

$$P_0 = D_0(1+g) / (k_s - g)$$

Where: P_0 = the value (estimated market price) at time 0.
D_0 = the current (time 0) total annual dividend.
g = the constant growth rate.
k_s = the required rate of return on stock.

- Note that this model takes the next dividend (estimated in the numerator) and divides it by the required rate minus the growth rate. Relating this back to our general model above, we note that the value of any period's dividend (D_i) is determined as the last known dividend (D_0) times $(1+g)^i$, or a growth factor for i periods at the growth rate g.

- This model estimates the current value of the infinite number of dividends discounted at the required rate of return. This is an important point to remember when the model is utilized with the next set of assumptions.

- Note that when the next dividend (D_1) is known, the term $D_0(1+g)$ could be replaced by D_1. This is usually the case in larger publicly traded firms, where the dividend is announced well in advance of the payment date.

- This model works best for established firms that pay regular dividends.

An important feature of the Gordon model is that if the decision-maker has estimates of the growth rates, the market's required rate can be estimated as:

$$K_s = D_0(1+g)/P_m + g$$

Where: K_s = the markets required rate for this stock.
D_0 = the current (time 0) total annual dividend.
P_m = the current market price.
g = the constant growth rate or proxy for capital gains rate.

Note that the first term [$D_0(1+g)/P_m$] represents return from dividend payments, and g should represent the constant growth rate, which is a proxy for capital gains return. This relationship can be useful in comparing similar companies.

3. **Non-Constant Growth:** Finally, the model to use when the final set of assumptions is made is:

$$P_0 = D_0(1+g_1)/(1+k_s)^1 + D_1(1+g_2)/(1+k_s)^2 + \ldots$$
$$+ D_{n-1}(1+g_n)/(1+k_s)^n$$
$$+ [D_n(1+g_c)/(k_s - g_c)] [1/(1+k_s)^n]$$

Where: P_0 = the value (estimated market price) at time 0.
D_n = the total annual dividend at time n.
k_s = the required rate of return on stock.
g_n = the growth rates estimated for periods 1 through n.
g_c = the constant growth rate.

The first portion of the equation is the discounted value of the dividends that occur during the period in which the decision-maker is estimating individual rates of growth. The second portion of the equation uses the constant growth model to estimate the remaining dividends during the period of constant growth. Note that this equation is still just a specific example of the general model presented earlier. This model could be easily programmed into a computer spreadsheet.

These models, especially the last one, can be utilized in most stock valuation situations. The only requirement for the last model is that at some point the decision-maker assumes that constant growth begins. These models, of course, provide the value of the cash flows to the decision-maker, not necessarily the market value of the stock. The market value may reflect other investors' estimates of the growth rates and required rates of return.

B. Risk and Rates of Return

An integral part of each valuation model described above is the required rate (by investors in the market) of return for each type of security. This section describes a method for determining the required rate of return for any asset. This required rate of return can then be used in valuation models like those previously described.

1. Defining and Measuring Risk

Risk refers to the chance that some unforeseen event will occur. The decision-maker needs to be able to define and quantify the amount of risk involved in investment in a specific asset. Statistical measures provide the capability to measure risk. The risk associated with investment in financial assets is the possibility that the realized return will be different from that expected by the investor.

In a slightly different example of risk, the investor realizes a return lower than that needed to compensate for the risk involved in the investment. The statistical concepts of expected value and standard deviation provide measures of expected return and the risk associated with it.

a. Expected Rate of Return: The expected rate of return for any asset can be estimated as:

$$K_j = \sum_{i=1}^{\infty} (P_i \times K_i)$$

Where: k_j = the expected return on asset j.
$\quad\quad\quad P_i$ = the probability of outcome i.
$\quad\quad\quad k_i$ = the return for outcome i.

Note: i has n possible outcomes.

Most business calculators will compute the expected return as formulated above. Statistical and spreadsheet applications for personal computers usually can make this computation. The problem, however, is in determining the appropriate estimated probabilities and returns. These will be different for different investors.

b. Standard Deviation (SD): Associated with the calculation of expected value is the standard deviation of the expected value. The standard deviation is the square root of the variance taken from the weighted average of the squared differences between the individual possible outcomes and the expected value. The standard deviation is denominated in the same units as the variable being measured. To calculate the standard deviation, use the following equation:

$$SD = \sqrt{\sum_{i=1}^{n} [(k_i - \overline{k})^2 \times P_i]}$$

Where: k = the expected value.
        k_i = the individual possibility.
        P_i = the probability of the individual possibility.

Note: i has n possible outcomes.

Taking the square root of the equation is necessary to put the SD in the same terms as the expected value. Standard deviation measures the spread around the expected value that is present in the distribution.

2. Risk Aversion

With the exception of small investments (e.g. wagers such as lottery tickets), most investors are risk-averse. This means that, given a choice between two investments with identical expected returns, the investor will prefer the investment with the lower risk or standard deviation. In some cases an individual may be risk-seeking (preferring the riskier investment) or risk-neutral (neither risk-averse nor risk-seeking). It may be the case an investor will be risk-averse for the bulk of his/her portfolio, but may be risk-seeking for a small "speculative" portion of it. There are several implications to risk aversion:

- First, the higher the security's risk, the lower the price, other being factors constant. In addition, the higher the security's risk, the higher the required rate of return.

- Therefore, these two factors operate with an inverse relationship between interest rates and the price of a financial asset. Higher risk means a higher required rate of return, which, in turn, means that the present value of the cash flows will be lower, resulting in a lower price.

- Also, as the risk of an asset increases, perhaps as a result of slowing economic growth, the required rate will increase and the price will decline.

3. Portfolio Risk and Return

Assets are almost never held in isolation. Investors prefer holding combinations of assets so that losses from one investment may be compensated by gains in another. This basic understanding of diversification is highlighted in Figure 4.1.

Stock W and Stock M are negatively correlated, which means that the two stocks move in opposite directions. Statistical correlation is defined as the tendency of two variables to move together. Losses in Stock W are made up by gains in Stock M. The two assets held together have a return similar to the return of the individual assets, while the risk has been eliminated. Risk-averse investors will prefer this portfolio to a portfolio containing a single asset, because, over time, it would provide the same total return but with lower risk due to the absence of large swings in the size of the return.

As discussed below, it is important to divide the total risk of an asset into the risk peculiar to that asset and its risk relative to overall risk in the market. While diversification significantly reduces asset-specific risk, it does little to reduce market risk.

a. Portfolio Expected Return: To calculate the expected return for a portfolio, the following equation is used:

$$k_p = w_1 \times k_1 + w_2 \times k_2 + ... + w_n \times k_n$$

Where: k_p = the expected return for the portfolio.
       w = the weight invested in assets 1 to n.
       k = the expected return for assets 1 to n.

- This is simply the weighted average of the returns of the individual assets in the portfolio. This expected return is not influenced by the correlation between the assets.

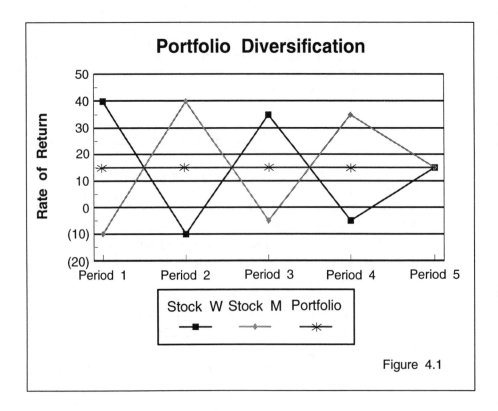

Figure 4.1

b. Portfolio Standard Deviation: Unlike expected return, the standard deviation of the portfolio is not a weighted average of the standard deviations of the individual assets. The portfolio standard deviation changes as the correlation between assets changes.

- Correlation as a statistical measure ranges between +1.0 and −1.0.
- If assets are correlated at +1.0, the standard deviation is a weighted average.
- If the assets are correlated below +1.0, but above −1.0, the standard deviation of the portfolio will be less than the weighted average, but above zero.
- With a correlation of −1.0 (perfect negative correlation), there is a weighting scenario that will achieve zero risk. With this type of correlation, as one asset decreases in value another asset increases in value by exactly the same amount, thus keeping the value of the portfolio constant. Essentially, this is the type of correlation provided by a perfect hedge or arbitrage.

It is important to understand the concept of portfolio risk and how it relates to individual asset risk.

- Total risk of the asset, as measured by the standard deviation of the asset's expected return, can be broken down into company-specific risk and market risk, an important concept.
- Company-specific risk is the risk to which an investor would be exposed if the company were the investor's only investment. Therefore, company-specific risk is essentially the diversifiable portion of total risk.
- The maximum diversification that can take place is to include all assets in the world in one portfolio. There would be no diversification left since there would be no remaining assets available for diversification. This is known as market risk, and the resulting portfolio is known as the market portfolio.
- Company-specific risk is, therefore, diversifiable (can be eliminated), and investors should not expect to be compensated for bearing this risk. For assets held in well-diversified portfolios, investors should only concern themselves with the market risk portion of total risk, not company-specific. The risk that an asset adds to a diversified portfolio is measured only by its market risk.

4. Beta

The market portfolio described above is exposed to non-diversifiable risk, also known as market, or systematic risk. As mentioned above, the total risk to which an asset is exposed is in part market risk. Beta risk measures the market risk of a given asset relative to the risk of the market portfolio. Beta is, therefore, a relative measure, and is defined as the percentage change in the return on an asset for a 1% change in the value of the market portfolio.

- The market portfolio has a beta of 1.0, signifying that it bears the base level of market risk. If an asset bears relatively more market risk, the asset will have a beta greater than 1.0. If an asset bears relatively less market risk, the asset will have a beta lower than 1.0.

- Stocks that have betas greater than 1.0 (signifying that the volatility of the stock is greater than the volatility of the market portfolio itself) are called "aggressive stocks." Stocks that have betas less than 1.0 (indicating that their volatility is lower than the volatility of the market portfolio) are called "defensive stocks."

- The beta can be calculated by estimating the regression relationship between the asset being evaluated and a proxy for the market portfolio. One of the typical proxies used is the S&P 500 Index.

- It is important to realize that beta is an *ex ante* relationship, meaning that it is a before-the-fact relationship, or a forecast. Most measurement techniques, however, use *ex post* (historical) data to determine the relationship. The decision-maker must take this into account when using the results of the measurement technique, as conditions may be different in the future than they were in the past.

- There are several investment services, notably the ValueLine Investment Survey and Standard and Poor's, that publish their estimates of beta for many publicly traded common stocks. These reports are generally found in public or university libraries, and are also available by subscription. Using these estimates may be useful when evaluating such stocks. Many investment companies and analysts also publish their estimates of beta.

- In the portfolio context beta is linear, meaning that the portfolio beta is the weighted average of the betas of the individual assets included in the portfolio. There are no effects from any correlation among betas.

5. Relationship between Risk and Rates of Return

Basically, because most investors are risk-averse, the higher the level of risk, the higher the required rate of return. The above discussion describes the risk that should be compensated, namely market risk. The Capital Asset Pricing Model described next provides the decision-maker with the ability to determine the required rate of return for any asset, based on its exposure to market risk.

a. Capital Asset Pricing Model (CAPM): The Capital Asset Pricing Model (CAPM) describes the relationship between risk and required rate of return. The model assumes a linear relationship between them and is expressed as:

$$k_i = k_{RF} + (k_M - k_{RF})b_i$$

Where: k_i = the required rate of return for asset i.
  k_{RF} = the expected rate of return on a riskless asset.
  k_M = the expected return on the market portfolio.
  b_i = the beta of asset i, described above.

- The return on the riskless asset is typically measured by the return on short-term U.S. Government securities, such as the T-Bill. Another approach is to use a risk-free rate with a maturity that matches the maturity of the asset. In this case, a long-term government security rate could be used as a risk-free rate for long-term bonds or stocks.

- Note that this is the equation for a line, where the riskless rate is the intercept, beta is the variable x, and the term in the brackets (k_M k_{RF}) is the slope of the line and is generally known as the market risk premium.

- The slope in Figure 4.2 represents the premium paid for bearing market risk. When the market risk premium is multiplied by the asset's beta, the risk premium for the specific asset can be determined.

- The line shown in Figure 4.2 called the Security Market Line, is described in the next section.

b. Security Market Line (SML): The Security Market Line shows the linear relationship between risk and return.

- The Y-axis of the graph is the required rate of return given the risk of the asset.

- The X-axis is the measurement of the level of risk, in this case beta.

- At a beta of 0, the risk-free rate is the required rate of return. This level of beta indicates that the asset is not exposed to systematic risk.

- As beta increases, the required rate of return also increases.

- To find the required rate for a specific asset, determine the beta for the asset, then find the level of y (required rate of return) that corresponds with that level of beta.

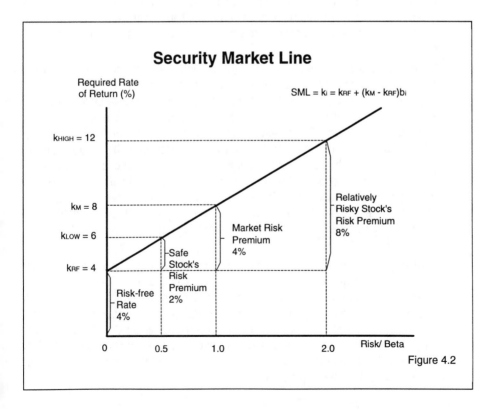

Figure 4.2

- According to this theory, under equilibrium conditions, all assets will be priced to lie along the SML. The model (CAPM) is an equilibrium model because forces exist to move assets that are mis-priced (not on the SML) onto the SML.

- If an asset is priced so that its rate lies above the SML, the asset has an expected return above its required return. This indicates that investors will find it desirable to hold, meaning that there will be buying pressure on the asset. This pressure will drive the price up (and the return down) until the asset is priced correctly (i.e., along the SML).

- If an asset is priced so that the expected return lies below the SML, investors will not want to hold the asset, causing downward pressure on the asset price and moving the return upward until it intersects with the SML. Therefore, in equilibrium, all assets will be priced so that they may be expected to provide their required rate of return.

6. Efficient Markets Hypothesis

The Efficient Markets Hypothesis (EMH) holds that market prices reflect available information and that it is impossible for investors to consistently receive returns above the required rate of return. There are three levels to this theory, reflecting different levels of information availability.

a. Weak Form Efficiency: The weak form of the EMH states that all information contained in past price movements is fully reflected in current market prices. This means that information about the recent (or historical) movement of the stock price will not aid the investor to achieve a return above the required return on a consistent basis.

b. Semi-Strong Form Efficiency: This form of efficiency states that current market prices fully reflect all of the information concerning an asset that is publicly available. This means that studying the financial reports and other types of publicly available information will not enable the investor to consistently earn a return above the required rate of return. This form of efficiency does not preclude insiders' earning returns above the required return when using information that is not publicly available. There is, however, some argument over exactly what constitutes publicly available information. In reality, there is a significant cost for obtaining the best public information, such as real-time electronic news services, or access to the floors of the securities exchanges. Thus, large traders and brokers will generally have the "best" publicly available information, while individual investors may not have such ready access.

c. Strong Form Efficiency: This form of efficiency states that market prices fully reflect all information, both publicly and privately available. Under this form, investors who are privy to inside information will not be able to consistently earn a return above the required rate of return. Empirical evidence seems to indicate that this form of the EMH is not valid in the "real-world" as insiders (management, directors, etc.) do appear to be able to earn excess returns (which is why the SEC places restrictions on insider trading). The other forms of efficiency, however, seem to be supported by the empirical evidence.

C. Cost of Capital

The cost of capital figures in many aspects of decision-making, especially capital budgeting, which is the topic of Chapter 12. The cost of capital reflects the cost of funds to the firm, and therefore represents the minimum required rate of return it needs in making capital investment decisions. It is important to recognize that these calculations represent only an estimate of the cost of capital. There are many factors that are difficult to incorporate into the analysis. For most firms, the estimation of cost of capital need only be reasonably accurate. This section describes the components that make up the cost of capital and then develops the firm's cost of capital.

1. Capital Components and Costs: The primary sources of funds for the firm, especially long-term funds, are debt, preferred stock and equity capital in the form of newly issued common stock and retained earnings. The costs associated with these components are found using the pricing models developed earlier and are discussed below.

It is important for the decision-maker to recognize that the most important item is the marginal cost of these components; that is, what the cost of raising new amounts of these forms of capital is expected to be. Using the marginal, or expected, cost of these components, provides the decision-maker with the market's current evaluation of the risk (and therefore required rate of return) to the company. There is an additional consideration, however, as changes in the firm's capital structure will impact the marginal costs of the individual capital components. Thus, trying to reach a specific capital structure may be like trying to hit a moving target.

It is also important to recognize that some of the funding will be repaid with before-tax cash flows (debt) and some with after-tax cash flows. Given the overriding goal of maximizing shareholder wealth, the analysis should be made using after-tax costs of the financing sources. Therefore, debt costs should be adjusted to an after-tax basis.

a. Cost of Debt: The relevant component in cost of debt is its after-tax cost. For any newly issued debt, the cost is the Yield to Maturity (YTM), described earlier. The following computation is made to determine the after-tax cost of debt:

$$k_D(\text{after-tax}) = k_D(1-T)$$

Where: $k_D(\text{after tax})$ = the after-tax cost of debt.
$\quad\quad\quad k_D$ = the YTM projected for newly issued debt.
$\quad\quad\quad T$ = the firm's marginal tax rate.

- In many firms with complicated tax liabilities, this may be difficult to estimate from standard financial statements. If the analysis is being done internally, the firm's tax accounting department may be able to provide an appropriate figure. The analyst could also use, as an estimate, the most recent year's taxes paid divided by the pre-tax earnings. Another approach is to use the average tax rate paid (as a percentage of pre-tax profits) over the last few years.

- The cost of debt is adjusted to an after-tax cost because outlays associated with debt financing are an expense for tax purposes.

- The flotation (issuance) costs associated with debt may be significant for some firms. If so, they should be included in the determination of the cost of debt. Firms with minimal issuance costs (usually large, well-established firms), may not have to include them.

- It is only necessary to be reasonably accurate in the estimation of these costs. Because of errors inherent in the estimation, it is impossible to determine the exact costs involved for any given component in the cost of capital.

b. Cost of Preferred Stock: The cost of preferred stock can be estimated using the pricing formula described earlier in this section. Recall that the cash flows from preferred stock take the form of dividends and, therefore, are made with after-tax cash flows. This means that there is no adjustment needed to convert the cost of preferred stock to an after-tax basis. The pricing formula described earlier can be modified to solve for the cost of preferred stock, as follows:

$$k_p = D_p/P_p$$

Where: k_p = the cost of preferred stock (after-tax).

D_p = the annual preferred dividend expected to be paid on newly issued preferred stock.

P_p = the price, net of flotation or underwriting costs, that the firm would receive on newly issued preferred stock.

Note that the price is adjusted to reflect the costs of the underwriting process in issuing the new preferred stock. This adjustment causes the component cost to reflect the fact that the expenses associated with issuing the new security effectively reduce the amount of funds available to the firm. The cost needs to reflect the reduced amount of funds received.

c. Cost of Common Equity: Funds from common equity can be raised from two sources:

1. Retaining earnings during the period (instead of paying them out in dividends).

2. Issuing new common stock.

This section describes in depth the cost associated with retained earnings.

- It is important to realize that the firm must apply a cost factor to the use of retained earnings and that these are not free funds. This is based on the concept of opportunity cost, which states that the firm should be able to earn at least the equity rate of return on any retained earnings.

- If the firm cannot find investment opportunities that meet this criterion, the earnings should be paid out to the shareholders as dividends so that they can find other investments that can satisfy their required rates of return.

- Applying the required rate of return on equity as a cost factor for retained earnings satisfies the opportunity cost principle.

Note that the process of valuing common stock is complicated by the fact that the dividends and stock price appreciation are not easily forecast by the decision- maker. There are many different ways to estimate the cost of retained earnings for the firm.

1) CAPM: The first method is to use the Capital Asset Pricing Model (CAPM) to estimate the required rate on these funds. The CAPM (adjusted to reflect that we are estimating the required rate of return on stock) is formulated as:

$$k_s = k_{RF} + (k_M - k_{RF})b_i$$

Where: k_s = the required rate of return for the stock.
  k_{RF} = the expected rate of return on a riskless asset.
  k_M = the expected return on the market portfolio.
  b_i = the beta of stock.

The concept and determination of betas was discussed earlier in this chapter. For most publicly traded companies, estimations of betas can be found in reports published by ValueLine, Standard and Poor's, Moody's and other investment analysis services.

One of the key assumptions of the CAPM is the estimation of the riskless, or risk-free, rate to be used in the equation. The return on the riskless asset is typically measured by the return on short-term U.S. Government securities, such as the T-Bill. It can also be argued that a long-term Treasury Note or Bond rate should be used because of the long-term nature of the stock investment. The significance of the risk-free rate is that it represents an investment rate on default-free assets of similar maturity. It should be noted that the term risk-free refers to lack of default risk (hence the use of U.S. Government securities as proxies for this rate) rather than lack of interest rate risk. Any long-term rate will be subject to risk as a result of fluctuating interest rates. This is one of the arguments for using a short-term rate (T-Bills) rather than a long-term rate (T-Bonds).

2) Discounted Cash Flow (DCF) Method: The second method for estimating the cost of equity is to use the pricing models developed above. The most commonly used would be the Gordon Model, which can be rearranged to solve for the required rate as follows:

$$k_s = [D_0(1+g) / P_0] + g$$

Where: k_s = the required rate of return for the stock.
  D_0 = the current annual dividend on the stock.
  P_0 = the current market price of the stock.
  g = the annual growth rate in earnings and dividends.

The decision-maker must have reliable estimates of expected growth and make the assumption that the growth rate will be constant for the foreseeable future (technically forever).

One technique for estimating growth rate is to measure the historical growth rate and simply assume that it will continue to prevail in the future. Another technique is to estimate earnings retention growth as:

$$g = b \times r$$

Where: g = the expected growth rate.
        b = the percentage of earnings expected to be retained.
        r = the Return on Equity (ROE) expected in the future.

This growth estimate takes into account the expected growth due to retained earnings and the return on those earnings. A final technique for estimating the future growth of the firm's dividends is simply to utilize market analysts' projections. Most investment banks have estimates of the growth rates for publicly traded firms.

3) Bond Yield plus Risk Premium Approach: A third method for determining the component cost of equity is to measure the bond yield and adjust for a risk premium. This method assumes that the cost of equity is determined as follows:

$$k_s = \text{Bond Yield} + \text{Risk Premium}.$$

The decision-maker determines the firm's cost of debt and adjusts for the premium that is usually present in the firm's equity over the cost of debt. A problem associated with this approach is the assumption that the historical premium is the appropriate premium for the future. Investment advisory services, such as ValueLine, publish information on historical risk premiums for many publicly traded stocks.

2. Cost of Newly Issued Common Stock: Newly issued common stock must be adjusted for issue costs just as preferred stock is adjusted. This adjustment is most easily made by using pricing models such as the Gordon Model. The price used in these models is adjusted for the issue costs before the computation of the cost of equity is made.

Adjusting for issue costs helps reflect the market's perception of the firm's risk and assets. The issue costs will increase as the underwriters' perception of the firm's risk increases. This means that the cost of the funds will increase with the increased risk. The cost of newly issued stock will, of course, be higher than the cost of internally generated funds (opportunity cost of equity) because of these issuance costs.

3. Weighted Average Cost of Capital (WACC): To determine the firm's cost of capital, the decision-maker calculates a weighted average of the component costs of funds for the firm. This computation is made as follows:

$$\text{WACC} = k_a = W_D \times k_D \times (1-T) + W_p \times k_p + W_s \times k_s$$

Where: WACC = k_a is the cost of capital of the firm.
        W   = the weight of the capital structure for each component D (debt), p (preferred stock) and s (common equity).

$k_D \times (1-T)$ = the after-tax cost of debt.
k_p = the cost of preferred stock.
k_s = the cost of common stock, either retained earnings or newly issued stock.

- Note that the cost of equity will be either the cost of retained earnings or new issues of stock. From a pure cost perspective, the preference would be to use retained earnings as their cost is lower than new issues. However, the dividend policy of the firm may restrict the amount of retained earnings available for reinvestment, or the firm may have limited earnings for the period.

- Depending on the size of earnings and the firm's dividend policy, there generally will be a limited supply of retained earnings. Thus, for large capital budgets or in times of low retained earnings, newly issued common stock will have to be used.

- The exclusive use of retained earnings only works if internal generation of funds exceeds 100% of capital needs at the target debt/equity level.

a. Marginal Cost of Capital (MCC) Schedule: A weighted average cost of capital can be calculated for any combination of capital components. Essentially, the marginal cost of capital is the weighted average cost (to the firm) of raising one additional dollar of capital for a given mix of capital components. The MCC schedule (shown in Figure 4.3) is the graph of different weighted average costs for various levels of capital raised. The X-axis represents the amount of funds raised by the firm, and the Y-axis represents the corresponding WACC for that amount.

Note that at some level (specifically at $15 million), the WACC shows a discrete increase or jump, and later shows a steady rise as additional dollars of capital are raised.

b. Breaks in the MCC Schedule: The jumps described in the MCC schedule shown above occur because, at some level of funds raised, it becomes necessary to raise higher-cost funds for that component cost of capital.

- This is illustrated by the firm's limited amount of retained earnings available during the period. To raise funds after using all of the available retained earnings, it is necessary to issue new common stock.

- Note that having to switch to more expensive sources of funds is possible within the other components of the capital structure. For example, a firm may only be able to raise a limited amount of debt capital at the lowest rates. Thereafter, the marginal cost of debt capital will increase to reflect the increased riskiness of the firm. To determine where these breaks occur, compute the break point as:

Break point = Amount of funds used/Component weight

- In this equation, the break point is defined as the level of funds raised when the break in the MCC occurs. The amount of funds used is defined as the amount of funds used from that component of funding before the break occurs. The component weight is defined as the percentage of the capital structure financed with the specific component.

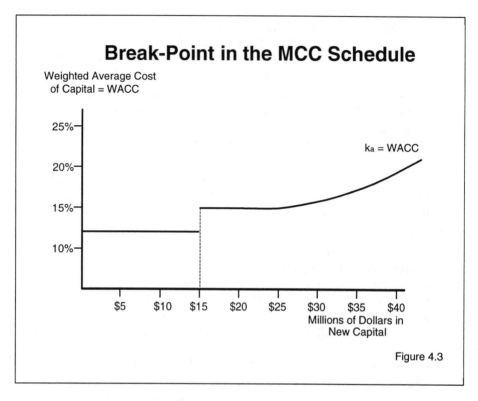

Break-Point in the MCC Schedule

Weighted Average Cost
of Capital = WACC

k_a = WACC

25%
20%
15%
10%

$5 $10 $15 $20 $25 $30 $35 $40

Millions of Dollars in
New Capital

Figure 4.3

- It is possible that there will be multiple break points in the MCC schedule. The decision-maker needs to know where these points occur so that the correct required rate of return will be used in capital budgeting decisions.

- The key challenge for corporate treasurers is to analyze the operational opportunities for the firm and obtain the required capital at the best mix and price to meet those opportunities. The question that treasurers need to ask continuously is: "How do the firm's operational risks and expected returns impact the available cost and mix of capital, and what is the best combination to maximize the firm's market capital value?"

D. Capital Structure of the Firm

One of the important inputs in the weighted cost of capital is the weight of the components. Firms tend to behave as if there were a specific breakdown of the capital structure they wish to maintain. This section briefly describes the major theories explaining this desire to operate at a certain capital structure, and discusses some of the key factors to be considered.

1. Capital Structure Theory

The primary theories of capital structure were developed in the seminal work of Modigliani and Millers (MM) in the late 1950s. Prior to MM, capital structure theories were based mainly on a loose set of assumptions about the behavior of investors.

a. Early Theories: MM's major contribution was a formalized development of capital structure theory. This theory was much more analytical and structured than its predecessors and made possible more serious discussion of the topic. MM devised a structured set of assumptions under which various theories of capital structures could be fairly evaluated. Essentially, these assumptions created an economic framework of perfect capital markets populated by knowledgeable investors with similar expectations.

The major conclusion of their research held that so long as the interest payments on debt were tax-deductible, due to this tax shield, there was an advantage to using debt.

b. Adjustments for Bankruptcy and Agency Costs: Most theories since MM take into account the cost of bankruptcy and other external factors (which are eliminated under the assumptions made by MM). When these costs are included in the model, an optimal capital structure is found to exist. While most theories tend to follow the lead of traditional approaches, they are more analytically rigorous than earlier developments before MM. The decision-maker needs to take into account the volatility of earnings, and therefore the risk of these earnings, when determining the optimal capital structure. This is the topic of the next section.

The other important adjustment to the theoretical capital structure models is agency costs associated with both debt and equity issues. With respect to debt use, the agency costs involved are a result of the additional monitoring and constraints placed on the management of the firm to protect the interests of the debt holders (debt covenants). With respect to the use of equity, there are agency costs involved in monitoring and restricting the actions of the managers to insure that they act in the equityholders' best interests.

c. Tradeoff Models: The general category of theoretical models discussed above is called "tradeoff models," meaning that the optimal capital structure is found by balancing (trading off) the tax shield benefits of debt (leverage) against the costs of financial distress and agency issues. Though tradeoff models may not be capable of determining the precise optimal capital structure for a firm, they do enable us to make several statements about the use of debt.

1. All else being equal, higher-risk firms (measured by variability or standard deviation of return on assets) should be able to borrow less than lower risk firms. The higher variability of returns would result in higher probability of financial distress and thus make high levels of debt more difficult to manage.

2. Firms that can take maximum advantage of the tax shield provided by debt (i.e., firms in high tax brackets) should use more debt than firms having lower tax rates.

If the tradeoff theories are correct, we should be able to observe debt levels at actual firms in accordance with the above statements. While there is some evidence that firms with high levels of tangible assets do indeed borrow more heavily than firms with low levels, there seems to be no empirical relationship between risk (as measured by betas) and the use of debt.

All in all, the empirical support for the tradeoff model is not strong, which suggests that other factors not included in these models are also at work.[2] In short, the tradeoff models do not tell the full story about capital structure.

d. "Pecking Order" Theory: The pecking order theory was first proposed by Gordon Donaldson in the early 1960s[3] and contained several important findings:

1. Firms prefer to raise capital through retained earnings (internally generated funds).

2. Firms generally derive their target dividend payout ratios from their historical earnings pattern, investor expectations, expected future investment opportunities and expected future cash flows. The target ratio is set at a level which allows the firm to meet capital expenditure requirements under normal conditions. This finding and the next are often attributed to the theory that dividends signal the firm's future earnings, making management reluctant to change dividends unless there is a major change in the opportunities available to the firm. This topic is covered in more detail in Chapter 5.

3. In the short term, firms are reluctant to make changes in dividends, especially dividend reductions (known as "sticky dividends"). However, if a firm were to experience less-than-normal cash flows during a given period, and dividends were not changeable, the result could be insufficient cash flows to fund desired capital expansion.

4. If a firm has cash in excess of that needed for capital investment purposes (due to sticky dividends and greater than normal cash flows) it will generally either retire debt or place the excess in short-term investments.

5. If a firm has insufficient internal cash flows to finance capital projects, it will first sell off short-term investments, and, if still more funds are needed, it will first issue the least expensive form of debt, then more expensive forms of debt or debt/equity hybrids, and, as a last resort, new common equity.

6. Thus, there is a "pecking order" in which new capital is raised, rather than some tradeoff between the benefits and costs of debt and equity. This means that the capital structure observed at any given firm is not necessarily a planned target; rather, it is the simple result of past cash flow fluctuations, dividend policy and investment opportunities.

e. Asymmetric Information Theory: One problem with the pecking-order theory was that it was based on observation of corporate activity rather than on a theoretical model which explained the behavior. In 1984, Stewart C. Myers proposed a new theory that helped form the theoretical basis for the pecking order findings.[4] Myers made the following observations:

1. The behavior of managers in the pecking order model can be explained in the context of asymmetric information. In this context, the management of the firm has better information on the firm's prospects than do the stockholders.

2. In a world with asymmetric information, corporations should only issue new shares if: (a) the firm has very profitable investments that cannot be postponed or financed by debt, or (b) if management thinks the shares of the firm are overvalued.

3. Investors recognize behavior of management cited above and consequently tend to mark down the price of a company's stock when it announces plans to issue new stock. This is especially true if investors believe that management considers the stock to be overvalued.

4. The financing pecking order as postulated by Donaldson is rational in this type of asymmetrical information environment. This is especially true as managers tend to place the interests of existing shareholders above those of prospective shareholders.

2. Business and Financial Risk

The decision-maker will take the firm's total risk into account when determining the firm's capital structure policy. Total risk comprises business risk and financial risk. These are discussed next, together with the ways they are measured.

a. Operating Leverage: Business risk is that associated with the firm's operating capabilities and policies, the volatility of its operating income, or earnings before interest and taxes (EBIT). Some of the factors that affect EBIT volatility are demand variability, sales price variability and resource cost variability. All such factors affecting business risk must be analyzed to gain a thorough understanding of its nature.

A good indicator of the firm's business risk is the use of operating leverage, which is the use of fixed costs in the production of the product. The presence of these fixed costs magnifies the impact of changes in other factors, such as price and variable costs.

b. Financial Leverage: Financial risk is best understood in the context of financial leverage. The fixed costs associated with financial leverage increase the impact of operating leverage discussed above. Changes in the variables of interest (i.e., price, demand for products and resource costs) will have more impact on firms that use financial leverage than on firms that do not. The firm's total risk is increased as it utilizes more financial leverage. Most analysts like to view total risk as the sum of business and financial risk; therefore, a distinction can be made between the risk of the firm's operations and that associated with its financing policies.

There is the problem of agency risk in the use of debt. The firm's managers act as agents for its shareholders (equityholders) and management's goal should be to maximize the firm's value to them. Management may take actions that will benefit the shareholders at the expense of the bondholders. The bondholders will protect themselves by introducing (or adding) covenants that restrict such management actions. These restrictions may cause the firm to be less efficient, thereby adding an agency cost to the overall management cost of the firm.

3. The Target Capital Structure

- The firm must operate in a manner enabling it to take on the desired level of total risk. Business risk and financial risk must be balanced in order to meet that total risk, or others will take over the company and maximize the capital structure.

- Firms that employ high levels of operating leverage will normally employ lower levels of financial leverage to compensate for risk. The reverse is also true. The decision-maker needs to know how much financial risk the firm is willing to take on in order to establish a capital structure consistent with the amount assumed.

- If the firm can assume a high level of financial risk, then a high level of debt will be used in the capital structure. If, however, the firm already uses high levels of operating leverage it may want to use relatively low levels of debt in the capital structure. This concept has also been described as determining the debt capacity of a firm, that is, how much debt it may safely take on before it has a significant impact on the overall riskiness. Thus, the setting of a firm's operating and financial risk is clearly a management decision.

- It is important to understand that the use of debt in a particular firm will change over time. As existing long-term debt is retired, the capital structure of the firm will change, unless new debt of a similar type is added. The acceptable target debt levels may change over time as the perceptions of debt by the financial markets change. During times of high growth, use of large amounts of debt may be more acceptable than during slow growth periods.

- Most managers prefer to use internal sources of funds rather than external sources of funds.[5] In practice, this means that during periods of high earnings, managers will tend to finance the firm's growth with retained earnings rather than by borrowing funds. As earnings slow, managers prefer to borrow rather than issue new equity. Over the long term, therefore, a firm's capital structure may stem more from its earnings history than from any conscious effort on the part of management to maintain a predetermined target debt level.

4. Other Considerations in the Capital Structure Decision

a. Using Common Stock as a Source of Funds:

- **Advantages:** The main advantage of common stock financing is that it does not obligate the firm to make fixed payments to investors. In addition, it has no specific maturity date. For the creditors, stock offers a cushion against losses, and, if the firm's future is bright, equity can often be raised at an attractive rate. Finally, as noted in the capital structure section, if a firm has sufficient equity, it may find that it is easier to issue debt.

- **Disadvantages:** Sale of common stock may extend voting rights and control to more people. This may be a problem for smaller firms where management is the primary owner. In the event the firm does well, the profits must be shared with new stockholders. The cost of underwriting common stock is considerable when compared to other sources of capital. Common equity financing does not enjoy the tax shield (deductibility of interest expense) that debt financing provides and, therefore often costs significantly more than debt.

- **Social Viewpoint:** In general, equity financing increases the overall stability of the stock market and the economy as a whole. The control of the firm rests with those investors willing to take on the residual risk (i.e., the holders of common shares). Shareholders demand that the value of their investment be maximized, and, in order to accomplish this, the firm's managers must operate as efficiently as possible.

b. Long-Run Viability: Managers of large firms that provide vital community services (such as utilities) have a responsibility to provide continuous service to their customers. This responsibility (and the regulatory agencies) may force them to use less than optimal levels of debt to ensure the firm's long-term viability.

c. Managerial Conservatism: In many cases, managers may be less willing to take on risk than the average investor. While the typical investor holds a firm's stock in a well-diversified portfolio, management actually has a non-diversified interest in the firm. If the firm were to fail, the investor might lose a small investment in a portfolio, but the managers would lose their jobs. As a result, management usually acts more conservatively in day-to-day operations of the firm than would the investors.

d. Lender and Rating Agency Attitudes: Since rating agencies and lenders often impose restrictions on the actions of management as part of the debt covenants, they are important in the determination of a firm's capital structure. Regardless of what management or equityholders may want as to optimal capital structure, the lenders are likely to require a more conservative level of debt in order to protect their interests. In some firms, the various debt covenants from different lenders may leave management with very little leeway in setting the capital structure.

e. Borrowing Capacity Reserve: In many cases, the management will restrict its use of debt simply to ensure that it will have debt capacity available should they "really" need it at some future time. To some extent, this is just a variation of the pecking order theory, with management preferring, if possible, to raise capital in the form of debt. Also, although this approach may seem less than optimal in the short run, it could actually benefit the firm in the long run by forcing it to save its debt capacity for the most important investment needs or for cushioning downside results.

f. Control: Control of the firm is definitely an important issue in the determination of capital structure. If management fails to use sufficient debt, the stock value may be depressed, increasing the risk that the firm may be taken over by others who would then restructure it to its optimum debt level. If the firm's management uses too much debt, it risks incurring bankruptcy or financial distress, resulting in the creditors taking control. Finally, if the firm issues additional equity, the existing majority shareholders (often the management in smaller firms) may lose control.

g. Additional Considerations: Various other factors should be considered in determining the capital structure of a firm:

- **Asset Structure:** Firms that invest in easily mortgageable assets often tend to use debt very heavily. Thus, real estate firms or large manufacturing firms will tend to use debt more heavily than service or high-technology firms.

- **Growth Rate:** Many firms with normal growth rates are able to fund needed investments through internally generated earnings. Firms with high growth rates, however, must often rely more heavily on external capital. Given the high flotation costs involved in new equity, the high-growth firms often use higher-than-normal levels of debt compared with other firms of the same size.

- **Profitability:** Firms with high levels of profitability generally need to raise less external capital those with lower levels. Given management's preference for debt over equity, we would expect to find that high-profit firms would have less debt than lower-profit firms, all else equal.

- **Taxes:** Interest is a tax deductible expense, while dividends are not deductible. This implies that firms in higher corporate tax brackets would have a greater incentive to use debt than those in lower brackets.

5. International Differences in Capital Structures:[6] Research into the capital structures of firms in foreign countries has shown significant differences, even in firms of similar size and industry group.[7] These differences may be explained by:

- Differences in tax codes, either on regular income, capital gains or the existence of value-added taxes.

- Differences in bankruptcy laws or agency costs related to bankruptcy (the cost of financial distress).

- A close linkage between banks and their customers (banks often hold ownership interests and serve on boards of directors in other countries).

- The debt ratios of multinational corporations (MNCs) in the United Kingdom and the United States tend to be lower than for those headquartered in most other industrialized countries. Possibly this is because the equity markets in other countries are not as well developed as those in the U.K. and U.S.

- Japanese companies tend to have greater degrees of financial leverage than comparable U.S. companies, but they are not perceived to have excessive risk because of potential backing from their government should they experience financial difficulties. In addition, the Japanese banks providing credit to Japanese firms are generally significant equity holders, and thus will make every effort to rescue a firm in trouble rather than force it into bankruptcy. It is also true that in Japan firms are often joined in large trading groups or "keiretsu" which typically include a bank as part of the group. The bank has both a lending and equity relationship with the other firms in the group.

IV. Chapter Checklists

A. Standard and Poor's Bond (Debt) Ratings

The listing below shows the most common ratings, along with a short description of each as used by Standard and Poor's.

AAA   Highest credit quality. Capacity to pay interest and repay principal is extremely strong.

AA   High credit quality. Very strong capacity to pay interest and repay principal.

A   Strong capacity to pay interest and repay principal. Is somewhat susceptible to the adverse effects of changes in economic and other circumstances.

BBB   Adequate capacity to pay interest and repay principal. Adverse economic conditions or changing circumstances can lead to insufficient capacity to pay interest and principal.

BB   Has less chance to default than some other bond issues. It faces ongoing uncertainties or exposure to adverse business, financial, or economic conditions which could lead to insufficient capacity to pay interest and principal.

B   Can meet current interest and principal payments but adverse business, financial, or economic conditions could impair capacity to pay interest and principal.

CCC   Uncertainty whether the bond can meet current obligations to pay interest and principal. Ability to meet obligations is based upon favorable business, financial, or economic conditions.

DDD to D   These ratings are used for bonds which are (1) either currently or about to be declared in default, or (2) in arrears for one or more interest payments. They generally indicate bonds that are highly questionable in value.

B. Duff & Phelps Bond (Debt) Ratings:

The listing below shows the most common ratings, along with a short description of each as used by Duff & Phelps.

AAA   Highest credit quality. The risk factors are negligible, being only slightly greater than for risk-free U.S. Treasury debt.

AA   High credit quality. Protection factors are strong. Risk is modest but may vary slightly from time to time because of economic conditions.

A   Protection factors are average, but adequate. However, risk factors are more variable and greater in periods of economic stress.

BBB   Below average protection factors, but still considered sufficient for prudent investment. Considerable variability in risk during economic cycles.

BB   Below investment grade, but deemed likely to meet obligations when due. Present or prospective financial protection factors fluctuate according to industry conditions or company fortunes. Overall quality may move up or down frequently within this category.

B   Below investment grade and possessing risk that obligations will fluctuate widely according to economic cycles, industry conditions and/or company fortunes. Potential exists for frequent changes in the rating within this category or into a higher or lower rating grade.

CCC   Well below investment grade securities. Considerable uncertainty exists as to timely payment of principal, interest, or preferred dividends. Protection factors are narrow and risk can be substantial with unfavorable economic/industry conditions, and/or with unfavorable company developments.

C. PVIF and PVIFA Tables[8]

PVIF – Present Value Interest Factors (for single cash flow)

PRESENT VALUE OF $1.00

$$P = 1/(1 + i)^n = PVIF (i, n)$$

Periods	4%	6%	8%	10%	12%	14%	20%
1	0.962	0.943	0.926	0.909	0.893	0.877	0.833
2	0.925	0.890	0.857	0.826	0.797	0.769	0.694
3	0.889	0.840	0.794	0.751	0.712	0.675	0.579
4	0.855	0.792	0.735	0.683	0.636	0.592	0.482
5	0.822	0.747	0.681	0.621	0.567	0.519	0.402
6	0.790	0.705	0.630	0.564	0.507	0.456	0.335
7	0.760	0.665	0.583	0.513	0.452	0.400	0.279
8	0.731	0.627	0.540	0.467	0.404	0.357	0.233
9	0.703	0.592	0.500	0.424	0.361	0.308	0.194
10	0.676	0.558	0.463	0.386	0.322	0.270	0.162
11	0.650	0.527	0.429	0.350	0.287	0.237	0.135
12	0.625	0.497	0.397	0.319	0.257	0.208	0.112
13	0.601	0.469	0.368	0.290	0.229	0.182	0.093
14	0.577	0.442	0.340	0.263	0.205	0.160	0.078
15	0.555	0.417	0.315	0.239	0.183	0.140	0.065
16	0.534	0.394	0.292	0.218	0.163	0.123	0.054
17	0.513	0.371	0.270	0.198	0.146	0.108	0.045
18	0.494	0.350	0.250	0.180	0.130	0.095	0.038
19	0.475	0.331	0.232	0.164	0.116	0.083	0.031
20	0.456	0.312	0.215	0.149	0.104	0.073	0.026
30	0.308	0.174	0.099	0.057	0.033	0.020	0.004
40	0.208	0.097	0.046	0.022	0.011	0.005	0.001

Source: From DICTIONARY OF ACCOUNTING TERMS by
Joel G. Siegel and Jae K. Shim.
Copyright © 1987 by Barron's Educational Series, Inc.,
Hauppauge, NY.

PVIFA – Present Value Interest Factors for Annuities

PRESENT VALUE OF ANNUITY OF $1.00

$$P_n = \frac{1}{i}\left[1 - \frac{1}{(1+i)^n}\right]$$

Periods	4%	6%	8%	10%	12%	14%	20%
1	0.962	0.943	0.926	0.909	0.893	0.877	0.833
2	1.886	1.833	1.783	1.736	1.690	1.647	1.528
3	2.775	2.673	2.577	2.487	2.402	2.322	2.106
4	3.630	3.465	3.312	3.170	3.037	2.914	2.589
5	4.452	4.212	3.993	3.791	3.605	3.433	2.991
6	5.242	4.917	4.623	4.355	4.111	3.889	3.326
7	6.002	5.582	5.206	4.868	4.564	4.288	3.605
8	6.733	6.210	5.747	5.335	4.968	4.639	3.837
9	7.435	6.802	6.247	5.759	5.328	4.946	4.031
10	8.111	7.360	6.710	6.145	5.650	5.216	4.192
11	8.760	7.887	7.139	6.495	5.938	5.453	4.327
12	9.385	8.384	7.536	6.814	6.194	5.660	4.439
13	9.986	8.853	7.904	7.103	6.424	5.842	4.533
14	10.563	9.295	8.244	7.367	6.628	6.002	4.611
15	11.118	9.712	8.559	7.606	6.811	6.142	4.675
16	11.652	10.106	8.851	7.824	6.974	6.265	4.730
17	12.168	10.477	9.122	8.022	7.120	6.373	4.775
18	12.659	10.828	9.372	8.201	7.250	6.467	4.812
19	13.134	11.158	9.604	8.365	7.366	6.550	4.844
20	13.590	11.470	9.818	8.514	7.469	6.623	4.870
30	17.292	13.765	11.258	9.427	8.055	7.003	4.979
40	19.793	15.046	11.925	9.779	8.244	7.105	4.997

Source: From DICTIONARY OF ACCOUNTING TERMS by
Joel G. Siegel and Jae K. Shim.
Copyright © 1987 by Barron's Educational Series, Inc.,
Hauppauge, NY.

V. Examples of Calculations

A. Basic Valuation Model

The present value of an asset (V_0) is equal to the cash flow expected from the asset. For an asset that has a 10-year life with no salvage value and an opportunity cost (required rate) of 7%, the present value can be found as follows:

Years:	Cash Flow
1–5	$10,000
6–8	$15,000
9–10	$17,000

$$V_0 = \$10,000/(1+.07)^1 + \$10,000/(1+.07)^2 + \$10,000/(1+.07)^3 +$$
$$\$10,000/(1+.07)^4 + \$10,000/(1+.07)^5 + \$15,000/(1+.07)^6 +$$
$$\$15,000/(1+.07)^7 + \$15,000/(1+.07)^8 + \$17,000/(1+.07)^9 +$$
$$\$17,000/(1+.07)^{10}$$

$$V_0 = \$9,346 + \$8,734 + \$8,163 + \$7,629 + \$7,130 + \$9,995 +$$
$$\$9,341 + \$8,730 + \$9,247 + \$8,642$$

$$V_0 = \$86,957$$

B. Bond Valuation Using PVIFA (Annuity) Tables

A 14%, $1,000 par value bond has annual payments and has ten years until maturity. If the required rate of return on the bond is 12%, the value of the bond (V_0) is calculated as follows:

$$V_0 = \$140(PVIFA_{12\%,10}) + \$1,000(PVIF_{12\%,10})$$
$$V_0 = \$140(5.650) + \$1,000(.322)$$
$$V_0 = \$1,113.00$$

If the bond has semiannual instead of annual payments, its value would be calculated as follows:

$$\$140/2 = \$70, 12\%/2 = 6\%, 10 \text{ years} \times 2 = 20 \text{ payments}$$
$$V_0 = \$70(PVIFA_{6\%,20}) + \$1,000(PVIF_{6\%,20})$$
$$V_0 = \$70(11.470) + \$1,000(.312)$$
$$V_0 = \$1,114.90$$

C. Impact of Change in Interest Rates on Bond Prices

A change in the interest rate inversely affects the current price of a bond. When interest rates fall, a bond's selling price rises. If interest rates rise, the price falls. This means that a bond carrying an annual rate of 10% will not have the same worth when interest rates change. Were interest rates to rise to 12%, a bond could be purchased in the open market that returns 12% for a par value. The 10% bond would then be less valuable than the 12% bond and would therefore cost less. The opposite occurs when interest rates fall; buyers are willing to pay more for a bond that returns 10% than for one that returns 9%.

D. Yield to Maturity (YTM) and Yield to First Call Calculations

YTM Calculations:

The YTM on a bond that currently sells for $1,368.31 with a $1,000 par value, a 15% coupon (making the coupon $150 per year) and 14 years remaining until the bond matures, would be calculated as follows (through trial and error):

Try 11%:

$$\$1,368 = \$150/(1+.11)^1 + \$150/(1+.11)^2 + \$150/(1+.11)^3 + \$150/(1+.11)^4 +$$
$$\$150/(1+.11)^5 + \$150/(1+.11)^6 + \$150/(1+.11)^7 + \$150/(1+.11)^8 +$$
$$\$150/(1+.11)^9 + \$150/(1+.11)^{10} + \$150/(1+.11)^{11} +$$
$$\$150/(1+.11)^{12} + \$150/(1+.11)^{13} + \$150/(1+.11)^{14} +$$
$$\$1,000/(1+.11)^{14}$$

$$\$1,368 = \$135 + \$122 + \$110 + \$99 + \$89 + \$80 + \$72 + \$65 + \$59 +$$
$$\$53 + \$48 + \$43 + \$39 + \$35 + \$232$$

$$\$1,368 > \$1,279$$

Since the current selling price is greater than the value when using 11%, the YTM must be lower. Try a lower YTM such as 9%:

$$\$1,368 = \$150/(1+.09)^1 + \$150/(1+.09)^2 + \$150/(1+.09)^3 + \$150/(1+.09)^4 +$$
$$\$150/(1+.09)^5 + \$150/(1+.09)^6 + \$150/(1+.09)^7 + \$150/(1+.09)^8 +$$
$$\$150/(1+.09)^9 + \$150/(1+.09)^{10} + \$150/(1+.09)^{11} +$$
$$\$150/(1+.09)^{12} + \$150/(1+.09)^{13} + \$150/(1+.09)^{14} +$$
$$\$1,000/(1+.09)^{14}$$

$$\$1,368 = \$138 + \$126 + \$116 + \$106 + \$97 + \$89 + \$82 + \$75 + \$69 +$$
$$\$63 + \$58 + \$53 + \$49 + \$45 + \$299$$

$$\$1,368 < \$1,467$$

Since the current selling price is less than the value when using 9%, in this case the YTM must be higher. Try a higher YTM such as 10%:

$$\$1,368 = \$150/(1+.10)^1 + \$150/(1+.10)^2 + \$150/(1+.10)^3 + \$150/(1+.10)^4 +$$
$$\$150/(1+.10)^5 + \$150/(1+.10)^6 + \$150/(1+.10)^7 + \$150/(1+.10)^8 +$$
$$\$150/(1+.10)^9 + \$150/(1+.10)^{10} + \$150/(1+.10)^{11} +$$
$$\$150/(1+.10)^{12} + \$150/(1+.10)^{13} + \$150/(1+.10)^{14} +$$
$$\$1,000/(1+.10)^{14}$$

$$\$1,368 = \$136 + \$124 + \$113 + \$102 + \$93 + \$85 + \$77 + \$70 + \$64 +$$
$$\$58 + \$53 + \$48 + \$43 + \$39 + \$263$$

$$\$1,368 = \$1,368$$

The YTM on this bond is thus 10%.

Yield to First Call Calculations:

Calculating the Yield to First Call is similar to the YTM calculation but instead of extending the bond life to maturity, you calculate to the callable date. Using the same bond, but with a callable price of $1,205, in five years the calculation would be as follows:

Try 10%:

$1,368 = $150/(1+.10)^1 + $150/(1+.10)^2 + $150/(1+.10)^3 + $150/(1+.10)^4 + $150/(1+.10)^5 + $1,205/(1+.10)5

$1,368 = $136 + $124 + $113 + $102 + $93 + $748

$1,368 > $1,316

Since the current selling price is greater than the value when using 10%, the YTM must be lower. Try a lower YTM such as 8%:

$1,368 = $150/(1+.08)^1 + $150/(1+.08)^2 + $150/(1+.08)^3 + $150/(1+.08)^4 + $150/(1+.08)^5 + $1,205/(1+.08)^5

$1,368 = $139 + $129 + $119 + $110 + $102 + $820

$1,368 < $1,419

Since the current selling price is less than the value when using 8%, the YTM must be higher. Try a higher YTM such as 9%:

$1,368 = $150/(1+.09)^1 + $150/(1+.09)^2 + $150/(1+.09)^3 + $150/(1+.09)^4 + $150/(1+.09)^5 + $1,205/(1+.09)^5

$1,368 = $138 + $126 + $116 + $106 + $97 + $785

$1,368 = $1,368

The Yield to First Call on this bond is 9% versus the YTM of 10%. A company will use the Yield to First Call to protect itself against interest rate changes.

E. Valuation of Preferred Stock

A preferred stock pays a $3.50 annual dividend and the required rate of return is 12%. The current value (price) of the preferred stock (V_{ps}) is calculated as follows:

$$V_{ps} = \$3.50/.12 = \$29.17$$

F. Stock Valuation Example

In order to properly value common stock, an assumption concerning its earnings and dividends growth must be made. The basic forms of growth are zero growth, constant growth and non-constant growth.

Zero Growth:

A common stock is expected to pay a $5.00 annual dividend with no growth in the future and the required rate of return stays at 8% for the life of the stock. The value of the common stock (P_0) is calculated as follows:

$P_0 = \$5.00/.08$

$P_0 = \$62.50$

Constant Growth:

A common stock just paid a $2.50 annual dividend and an investor expects the dividend to grow at 5%, and the required rate of return is 8%. The value of the common stock (P_0) is calculated as follows:

$P_0 = \$2.50(1+.05)/(.08-.05)$
$P_0 = \$87.50$

Without knowing the required rate of return (K_s) on a stock, and using the assumptions above, the required rate of return is calculated as follows:

$K_s = [\$2.50(1+.05)/\$87.50] +.05$
$K_s = 8\%$

Non-Constant Growth:

A common stock has just paid a $2.50 annual dividend (D) and an investor expects the dividend to grow at 15% for the next three years, then settle at a constant growth rate of 5%. The required rate of return is 8%. The value of the common stock (P_0) is calculated as follows:

$D_1 = \$2.50 \times (1+.15)^1 = \$2.88$; $D_2 = \$2.50 \times (1+.15)^2 = \$3.31$
$D_3 = \$2.50 \times (1+.15)^3 = \$3.80$; $D_4 = D_3 \times (1+.05)^4 = \$3.80 \times (1+.05)^4 = \$4.62$

$P_0 = \$2.88/(1+.08)^1 + \$3.31/(1+.08)^2 + \$3.80/(1+.08)^3 +$
$\qquad [\$4.62/(1+.08)^4]/(.08-.05)$
$P_0 = \$2.67 + \$2.84 + \$3.02 + \$113.20$
$P_0 = \$121.73$

G. Cost of Debt

A firm sells a $1,000 bond at par that has 8% annual payments bonds for 10 years. Assuming the marginal tax rate is 34%, the cost of debt is calculated as follows:

k_d (after-tax) $= .08 \times (1 - 0.34)$
k_d (after-tax) $= 5.28\%$

If the firm sells the bond for $900, at a discount, the cost of debt is calculated as follows:

Use the YTM calculation to find k_d:

| Present Value(PV) = $900 | Future Value | = $1,000 |
| Annual Payments = $80 | Number of Periods = 10 | |

Using a calculator, the YTM = 9.60%

k_d (after-tax) $= .096 \times (1 - 0.34)$
k_d (after-tax) $= 6.30\%$

H. Cost of Preferred Stock

A company issues 11% annual dividend preferred stock with a par value of $100 and net proceeds (less $5 underwriting cost) of $95 to the company. The cost of the preferred stock (k_p) is calculated as follows:

$$k_p = \$11/\$95$$
$$k_p = 11.57\%$$

I. Cost of Retained Earnings

Depending on the information available, the cost of retained earnings may be calculated by using either the capital asset pricing model (CAPM) or the discounted cash flow (DCF) approach. Both are outlined below:

Capital Asset Pricing Model (CAPM):

A government T-Bill return rate is 8% (risk free rate or k_{rf}) and the expected return on the market stated by an investment firm (k_{rf}) is 11%. The company's beta (b_i) is 1.05. The cost of retained earnings (k_s) using the CAPM method is calculated as follows:

$$k_s = .08 + (.11 - .08) \times 1.05$$
$$k_s = .08 + .032$$
$$k_s = 11.2\%$$

Discounted Cash Flow (DCF):

A company's current annual dividend is $2.50 ($D_0$) and the current selling price of the stock is $35 ($P_0$). The company's expected constant annual growth is 5% (g). The cost of retained earnings (k_s) using the DCF method is calculated as follows:

$$k_s = [\$2.50 \times (1+.05)/35] + .05$$
$$k_s = .075 +.05$$
$$k_s = 12.5\%$$

J. Cost of New Equity

A company's common stock with a value of $65 has just paid a $2.50 annual dividend and an investor banker expects the dividend to grow at 5%. The required rate of return is 8% and the new issue cost is 12% of the stock's current value. The net proceeds from the sale of the common stock (P_0) is calculated as follows:

$$P_0 = [\$2.50(1+.05)/(.08-.05)] \times (1-.12)$$
$$P_0 = \$87.50 \times (1-.12)$$
$$P_0 = \$77$$

K. Determination of Marginal Cost of Capital and Breakpoints

A company's capital structure is as follows:

Debt	$ 6,000,000	30%
Preferred Stock	2,000,000	10%
Common Stock	12,000,000	60%
Total Market Value	$20,000,000	100%

To raise an additional $5,000,000 of capital the firm would need to issue the following amounts of each component in order to keep the same capital structure:

Debt	$5,000,000 \times .30 =$	$1,500,000
Preferred Stock	$5,000,000 \times .10 =$	500,000
Common Stock	$5,000,000 \times .60 =$	3,000,000
		$5,000,000

Breakpoints:

Assume that the firm has estimated it will have $1.2 million in retained earnings available to satisfy a portion of the common equity requirements listed above. Since retained earnings are a less expensive source of capital than issuing new common stock, due to the flotation costs of new stock, a breakpoint will occur in the marginal cost of capital (MCC) schedule when the firm exhausts the retained earnings and begins to issue the new stock. The resulting breakpoint (X) can be calculated as

$$X = \frac{\text{Amount of Retained Earnings}}{\text{Percentage of Common Equity in the Firm's Capital Structure}}$$

$$X = \$1,200,000/.60$$

$$X = \$2,000,000$$

A total of $2 million in additional financing can be raised using only retained earnings as the common equity component. Any capital above this level will require the issuance of new common stock, whose higher cost will cause a breakpoint in the MCC schedule and shift it upwards.

VI. Endnotes

1. This type of preferred stock is discussed in greater detail both as a source of funds and a short-term investment in the Fourth Edition 1992 of *Essentials of Cash Management*, Henry A. Davis and Paul J. Ruggeri, CCM.

2. For background on the empirical evidence in this area, see: Robert Taggart, "A Model of Corporate Financing Decisions," *Journal of Finance*, December 1987; and Paul Marsh, "The Choice between Equity and Debt: An Empirical Study," *Journal of Finance*, March 1982.

3. See: Gordon Donaldson, *Corporate Debt Capacity: A Study of Corporate Debt Policy and the Determination of Corporate Debt Capacity*, Harvard Graduate School of Business Administration Research, Boston, 1961.

4. See: Stewart C. Myers, "The Capital Structure Puzzle," *Journal of Finance*, July 1984, pp. 575–592 (presented as a presidential address to the American Finance Association).

5. For more information on this theory of capital structure, see Stewart C. Myers, "The Theory of Capital Structure Revisited," *Journal of Finance*, July 1988.

6. See: *International Financial Management: Second Edition*, Chapter 16, "Multinational Capital Budgeting," Jeff Madura, West Publishers, St. Paul, MN, 1989.

7. A study by Markham Collins and William Sekely ("The Relationship of Headquarters Country and Industry Classification to Financial Structure," *Financial Management*, Autumn 1993) found that capital structures of MNCs tend to vary among the countries in which they are headquartered.

8. These tables are taken from: *Dictionary of Accounting Terms*, Barron's Business Guides, 1987.

5 Dividend Policy

I. Outline of the Chapter

A. Theories of Dividend Policy
    1. Dividend Irrelevance
    2. "Bird-in-the-Hand" Theory
    3. Tax Differential Theory
    4. Tests of Dividend Theories

B. Other Dividend Policy Issues
    1. Information Content of Dividends
    2. Clientele Effect
    3. Stability of Dividends

C. Dividend Policy in Practice
    1. Residual Dividend Model
    2. Constant or Steadily Increasing Dividends
    3. Constant Payout Ratio
    4. Low Regular Dividend plus Extras (Extra Dividends)
    5. Payment Procedures
        a. Declaration Date
        b. Holder-of-Record Date
        c. Ex-Dividend Date
        d. Payment Date
    6. Dividend Reinvestment Plans
    7. An Approach to Setting Dividend Policy

D. Factors That Influence Dividend Policy
    1. Constraints on Dividend Policy
        a. Bond Indentures and Loan Covenants
        b. Preferred Stock Restrictions

II. Introduction

This chapter discusses both the theory and the practice of dividend policy for corporations. Dividends are a primary means of providing returns to shareholders and serve as a measure, or "signal," of the financial health of the firm. Dividends are of great concern to the treasurer because they often represent a substantial outflow of company funds for the firm, and may have a significant impact on the financial structure of the firm. The treasurer must know what kinds of investors hold the firm's stock and what they expect in terms of risk and return. Accordingly, the material in this chapter is closely related to Chapter 4, Capital Structure.

III. Coverage of the Chapter Material

A. Theories of Dividend Policy

Dividend policy decisions are critical for the firm because they will impact its earnings ability as well as its ability to raise capital in the future. The changing of dividends may have several consequences:

1. Steadily increasing dividends may make the firm's stock more attractive to certain institutional investors, and perhaps increase the stock price,[1] however,

2. Increasing dividends reduces the amount of retained earnings the firm will have available for expansion. This may slow the firm's growth, and thus its ability to provide capital gains for its investors. The firm may then become less attractive to investors who prefer high levels of capital gains to regular income in the form of dividends.

Therefore, to some extent dividend policy will determine the types of investors who may be interested in becoming shareholders.

The optimal dividend policy is one that maximizes the value of the firm (shareholder value) while maintaining adequate retained earnings for future expansion, and possibility for equity capital gains for their investors.

1. Dividend Irrelevance: In a theoretical world without taxes and with perfect capital markets, Miller and Modigliani[2] argued that dividend policy would have no effect on the value of the firm. Unfortunately, we don't live in a perfect world, and dividend policy does seem to have an effect on value.

2. "Bird-in-the-Hand" Theory: This theory developed by Gordon and Lintner[3] held that investors preferred dividends because future retained earnings were more uncertain. Therefore, investors would prefer current dividends to future dividends and, all else being equal, would value firms that paid dividends more highly than firms that did not. Other financial theoreticians argued that this was not the case, because investors would simply reinvest any dividends in other stocks that had the same basic cash flow stream and risk as those of the original firm, or because tax regulations would impact the investment decision, making receipt of dividends and later investment a tax-disadvantaged strategy.[4]

3. Tax Differential Theory: This theory was proposed by Litzenberger and Ramaswamy[5] and is based on the fact that, periodically, there are changes in the tax codes which may have an impact on dividend policy. Under previous tax codes there was some advantage to paying investors in the form of retained earnings and stock price appreciation rather than dividends because of the lower tax rates on capital gains versus ordinary income (dividends). Those codes have since been amended to make the tax rates equivalent; however, there is now discussion about reinstating the tax differential on capital gains. Depending on the type of investors holding a firm's stock, tax regulations may have an effect on the firm's dividend policy.

4. Tests of Dividend Theories: Although there are several competing theories of dividend policy, and there have been numerous empirical tests of these theories, the results to date are inconclusive. This is a prime example of a classic problem in empirical tests of market phenomena: We can observe that dividend policy does have some impact on the value of the firm, but no one theoretical model can adequately explain why.

B. Other Dividend Policy Issues

There are several important issues relating to dividend policy that need to be addressed. These issues have arisen as the result of actual observations of company and investor behavior.

1. Information Content of Dividends: There is significant evidence that dividends contain information for the stockholder and can send "signals" of the intentions of the management of the firm.

- For most firms, it has been noted that dividends tend to be fairly stable or exhibit a constant growth rate. Even firms that have periods of abnormal dividend growth usually settle down to constant growth at some point.

- The general hypothesis is that when a firm's management declares an unexpected increase in the upcoming dividends (higher than expected growth), it is signaling good news to the stock market.

- This good news translates into a higher price for the firm's stock. Management would not announce higher dividends unless it was certain that it would be able to maintain the higher level indefinitely.

- Similarly, if dividends are announced that are unexpectedly low or are eliminated altogether, this would signal bad news, and the price of the firm's stock would drop. Management can, therefore, use dividends as a signal to investors concerning the firm's future earnings potential.

- Although the existence of the information content of dividends has been substantiated, the empirical studies have been unable to show a strong linkage between a change in dividend policy and stock prices. One theory regarding this relationship holds that while dividend policy may determine the type of investors holding a firm's stock (see Clientele Effect below), it does not necessarily have a significant impact on the overall value of the firm.

2. Clientele Effect: This theory holds that different groups of investors (or different institutional investors and mutual funds) prefer different payout policies, and that they will invest in those firms that give them the dividend payouts they prefer.

- Investors with low tax rates and a preference for current income (some pension funds, retired persons, endowment funds, etc.) will tend to purchase stocks with high regular dividends.

- Investors in higher tax brackets or those looking for a high long-term return will tend to purchase stock in companies which regularly reinvest high levels of earnings in the firm to stimulate growth. Such firms will tend to pay low dividends over time with investors receiving their return from the long-term appreciation of the stock price.

- The implication for management is that it can change its dividend policy so long as it is willing to have new investors hold the stock and deal with temporary problems with the current set of investors.

- There is some empirical evidence of a clientele effect,[6] but most tests have been inconclusive about how important this factor really is.

3. Stability of Dividends: Due to both the information content of dividends (signaling effect) and the clientele effect, most firms attempt to maintain a fairly stable dividend policy.

- There is generally a real tradeoff that managers must consider between paying stable dividends and retaining earnings in the firm for needed reinvestment. This is especially difficult for firms with historically high levels of fluctuation in their earnings.

- Another factor encouraging firms to maintain a stable dividend policy is that many institutional investors with a need for steady income (especially pension funds) may only purchase stocks that maintain stable dividend payments.

- Given the above factors, dividends are rarely reduced unless there are significant reasons to do so.

- The general practice for management in setting dividends is to:

    1. Determine the long-term profits for the firm
    2. Determine the growth rate of these profits
    3. Determine the firm's need for reinvested earnings
    4. Set dividends so that the firm will be able meet its needs for reinvestment under most economic scenarios
    5. Leave dividends at this level (or growing slightly based on the projected long-term growth rate) unless very dire circumstances necessitate a change.

C. Dividend Policy in Practice

The preceding section discussed how dividends should be set, not how they are actually set. This section will look at several factors that influence dividend policy in actual practice.

1. Residual Dividend Model: This policy argues that any dividends paid out by a firm should be made from funds left over after all capital expansion is completed. The steps are as follows:

1. The firm determines its optimal capital budget by matching its investment opportunities with its marginal cost of capital. That is, the firm continues to plan investment projects so long as the marginal rates of return are greater than the marginal cost of capital. This topic is covered in greater detail in Chapter 12, Capital Budgeting.

2. The firm determines the amount of equity needed to finance this budget based on current capital market conditions and its target capital structure. This topic is covered in greater detail in Chapter 4, Cost of Capital and Capital Structure. The firm then uses available earnings to the extent necessary to fund this equity requirement.

3. The firm pays dividends only if there are excess earnings after the capital budget investment. For example, if a firm had $100 million in after-tax earnings and needed $75 million in new equity for its capital budget, it would fund the capital budget first, then use the remaining $25 million to pay dividends.

4. Dividends, therefore, are paid only if the firm has residual earnings after meeting all equity capital needs. If the equity capital needs exceed the amount of earnings available, no dividends would be paid.

This approach is based on the opportunity cost principle, which holds that the firm should pay dividends only if there are no other acceptable investment opportunities available.

- Stockholders of this type of firm should prefer this action, as long as the firm can earn the required equity rate of return on any retained earnings. Note: this would be an example of the clientele effect in that investors desiring this type of return would gravitate towards a firm with this type of dividend policy.

- As earnings and available investment opportunities change, this policy would lead to fluctuating dividends.

- If dividends do contain a signal, a firm observing this policy would be constantly sending mixed signals to the market as dividends were raised and lowered.

- For this reason, the residual dividend policy is primarily observed by newer, high-growth firms that need to maintain maximum retained earnings to fuel their rapid rate of expansion.

2. Constant or Steadily Increasing Dividends: For most established firms, this is the policy of choice for dividends. By keeping dividends stable or on a steady increase, management accomplishes two basic objectives:

1. It sends a consistent signal to the market.

2. It maintains the firm's listed status, its shares eligible for purchase by institutional investors. Many states require that financial institutions (mutual savings banks, insurance companies, and mutual funds) invest only in those stocks with good dividend records. Federal laws covering pension plans encourage the purchase of stocks with high, stable dividends. The exact requirements vary by state and by type of pension fund. A constant or steadily increasing dividend policy would probably be inappropriate for a new firm going through high initial growth; it

would suffer a continuing leakage of capital from just when it needs all of the capital it can find.

3. Constant Payout Ratio: This policy sets a constant percentage of earnings that are paid out in dividends.

- The problem with this policy is that dividends will fluctuate constantly as earnings fluctuate, which makes it inappropriate for most publicly traded firms because the stock price will not be maximized.

- It is, however, an appropriate and widely used dividend policy for wholly owned subsidiaries of large firms. In such cases, dividends are simply a means of moving earnings (cash) from the subsidiaries back to the parent firm, and a constant payout ratio of dividends to earnings is the easiest way to accomplish this.

4. Low Regular Dividend plus Extras (Extra Dividends): This approach is utilized by firms that want to maintain a constant dividend policy but have widely fluctuating earnings.

- In order to pass additional earnings to its shareholders during good times, a firm can simply declare an extra dividend, which is paid in addition to the regular dividend, and still maintain a stable record of regular dividends.

- Because it is declared as an extra (special) dividend, it does not send the same signal as an increase in the regular dividend. Investors recognize that an extra dividend is only a one-time event. Another device for providing a one-time bonus for shareholders is the stock dividend, covered later in this chapter.

5. Payment Procedures: There are several important dates in the declaration and payment of a dividend:

a. Declaration Date: The date on which the board of directors announces (declares) the dividend.

b. Holder-of-Record Date (Also referred to as the record date): The date specified by the board of directors when the holders-of-record on that date are entitled to receive the dividend declared.

c. Ex-Dividend Date: The date on which the stock is sold without the upcoming dividend attached. This is usually four business days prior to the holder-of-record date and allows the brokerages to get the updated list of stockholders to the firm before that day. Theoretically, there is a drop in the price of the stock equivalent to the dividend on the ex-dividend date. This is difficult to measure because of other factors that may influence the market price.

d. Payment Date: The date on which the dividend is paid.

6. Dividend Reinvestment Plans: During the 1970s, many firms instituted these plans, through which stockholders could elect to reinvest their dividends automatically in the stock of the firm paying the dividends.

- Firms can either buy the stock on the open market, use treasury shares or issue new stock.

- These plans benefit smaller stockholders because of the low (or non-existent) transaction (brokerage) costs involved.

- In addition, when firms issue new stock in this manner, they may offer a discount off the market price to the reinvesting shareholder.

- From the firm's point of view, this method of raising capital is significantly less expensive than issuing new stock to the general public, thus saving cash for the issuing firm.

- On the negative side, this type of plan may lead to an increased number of small shareholders which could be expensive in terms of maintaining shareholder relations and records.

7. An Approach to Setting Dividend Policy: Dividend policies can vary widely from firm to firm, depending on a variety of factors and considerations. In general, firms set dividend policy within the framework of their overall financial plans. For established firms, setting dividend policy is typically done in two steps:

1. The first, and most important, step for the firm's management is to determine the long-term needs for equity capital or for capital expansion. This involves:

    - An analysis of the firm's future investment opportunities
    - The ability of the firm to raise other forms of capital (debt, preferred stock, new common stock)
    - The target capital structure of the firm
    - The ability of the firm to generate earnings over the planning period

2. The second step is to set dividends at a steady (or steadily increasing) level, so that there is reasonable expectation that the firm can maintain both its level of investment and its dividends. Obviously, actual earnings will fluctuate over time, but management will usually not change its dividend policy unless it believes that there is a permanent change in the firm's long-term opportunities, sources of capital, or costs of capital.

D. Factors That Influence Dividend Policy

There are many factors that affect the dividend policy of the firm.

1. Constraints on Dividend Policy:[7] Most of these factors are constraints on the firm's management in setting and paying dividends, as outlined below:

a. Bond Indentures and Loan Covenants: Most debt contracts contain protective covenants that limit the ability of the firm to pay dividends. These are usually related to specified levels for certain financial ratios and prevent the stockholders from draining assets from the firm at the expense of the bondholders and other creditors.

b. Preferred Stock Restrictions: Preferred stock is often cumulative in nature, which requires all past preferred stock dividends (arrears dividends) be paid in full before any common dividend can be paid. There are many forms of preferred stock which are non-cumulative in nature, and thus do not have this type of restriction.

c. Impairment of Capital Rules: Dividend payments cannot usually exceed retained earnings on the balance sheet. This serves as protection for the creditors of the firm. Dividends can, however, be paid out of capital, but they must be indicated as such and must not reduce capital below limits stated in the firm's debt contracts.

d. Availability of Cash: A firm must have cash to pay cash dividends. The treasurer must make certain that adequate cash is available to fund the dividend payments. The firm may also utilize unused borrowing capacity to raise cash for the dividend.

e. Penalty Tax on Improperly Accumulated Earnings: To prevent wealthy individuals from using corporations they own to avoid personal taxes, the Tax Code provides for a special surtax on improperly accumulated income. Thus, if the IRS can demonstrate that the dividend payout ratio is being deliberately held down to help stockholders avoid personal taxes, heavy penalties will be imposed on the firm or the individuals. As a practical matter, the penalty has been applied only to privately owned firms.

f. Control: This is more a concern for smaller, closely held firms than for large publicly held corporations. The current management (usually the owners) is reluctant to sell new common stock as it may dilute its ownership and control of the company. As a result, management may decide to pay very low or no dividends in order to keep as much cash in firm as possible for reinvestment and growth.

2. Investment Opportunities: The investment opportunities available to the firm will affect the dividend policy. If there are many acceptable investment opportunities, it may want to limit the size of dividends in order to increase the amount of available capital. If the firm can easily change the timing of investment projects, then it may have more flexibility in its dividend policy, delaying projects when earnings are low or accelerating them when earnings are high.

3. Alternative Sources of Capital: The availability of alternative sources of capital makes the dividend decision less critical. This is especially true for firms with good access to capital markets; if it is easy to raise new equity in the capital markets, the firm's flexibility and ability to pay a cash dividend are greater. For a new, high-growth firm, however, this may not be the case. The firm would not typically have good access to new sources of capital and would be most likely to retain almost all of its earnings to fund expansion.

4. Effects of Dividend Policy on Cost of Capital: Because dividend policy can affect the perception (and ultimately the price) of the firm's stock in the market, it will have an impact on the firm's cost of capital. Firms that pay regular dividends are more attractive to certain institutional investors, and thus may enjoy a more stable stock price over time. Dividend policy has an impact on the firm's cost of capital because it changes the ratios of the capital components. As the stock price increases, the value of the equity increases relative to the debt, thus decreasing the firm's market-based debt ratios.

E. Stock Repurchases

This section specifically covers the area of "non-targeted repurchases," which differ from "targeted repurchases" (also known as "greenmail") in that shares in a standard non-targeted repurchase are purchased from the corporation's shareholders generally, rather than from a single shareholder or specific group of shareholders.

As an alternative to paying cash dividends, a firm can elect to repurchase its own stock. By taking some of its stock out of circulation, the firm may increase the price of the stock, and if earnings are constant the earnings per share will be increased. An added benefit to the remaining shareholders is that any capital gains made from the increase in stock price will not be taxable until the shareholder elects to sell the stock. Repurchases are useful to the firm for accomplishing a large modification of its capital structure or for reducing the number of small holders of the stock. The disadvantages are: (1) firms may have difficulty using stock repurchases on a regular basis because they send conflicting signals, and (2) IRS and SEC regulations affect repurchases. Full disclosure of all relevant information is required by the SEC in any type of stock repurchase plan. In general, however, most firms have found that stock repurchases offer an attractive alternative to dividends and a way to control shareholder demographics and earnings per share.

    1. Stockholders' Viewpoint: From the stockholders' point of view there are several advantages and disadvantages to stock repurchases:

    a. Advantages: The advantages of using stock repurchases to the shareholders are as follows:

        1. Repurchase agreements may be viewed as a positive signal by investors because the repurchase could be motivated by management's assessment that the firm is undervalued.

        2. The stockholders have the choice either to sell their stock or to hold onto it in anticipation of an increase in the stock price. Those retaining the stock would have the advantage of deferring any tax liabilities, while those reselling the stock would have immediate tax consequences.

        3. Earnings per Share (EPS) will generally increase due to the smaller number of shares outstanding.

    b. Disadvantages: The disadvantages of stock repurchases from the shareholders' viewpoint are as follows:

        1. Because dividends are more dependable, the price of the stock may actually benefit more from regular payment of dividends (or an increase in the dividends) than from a stock repurchase plan.

        2. The repurchase plan will reduce existing capital and, may result in lower growth in the future or missed investment opportunities.

        3. If the firm's stock is not actively traded (thinly traded), or if the firm is trying to repurchase too large an amount of stock, the price may be bid up excessively. Consequently, the firm will pay too high a price for the stock, resulting in an overall reduction in its value to the remaining shareholders.[8]

2. Management's Viewpoint: There are also advantages and disadvantages to stock repurchase plans from management's point of view:[9]

a. Advantages: The advantages to management from a stock repurchase plan are as follows:

1. Because management is reluctant to increase dividends unless there is a long-term justification, and assuming that the firm has some excess earnings, it may prefer simply to repurchase some of its stock. This gives the shareholders who want immediate returns the opportunity to obtain them; and those who are looking for future growth will generally benefit from an increased stock price due to the repurchase.

2. The repurchased stock can be used for acquisitions, or can be released when stock options or warrants are exercised, or when convertibles are converted. By using repurchased stock for these operations, the dilution of per-share earnings can be avoided.

3. If management has decided to undertake a major restructuring (large asset sale, increase in debt ratio, etc.), repurchases may be the only practical choice.

4. Treasury stock may be resold in the open market if the firm needs additional funds at a later date.

5. Management may decide to repurchase the firm's stock in an attempt to thwart a takeover attempt. The repurchase would divert shares from both hostile bidders and arbitrageurs looking to accumulate blocks of shares. It would also make the corporation less attractive to a potential acquiror by depleting the corporation's cash or other liquid assets, or burdening it with debt.

6. If management feels that the firm's stock is truly undervalued by the market, it may elect to repurchase its stock because (1) it is a "good deal," and (2) reducing the number of shares on the market will increase its value for the remaining shareholders.

b. Disadvantages: The disadvantages to management in using stock repurchase plans are as follows:

1. Management may use repurchase plans because the firm has a poor expected growth rate and few good investment opportunities.

2. There are legal considerations in a stock repurchase operation, primarily for closely or privately held corporations. If the IRS ruled that the repurchase plan was set up primarily to avoid taxes on dividends, penalties could be imposed on the firm. Generally, this falls under the Internal Revenue Code regulations regarding the improper accumulation of earnings.

3. If the management of the firm appears to be using stock repurchases to directly manipulate the price of the firm's stock, the Securities and Exchange Commission (SEC) will intervene. This is especially true if a firm plans offerings of other securities in the near future, or if it is planning merger negotiations using the firm's stock in exchange for that of another company. Management is required

to disclose this type of information and all other material information, to all shareholders prior to any repurchase action.

3. Conclusions on Stock Repurchases: A review of the advantages and disadvantages of stock repurchases from various viewpoints leads to several conclusions:

- Stock repurchases on a regular basis may not be feasible due to tax consequences and the long-term impact on stock price.

- Stock repurchases offer some tax deferral advantages over dividends for the stockholders who do not sell their shares.

- Under some circumstances, such as abnormally high earnings, a highly undervalued stock price, or temporary shortage of suitable investment opportunities, stock repurchases may be the best option to provide "one-time" earnings to shareholders.

- Stock repurchases offer a way to increase financial leverage without directly increasing the amount of debt, provided that the company has cash on hand.

- The stock repurchase decision is similar to an internal investment decision, and the question for the firm's management is whether or not the firm's stock is truly undervalued in the market. If it is, management may want to consider the value of using some funds for the repurchase of stock rather than investing in new capital projects.

4. Steps in Managing a Repurchase Operation: As discussed earlier, a stock repurchase plan requires full disclosure to the shareholders and SEC notification.

a. Methods Used in Repurchasing Stock: There are three ways in which a company can repurchase stock after notifying the SEC:

- The company can purchase its own stock in the open market.
  - No forms are required by the SEC unless the firm is purchasing more than 5% of the outstanding stock (tender offer).
  - The firm can announce the repurchase by a standard press release.
  - There are limitations on the purchase price (to avoid "greenmail" problems).

- The company can make a tender offer to its stockholders.
  - Tender offers must be used if more than 5% of the firm's stock is repurchased, and must be registered with the SEC.
  - An investment banker usually is involved to help persuade stockholders and manage the stock repurchase.

- The company can negotiate directly with a major stockholder (often an institutional investor, such as an insurance company or pension fund) to purchase its stock.

The repurchased shares become treasury stock and can be (1) retired, (2) resold at a later date to raise additional capital, or (3) used for stock option or warrant programs.

b. IRS and SEC Regulations for Stock Repurchases: Both the IRS and the SEC have regulations concerning the use of stock repurchases by firms.

- IRS Regulations:
  1. Stockholders who sell their shares in a repurchase operation are required to report and pay taxes on any capital gains.
  2. From the point of view of the firm, a stock repurchase may be treated as a dividend payout, especially if the IRS rules that a closely held firm is using a stock repurchase as a means to avoid the payment of dividends and thus avoid taxes.
- SEC Regulations:
  1. When stocks are repurchased on the open market the company cannot at the same time issue other stock or be involved in private negations to buy stock.
  2. The repurchase cannot exceed a stated proportion of the outstanding stock of a company that is currently trading on the market (without invoking SEC regulations on tender offers).

F. Other Types of Dividends

1. Stock Dividends:

- In this case, the firm pays the shareholders additional shares of stock rather than paying out cash dividends. In actuality, the economic impact of a stock dividend is the same as that of a stock split. That is, the per-share price of the stock is reduced because additional shares are in circulation, but there is no real impact on shareholder wealth. However, there may be additional costs to the firm for managing and record-keeping for the new shares.
- If the firm is in a high-growth stage but needs to keep all earnings for growth, then, in the long long-range, this may be a viable means to keep the shareholders happy.

2. Stock Splits:

- The basic idea behind a stock split is that an optimal trading range exists for a stock's price. When the per-share price of a stock gets too high, trading in the stock may be affected because of the large dollar amount needed to trade an even lot (100 shares).
- By splitting the stock, the trading price can be brought down to the desired trading range. Because there is no real impact on value to the shareholders, stock splits are generally not a critical consideration in dividend policy.
- It is true, however, that stock splits are often caused and followed by significant dividend increases. Therefore, if the stock is generally on a strong upward trend, the prices may not drop by exactly the same ratio as the stock split.
- There may, however, be increased costs for managing shareholder records.

3. Extraordinary Dividends:

- In situations where the firm has high short-term or "one-time" earnings, management may want to declare a special or extraordinary dividend to put some of those earnings in the hands of the shareholders.
- Because such special dividends are designated as one-time only, they do not carry the same dividend information as increasing in regular dividends.

4. "Building Down" Dividends: Some firms in a seriously declining industry (such as weapons/defense contractors) may choose to "build-down" the firm through the use of high dividends or regular repurchases of the its stock. A good example would be a company that has decided to slowly liquidate by selling off assets and giving the money back to the shareholders in the form of "one-time" dividends.

5. "Dividend Out" Shares: In cases where an existing company is split or "spins off" a new company, the existing shareholders of the old company may be given shares in the new or spin-off company as dividends. If there is a net increase in value, the stockholders may be liable for additional taxes due to the stock dividends.

6. Intra-Company Dividends: Large companies with wholly-owned subsidiaries will generally use intra-company dividends to move profits from the subsidiaries to the parent. In many cases, subsidiaries are simply required to pay some stated percentage of earnings (often 100%) to the parent. Since intra-company dividends are only a movement of funds within the company, they are not subject to IRS or SEC regulations.

G. Dividend Policy in Multinational Companies (MNCs)

For multinational companies (MNCs), dividend policy may be constrained by foreign government regulations and tax laws. The intent of most of these regulations is either to prevent the firm from removing capital from the country or to make sure that the MNC pays its fair share of taxes on profits earned within the country. The policies covered below are primarily related to the movement of funds from wholly- or partially-owned foreign subsidiaries of U.S. MNCs back to the U.S. parent. Foreign governments will often restrict, block, or tax this movement of funds in order to force the MNC to reinvest the funds locally, rather than repatriate them.

1. Dividends: The use of dividends for the transfer of profits from foreign subsidiaries is often restricted by foreign governments. Usually there are either significant taxes charged on cross-border dividends or outright restrictions on the repatriation funds through dividends. Foreign governments often view dividend payments to the parent as a means of taking the profits from the subsidiary out of the country, when they would rather have them reinvested locally. To counter this problem, the managements of MNCs now generally "unbundle" the cash flows from their subsidiaries into separate items that can be more easily justified to foreign governments than dividends. The techniques are discussed below.

2. Management Fees: Many MNCs now charge their foreign subsidiaries licensing and/or management fees in order to justify to host governments the flow of funds from subsidiary to parent. These fees are often negotiated with the foreign governments prior to the MNC's investing on its soil. The objective is to ensure the MNC is fairly compensated for the foreign investment, but that the host country benefits from some local reinvestment of funds.

3. Transfer Pricing: Transfer pricing is the price which subsidiaries of a large corporation charge each other for components sold among themselves. The benefit for MNCs is that transfer pricing can be manipulated to locate profits in subsidiaries in low-tax countries and move them out of subsidiaries in countries with high tax rates.

Foreign governments, of course, resent these actions and will generally place restrictions on transfer pricing, or changes in transfer pricing, by MNCs within their jurisdictions. The implication for MNC management is that most transfer pricing for foreign subsidiaries must be done at "arm's length." This means setting transfer prices at the same level at which the firm would buy or sell similar products from an unaffiliated company. This assures foreign governments that the profits from the MNC will be fairly distributed among all of its foreign subsidiaries.

4. Intra-Company Loans: Another approach to moving funds between foreign subsidiaries is to utilize intra-company loans. In this case, the parent (or another subsidiary) would loan funds to a foreign subsidiary in a country whose government has blocked dividends or other transfers from the subsidiary. These loans often engage a multinational bank as an intermediary in the process, thus making the loan appear to be a legitimate banking arrangement. The interest payments on the loan are essentially a net transfer of funds from the foreign subsidiary back to the parent. The assumption in this type of arrangement is that the foreign government will be more likely to approve the transfer of funds for a loan repayment than for dividends or other types of transfers. Also, there may be a tax advantage as the firm may avoid taxes imposed by foreign governments on dividends paid to a parent company in another country. This practice may be affected by tax treaties between the countries involved.

IV. Endnotes

1. Though cash flow theory implies that increasing dividends would not result in an increase in the stock price, this theory does not take into account market segmentation adjustments which may restrict certain classes of investors to certain types of stocks.

2. See: Merton H. Miller and Franco Modigliani, "Dividend Policy, Growth, and the Valuation of Shares," *Journal of Business,* October 1961, pp. 411–433.

3. See: Myron J. Gordon, "Optimal Investment and Financing Policy," *Journal of Finance,* May 1963, pp. 264–272; and John Lintner, "Dividends, Earnings, Leverage, Stock Prices and the Supply of Capital to Corporations," *Review of Economics and Statistics,* August 1962, pp. 243–269.

4. See: Michael Brennan, "A Note of Dividend Irrelevance and the Gordon Valuation Model," *Journal of Finance,* December 1971, pp. 1115–1121.

5. See: Robert H. Litzenberger and Krishna Ramaswamy, "The Effects of Personal Taxes and Dividends on Capital Asset Prices," *Journal of Financial Economics,* June 1979, pp. 163–196.

6. For an example, see: R. Richardson Pettit, "Taxes, Transaction Costs and the Clientele Effect of Dividends," *Journal of Financial Economics,* December 1977, pp. 419–436.

7. See: Chapter 14: Dividend Policy, *Financial Management: Theory and Practice, Sixth Edition,* Brigham and Gapenski, Dryden Press, 1991.

8. See: Larry Y. Dann, "Common Stock Repurchases: An Analysis of Returns to Bondholders and Stockholders," *Journal of Financial Economics,* June 1981, pp. 113–138.

9. See: *The Battle for Corporate Control,* Edited by Arnold W. Sametz, Business One Irwin, Publisher, 1991, pp. 445–460. This reference also provides extensive listings of case law in this area.

6 Mergers, Acquisitions, and Divestitures

I. Outline of the Chapter

A. Rationale for Mergers
   1. Synergy
      a. Economies of Scale in Operations
      b. Financial Economies of Scale
      c. Improved Managerial Efficiency
      d. Increased Market Power
      e. Completion of Product Line
   2. Tax Considerations
   3. Undervalued Assets
   4. Diversification
   5. Management's Incentives
   6. Breakup Value
   7. Growth

B. Types of Mergers
   1. Horizontal
   2. Vertical
   3. Congeneric
   4. Conglomerate
   5. Friendly versus Hostile Takeovers
      a. Friendly Mergers
      b. Hostile Mergers
C. Issues in Mergers
   1. Merger Regulation

    b.   Lack of Analyst/Investor Knowledge

    c.   Need for Funds

    d.   Elimination of Unprofitable Business Operations

    e.   Antitrust Compliance

    f.   Cleaning Up Past Merger Activity

    g.   Monetizing Assets for Shareholders

    h.   Different Perceptions of Value

Chapter Checklists

A.   Antitrust Regulations in Mergers

B.   Required Steps in Merger Approval

C.   Important Elements of the Williams Act

D.   Pooling versus Purchase Accounting for Mergers

E.   Listing of Terms Used in Mergers and Acquisitions

Calculations and Examples

A.   Purchase versus Pooling Merger Calculation

B.   Merger Valuation Example

II. Introduction

This section provides an overview of mergers and acquisitions.[1] Mergers are defined as the combining of two or more companies into one, usually with only one company retaining its identity. Typically, the larger firm is the one whose identity is maintained. The term merger is generally used to indicate a friendly joining of companies, while the term acquisition is used for unfriendly takeovers or combinations where one company is much larger than the other. Mergers have increasingly been used to accomplish strategic goals, e.g., enter new markets, expand product lines, diversify into different businesses, or acquire technological or labor expertise. It is important to understand both the motives behind mergers and the methods used to analyze the merger decision.

While most of the merger literature is written from the buyer's perspective, it is also necessary to remember that for every buyer there must be a seller. Although the methods of analysis for selling are the same as for buying, the selling process usually has its own name, divestiture.

There have been four major periods of heavy merger activity in the United States. The first occurred in the late 1800s when there were major consolidations in several basic industries such as oil, steel, railroads and tobacco. The second period was during the stock market boom of the 1920s, when consolidation occurred in the utilities, communications and auto industries. In the 1960s, many corporations tried to become everything to everybody in a rash of conglomerate mergers.

The most recent period of merger activity was in the mid-to-late 1980s, and was characterized by hostile takeovers and highly leveraged transactions. This activity resulted from several factors:

- The stock market in the early 1980s was fairly depressed, resulting in relatively low stock prices.

- High inflation during the late 1970s and early 1980s had increased the replacement value of a firm's assets, while at the same time reducing its market value.

- The development of the high-yield bond ("junk-bond") market provided ready access to large amounts of capital for merger activity.

- The above factors, plus the laissez-faire attitude of the Reagan administration towards mergers made it easier for firms that wished to expand their operations or markets to "buy assets" through mergers and acquisitions. This was especially true for natural resource companies and other industries with substantial overcapacity.

- In addition, the U.S. dollar was at historic lows relative to other currencies, making U.S. companies attractive investments (takeover targets) for foreign companies.

- As takeover fever on Wall Street mounted during the 1980s, the number of deals jumped from 1,558 (valued at $33 billion) in 1980 to 3,484 ($146 billion) in 1985; 4,000 deals (a record $236.4 billion) in 1988; 3,415 deals ($231 billion) in 1989; and 3,590 ($158.8 billion) in 1990. Altogether, 34,702 deals, valued at $1.5 trillion were completed between 1980 and 1990.[2]

This chapter will discuss the rationale for mergers and identify the different types of mergers. Merger analysis will be examined, including a discussion of the role of various advisors in this process. The last part of the section will address leveraged buyouts and divestitures.

III. Coverage of the Chapter Material

A. Rationale for Mergers

There must be motive for the merger. While a merger may be the most glamorous method of expansion, there must be a rationale to justify the merger's cost if it is to provide benefits to the acquiring firm's shareholders.

    1. Synergy: Synergy can make the value of the combined firm greater than the sum of the values of the two companies operating independently. Synergies can come from:

        a. Economies of Scale in Operations: These may be cost savings in management, marketing, production or general overhead.

        b. Financial Economies of Scale: These can include an improved price/earnings ratio, reduced cost of capital, greater access to capital markets or a larger debt capacity.

        c. Improved Managerial Efficiency: The replacement of existing management may improve profitability and efficiency and increase the value of the firm.

        d. Increased Market Power: A merger may eliminate a competitor, although this may be subject to anti-trust considerations.

e. Completion of Product Line: A merger may increase sales if the combined firm can provide a complete or expanded product line to its customers. This case and the preceding one are examples of a synergistic merger, where the combined company is worth more than the sum of the parts.

2. Tax Considerations: Operating losses from an acquired firm might be used to offset positive income of the acquiring firm. This could result in substantial tax savings which, in conjunction with synergies, could be very beneficial.

The classic example of this type of merger was GE's acquisition of RCA in 1990. At the time, GE was generating high levels of revenues and profits, while RCA had high operating expenses (primarily from its NBC division) and had posted significant recent losses. Through the merger, GE was able to reduce its overall tax liability, as well as provide needed capital to RCA. Both companies were in a better position (lower overall taxes) after the merger than before.

3. Undervalued Assets: It may be possible to acquire a firm for a price below the replacement value of its assets. However, there still must be sufficient value associated with the use of the assets to justify the cost of the merger.

4. Diversification: A merger may enable a firm to reduce the variability of its earnings stream, or to expand into new product lines or into new geographic areas with existing products.

- For example, this can be accomplished by an acquiring firm with sales that are counter-cyclical to those of the acquired firm. This may reduce risk and cause a decrease in its cost of capital.

- The problem with this approach is that the shareholders of publicly traded firms may not want that kind of diversification. These shareholders can form their own portfolios of investments, matching the diversification of the merger by buying stock in both companies.

- The major beneficiary of this type of mergers may be the firm's management. Senior managements' compensation is often based on its ability to deliver a steady stream of cash flows and/or earnings over time. Diversifying the firm's operations into different areas can make this stream more stable.

- Diversification as a motive for mergers may be especially appropriate for private or closely held firms, as the owners of these firms may not have the same opportunities for diversification through portfolios that independent investors have.

5. Management Incentives: Management may seek a merger to protect its position. A merger under terms favorable to management's continuing employment may prevent an unplanned, hostile takeover that could cause managers to lose their jobs.

6. Breakup Value: There are many ways to value a firm (book value, economic value or replacement value), and one of the most recent forms is called breakup value.

- This value is defined as the value of the firm's assets (or divisions, product lines, etc.) if they were split up and sold to other firms which utilized or managed them more efficiently. This has also been referred to as finding the "highest optimum value for each asset."

- The analyst must consider the potential tax impact from various federal and/or local laws concerning plant closings. In some cases, tax exemptions granted by state and local authorities must be refunded when a firm closes a plant prior to some agreed-upon schedule.

7. Growth: Some firms utilize mergers as a primary vehicle for growth. For example, a company could expand over time by buying out smaller competitors in the market.

B. Types of Mergers

1. Horizontal: A horizontal merger is a combination of two firms that are in the same line of business. For example, if two large airlines, such as American Airlines and United Airlines, were to propose a merger, it would be a horizontal merger. Since these types of mergers reduce competition, they may be subject to antitrust review. A listing of the required documentation and notifications to the Justice Department is provided at the end of this chapter.

2. Vertical: A vertical merger involves firms that have a buyer-seller relationship with each other. For example, a producer may acquire the firm from which it obtains its raw materials. The purchase of Conoco by DuPont was an example of a vertical merger.

3. Congeneric: A congeneric merger involves firms in related enterprises but not producers of the same product nor those firms with a buyer-seller relationship. An example would be a bank holding company acquiring a discount brokerage firm. Specific examples of congeneric mergers were American Express's takeover of Shearson Hammill (a stock brokerage firm) and Philip Morris's acquisitions of General Foods and Kraft.

4. Conglomerate: A conglomerate merger involves firms that are completely unrelated. This is often the riskiest type of merger, since synergies are less likely in such a case. In addition, the managements of the two firms may not be able to interchange skills, or there may be conflicting corporate cultures. An example of this type of merger would be an oil company purchasing a chain of department stores.

5. Friendly versus Hostile Takeovers: In the great majority of mergers, the companies involved are willing participants and the details of the merger can be easily negotiated. In fact, many firms (often smaller closely held firms) actively seek others as buyers.

   a. Friendly Mergers: The steps involved in a friendly merger or tender offer are as follows:

- The acquiring firm (the buyer) and the target firm (the one bought) are brought together for initial negotiations. This is often done by an investment banker specializing in mergers.

- The parties to the merger establish a suitable price (or range of prices) and set tentative terms of payment (cash, stock, bonds, etc.).

- The management of both firms issue statements to their shareholders that they approve of the merger, and the shareholders of the target firm are asked to tender (sell) their shares to the acquiring firm (usually through a financial institution acting in a trust capacity). The general procedures for management and share-holder approval of mergers are outlined at the end of this chapter.

- The target firm's shareholders then receive some specified payment (cash, shares of the acquiring firm, etc.) and the merger is completed.

b. Hostile Mergers: In some cases the management or stockholders of a firm will resist an "unfriendly" or hostile takeover of their firm. There may be any number of reasons for this, such as: the price offered is too low, management does not want to lose control of the firm, or workers and/or unions may object to the change in ownership and management. Although there are many approaches to a hostile takeover, generally they are as follows:

- The acquiring firm decides which firm it wants to acquire. As in the case of a friendly merger, an investment banker specializing in mergers may help in this process. Many firms active in the acquisition market may have large staffs of their own that continuously seek new investment opportunities for the company.

- The merger may start on a friendly basis if there is a chance that the target firm's management will agree to the merger. In other cases, the acquiring firm may decide that the target firm's management would never agree to the merger and they will go on tp the next step.

- The acquiring firm appeals directly to the shareholders of the target firm with a hostile tender offer at an attractive price.

- The management of the target firm typically begins defensive actions to try to prevent the merger (or at least to get a higher price for the firm's shareholders). The role of the firm's management and board of directors in a takeover attempt is covered in greater detail in Chapter 3. The management of the target firm may use such defenses as "poison pills" which would make the target firm very unattractive in a hostile takeover. A listing of many of the terms used in hostile acquisitions is provided at the end of this chapter.

- The ultimate result of this process is often a "proxy fight" in which the acquiring firm and the management of the target firm both try to convince the target firm's shareholders to send their proxies to them so that they can vote the shares at a stockholders' meeting. The party that gathers the most shares or proxies "wins" control of the firm.

C. Issues in Mergers

1. Merger Regulation: During the merger activity in the 1960s, many hostile mergers were accomplished by the acquiring firms' use of public announcements of tender offers to a target firm's shareholders. A well-coordinated effort on the part of the acquiring firm often overwhelmed the management of the target, which was not able to properly inform the stockholders that the particular tender offer might be undervalued. In some cases, the management of the target firm or other parties were able to raise the issue of antitrust regulations to attempt to block the merger. To deal with this situation, in 1968 Congress passed the Williams Act, which established regulations concerning how acquiring firms may structure takeover offers, and forced acquiring firms to disclose more information about their offers.

The Williams Act (additional information is provided at the end of this chapter) placed three major restrictions on the actions of acquiring firms in a hostile merger:

1. Acquiring firms must disclose their current holdings and future intentions within 10 days of amassing at least 5% of a firm's stock (SEC Rule 13D for most investors, SEC Rule 13G for institutional investors and insurance companies). In addition, they must disclose the source of funds to be used to finance the acquisition.

2. The target firm's shareholders must be allowed at least 20 days to tender their shares (called the "open period").

3. If the acquiring firm increases the offer price during the open period, all shareholders who tendered prior to the new offer also must receive the higher price.

2. Corporate Alliances (Non-Merger Mergers): In some cases firms that want to work more closely together will cooperate in an alliance rather than doing a formal merger. There are many forms of alliances, but the most common is the joint venture, in which parts of different companies are joined together to achieve limited, specific objectives. This joint venture is often managed by a joint team consisting of representatives from all of the firms involved. Some of the more recent joint ventures are:

- GM and Toyota joining forces to produce automobiles in Fremont, California.

- IBM and Apple joining forces to produce their new "Power Chip" to run both IBM and Apple software on the same computer platform.

- Whirlpool and Philips, the Dutch electronic firm, to produce appliances under Philips' brand names for sale in the European Economic Community (EEC).

3. Empirical Evidence about Mergers: The question here is who benefits from a merger, and if there are benefits, how are they distributed to the parties involved. Some evidence about mergers is as follows:

- Most research proves that takeovers generally do benefit the shareholders of the target firm. Generally, if a tender offer does not provide benefit to the target firm's shareholders, they will not agree to it.

- For the shareholders of the acquiring firm, however, there is a different ending to the merger story. Extensive research of both friendly and hostile takeover activity has shown that the shareholders of the acquiring firm rarely benefit from mergers because in almost all cases the stock price of the acquiring company remains unchanged or increases only very slightly.[3]

D. Merger Analysis

Analyzing a merger is comparable to the capital budgeting process used to evaluate acquiring a capital asset; the only difference is that in a merger, instead of analyzing a single asset acquisition, the analysis involves the acquisition of an entire business.

- The process is the same as calculating any net present value. Cash flows arising from the acquisition must be determined, as well as capital expenditure requirements of the firm for purchasing new equipment and plants or refurbishing acquired facilities. In addition, an appropriate discount rate must be agreed upon, and the value of the initial investment must be calculated (shown later in this chapter). Due the existence of possible synergies, consolidation of facilities, and combination of management teams, the capital budgeting process in mergers tends to be fairly complex.

- The cash flows involve estimating the synergistic effects. The discount rate must consider any impact the merger will have on the firm's cost of capital. The initial investment in a merger determines the method of payment; it may involve cash, an exchange of common stock shares, debt issues, some combination of all three of these, or some other payment package.

- All of the foregoing involve the application of capital budgeting techniques to mergers, a difficult and complicated task. Further complications may occur if the firms issue new classes of stock specifically to finance the merger.

   1. **Operating versus Financial Mergers:**

   a. Operating Merger: The two firms are combined and operated as a single entity with the expectation of synergistic benefits. Often, in operating mergers, there is a consolidation of both management and facilities for the combined firm. Because this type of merger is essentially the creation of a new operating entity, considerable effort is required to forecast cash flows for the merged firm. Once the post-merger cash flows and an appropriate discount rate have been determined, it is possible to calculate the Net Present Value (NPV) of the acquisition. In some cases, if the new combined firm has a truly different operating risk, it may be difficult to determine the required discount rate.

   b. Financial Merger: In many mergers, the merged firms do not operate as a single entity, but continue to operate independently. This is often the case where one firm buys another for diversification purposes or when one is purchased in another country. In a financial merger, therefore, the purchase of one firm by another is more an investment than a combination of operations. This usually means that no (or only limited) operating synergies are expected from a financial merger. The analysis of a financial merger is often easier than for an operating merger, as both the cash flows and discount rate for the acquired firm can be discretely determined.

   2. Valuing the Target Firm:[4] A primary approach to determining the value of the target firm is the discounted cash flow (DCF), where the value is calculated by discounting the stream of annual cash flows and the terminal cash flow by an appropriate discount rate. There are other approaches which can be used in the valuation process, and in many cases several may be used to determine the potential value of a merger, as outlined below.

   a. Discounted Cash Flow (DCF) Analysis: This is the most fundamental method of measuring value, since it measures the ultimate source of value: cash. It can be used in most situations, provided that the underlying assumptions used in projecting the cash flow stream reflect the likely (high probability) course of events. The steps involved in this process are as follows:

1) Determine Pro Forma Cash Flow Statements: The forecast for cash flows must include both the acquired firm and any cash flows arising out of synergies.[5]

- The cash flow should include the cash flow from operations less any cash that needs to be retained by the firm for capital expenditures or increasing working capital.

- Cash flow from operations can be significantly affected by the tax treatment of an acquisition. The prime tax issue is whether the pooling or purchase accounting method will be used for the tax valuation of the merger. This is especially true in determining the value of goodwill, which, in the case of purchase accounting, must be amortized over a 40-year horizon. The accounting methods for mergers are covered at the end of this chapter.

- The pooling method of merger accounting allows the financial statements of the two firms to be simply combined in a new consolidated set of statements. This method can only be used if the acquirer is using its own stock as payment for the acquired firm.

- The purchase method of merger accounting assumes that an investment has taken place on the part of the acquirer, and that the investment must be recorded at the acquiror's full cost, including booking goodwill if necessary.

- At the end of the forecast horizon (the length of time for which detailed annual cash flows are forecast—usually 5–15 years), a terminal value must be determined.

- This terminal value represents the value at the end of the forecast horizon, of all the cash flows beyond that point in time. As in any capital budgeting analysis, cash flow probability distributions should be identified and risk assessments performed through sensitivity testing and computer simulation.

2) Determination of Discount Rate: The cash flows should be discounted using a cost of capital that reflects the cost of raising the capital to acquire the target firm (marginal cost of capital). This cost of capital should reflect the risk of the merger and the implied risk of the cash flows (both the flows from the acquired firm and from the synergistic effects). The starting point for the determination of this rate is the cost of capital for the acquiring firm, but the cost of capital from the acquired firm, as well as other risk factors must be considered. When an acquisition is large relative to the size of the acquiring firm, the estimated combined cost of capital for the merged company may be the most appropriate rate to use.

3) Valuation of Cash Flows: The value of the target firm is the present value of the expected cash flows, discounted by the appropriate cost of capital. This valuation equation is shown below:

$$V = CF_1/(1+k) + CF_2/(1+k)^2 + \ldots + CF_n/(1+k)^n + TV_n/(1+k)^n$$

Where: V = The value of the acquired firm and the synergistic benefits.

CF_i = The cash flow from the acquired firm and from the synergistic effects for period i. This estimate is essentially the projected cash flow stream for the merged entity.

TV_n = The terminal value at time n; that is, the present value at time n of all future cash flows from time n + 1 and beyond. If it is assumed that cash flows will grow at a constant rate (g) into perpetuity, then TV_n can be calculated as:

$$[(CF_n) \times (1+g)] / (k-g).$$

Where: CF_n = The annual cash flow from the merged firm, which is assumed to be constant from period n into the future.

g = The assumed constant annual growth rate from period n to infinity.

k = The cost of capital, appropriate for the riskiness of the cash flow stream.

- The value for V shows the maximum that one would be willing to pay for the target firm to receive a return equal to k.

- If the firm can be acquired for a cost less than V, the merger will provide a return greater than k. Obviously, the acquiring firm should not pay more than V for the target firm.

- The final cost of the merger will be settled through the negotiation process between the buyer and the seller, but the value for V does set an upper limit on how much should be paid for the target firm.

b. Acquisition Multiples Valuation:[6] This valuation approach is a means of establishing benchmark values for a company based on multiples of earnings, book value, annual cash flows, etc., paid by other acquirers for similar companies. From the prospective seller's point of view, the multiples suggest a target price range at which other buyers have been willing to deal; conversely for a potential buyer, they suggest price ranges that are acceptable to other sellers. In most cases, multiples suggest a range of possible values and can be used as a starting point for price negotiation. There are several different multiples commonly used in the merger arena.

1) Earnings Multiples: Prices paid as a multiple of earnings are typically the most useful for a broad range of industrial companies. For example, a firm may sell for six times pre-tax earnings or 10 times after-tax earnings. Earnings may be defined in a variety of ways, such as: earnings per share, net profits, gross earnings, etc. Care must be taken to ensure that accounting conventions are comparable across a sample of merger transactions, and that proper adjustments are made for the use of debt, which distorts earnings figures.

2) Book Value Multiples: Although book value (total common stock equity) is an accurate measure of the historical cost of the investments made in a company, it is unlikely to have a meaningful relationship to acquisition value. There are, however, industries where book value plays an important role in determining the firm's future profitability and is thus a meaningful valuation technique. For example, in rate-of-return regulated industries, such as telephone, electric, and gas utilities, a firm's future earnings are limited to a defined return on the firm's equity. In such cases, book value may play a major role in determining acquisition value.

3) **Cash Flow Multiples:** In some industries, cash flow multiples are a common form of valuation, but it is important to properly define what cash flows entail. The most typical definition is "cash flow from operations": net income plus noncash charges (depreciation, amortization of intangibles and deferred tax expense). Industries such as real estate and oil and gas, which tend to make project-type investments, are typical candidates for this type of valuation. In these industries, massive amounts of capital tend to be invested initially, after which a steady stream of earnings and operating cash flows results, with relatively small investments required to maintain them.

c. Premiums over Market Trading Value: This valuation technique typically measures the premium percentage paid to public stockholders. This measure is important in drawing support from shareholders to ensure the success of a tender offer or merger vote. When an acquisition candidate is publicly traded, the market price of the stock is very important to the determination of a feasible acquisition price. The buyer must pay a premium over the market price in order to induce shareholders to tender their shares. In the period 1978–1987, the average premium (over an unaffected market price) paid on successful acquisitions was 49% from friendly bidders and 52% from hostile bidders. These premiums will vary by industry group and size of company involved in the acquisition.

d. Liquidation Value: This valuation technique measures the amount of cash that could be realized if a firm sold all of its assets and paid off its liabilities in the near future. Broadly speaking, the liquidation value represents the minimum value for a company, because the liquidation alternative is always available to its owner. Liquidation value would be appropriate if the acquirer were buying a highly-under-valued firm with significant amounts of marketable assets.

e. Replacement Value: This valuation technique measures the cost of starting up a similar company from scratch. In practice, the replacement value concept is awkward for most types of companies. It is potentially most useful in industries with fairly standard manufacturing technology where the value of existing plants can be easily compared to the cost of building new plants. Other examples are in the oil exploration arena, where the cost of buying proven reserves can be compared to the cost of exploring for new reserves.

In trying to make a valuation estimate, it is important to apply the methods most pertinent to the particular circumstances of the company under review.

- If a target company has vast under-utilized resources or other property (e.g., oil and gas, real estate, patents, copyrights, and broadcasting licenses), a liquidation approach would be material to the formation of a valuation judgment, even if the buyer does not plan to liquidate the company.

- If a target company has little in the way of marketable assets, but has an important brand name and strong management skills, a DCF (discounted cash flow) analysis will be much more relevant than a liquidation analysis.

- The purpose of having a variety of valuation techniques is to enable the participants to choose those methods which best suit the nature of the company in question. Also, analysts may be able to confirm values generated by one technique with those generated from another.

- There are many viewpoints to consider in the analysis of a merger and its valuation. The acquired (target) firm needs to determine its own value, the acquiring firm must determine what it is willing to pay for the target firm and, finally, the impact of potential competitors in the acquisition process must be considered. Most of these participants will determine a range of prices they are willing to assign to the valuation and will negotiate within those ranges.

3. Post-Merger Control: After the merger agreement, it is imperative to monitor the performance of the merged firm.

- To achieve the expected benefit from the merger, the actual cash flows must equal or exceed what was originally expected. The control process is important to determine whether results were as planned.

- The continuity of past management can influence these results. New management may not operate in the same style as the old, and this can affect performance. Additionally, former owners who continue as management may not manage in the same manner precisely because they are no longer owners.

4. Structuring the Takeover Bid: The bid for the target firm's shares may be in the form of cash, stock of the acquiring firm, debt of the acquiring firm, hybrid securities (options, warrants, convertibles, etc.) or some combination of all. The structure of the bid is very important and will ultimately affect the following:

- The capital structure of the merged firm will be impacted by the merger if stock or bonds are used either as direct payment for the target firm or to finance a cash acquisition. There will be either dilution of equity or increased leverage by the use of debt.

- The structure of the bid will be affected by the expected tax treatment of the merger. Generally, the target's shareholders do not have to pay taxes on the transaction if they maintain a substantial equity position in the merged firm. The IRS generally holds that at least 50% of the payment to the target's shareholders should be in the form of acquiring shares (common or preferred) in order to make the offers non-taxable. If shareholders receive equity securities of the acquiring firm, they maintain a carryover basis in the new security. If they receive cash or debt, they will owe capital gains tax on any gain. If they receive a mixture, the cash portion may be taxed as dividends. The tax issues involved may be very complex and change frequently; therefore, tax experts should be consulted to determine their potential impact.

- Both state and federal securities laws may influence the structure of merger bids. The SEC has oversight over any new stock or bond issues and this requires a substantial amount of time and effort on the part of the acquiring firm. Also, tender offers (cash or otherwise) are extensively regulated by the SEC under the Williams Act. Some of the more important provisions of this act are provided at the end of this chapter.

5. Tender Offers versus Mergers:[7] A tender offer is a broad solicitation to the shareholders of a target company requesting the tendering of their shares for purchase by the bidder.

- Cash is offered in most tender offers today, but there are also offers in which shares of the acquiring firm are offered in exchange for shares of the target firm. The ratio of exchange will be determined as a function of the market value of the acquiring firm's stock and the estimated value of the target firm's stock. Tender offers may be partial offers (less than 100%) or for all shares of the target firm.

- A bidder may establish conditions under which it will not purchase tendered shares, as, for example, if fewer than 50% of the outstanding shares are tendered or the target firm's board fails to revoke some restrictive provision (poison pill, golden parachute, etc.).

- Unlike a merger, a tender offer does not require the approval of the board of directors of the target firm. Instead, the offer is made directly to the shareholders of the target. It is often a means for accomplishing a hostile takeover, in which the board of directors and management of the target firm oppose the acquisition.

- Tender offers can be used in friendly acquisitions. Where the acquirer fears a competing offer, the tender offer presents the fastest route to ownership of the target because no proxy statement is prepared and no shareholder vote need be obtained.

E. Role of Investment Bankers

Investment bankers help to analyze and facilitate mergers and are important participants in the merger process. Their roles are discussed below.

1. Arranging Mergers: Investment bankers identify potential buyers, identify firms that want to be acquired, and identify other potential acquisition candidates. Investment bankers can work with both buyers and sellers to design an agreement, deal structure and method of payment.

2. Resisting Mergers: Investment bankers may provide advice and suggestions to help resist an unwanted takeover attempt. They may help to: (1) issue securities that will prevent a merger, (2) find desirable merger partners, (3) suggest changes to corporate by-laws or (4) raise legal issues to impede the merger. The role of the board of directors and its responsibilities in mergers and acquisitions is covered in detail in Chapter 3 of this text.

3. Establishing Prices: Investment bankers may be asked to do the merger analysis and to calculate the value for the target firm. The actual price paid in the merger will be a result of negotiations in which investment bankers may be active participants. Investment bankers provide "fairness opinions" for potential mergers. These are comments by an expert in mergers, acquisitions, or leveraged buyouts that the tender price is reasonable and in the best interest of the shareholders. These opinions are generally provided (for a fee) by an independent investment banker to the potential acquirer to forestall litigation about the terms of the deal.

4. Financing Mergers: Although many mergers are financed with excess cash the acquiring firm has stored up, some firms must raise additional capital for the financing. A primary reason for the high level of merger activity in the 1980s was the development of the high-yield (junk) bond market. This market allowed firms (or investment bankers) to raise large amounts of cash quickly on a speculative basis in order to fund friendly or hostile takeovers.

5. Arbitrage Operations: Investment banking firms will often speculate in the stocks of firms expected to be takeover candidates. While the benefit of this activity is widely debated, it does provide an active market for the stocks of those companies. It presents potential problems for the investment bankers because other parts of the bank may be working to arrange a merger while the arbitrage area is speculating on it. Investment banks must take great care to maintain the "Chinese wall" (no contact) between these areas; otherwise they are in violation of SEC insider trading rules.

F. Leveraged Buyouts (LBO)

A leveraged buyout (LBO) occurs when a group of equity investors acquires a firm, financing the acquisition largely with debt. Normally, the assets and cash flow stream of the acquired firm are pledged against the debt obligations. The equity investors usually plan to operate the firm for a period of time, after which they may be able to sell their equity position for a significant return. This topic is also covered in detail in Chapter 3.

1. Leveraged and Management Buy Outs: Many of the LBOs in recent years have actually been management buyouts, where the existing management purchases and operates the firm as private owners.

2. Advantages/Disadvantages: The primary advantages to a management buyout are: (a) administrative cost savings, (b) increased managerial incentives, (c) increased managerial flexibility, (d) more focused management attention due to high levels of debt service, (e) increased shareholder participation, and (f) increased returns to shareholders as a result of financial leverage. The primary disadvantage is the large amount of debt which allows management to make very few mistakes in its operations and provides little cushion from a business downturn. One bad period could result in defaulting on the debt and the loss of the business.

G. Divestitures

For every buyer, there must be a seller. The types of divestitures and the motives behind divestitures are discussed below.

1. Types of Divestitures: A divestiture does not necessarily have to be the sale of a complete firm. There are four primary types of divestitures:

a. Sale to Another Firm: This usually involves the sale of an entire division or business, usually for cash or an exchange of common stock. These sales may be in the form of an "earnout," where a small percentage is paid upfront and the remainder (usually a multiple of future year earnings) is paid after several years.

b. Managerial Buyout: The managers of a business unit purchase it to run by themselves, as a separate business.

c. Spin-Off: The ownership of a part of the firm is spun off to the firm's existing shareholders. The stockholders end up owning shares of two separate firms instead of one.

d. Liquidation: The assets of a business unit are sold piecemeal, and the business unit no longer exists.

e. IPO-Partial Divestiture: A firm may decide to spin off one of its subsidiaries or some other part of the firm as an initial public offering of a new company. Initial public offerings (IPOs) are covered in detail in Chapter 3.

2. Reasons for Divestitures; There may be a variety of motives for divestiture:

a. Conglomerate Discount: Sometimes management may feel that the market does not recognize the value of the firm's assets when they are part of a conglomerate. A divestiture may allow the market to value the business units separately, and its true (higher) value may now be recognized.

b. Lack of Analyst/Investor Knowledge: Sometimes management may feel that a firm is so complex and diverse that analysts and investors cannot understand it. A divestiture may allow for smaller, less diverse companies that analysts and investors can better understand and value. They may, therefore, be wiling to pay a higher price for the "pieces" of the company than for the company as a whole.

c. Need for Funds: A firm may need cash to finance expansion and activities in its major business line, or it may need cash to reduce an excessive amount of debt. A divestiture can raise the cash required.

d. Elimination of Unprofitable Business Operations: Liquidation may be a last resort for eliminating unprofitable business units that can significantly harm the value of the rest of the firm.

e. Antitrust Compliance: A divestiture may not be voluntary; it may be the result of legislation, regulation or an antitrust settlement.

f. Cleaning Up Past Merger Activity: In many cases, firms that have recently gone through a series of acquisitions will find that some of the operations acquired (or parts of them) do not fit into the firm's strategic plans. These operations will be sold off, as necessary, following their acquisition.

g. Monetizing Assets for Shareholders: In cases where some business units of a firm may provide greater value to the shareholders by being sold than by continuing to be owned and operated, management should divest these assets and pass the proceeds along to the shareholders.

h. Different Perceptions of Value: Sometimes there are other firms in the market with a different view of the future prospects for certain assets of the firm. In such cases, those parties may be willing to pay a premium to acquire the assets.

IV. Chapter Checklists

A. Anti-Trust Regulations in Mergers[8]

The principal federal antitrust law applicable to acquisition transactions is the Clayton Act, particularly Sections 7 and 7A. Section 7A of the Clayton Act contains the pre-merger notification requirements that were added to the Hart-Scott-Rodino-Federal Trade Commission Improvements Act of 1976. The federal antitrust laws are enforced by the Antitrust Division of the Department of Justice (DOJ) and the Federal Trade Commission (FTC), whose jurisdictions overlap, and are shared on a basis of prior experience, available resources and other factors.

Reporting Requirements

Section 7A of the Clayton Act imposes pre-notification and reporting requirements and waiting periods on larger mergers and acquisitions affecting interstate commerce if:

1. One party to the acquisition has annual net sales or assets of over $100 million, while the other party to the acquisition has annual net sales or assets of over $10 million,

2. And, as a result of the acquisition, the acquiring party would hold 15% or more of the voting securities or assets, or the total amount of the voting securities or assets is over $15 million.

Exemptions

There is a variety of exemptions to the above requirements, mostly relating to small acquisitions (under $15 million) or where the acquisition of the voting securities does not confer control of the company. Other important exclusions are acquisitions through management buyouts (MBOs) and IRS-qualified employee stock ownership plans (ESOPs).

Waiting Periods

Parties subject to notification and reporting requirements are bound by a 30-calendar-day waiting period before the acquisition can be consummated. DOJ or FTC can extend this waiting period an additional 20 days. For a cash tender offer, the waiting period is 15 days, which may be extended up to an additional 10 days. These waiting periods run from the time the completed notification is filed with the FTC, or when an incomplete notification is filed with a statement of reasons for noncompliance. In practical terms, this often means that waiting periods may be significantly longer than those stated above.

Reports

A notification and report must be filed with the DOJ and FTC by both parties to a voluntary acquisition and by the acquiring party in a tender offer. The acquired party in a tender offer is required to file a response to DOJ or FTC rules, and in a hostile takeover, usually cooperates eagerly in an effort to get the offer enjoined. The report forms require the filing of extensive information about the businesses of both parties to the acquisition, including documents obtained or prepared to evaluate the acquisition. Products are reported in accordance with the Standard Industrial Code (SIC), and the heart of each report is a section that lists overlapping products of the two companies. In their requests for information, the DOJ and FTC typically focus their inquiries on the overlapping products, requiring further detail about sales volumes and territories, pricing, plant capacities, competitors, substitute products, recent acquisitions and divestitures in the industry, foreign and potential competition, uses of the products by customers, capital and technology required by potential new entrants, and numerous other matters.

The form most commonly used for this reporting is the Notification and Report Form for Certain Mergers and Acquisitions (FTC Form C4). Copies of the most current version of this form may be obtained from the FTC.

Resolving Substantive Objections by DOJ or FTC

At times, the DOJ or FTC may find potentially adverse effects on competition of a nature critical to the objectives, structure, or financing of the acquisition. If so, the seller and buyer must face a choice either to terminate the acquisition or defend a lawsuit by the DOJ or FTC. More often, however, only limited adverse effects are identified which impact only a single product or subproduct line, or perhaps only a limited geographic area. These limited problems can sometimes be resolved by negotiating a consent decree which permits the acquisition to proceed followed by "hold separate" and divestiture arrangements designed to preserve competition. These arrangements require that the acquiring party hold separate and preserve the business to be divested and to accomplish the divestiture within a specified time. Failure to accomplish the divestiture can result in civil penalties, appointment of a trustee to operate the business, and even instructions to make capital and operating expenditures that make the divestiture more attractive to buyers.

B. Required Steps in Merger Approval[9]

In the United States, corporations are private entities established at the behest of their founding shareholders and governed in the context of a system that includes:

- A body of state statutory and judicial corporation law, which makes possible a corporation's formation, recognizes its rights as a legal entity and offers "default" rules for internal governance. In choosing a state of incorporation, the founding shareholders seek one whose body of law best suits the needs of their corporation and its shareholders.

- Articles of incorporation, or the corporate charter, which define the basic rules of corporate governance and supplement or override the default provisions of state law.

- Bylaws that provide rules of governance for the board of directors in some detail.

This section describes the legal mechanics of a business combination of two Delaware corporations, which is perhaps the single most common type of combination. Other state laws governing combinations generally parallel the Delaware rules.

In a merger of two corporations (A and B), the basic steps taken in the approval process are as follows:

1. The directors of corporations A and B approve an agreement of merger which specifies, among other things:
   - The terms and conditions of the merger
   - Designation of one corporation (A, for example) as the survivor
   - The number of shares of A or other consideration (e.g., cash) into which each share of B is to be converted as a result of the merger
   - The timing and means by which the merger is to be carried out

2. The shareholders of each corporation hold meetings at which the proposed merger is voted upon and, hopefully, approved. The percentage of each corporation's outstanding shares that must approve the merger is 50% plus one vote, unless the charter specifies a higher percentage.

3. The surviving corporation files a certificate of merger with the Secretary of State of Delaware.

4. As a result of the filing, B ceases to exist and each share of B becomes a right to receive the consideration provided in the agreement of merger.

5. All assets and liabilities of B, by law, become assets and liabilities of A, the survivor.

A consolidation is simply a merger in which there is no designated survivor but, rather, a newly created corporation that represents the combined A and B.

C. Important Elements of the Williams Act[10]

As discussed earlier in this chapter, the Williams Act placed important constraints on the actions of firms in mergers and granted key rights to the shareholders involved in a tender offer. Some of the more important elements of the Williams Act are as follows:

- **Notification:** Acquirers must disclose their current holdings and future intentions to the SEC within 10 days of amassing at least 5% of a company's outstanding stock, and they must disclose to the SEC the source of the funds to be used in the acquisition.

- **Prorating:** In a partial tender offer, the offerer must accept all shares tended on a pro-rata basis from each shareholder. For example, if the bidder is seeking 50% of the target's shares, and 80% are tendered during the proration period, each tendering shareholder will have $5/8$ of his/her share taken up under the offer.

- **Withdrawal:** An offeror must allow tendering shareholders to withdraw their shares for the entire period the offer is open, including any extensions.

- **Minimum Offer Period:** Under current rules a bidder must keep its offer open for a minimum of 20 business days (approximately 27 calendar days).

- **Price Protection:** If the acquiring firm increases the offer price during the 20-day open period, all shareholders who tendered prior to the new offer must receive the higher price.

- **Amendments:** A tender offer is required to remain open for 10 business days after a change in the percentage of shares being sought or the consideration being offered.

- **Purchases Outside the Offer:** A bidder is prohibited from purchasing the stock of the target during the tender offer except pursuant to the offer upon its expiration.

D. Pooling versus Purchase Accounting for Mergers[11]

The method used in accounting for mergers is determined on the basis of certain characteristics of the merging firms. Qualifying for the pooling-of-interests method means meeting several general accepted accounting principles (GAAP) requirements. Meeting all of these requirements means one must use the pooling method. If the merger does not meet all of the requirements it must be treated using the purchase method. Listed below are the GAAP requirements for accounting for a merger:

Pooling-of-Interests Method: The pooling-of-interests method generally is used if the acquiring company issues voting common stock in exchange for voting common stock of the acquired company. It is a tax-free merger or exchange. To use the pooling method all of the following criteria must be met at the time of merger:

1. A combining company is autonomous in that it must not have been a subsidiary of any other company within two years before the initiation date of the merger.
2. A combining company is independent, meaning it does not own 10% or more of another company's common stock at the initiation or consummation date of the merger.
3. The combining companies come together in a single transaction or within one year after initiation of the merger.
4. The acquired company issues voting common stock for substantially all (90% or more) of the voting common stock of the other company.
5. Neither of the combining companies changes the equity interest of voting common stock in anticipation of the combination within two years prior to its consummation.
6. Reacquisition of shares is for reasons other than the business combination.
7. The relative percentage ownership of each stockholder remains the same.
8. Stockholders are not restricted in voting rights.
9. The combination is completed at the consummation date with no pending provisions.
10.–12. There is an absence of planned transactions after the combination relating to (10) treasury stock acquisition, (11) financial arrangements to benefit former combining stockholders, and (12) disposal of a significant part of the combining company's assets within two years after combination.

The accounting entries under the pooling-of-interests method are as follows:
1. The acquired company's net assets are brought forward at book value.
2. The retained earnings and paid-in capital of the acquired company are brought forward.
3. The net income of the acquired company is picked up for the entire year regardless of acquisition date.
4. Expenses of the pooling are immediately charged against earnings.

Therefore, when a merger qualifies for the pooling method the acquired company's assets are recorded on the acquiring company's books at their book value (less depreciation). There is no goodwill available when using the pooling of interest method. Under the purchase method, the assets are recorded at fair market value on the acquiring company's books and any difference is recorded as goodwill.

Purchase Method: The purchase method of accounting for a business combination is used when cash and other assets are distributed, or liabilities are incurred to effect the combination. This method must be used when one or more of the 12 criteria for the pooling-of-interests method are not met. Under the purchase method, the acquiring corporation records the net assets acquired at the fair market value of the asset purchased. Any excess of the purchase price over the fair market value of the net identifiable assets is recorded as goodwill. The acquiring corporation then records periodic changes to income for the depreciation of the excess price over book value of net identifiable assets and for amortization of goodwill. Note that goodwill already on the books of the acquired company is brought forward from the acquisition date to year-end. Direct costs of the purchase reduce the fair value of securities issued. Indirect costs are expensed.

E. Listing of Terms Used in Mergers and Acquisitions[12]

Black Knight: In corporate finance, a party who makes a tender offer or merger proposal that is hostile to present management of a company.

Cramdown Deal: Expression used by investment bankers if a merger is so arranged that shareholders have no option but to accept the compensation offered.

Crown Jewel Defense: A management strategy to thwart a hostile takeover. The strategy centers on an agreement to sell to a third party the company's most valuable asset, or assets—hence the term—to make the company less attractive to the raider. Such a defense may bring stockholder suits if the asset is sold for less than its fair market value.

Golden Parachute: One uses a parachute in the event of an air disaster to descend to the ground safely. Analogy: A company anticipates a takeover or other financial adversity that may "ground" present executives. Thus, the executives vote themselves termination or other retirement benefits that will—no matter what the fortunes of the company—provide them a safe passage to financial security.

Greenmail: Used in conjunction with takeover bids, tender offers or unfriendly proxy fights. The concept is similar to blackmail. Greenmail involves the purchase of a significant block of stock for one of two purposes: either to sell the block to a corporate raider, or to tender it to the company for a premium price. Because the sale of the block to a raider would threaten the continuity of management, management feels impelled to buy the shares at a premium above the current market price, rather than have the shares sold to the unfriendly corporate raider.

Highly Confident Letter: A letter, pioneered by Drexel Burnham Lambert in conjunction with certain issues of "junk bonds," stating that they were highly confident (but without official commitment) that they would be able to successfully market an offering of a particular type of security. Such a letter usually arises in connection with a tender offer, or a leveraged buyout, where significant amounts of money would be needed from an issue to obtain the funds needed to purchase control of a company.

Mezzanine Financing: Term used in conjunction with leveraged buyouts. As opposed to pure debt financing, the term refers to financing a takeover by preferred stock or convertible subordinated debentures. In this way, the resulting company's equity capital is expanded, rather than its debt, and it satisfies important creditors that the new owners will have a larger financial commitment to the merged corporation.

Pac-Man Defense: Named for the Atari video game owned by Warner Communications Corporation to designate a financial maneuver that is used to thwart an unfriendly merger. Under Pac-Man defense, the reluctant target runs toward rather than away from an unfriendly suitor and tries to purchase control of the raider before the raider can gain controlling influence over the target.

Poison Pill Defense: A corporate finance tactic to defend against unfriendly takeovers. Generally, the "poison pill" is an issue of convertible preferred stock distributed as a stock dividend to current stockholders. The preferred stock is convertible into a number of common shares equal to or greater than the present number of outstanding shares. However, because of dividend adjustments, there is little incentive to convert unless there is a takeover. The takeover attempt, therefore, becomes its own poison because it will vastly increase the price that will have to be paid for the company.

Schedule 13D: An SEC form that must be filed within 10 business days by anyone who acquires 5% or more of an equity security registered with the SEC. The purpose is to disclose the method of acquisition of the shares and the purchaser's intentions regarding management control of the company.

Schedule 13G: A short-form version of Schedule 13D. The short form is to be filed by a person who, at the end of a calendar year, owns 5% or more an equity security registered with the SEC. This short-form filing is permitted if the person acquired the securities in the ordinary course of business and if the owner does not intend to change or influence control of the company. Broker/dealers, banks, investment companies and insurance companies are typical filers of Schedule 13G. It is due within 45 days after year's end.

Scorched Earth Tactic: A corporate defense tactic whereby an unwilling takeover target discourages bidders by selling off attractive assets or by entering into long-term contractual commitments. The company thereby makes itself less attractive to the buyer.

Self-Tender Offer: An offer by the issuing company to repurchase a specific number or percentage of its outstanding shares. Using cash or other assets in exchange for these shares, companies sometimes use this tactic to equal or to top the bid made by a corporate raider endeavoring to take over the company.

Shark Repellent: Designates a change in a corporation's charter designed to make that company more difficult to acquire.

Supermajority: A stockholder vote in which 80% or more of the outstanding shares must be voted to approve a motion. To thwart takeover attempts, some companies have written into their corporate charters a requirement for a supermajority for certain corporate decisions.

Super Voting Right: Management-accorded privilege permitting a select class of voting stock a greater voice in corporation management. Before the SEC implemented its "one share—one vote" rule, the use of a "time-phased" super voting right was a popular defense against a hostile takeover. Under this concept, when an unwanted suitor acquired a specific percentage of stock, a new class of voting stock was initiated for earlier shareholders. This stock carried a greater voice in corporate affairs, thereby discouraging the predator.

War Chest: A picturesque term used in corporate circles to designate a fund set aside by a company to defend itself against a hostile tender offer. Such funds would be used to pay for legal fees and other costs deemed essential for preserving the company's independence.

White Knight: A person or corporation that saves a target corporation from an unfriendly takeover by taking over the target.

V. Calculations and Examples

A. Purchase versus Pooling Merger Calculation

The calculations below are for both the pooling of interest and purchase method. Company A acquires all of Company B's outstanding stock for $100,000 (i.e., the price paid is the total asset minus the debt). Company B's common stock book value is $70,000 prior to the merger and the market value of the assets is $110,000. The $30,000 difference between the book value and the purchase price is not accounted for on the acquiring companies' book using the pooling of interest method. Using the purchase method for the merger the difference is recorded as an increase to total assets and stockholders' equity. The acquiring firm is paying $100,000 to purchase assets with a net value (after debt claims) of $80,000 ($110,000 – $30,000). The amount of goodwill, therefore, is computed as the excess of the price paid ($100,000) over the $80,000 net value, or a total of $20,000. The value of the shareholders' equity is higher by $30,000 under the purchase method to reflect the $10,000 increase in assets (market value versus book value) and the $20,000 extra paid as a result of goodwill.

	Before Merger		Firm A—After Merger	
	Firm A	Firm B	Pooling of Interest	Purchase Method
Total Assets, book value	$500,000	$100,000	$600,000	$610,000
Goodwill				20,000
Total Assets under Purchase Method				$630,000
Liabilities, book value	150,000	30,000	180,000	180,000
Stockholders' Equity book value	350,000	70,000	420,000	450,000

B. Merger Valuation Example

Assume a firm is contemplating the acquisition of another firm. As a result of the merger, the net after-tax cash flows of the merged firm will increase by the amounts shown in the table below over the next five years. For the terminal value assume the year 5 cash flow will grow at 5% into the future. The firm will use a 12% cost of capital in evaluating this merger. Calculate the value for this merger.

Year	Cash Flow
1	$10 Million
2	$11 Million
3	$12 Million
4	$13 Million
5	$15 Million

Terminal Value   =[Yr 5 CF × (1 + Growth Rate)] / (Cost of Capital − Growth Rate)
                 = [$15M × (1.05)] / (.12 −.05) = $225 Million
Value of Merger = PV of Cash Flow Stream + PV of Terminal Value
Value of Merger = $10M / (1.12) + $11M / (1.12)^2 + $12M / (1.12)^3
                 + $13M / (1.12)^4 + $15M / (1.12)^5 + $225M / (1.12)^5
Value of Merger = $170,683,247

VI. Endnotes

1. Additional background and more detailed information on mergers and acquisitions can be found in *Acquisitions Yearbook: 1991,* Edward E. Shea, Editor, The New York Institute of Finance and Simon and Schuster, 1992.

2. Source: *Louis Rukeyser's Business Almanac,* Simon and Schuster, New York, 1991, p. 233.

3. A detailed discussion of the research related to the benefits of mergers can be found in *Handbook of Modern Finance, Second Edition,* pp. 31–35 to 31–48; Dennis L. Logue, Editor, Warren, Gorham & Lamont, Publishers, 1990.

4. See: Chapter 30, Mergers and Acquisitions, *Handbook of Modern Finance, Second Edition,* Dennis E. Logue, Editor, Warren, Gorham & Lamont, Publishers, 1990.

5. If these pro forma statements are being used in a proxy campaign, the valuations and projections must be supported by factual data. In addition, these statements must disclose any limitations and qualifications, and must be prepared in accordance with recognized standards of financial analysis. (See Rule 14a-9 and SEC Release # 34-16833—May 23, 1980.)

6. See: Chapter 30, Mergers and Acquisitions, *Handbook of Modern Finance, Second Edition,* Dennis E. Logue, Editor, Warren, Gorham & Lamont, Publishers, 1990.

7. Ibid.

8. See *Acquisitions Yearbook: 1991,* Edward E. Shea, Editor, The New York Institute of Finance and Simon and Schuster, Publisher, 1992.

9. See: Chapter 30, Mergers and Acquisitions, *Handbook of Modern Finance, Second Edition,* Dennis E. Logue, Editor, Warren, Gorham & Lamont, Publishers, 1990.

10. Ibid.

11. This section is taken from: *Dictionary of Accounting Terms,* Barron's Business Guides, 1987.

12. These definitions are taken from: *The Complete Words of Wall Street,* Allan H. Pessin and Joseph A. Ross, Business One Irwin, Publisher, 1991.

7 Working Capital Management Strategies

I. Outline of the Chapter

A. Overview of Working Capital Management
1. Concepts
   a. Working Capital
   b. Net Working Capital
   c. Current Ratio
   d. Quick Ratio (Acid Test Ratio)
   e. Working Capital Policy
   f. Working Capital Management
2. External Financing of Working Capital
   a. Changes in Current Assets
   b. Changes in Current Liabilities
   c. Required External Financing
3. Working Capital Cash Flow Cycle
   a. Inventory Conversion Period
   b. Receivables Conversion Period
   c. Payables Conversion Period
   d. Cash Conversion Cycle

B. Impact of Differing Levels of Current Asset Investment and Financing Policies
1. Current Asset Investment Policies
2. Current Asset Financing Policies
   a. Maturity Matching
   b. Aggressive Strategy
   c. Conservative Strategy

C. Financing Current Assets
1.   Operational Advantages of Short-Term Credit
a.   Speed
b.   Flexibility
c.   Financing Seasonal Needs
2.   Sources of Short-Term Credit
a.   Accounts Payable (Trade Credit)
b.   Accruals
c.   Short-Term Bank Loans
d.   Commercial Paper
e.   Secured Short-Term Loans

D. Costs and Risks of Alternative Debt Maturities
1.   Cost
2.   Risk

Calculations and Examples
A. Cash Conversion Cycle
B. NPV Cost of Cash Conversion Cycle
C. Cost of Not Taking Cash Discount
D. Benefit of Cash Discount to Seller

II. Introduction

Because a firm's daily activities can cause the working capital accounts to change dramatically, the management of these accounts may be critical to the firm's liquidity, survival, and ultimate success. It is important to understand the causes of these changes and the interrelationships among the working capital accounts.

This chapter will define the terms involved in working capital management and, through the cash flow cycle, illustrate the important interrelationships. Alternative current asset investment strategies will be discussed. The sources, the costs and the risks of alternative current asset financing strategies will also be treated.

Working capital decisions affect many of the financial ratios used to evaluate financial conditions. In addition, the risk posture implied by the working capital strategies may influence the firm's cost of capital. Also, working capital can be positively or negatively impacted by a firm's credit and cash management practices. For example, use of controlled disbursement and concentration of excess balances has an impact on working capital management, as well as on the credit and collection departments.

III. Coverage of the Chapter Material

A. Overview of Working Capital Management

Working capital management refers to the decisions and strategies concerning amounts and types of investment in current assets and amounts and types of financing from current liabilities. The daily activities of the firm result in a flow of cash through the working capital accounts.

- Working capital management involves the analysis of the risk/reward relationship. The calculation and interpretation of the current ratio and the quick ratio are discussed in greater detail in Chapter 10, Financial Analysis. A high value for the current ratio suggests a strong liquidity position and relatively low risk. However, in general, current assets have low rates of return, while current liabilities have relatively low interest costs. Therefore, there is a high cost to having strong liquidity.

- For most profitable companies, investing in cash generates less of a return than investing in capital projects that generate future sales and revenues.

- It must also be noted that there may be loan covenants in long-term borrowings which may require a minimum level for the current ratio.

- One of the primary problems in the continuing use of short-term debt is that the lender may decide not to roll-over the loan or renew the credit line at its maturity. In addition, many short-term lenders require that loans used to finance seasonal needs be closed out for a short period each year (known as a bank loan "clean-up" period). For these reasons, many firms find that the use of short-term loans for the financing of permanent asset requirements involves significant risk.

- There are, however, some approaches to continued use of short-term debt that carry lower risk and should be considered. These generally involve revolving loans which may be secured by accounts receivable or inventory (secured loans). Later in this section, the viewpoint of both the lender and borrower with respect to short-term financing will be discussed.

1. Concepts

a. Working Capital: This is defined as current assets, typically: cash, marketable securities, pre-paid assets, accounts receivable and inventory.

b. Net Working Capital: This is defined as current assets minus current liabilities, where current liabilities are represented by accounts payable, notes payable, and accrued liabilities.

c. Current Ratio: This is generally defined as the ratio of current assets to current liabilities, but may be more specifically defined under certain loan agreement covenants. This ratio measures the extent to which a firm has current assets to cover its current liabilities. For example, a current ratio of 1.58:1 implies that for every dollar of current liabilities there is $1.58 of current assets.

d. Quick Ratio (Acid Test Ratio): This is defined as the ratio of cash, near-cash investments and accounts receivable to current liabilities. It is considered a better measure of a firm's liquidity than the current ratio because it excludes the least liquid of the current assets (pre-paid items and inventories) from the calculation. In essence, it measures the ability of the firm to cover short-term liabilities using only those assets most readily converted into cash (i.e., the most liquid of the assets).

e. Working Capital Policy: This is defined as basic policy decisions regarding the amounts invested in each category of current assets and how these amounts will be financed.

f. Working Capital Management: This is defined as the execution and administration of the policy decisions regarding current assets and current liabilities.

2. External Financing of Working Capital: Many current asset and current liability accounts vary directly with sales activity, and these accounts are said to be spontaneous. That is, there are no specific decisions to increase these accounts, but the changes will occur spontaneously with the change in sales. The magnitude of the spontaneous changes will have a significant impact in determining the amount of external financing necessary for working capital.

a. Changes in Current Assets

- Increases in non-cash current assets must be offset either by reducing cash or increasing liabilities or debt.

- Assuming no change in working capital policies, as the volume of sales activity increases, credit sales should increase, resulting in larger dollar amounts invested in accounts receivable.

- Also, generating additional sales may require expanded inventories of production materials, work in process and finished goods to support the increases, thus also increasing both inventory and accounts payable.

- Finally, if the increased level of sales activity is permanent, it may necessitate a larger cash (and/or marketable securities) balance in order to cover current asset buildups. An increase in accounts receivable and inventory may actually cause the cash account to decrease or borrowing to increase to fund the working capital requirement. Obviously, a decrease in sales activity should cause a corresponding decrease in those current asset accounts. In the short run, however, inventories might go up as production continues and sales decline.

b. Changes in Current Liabilities

- Decreases in current liabilities must be offset by decreases in an asset account or increases in other liability accounts. A decrease in accounts payable requires either a decrease of cash or an increase in debt to pay off the accounts.

- A larger volume of sales activity would typically require a higher volume of materials purchased. If these materials are purchased on credit, the accounts payable account will increase.

- Likewise, the additional labor expenses associated with increased production will cause the accrued wages account to increase.

- The increase in taxes due to a higher level of taxable income will cause the accrued taxes account to increase. Again, a decrease in sales activity should cause corresponding decreases in these accounts.

c. Required External Financing

- The total of the above net increases in the current asset accounts (excluding cash) represents the total amount of financing necessary for the incremental working capital, assuming there are no net changes in cash flows from changes in long-term assets or liabilities.

- Many of the current liabilities, such as accounts payable and accrual items, can be considered "spontaneous" in that they will generally automatically increase with increasing sales. For example, as a firm increases its sales level, purchases and production will rise, thus increasing the amount of accounts payable, accrued wages and taxes. In addition, as the firm generates additional profits, the retained earnings account will increase. If the incremental working capital exceeds the increase in internally generated funds, the difference must be financed from external sources.

- If the level of current assets (excluding net cash) decreases, this amount represents funds that have been "freed up" or no longer need to be financed (i.e., lower inventory or lower accounts receivable under rising sales results in increased liquidity for the firm).

- If the level of current liabilities decreases, this amount represents the reduction in funding available to support the current assets. The firm would then have to utilize external sources (such as long-term debt or other capital) to support the working capital investment.

3. Working Capital Cash Flow Cycle: The flow of cash through the working capital accounts can be illustrated with the cash flow cycle. This cycle shows how the strategies concerning inventory, receivables and payables all interact to affect the flow of cash through the firm. A diagram of the cash flow cycle appears in Figure 7.1.

a. Inventory Conversion Period: This period is the average number of days, from the acquisition of raw materials until the sale of the finished goods produced from these materials, that usually generates accounts receivable. Inventory management techniques such as just-in-time (JIT) can help to reduce significantly the absolute levels of inventory. This topic is covered in detail in Chapter 9.

- For a manufacturing firm, this period of time is the sum of:
  1. The average number of days that raw materials remain in inventory
  2. The average number of days necessary to convert these raw materials into finished goods
  3. The average number of days the finished goods remain in inventory

Therefore, any decision that affects either the raw materials, the work in process or the finished goods inventories will affect the inventory conversion period. The

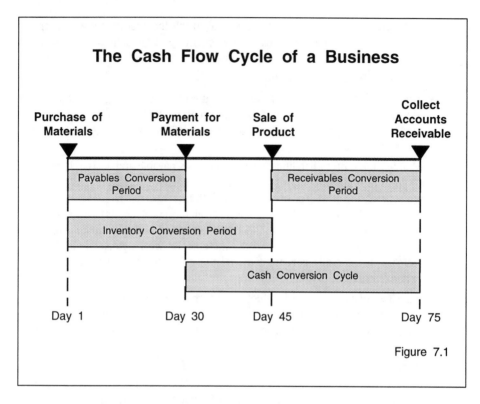

The Cash Flow Cycle of a Business

| Purchase of Materials | Payment for Materials | Sale of Product | Collect Accounts Receivable |

Payables Conversion Period

Receivables Conversion Period

Inventory Conversion Period

Cash Conversion Cycle

Day 1   Day 30   Day 45   Day 75

Figure 7.1

inventory conversion period, when divided into the number of days in a year, gives the number of inventory turns, or turnover, in a year. This topic is covered in greater detail in Chapter 10.

- For a service firm, the inventory conversion period will be determined only by the average length of time that any materials used in the service process remain in inventory until they are used to provide services.

b. Receivables Conversion Period

- This period is the average number of days required to convert the accounts receivable into cash.

- Any change in accounts receivable policies, such as credit standards, credit terms or collection efforts, will impact the receivables conversion period.

- Changes in the competitive marketplace or general business conditions could also impact the receivables conversion period. The receivables conversion period is also referred to as Days Sales Outstanding (DSO) or average collection period and is covered in greater detail in Chapter 10.

c. Payables Conversion Period

- This is the average number of days between the purchase of materials and supplies and payment for them. The ability to purchase materials on deferred payment terms allows the firm to delay the outflow of cash.

- Any strategy that affects payables, such as stretching payables or taking cash discounts, will affect the payables conversion period. The stretching of payables enables a firm either to use cash to reduce debt (thus reducing interest expense) or to invest cash on a short-term basis to increase interest income.

d. Cash Conversion Cycle

- This is the average number of days between the actual cash outflow for the acquisition of materials and supplies and the actual cash inflow from the sale of the products or services.

- The cash conversion cycle can be expressed by the following formula:

$$
\begin{array}{cccc}
\text{Cash} & \text{Inventory} & \text{Receivables} & \text{Payables} \\
\text{Conversion=} & \text{Conversion} + & \text{Conversion} - & \text{Conversion} \\
\text{Cycle} & \text{Period} & \text{Period} & \text{Period}
\end{array}
$$

- The cash conversion cycle tells the firm how long, on average, it must finance the cash outflow before it receives the cash inflow. Examples of calculations concerning the cash conversion cycle appear at the end of this chapter.

- This cycle can be considered in a net present value framework. The treasurer should examine the timing of cash inflows and outflows as they relate to the conversion of raw materials into the receipt of available funds from sales.

- Each of the events outlined above can be placed on a time line, and the net present value of inflows minus the net present value of the outflows can be computed. The treasurer can, therefore, determine the precise cost of the cash conversion cycle.

- The cash conversion cycle can be shortened by reducing the inventory conversion period, by reducing the receivables conversion period or by lengthening the payables deferral period.

- The firm may be able to improve profits by reducing financing costs if it can shorten the cash conversion cycle. However, the trade-offs that must be compared with these financing cost savings are the possible costs from strategies that shortened the cycle.

- Examples of these costs include:
  1. Lost sales caused by tightened credit and collection standards
  2. Costs of production stoppages from depletion of materials (stock-outs)
  3. Penalties for stretching payables beyond the due date (i.e., lost discount or charges on late payments)
  4. Higher price charged by suppliers to "slow-payers"
  5. Lost sales from not selling to "slow-payers" for fear of non-payment
  6. Extending open credit terms to slow or non-payers

- Benefits from lower cash financing costs resulting from these strategies must be compared with increased costs and lost sales caused by the strategies. If the benefits exceed the costs of the strategies, including the lost profit from lost sales, the strategies should be implemented.

- When analyzing any working capital strategy, it is important to determine how all decisions regarding inventory, receivables or payables will impact the cash conversion cycle.

B. Impact of Differing Levels of Current Asset Investment and Financing Policies

The answers to two basic questions establish the framework for the risk/return trade-off analysis involved in working capital management. The two questions are:

1. What is the appropriate level for current assets?
2. How should the current assets be financed?

1. Current Asset Investment Policies: A firm can choose among alternative policies regarding the total amount of current assets to support a given level of sales. It is important to note that the normal range of ratios of current assets to sales will vary by industry and by size of firm. The various policies discussed below reflect the current asset policy of a given firm relative to its industry and competitors.

- Under a liberal current asset policy, a firm would hold high levels of current assets relative to sales. Typically, these current assets would consist of inventories and accounts receivable resulting from either liberal credit policies or high inventory carrying levels (usually to maintain low risk of stockouts).

- Under a conservative current asset policy, a firm would hold low levels of current assets relative to sales. Inventories would be managed as tightly as possible and the accounts receivable investment would be small, reflecting conservative or aggressively managed credit policies.

- A moderate strategy would result in current asset investment between the liberal and conservative strategies.

- The current asset investment decision is necessary, in part, because of the uncertainties associated with sales levels, costs, production time, lead times for inventory replenishment, desired customer service levels, collection periods and payment periods.

- If there were no uncertainty, firms would need to hold only minimal levels of current assets. The extent of the uncertainty and the firm's risk tolerance will determine the investments in the current asset accounts. For example, if suppliers are unpredictable in their delivery patterns, or if customers are unpredictable in their buying patterns, large safety stocks of raw materials or finished goods may be desirable. Greater uncertainty in cash flows or the lack of available credit lines may result in a decision to extend the payables period, or to hold extra dollars in cash or marketable securities as a "safety cushion."

- A conservative current asset investment policy could have relatively higher risks associated with (1) inventory stock-outs, and (2) not having the cash to make necessary payments. A conservative credit policy could have a negative impact on sales. Many firms, especially small ones, may have to pursue a conservative policy due to limited availability of short-term credit or limited overall capitalization.

- A conservative policy, however, may be the most profitable policy. Since relatively fewer dollars are invested in current assets, the amount of total funds invested in the firm may also be small. A conservative policy, therefore, may result in a larger expected return on investment, as long as the tightened credit policy does not lose more sales than the resulting savings.

- With its larger investment in current assets, a firm using a liberal current asset policy may have a relatively lower return on investment. However, the larger investment in current assets combined with the liberal policy may result in a larger current ratio and, subsequently, in lower credit and stock-out risk.

- A firm's current asset policy may be a function of its industry. In industries with generally high gross profit margins (contribution margin) on sales, a liberal policy may offer substantial benefits, especially if the potential for additional profit greatly outweighs the potential costs; that is, if the profits gained from the additional sales are greater than the costs of carrying the additional receivables and any additional bad debt loss.

- Obviously, the moderate policy falls between the two extreme policies in terms of expected return and risk. Managements choice of a specific current asset investment policy depends upon the risk/return trade-off characteristics that it wants.

- It is important to understand the viewpoint of the firm's creditors in the management of current assets. For banks and institutional creditors relying on current assets as security for short-term lending, the current asset policy of the firm is a very important consideration. The quality of the current assets used as security (generally accounts receivable and inventories) is also important to the firm's creditors.

- Sales and operating managers may take a different view of current asset management than do financial managers. Sales managers want a good inventory of finished goods to avoid having stock-outs, and thus losing sales, as well as easy credit policy to stimulate sales. Operating managers want to make sure they have the materials on hand needed to maintain production. Financial managers, on the other hand, must worry about financing these assets and, therefore, they try to minimize their levels wherever possible.

- A conservative policy may be risky, but it generally offers a higher rate of return. Subject to any ratio restrictions in the debt covenants, assessment of the proper level of current assets rests with the firm, not with its creditors.

2. Current Asset Financing Policies: The firm's need for current assets will typically fluctuate with variations in its sales.

- While any firm may have a sales cycle with major fluctuations over time, it is rare for sales to fall below some minimum level. There is usually a need for a base level of current assets at all times during the sales cycle. This minimum required current assets investment is generally referred to as the firm's permanent current assets.

- The level of permanent current asset investment can be determined by examining a firm's sales cycle and related levels of current assets over time. The average of the current asset investments at the bottom of several sales cycles can be used as an estimate for the necessary permanent current asset level.

- Another approach to determining permanent current assets is to monitor the relationships between individual current asset accounts (cash, accounts receivable and inventory) and the sales cycle over time. A desired minimum level for each type of current asset can be found.

- Expansion of temporary current assets represents the additional dollars necessary to support the sales increases that occur during upswings in the cycle (i.e., retailers during the Christmas season). The decisions regarding the financing of permanent and temporary current assets define the firm's working capital financing policy.

- The basic decision in the financing of a firm's current assets is whether to use short- or long-term sources of funding. Since the source of funds is generally debt, the basic question is whether it is less expensive over the long run to continuously borrow in the money markets or to lock in a long-term rate in the capital markets. Generally, the yield curve of debt is upward-sloping, indicating that short-term funds can be obtained at a lower cost than long-term rates. There are times, however, when the yield curve is downward-sloping. In these instances, long-term rates may be more attractive. Before the funding decision is made, it is important to accurately forecast the movements in interest rates, the shape of the yield curve in the future, and the future availability of credit for the firm.

- The basic approaches to the financing of a firm's permanent assets can be generally classified as maturity matching, aggressive, and conservative. These policy approaches are shown in Figure 7.2 and are discussed. Depending on the shape of the yield curve, the movement of interest rates, the forecast of future rates, and the risk posture of the firm's management, any of those approaches may be appropriate at a given point in time.

- A firm may also decide to try to smooth out its use of short-term debt over time, borrowing on a regular basis whether or not it needs funds at a particular time. This approach may yield more stable borrowing rates, especially if more favorable rates from the bank can be negotiated.

a. Maturity Matching

- The firm's total permanent assets are defined as its fixed assets plus its permanent current assets. Under maturity matching, the total permanent assets are financed with long-term financing.

- Short-term financing is used to finance the temporary current assets. The need for short-term financing follows exactly the pattern of fluctuation of the temporary current assets. This is generally considered a traditional or moderate policy.

b. Aggressive Strategy

- Under the aggressive approach, the firm finances all of its fixed assets, but it finances only a portion of its permanent current assets with long-term financing.

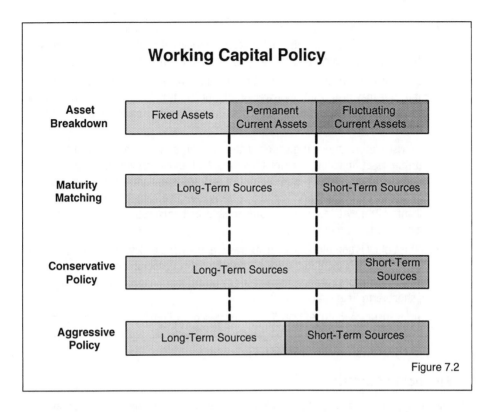

Figure 7.2

- Short-term financing is used for the remainder of the permanent current assets and for all of the temporary current assets. In comparison with other policies, this policy uses a larger amount of ongoing short-term financing.

- Since short-term financing often costs less than long-term financing, this strategy is usually less costly. However, greater use of short-term financing will result in a lower current ratio and greater risk. This risk arises from both interest rate risk (changing rates) and the risk that the loan may not be renewed.

- There are certain types of multi-year (usually 3 to 5 years) revolving credit agreements that allow a firm to borrow on a short-term basis, but classify the loan as long-term for accounting purposes. This type of borrowing arrangement does not reduce the current ratio as does borrowing under a true short-term loan. These credit agreements are covered in greater detail in Chapter 8.

c. Conservative Strategy

- Under the conservative approach, long-term financing is used for the fixed assets, the permanent current assets and some portion of the temporary current assets.

- Generally, the treasurer will try to finance the average level of temporary current assets with long-term sources. Short-term financing is used for the remainder of the temporary current assets.

- Since short-term financing is used for only a portion of the temporary current assets, this policy will generally involve the least use of short-term financing. Therefore, it will have higher financing costs than other approaches.

- The relatively smaller use of short-term financing will result in a larger current ratio, but may also result in lower profits for the firm. There may, however, be less interest rate risk if the long-term debt is on a fixed-rate basis and the short-term financing is on a variable-rate basis.

- The risk/return trade-off must be analyzed in both current asset investment and current asset financing decisions. As discussed above, an aggressive investment policy will have a higher expected return on investment and a higher risk because of its lower current ratio. The use of derivative financing products (covered in Chapter 2) may allow the treasurer to shift or hedge some of the risk from an aggressive investment policy.

- If this policy is combined with an aggressive financing policy, the expected return on investment is increased through the relatively cheaper financing costs, but the risk also increases because of the smaller current ratio associated with a larger use of short-term financing.

- In this instance, both policies lead to increased profitability and increased risk. It is important that the firm analyze the combined risk/return impact from the investment and financing decisions.

C. Financing Current Assets

The choices among the alternative sources of current asset financing are differentiated by speed, flexibility, cost and risk. Speed and flexibility are discussed in this section; cost and risk are discussed in Section D.

1. Operational Advantages of Short-Term Credit: When choosing between short-term (credit facilities of 360 days or less) and long-term credit, it is necessary to understand the advantages and disadvantages of each. Besides the basic differences due to cost and risk, there are also operational differences in using short-term versus long-term debt for the financing of current assets. The primary operational advantages of short-term credit are its speed, flexibility and ability to efficiently finance seasonal credit needs. An operational disadvantage of short-term debt is the continuing need to renegotiate or roll over the debt.

a. Speed: Short-term loans generally can be obtained much faster than long-term loans. Some sources of short-term financing occur spontaneously with sales. Therefore, there is a correlation between when the financing is required and when it is obtained.

b. Flexibility: Long-term loan agreements often contain restrictive covenants that are less common in short-term loans. If funds are necessary for only a short time, borrowing on a short-term basis will enable the firm to maintain its flexibility for future borrowing decisions. This flexibility may not exist if the firm is locked into a long-term borrowing arrangement with substantial pre-payment costs and/or initial fees for the credit placement.

c. Financing Seasonal Needs: One of the major uses of short-term credit is the financing of current assets in seasonal industries. In order to meet seasonal needs, a firm must build up inventory and/or accounts receivable (sometimes through seasonal dating of invoices). Short-term loans are generally the vehicle of choice for financing such temporary increases in current assets. This process is sometimes referred to as "gapping" or matching maturities (i.e., using short-term vehicles to finance short-term needs and using long-term vehicles to finance long-term needs).

2. Sources of Short-Term Credit: Different sources of short-term credit have different speeds of acquisition, flexibility, cost and risk. The four major types of short-term credit are discussed below.

a. Accounts Payable (Trade Credit)

- Suppliers of goods and services may allow their purchase on credit. The firm need not pay for them until the time specified by the supplier's credit terms.

- Accounts payable (trade credit) often represent the largest source of short-term credit for some firms. Increases or decreases in the current liability account are spontaneous and quickly accessed.

- Increased sales activity usually results in larger orders from suppliers which leads to larger accounts payable balances. As long as the obligation is paid within the credit period allowed by the supplier, there is no direct cost associated with trade credit. In a sense, it is an interest-free loan from the supplier. However, if a supplier offers a discount for payment in cash, there is a cost associated with not taking the discount. This cost is approximated using the following formula (an example of this calculation is provided at the end of this chapter):

$$\frac{\text{Approximate}}{\text{Percentage}} = \frac{\text{Discount Percent}}{100 - \frac{\text{Discount}}{\text{Percent}}} \times \frac{360}{\text{Days Credit} - \frac{\text{Discount}}{\text{Outstanding Period}}}$$

This represents the approximate interest rate applicable to the use of the firm's dollars resulting from *not* taking the discount. This interest rate should be compared with the cost of obtaining funds from other sources. Ideally, if funds can be obtained more cheaply, the firm should borrow at the cheaper cost and then take the cash discount by paying for the goods or services on the discount date.

- The cost of the average collection period for the supplier is built into the price. If the buyer has a cheaper cost of funds, a lower price with a shorter payment period (i.e., cash discount) could be better for both parties.

- Unless the firm is willing to pay penalties for late payment (and risk losing the privilege of trade credit), accounts payable are generally not flexible. Payment dates are negotiated with the supplier, and this source of short-term credit can only exist when goods and services are purchased. A supplier will not generally lend dollars for purposes other than purchases from the supplier.

- In some supplier/buyer relationships where the market for supplies is highly competitive, the buyer may be able to dictate or influence the terms of the sale. In that case, the seller may reluctantly lend money to the buyer for purposes other than the purchase of supplies. In some industries the terms may be considered "flexible" or negotiable between supplier and customer. For example, a seller may offer more flexible terms to a safe credit risk purchasing a large volume of supplies to gain a volume discount.

b. Accruals

- Wages are generally paid on a weekly, biweekly or monthly basis; taxes are generally paid on a weekly, monthly, or quarterly basis. Until these payments are actually made, the firm will have accrued wages and taxes. These current liabilities are spontaneous and will typically increase in relation to increases in sales, expenditures or inventories.

- There is usually no cost associated with the deferral of wages and taxes. For example, the firm does not need to pay interest to its wage earners to compensate them for being paid at the end of the month instead of daily.

- Accruals, however, are not considered flexible and are generally static. The firm does not have the ability to change the due dates for taxes, and many wage payment patterns are dictated by industry practice or labor negotiations. Within these constraints, the firm should utilize these cost-free sources whenever possible.

c. Short-Term Bank Loans: Loans from banks or other financial institutions can appear in the liabilities section of a firm's balance sheet as loans payable, notes payable, promissory notes or lines of credit.

- This short-term source of financing is not spontaneous. Increases must be negotiated with and approved by the lender; specific decisions to borrow and lend must accompany any increase in the firm's short-term borrowing position.

- Lines of credit are arranged in advance and can be accessed up to the specified limit. While these bank loans have a cost, the fact that they are negotiated provides flexibility as to cost and maturity.

- In addition, repayment patterns, collateral, compensating balances, credit limits and commitment fees on lines of credit are also negotiated items. Since all of these must be negotiated, this source of financing is not as spontaneous as accruals and accounts payable.

- There are non-bank costs involved in establishing bank credit facilities, such as those related to outside counsel, independent auditors, internal administration and asset monitoring.

d. Commercial Paper: Commercial paper is an unsecured promissory note issued by corporations that pays a competitive market rate with maturities of up to 270 days. Commercial paper is normally issued at a discount through dealers. For large firms active in the market, it is usually a quick source of low-cost, short-term financing. The cost of commercial paper for the issuing firm is based on its credit rating on the issue, which is a function of the firm's estimated default risk. This topic is covered in detail in Chapter 8.

e. Secured Short-Term Loans: These are short-term loans that are secured by some form of collateral, usually accounts receivable, inventories or securitized assets. They are generally referred to as asset-based loans.

- These types of loans are generally formula-based, with the lender agreeing to lend some percentage of the value of specified assets (usually accounts receivable, inventory, or some combination), with the assets used as security for the lending arrangement.

- These loans have explicit costs (usually high). While they are flexible, it does take time to negotiate them and to receive loan approval.

- One of the most common types of asset-based loans calls for the pledging of accounts receivable to provide security on a short-term loan or line of credit. This type of arrangement may be made through a bank or through a third-party financial intermediary.

- Factoring involves the outright sale a firm's accounts receivable to a third party. This sale can be with or without recourse to the originating firm in the event of default (non-collection) on the receivables. This sale of accounts receivable is, in effect, a proxy for a short-term loan.

- Securitization is the general term used for the creation of new securities based on financial assets such as accounts receivable. In essence, the receivables are bundled into packages and resold to other investors, providing the firm with increased liquidity.

- An inventory loan is a loan secured by providing the lender with a claim on the firm's inventory. This claim on inventory can be general (an inventory blanket lien) or it can identify specific items of inventory as the collateral (a trust receipt loan). These types of loans are also called "formula-based" loans, meaning that the amount of the loan is usually based on a percentage of eligible receivables or inventory, depending upon the age and/or dollar level of the asset(s).

- A warehouse loan usually involves storing the pledged inventory in a third-party-controlled warehouse, with the lender's approval required for release of the inventory.

D. Costs and Risks of Alternative Debt Maturities

Economic conditions and yield curves determine the general levels of interest rates and, therefore, the basic cost of borrowing, such as LIBOR or Prime Rate. In addition, risk or creditworthiness impact the costs of borrowing for individual firms. The specific types and costs of the various types of short-term credit arrangements are covered in greater detail in Chapter 8.

1. Cost

- Under normal financial market conditions, yield curves are upward-sloping, meaning that short-term interest rates are lower than long-term interest rates. This implies that there is generally a cost advantage to the use of short-term credit. There are several short-term financing sources, such as accounts payable and accruals, that have little or no implicit interest cost.

- Depending on interest rate cycles and the prevailing term structure of interest rates (yield curve), the firm may be able to lock in long-term, low-rate bank or institutional financing and fixed versus floating rate financing.

- A significant part of treasury management is the monitoring of interest rate cycles and the yield curve in order to make the proper decision on short-term versus long-term financing.

2. Risk: Borrowing on a short-term basis carries two types of risk that may be avoided in longer-term borrowing.

- The first risk is related to fluctuations in the market interest rate. Long-term borrowing on a fixed (or limited variable) rate basis locks in an interest cost, or at least provides a narrow range for fluctuation in the interest cost. If a firm borrows on a short-term basis, it will borrow at whatever the interest rate happens to be at that time. There is always a chance that interest rates may change dramatically. As discussed in Chapter 2, many firms utilize risk reduction techniques, such as interest rate caps, collars and floors, to reduce this type of risk.

- The second risk concerns the availability of funds. Borrowing on a long-term basis commits funds from the lender for a long period of time. If a firm relies heavily on short-term borrowing, there may come a time when the short-term funds may not be available due to a credit crunch or "flight to quality" on the part of the lenders. Also, the firm runs the risk that its credit quality will decline, thus endangering the future rollover of the credit arrangement. Firms may counter this risk by utilizing multi-year credit line commitments which guarantee the availability of funds over a longer term.

- Both of these risks are especially relevant for firms that rely on short-term borrowing for long-term uses. This is accomplished by rolling over short-term borrowing at each maturity to make it, in a sense, long-term borrowing. The relevant risk is that each time a rollover occurs, the firm faces whatever interest rate and availability conditions exist at the time of the rollover.

IV. Calculations and Examples

A. Cash Conversion Cycle

Given the following financial statements (in millions of dollars), determine the firm's cash conversion cycle.

Cash	$ 100	Accounts Payable	$ 150
Accounts Receivable	150	Notes Payable	100
Inventory	250	Long-Term Debt	350
Fixed Assets	500	Owners' Equity	400
Total Assets	$1,000	Total Liabilities and Equity	$1,000

Assume the firm has annual sales of $1,750 and cost of goods sold (COGS) equal to $1,095. Also assume that beginning inventory was $225. (All figures are in millions of dollars.)

Purchases   = Ending Inventory + COGS – Beginning Inventory

Purchases   = $250 + $1,095 – $225 = $1,120

Inventory Conversion Period   = (Ending Inventory/COGS) × 365
= ($250/$1,095) × 365 = 83.3 days

Receivables Conversion Period   = (Accounts Receivable/Sales) × 365
= ($150/$1,750) × 365 = 31.3 days

Payables Conversion Period   = (Accounts Payable/Purchases) × 365
= ($150/$1,120) × 365 = 48.9 days

Cash Conversion Cycle   = Inventory Conversion Period
+ Receivables Conversion Period
– Payables Conversion Period

Cash Conversion Cycle   = 83.3 days + 31.3 days – 48.9 days = 65.7 days

NOTE: In this calculation each of the periods is based on annualized information. When used for a shorter period (such as a quarter), the COGS, Sales, and Purchases figures must be adjusted to reflect data only for the quarter. Similarly, quarter-ending, rather than year-end information must be used for Inventory, Accounts Receivable and Accounts Payable. Finally, rather than multiplying by 365, the number of days in the quarter should be used.

B. NPV Cost of Cash Conversion Cycle

Using the information from the previous example, the firm must finance approximately 66 days of sales. Assuming a cost of capital of 12%, the NPV cost of the conversion cycle is:

NPV Cost   = 66 days × Average Daily Sales × (Cost of Capital)
= 66 × (1,750,000,000 / 365) × (.12)
= $37,972,603

This represents the cost of having to finance the net investment in inventory and accounts receivable, less accounts payable.

C. Cost of Not Taking Cash Discount

You are offered credit terms of 2/10, Net 90. Assuming your cost for short-term funds is 8%, should you take the discount?

Effective Cost of Discount $= i = d/(1-d) \times 365/(n-t)$
Where: $d = .02$, $n = 90$, and $t = 10$
Effective Cost of Discount $\quad = .02/(1-.02) \times 365/(90-10)$
$\qquad\qquad\qquad\qquad\qquad = .02/.98 \times 365/80 = .0931 = 9.31\%$

Compare the cost of not taking the discount to the short-term cost of capital or the opportunity cost for investing short-term funds. Here, the company should take the discount, as the cost of not taking the discount is 9.18% versus the firm's short-term borrowing costs of 8%. The firm would, therefore, borrow funds at 8% and take the discount. If, however, the firm's short-term cost of funds was 10%, it should not take the discount but pay the net amount on day 90. This would be less expensive than borrowing the funds at 10%.

D. Benefit of Cash Discount to Seller

From the seller's point of view, the benefit of offering a discount is receiving the funds earlier, while the cost is the discount given to the buyer in order to encourage early payment.

Assume that the seller has a cost of capital of 15%, the average credit sale is $100,000, and the offered terms are 3/10, Net 90.

The present value of receiving the discounted payment on day 10 is:

$\quad$ PV10 $= [\$100,000 \times (1 - .03)] / [1 + (10/365) \times .15] = \$96,603$

The present value of receiving the full payment on day 90 is:

$\quad$ PV90 $= [\$100,000] / [1 + (90/365) \times .15] = \$96,433$

$\quad$ Net Benefit $=$ PV10 $-$ PV90 $= \$96,603 - \$96,433 = \$170$

Thus, the seller is better off by $170 per payment if the buyer takes the discount and pays on day 10, rather than paying the full amount on day 90.

8 Short-Term Financial Management

I. Outline of the Chapter

A. Short-Term Investment Management
   1. Money Market Investments
      a. The Money Market
      b. Characteristics of Money Market Securities
      c. Types of Money Market Securities
   2. Managing the Investment Portfolio
      a. The Portfolio Management Process
      b. Yield Calculations
      c. The Term Structure of Interest Rates
      d. Tax-Based Strategies
   3. Hedging Uncertain Cash Flows
      a. Commodity Forward and Futures Contracts
      b. Financial Forward and Futures Contracts
      c. Interest Rate Swaps

B. Management of Short-Term Borrowing
   1. The Role of Short-Term Borrowing
      a. Planning Borrowing Requirements
      b. Steps to Successful Borrowing
      c. Preparing the Financing Proposal Package
   2. Borrowing from Commercial Banks
      a. Bank Credit Arrangements
      b. Unsecured Loans
      c. Secured Loans
      d. Loan Agreements

Chapter Checklists

A. Listing of Federal Treasury and Agency Obligations

B. Sample Listing of Typical Investment Guidelines

C. Accounting Principles for Swaps

D. Listing of Sample Loan-Term Sheet

Calculation and Examples

A. T-Bill Pricing and Yield Calculations

B. Tax-Exempt versus Taxable Yield Calculations

C. Yield Curve Examples

D. Average Effective Cost Calculation on Line of Credit

E. Effective Interest Cost for Commercial Paper Calculation

F. Credit Policy Evaluation Calculation

G. DSO (Days Sales Outstanding) Calculation

H. Forecasting Accounts Receivable Calculation

II. Introduction

The area of short-term financial management is often defined in terms of managing the key short-term assets and liabilities of a firm. If a firm is a net short-term investor, the management of short-term investments (most often referred to as marketable securities) is very important to the success of the firm. These assets generate interest income, provide a cushion against fluctuations in cash flows, and can provide a temporary store of funds for future capital investments, repayment of long-term loans, dividends, working capital build-up and/or acquisitions.

If a firm is a net short-term borrower, the most critical area of short-term financial management is management of the borrowing. This includes bank loans, lines of credit, letters of credit, commercial paper, and receivables and inventory-based borrowing. For many firms, short-term borrowing is an important permanent source for financing working capital requirements and provides interim financing between long-term debt or equity issues. In addition, unused short-term borrowing capacity serves as a source of backup liquidity.

The other component of short-term financial management encompasses the management of accounts receivable and accounts payable. In many companies, accounts payable are a major source of funds; similarly, many firms find that accounts receivable and inventory are the major working capital investments.

III. Coverage of Chapter Material

A. Short-Term Investment Management

- Short-term investments can serve as a source of liquidity for the corporation while earning a return.

- The marketable securities portfolio provides a cushion against unexpected, negative operating cash flows. It is a temporary store of funds to be used for future capital investments and/or acquisitions.

- For a firm with cyclical financing needs, this portfolio can provide a degree of insulation from the need to approach the capital markets during times of high interest rates.

- The main disadvantage of holding marketable securities is that their rate of return is generally lower than investments in other assets of the firm.

- The first step in managing a short-term investment portfolio is to establish investment objectives and management guidelines. In most firms, these investment policies need to be approved at the board of directors' level. Once such policies are in place, securities and management strategies can be chosen to meet the objectives.

- Some large and very creditworthy firms may be able to use their balance sheets to produce investment income by borrowing at attractive rates and then investing at higher rates. This is generally considered an investment strategy or speculation rather than a true working capital strategy, and it may require making riskier investments that may adversely affect the company's credit rating.

This section includes a discussion of appropriate types of securities for the short-term investment portfolio. Portfolio management includes strategies and security selection criteria to provide a desired yield and control the degree of risk. Also discussed are techniques for hedging risk in the short-term portfolio and how to set and maintain proper management controls and reporting standards.

1. **Money Market Investments:** The short-term investment portfolio is a major source of liquidity as well as a temporary store of value on which a return is earned. Short-term securities are traded in the money market. This section discusses the characteristics of money market securities, and the steps and considerations in establishing short-term investment policy, strategies and methods for managing portfolio risk.

a. **The Money Market:** This is an over-the-counter market for short-term securities conducted by telephone and other electronic means among borrowers, brokers, dealers and investors.

1) **Market Characteristics**

- The money market refers to the market for securities with less than one year remaining to maturity. However, most of the securities traded have maturities of 90 days or less.

- The market is very large and efficient with no single participant being large enough to affect prices. While the primary traders are located in the money center cities, such as New York, London, Tokyo, and Hong Kong, trading can occur wherever there is a telephone.

- The transaction agents are brokers, who match buyers and sellers, and dealers, who stand ready to buy for their own accounts at the bid price or to sell for their own accounts at the ask price.

- Brokers make their money primarily from the commission they charge, while dealers profit primarily from the spread between purchase and sale price.

- The large denomination of these transactions (a round lot is $1 million for many securities) helps to keep transaction costs small as a percentage of the total value of the securities.

2) Market Participants

- Although we generally think of the money market in terms of investment, it is important to realize that parties issuing the securities are essentially borrowing funds on a short-term basis. The largest borrower in the market is the U.S. Treasury. Other large borrowers are commercial banks, finance companies, industrial firms, utilities, and state and local governments.

- Investors in the market include many of the same entities that are borrowers with the exception of the U.S. Treasury. In recent years, individuals have become active investors in the market either through direct purchase of T-Bills and CDs, or indirectly through the purchase of mutual funds, which in turn buy T-Bills, Certificates of Deposit (CDs), etc.

- The Federal Reserve, through its Open Market Committee, is one of the largest participants. It attempts to control the money supply, and therefore short-term interest rates, through its purchase and sale of securities.

b. Characteristics of Money Market Securities: Money market securities are issued by borrowers who need funds and purchased by investors with excess liquid funds. In choosing securities, investors must be aware of their differing characteristics, and should keep in mind that the securities may need to be sold on short notice to meet cash flow or other funding needs.[1]

1) Liquidity: A liquid security is one that can be converted into cash easily and quickly at a known price and at a small transaction cost. The existence of a large, active secondary market is necessary for a security to be considered liquid.

2) Maturity: The maturity of money market securities ranges from overnight to one year. Securities with shorter maturities tend to be traded more actively and, therefore, have better liquidity. In making maturity decisions, investors consider the timing of their potential cash needs and/or their planning horizon.

3) Yield: The yield represents the expected return that the investor earns from holding the security. It is a function of the maturity, marketability, risk and taxability of the security. In addition, overall market and economic conditions will have a major impact on the general level of yields.

4) Taxability: The taxability of a security depends upon the issuer and the taxing agency.

- Securities issued by state and local governments, such as municipal bonds, are generally exempt from federal taxation. Some Federal Government securities, such as Treasuries, are exempt from state taxation.

- Taxability of foreign securities is a function of the tax treaties between the countries involved during the holding period of the security. Since tax laws change frequently, it is always advisable to check current tax codes.

5) Risk: The yield on securities is inversely related to the perceived risk. Two types of risk apply to money market securities.

- **Default Risk** is uncertainty that the required payments will be made at the maturity date. In general, only high-quality firms issue money market securities, so default risk is fairly low. These firms are usually rated in the top categories by a recognized rating agency. Firms may be able to obtain low-cost financing with the backing of a letter of credit provided by a bank or other financial intermediary (known as credit enhancement). In this case, the credit rating would be determined primarily by the financial strength of the institution providing the letter of credit.

- **Price Risk** is uncertainty over the price at which a security can be sold prior to maturity. This risk is a function of interest rates. An increase in rates will cause the price to fall. A decrease in the rates will cause the price to rise. Methods for managing price risk are discussed later in this section.

c. Types of Money Market Securities

- Money market securities are issued in the primary market either as discount securities (issued at less than face value with face value paid at maturity) or coupon-bearing securities (issued at face value with periodic interest payments and face value paid at maturity). After the initial issue, these securities may sell at a discount (below face value), at par (at face value), or at a premium (above face value) depending on general levels of interest rates and market conditions.

- Outstanding money market securities are typically quoted at discount interest rates with various conventions used to calculate the price and expected income at maturity. When considering securities whose yields are calculated according to different conventions, it is advisable to convert all of the yields to some common basis, such as a bond-equivalent yield or a taxable annualized yield. A further discussion of yields is provided later in this chapter.

U. S. Government and Agency Securities: The U. S. Government is the largest issuer of money market securities.

- These securities can be either Treasuries (direct obligations of the Federal Government) or Agencies (obligations of a federal agency and not direct obligations of the Federal Government). While most Agencies are not backed by the Government's full faith and credit, the Federal Government has historically taken actions necessary to prevent default on Agency securities.

- Most government securities are sold at auction on specified dates. A listing of the various U.S. Government treasury and agency obligations is provided at the end of this chapter.

- Treasury securities that trade in the money markets include T-Bills (discount securities issued in 13- and 26-week maturities on a regular schedule), T-Notes (coupon-bearing securities with an original maturity from two to ten years) and longer-term T-Bonds. All Treasuries are exempt from income tax at the state and local levels.

- Agency securities are issued by the Federal Home Loan Bank, the Federal National Mortgage Association (FNMA), the Government National Mortgage Association (GNMA), the Federal Home Loan Mortgage Corporation (FHLMC), the Bank for Cooperatives, the Federal Land Banks, and the Federal Intermediate Credit Banks.

- While many of these securities are issued with an original maturity of more than one year, they are actually traded on the secondary market as money market securities when they have less than one year remaining to maturity.

Financial Institution Obligations: Banks and other financial institutions issue negotiable Certificates of Deposit (CDs) to finance their short- and intermediate-term needs.

- CDs are generally coupon-bearing securities that pay interest at maturity.

- Banks create and sell Banker's Acceptances (BAs), which are discounted time drafts arising out of commercial transactions. These may be issued on either a fixed- or variable-rate basis, although a fixed rate is generally the norm.

Commercial Paper: This is an unsecured promissory discount note issued by a corporation (including bank holding companies) for a specified time period (from 2 days to 270 days due to SEC regulations).

- The largest commercial paper issuers place their paper directly with investors, while most issuers use commercial paper dealers to sell their paper.

- Most commercial paper is held to maturity.

Adjustable Rate Securities: Generally these refer to adjustable rate preferred stock, but certain CDs and municipal securities have adjustable rates.

- Adjustable rate preferred stock and auction rate preferred stock are long-term securities that have some of the features of money market securities. Since the rate is set at short periodic intervals, there is much less interest rate risk than would otherwise be present in preferred stock.

- Adjustable rate preferred stock also generally offers a tax advantage from the partial exclusion of dividends (70%) from federal corporate taxes if the stock is held for more than 46 days by another corporate entity. There are, however, some risks incurred in the auction process and in the marketability of the securities.

Eurodollar Securities: Eurodollar time deposits and Eurodollar CDs (Euro-CDs) are dollar-denominated investments outside the U.S., usually purchased from foreign banks or foreign branches of U.S. banks. These types of deposits may also be issued by banks in off-shore tax havens such as Nassau, Bahamas, or the Grand Cayman Islands.

- These time deposits are typically non-negotiable and are usually held to maturity.
- A secondary market is maintained in London for Eurodollar CDs.
- The yields on Euro-CDs are generally higher than those on domestic CDs to compensate for the higher risk associated with deposits outside the U.S., and also because of the lack of reserve requirements for dollar deposits held outside the U.S. and the wholesale nature of the market.

Money Market Mutual Funds: These investment pools are professionally managed portfolios of money market securities.

- Liquidity is provided by daily withdrawal privileges through wires or checks at the end-of-day net asset value.
- Money market mutual funds can provide the treasurer of a small corporation with a professionally-managed marketable securities portfolio at a low management cost. These funds can be useful to the treasurer of a large corporation by providing a minimum benchmark for judging investment performance.
- In most cases, these funds are open-ended (no fees to open the account or add funds), but may in some cases be closed-ended (fees are charged to open the account or to add funds). There may be different management fees or service charges depending on the investor's balance, level of activity, or services received.

Repurchase Agreements (Repos): A Repo is an agreement between a seller and a buyer, usually of U.S. Government securities, whereby the seller agrees to repurchase the securities at an agreed-upon price and, usually, at a stated time. It is widely used as a money market investment vehicle and as an instrument of the Federal Reserve's monetary policy.

- Repos are usually for very short terms, an overnight Repo being the most common.
- Depending on the underlying security involved (usually a T-Bill), the market value of the Repo may fluctuate. Since Repo arrangements are essentially collateral-type lending, and are "marked to market," the borrower may be required to post additional assets if the value of the underlying security falls.
- Marking to market involves adjusting the value of the underlying Repo security as interest rates change. Rising interest rates will cause the value of the security to drop, while falling interest rates will cause the value to rise. If the value of the security declines below a certain amount, the borrower must post additional assets (collateral) in order to protect the investor's position.
- Recent court rulings have raised some questions regarding the status of the collateral in the event of a failure of the bank or securities dealer. Investors must be cautious in executing Repos and related safekeeping agreements. Safekeeping of the documents involves a third party (usually the trust department of a bank) who takes legal possession of the securities in order to protect the position of the

investor. Many loan covenants specify safekeeping arrangements and/or custodial agent agreements relating to investments in Repos.

Other Short-Term Investments: Other investments may be suitable under some circumstances for a firm's money market portfolio. However, they generally tend to be riskier and less liquid than the standard money market investments detailed above.

- Many banks offer loan-participation agreements in which investors can invest in a portion of the bank's short-term loan portfolio or a portion of a specific loan.

- Another type of short-term investment is the financial future, which is used for hedging of interest risk on municipal securities close to maturity, and on corporate notes and bonds close to maturity. These financial futures are available from banks and various futures and commodity exchanges.

2. Managing the Investment Portfolio

- Managing the short-term investment portfolio requires information about the firm's investment policies, the characteristics of investment alternatives and the economic environment.

- Proper management of the short-term investment portfolio requires establishing and maintaining a set of objectives and guidelines to be used when selecting investment options under time constraints. The senior management of the firm, including the treasurer, must perform these tasks. A sample of typical investment guidelines is provided at the end of this chapter.

- Part of this investment policy includes a determination of the firm's preference for risk (or risk tolerance). This permits selection of securities with risk/return tradeoffs at the level of risk acceptable to senior management.

- The manager of the firm's money market portfolio should exercise caution before including speculative securities in a portfolio that is supposed to be a substitute for cash.

a. The Portfolio Management Process: This process should identify the firm's liquidity needs, establish an investment policy and culminate in the creation of an investment portfolio consistent with those needs.

1) Liquidity Needs: A firm's liquidity is measured by its ability to meet its obligations as they become due without causing financial distress.

- Identifying liquidity needs includes preparing a cash flow forecast, assessing unused borrowing capacity and determining the amount and duration of needs under different economic scenarios.

- An internal liquidity analysis typically goes well beyond the examination of liquidity ratios (see Chapter 10, Financial Planning and Analysis) used by analysts outside the firm.

- There is some disagreement about the need to determine a firm's liquidity needs. One school of thought holds that the firm's liquidity level should be planned in order to manage the overall financial health of the firm more properly. Short-term investments are viewed as substitutes for cash and as a cushion for possible cash flow shortages; therefore, the firm's management has a specific target in mind for the level of short-term investments.

- The more commonly utilized approach, however, has not been to plan specifically for a given level of short-term investments, but rather, to invest any excess funds the firm happens to have at any given time. This excess liquidity can occur for a variety of reasons but is not generally planned. For many firms, available sources of short-term borrowing more often provide needed access to funds or liquidity.

2) Investment Policy: An investment policy should be developed to help the firm select investments that meet the desired risk and return characteristics for the short-term portfolio.

- The investment policy statement includes investment portfolio objectives and any constraints, such as the type and maturity of eligible securities, the dealers or brokers to be used, the relative portfolio concentration allowed, reporting requirements and safekeeping requirements.

- The investment policy may include a reporting and monitoring procedure to assess portfolio performance with respect to the stated objectives. Generally, the portfolio's performance may be measured relative to money market mutual funds or some fund index published by an independent party.

3) Portfolio Construction and Revision: The planned size of the portfolio will be dictated by the liquidity needs identified for the firm.

- The actual size of the portfolio will vary depending on day-to-day cash flows and liquidity needs. The portfolio's overall risk and return criteria should be examined, as well as those of individual securities.

- Adequate information on changing cash flows and interest rates, acquired early in the day while the money markets are still active, is necessary to revise the portfolio to meet changing conditions.

b. Yield Calculations:[2] Yield calculations for short-term investments are usually made on a simple interest basis. The holding period yield is the yield for the time that a security is held. It is calculated as:

$$\text{Holding Period Yield} = \frac{\text{End-of-Period Cash Flow} - \text{Investment Amount}}{\text{Investment Amount}}$$

In this example, the end-of-period cash flow includes both the maturity value and interest payments (if any). Examples of the previous and following yield calculations are provided at the end of this chapter.

The money market yield and bond equivalent yield are more useful calculations for comparing investment alternatives. In both cases, they can be computed by annualizing the holding period yield. In the case of money market yields, the adjustment is to a 360-day year; for the bond equivalent yield, the adjustment is to a 365-day year.

$$\begin{matrix} \text{Money} \\ \text{Market} \\ \text{Yield} \end{matrix} = \begin{matrix} \text{Holding} \\ \text{Period} \\ \text{Yield} \end{matrix} \times \frac{360}{\text{Number of Days}}$$

$$\begin{matrix} \text{Bond} \\ \text{Equivalent} \\ \text{Yield} \end{matrix} = \begin{matrix} \text{Holding} \\ \text{Period} \\ \text{Yield} \end{matrix} \times \frac{365}{\text{Number of Days}}$$

There is a question of when to use 360 days versus 365 days in determining yield and cost calculations for various money market instruments. Generally for discount-type securities (T-Bills or commercial paper), 360 days is used for determining price and money market yield, but 365 days is used for bond-equivalent yield. Instruments such as bank CDs and BAs also use 360 in computing pricing and money market yield. Coupon-type instruments (T-Notes, T-Bonds, and municipal securities) generally use 365 days in their interest rate calculations.

1) Coupon Securities: For a coupon-bearing security, the end-of-period cash flow is the face value plus the total interest payment. The investment is either the face value (if purchased in the primary market when issued) or the total purchase price, including any accrued interest paid to the seller (if purchased on the secondary market).

2) Discount Securities: The end-of-period cash flow for a discount security is the face value. The purchase price is the face value minus the dollar discount for the remaining time to maturity. The effective yield for a discount security is higher than the quoted rate because the investment is less than the face value.

c. The Term Structure of Interest Rates: The term structure of interest rates is the relationship between yield and maturity for securities of the same degree of default risk. The theories and management approaches related to the term structure of interest rates are as follows:

- **Expectations Theory:** The pure expectations theory states that the expected yield from holding a sequence of short-term securities is the same as that from holding a long-term security. This theory only helps in determining the general shape of the yield curve, whether upward- or downward-sloping. Generally, if interest rates are "expected" to rise in the future, the yield curve will be upward-sloping; if interest rates are "expected" to fall in the future, the yield curve will be downward-sloping. There are other factors present, such as liquidity preference and supply and demand in the financial markets, that will determine the ultimate shape of the yield curve.

- **Liquidity Preference Theory:** The liquidity preference theory states that investors demand a premium to sacrifice liquidity. Higher yields can be earned by investing in longer-term securities versus shorter-term securities. When the liquidity preference theory is used in addition to the expectations theory, it generally results in the upward slope being increased (or downward slope decreased) as a result of investors' preferences for short-term investments versus long-term investments.

- **Riding the Yield Curve:** This strategy involves buying highly liquid and marketable securities such as T-Bills that mature on a day different from the day a payment is to be made. With such a strategy, the investor aims to take advantage of the current yield curve. There are two ways that this can be done (an example is provided at the end of this chapter):

  - **Normal Yield Curve/Long Maturity:** With a normal yield curve, longer-term securities offer higher yields. To take advantage of this, the firm purchases a security that matures at a time after a known cash need. At the time of sale, the security has a shorter maturity than it did when it was purchased. Unless interest rates have risen more than projected, the price of the security will be higher when it is sold than when it was purchased. The investor's yield is higher than it would have been with a security that matured the date cash was needed.

  - **Inverted Yield Curve/Short Maturity:** With an inverted yield curve, short-term securities offer higher yields. The investor buys a security that matures before the known cash needs, and reinvests the proceeds when it matures. As long as the yield curve does not shift, the investor earns higher rates by rolling over shorter-term investments than on an investment whose maturity occurred at the time cash was required.

d. Tax-Based Strategies: With the recent increase in the types of tax-exempt and other tax-favored securities, and the increased supply of these securities, tax-based strategies have taken on a more important role in the investment policies and strategies of many corporate and individual investors.

1) Tax-Exempt Securities: To decide between a tax-exempt security and a taxable security, an investor must compare their after-tax returns. Then, taking the comparative after-tax returns and other factors into consideration (including other alternatives) the investor can select the more advantageous security.

2) Other Tax-Favored Securities: Common stock (utilized in dividend capture programs), adjustable-rate preferred and auction-rate preferred stock are the most popular tax-favored securities due to the dividend exclusion available to corporations holding stock in other corporations. As with tax-exempt securities, a comparison of after-tax returns is a necessary step in deciding among alternative investments. It must be strongly emphasized, however, that a significant increase in risk is often inherent in these plans due to the highly variable nature of stock prices.

3. Hedging Uncertain Cash Flows: Two types of risks related to interest rate fluctuations can be managed through the use of forward or futures contracts. One is the price risk from the threat that interest rates will rise during the holding period, coupled with the need to sell a security at a loss prior to maturity to cover an unexpected cash need. The second is the uncertainty of the interest rate level in the future, when money is expected to be needed for investment.

a. Commodity Forward and Futures Contracts: The general forms of forward and futures contracts are presented here to provide the reader with background that may be useful in later discussions of specific financial forward and futures contracts.

- Commodity forward and futures contracts are obligations either to buy or sell a commodity at a set price at a specified time in the future. The contract includes a detailed description of the commodity, the price, the delivery location and the delivery time. Since either type of contract is a promise to perform, good faith money (usually placed in a margin account) is required to secure the promise.

1) Forward Contracts: A forward contract is a commitment either to sell (make delivery of) or to buy (take delivery of) a commodity at a set price at a specified time in the future. Financial forward contracts are generally available from large money-center banks.

- Forward contracts are agreements between the two sides of the transaction and, therefore, are very flexible with regard to time of delivery and amount.

- Most forward contracts are terminated by the delivery of the commodity at the specified date.

2) Futures Contracts: A futures contract is a standardized forward contract that is traded on an organized exchange. These exchanges are covered in detail in Chapter 2.

- The exchange performs a brokerage service in bringing the contract parties together. The exchange takes the opposite side of both contracts, so buyers and sellers do not have to meet. This also eliminates credit risk, because the exchange is the counterparty to both sides of the transaction.

- Most futures contracts are terminated by closing out the positions of the two parties, rather than by making or taking delivery of the commodity. The closing of the positions is accomplished by valuing them at the end of the contract and having one party pay cash to the other party equal to the differences in market positions. Holders of futures contracts have to mark to market by adjusting the collateral in the margin account on a daily basis.

3) Speculation versus Hedging

- The key to determining whether a particular transaction is speculation or hedging is to ascertain whether or not there is any underlying business risk involved. Transactions without such underlying risk are speculation rather than hedging.

- Forward and futures contracts can be used to hedge risk by arranging a set price for a commodity.

- For example, at planting time a farmer could arrange a selling price for a corn crop by using either a forward or futures contract. Once the contract is made, the farmer has eliminated the price risk by locking in a selling price.

- The same contracts could be used to speculate on the price of corn by a trader who had no corn; instead, the trader would plan to buy corn on the cash market at the delivery date. The trader who agreed to deliver under the contract would be speculating that the price of corn in the cash market would be less than the contract price. The speculative profit (or loss) would be the difference between the price paid in the cash market and the selling price stipulated in the contract.

- Treasurers must be careful in accounting for forward and future contracts. A discussion of current Financial Accounting Standards Board (FASB) and GAAP guidelines on accounting for hedging instruments is covered in the checklist section at the end of this chapter.

b. Financial Forward and Futures Contracts: Financial forward and futures contracts are the same as commodity contracts, with the commodities being a financial instrument, such as a T-Bill or a T-Bond.

1) Types of Contracts: Financial forward contracts can be arranged for any financial instrument agreeable to the two parties. A listing of the various types of financial futures contracts and the markets on which they are traded is provided at the end of this chapter.

- Financial futures contracts exist for T-Bills, T-Notes, T-Bonds, GNMA pass-throughs and Eurodollar time deposits.

- There are also futures contracts based on market indexes such as the S&P 500, the Municipal Bond Index and the Major Market Index.

- Financial forward contracts are usually offered by most major money-center banks, and futures contracts are typically traded on organized exchanges, such as the Chicago Mercantile Exchange.

- Forward rate agreements (FRAs) are contracts by which two parties agree on the interest rate to be paid at a future settlement date. The contract period is quoted as, for example, six against nine months, the interest rate for a three-month period commencing in six-months time. The principal amounts are agreed, but never exchanged, and the contracts are settled in cash; exposure is limited to the difference in interest rates between the agreed and actual rates at settlement. The majority of FRAs are based on Eurodollar rates, although others are available. A party that is seeking protection from a possible increase in rates would buy FRAs, while a party interested in protection from a possible decline in rates would sell FRAs.

2) Hedging Investment Risk: Financial futures and forwards can be used to hedge investment risk on portfolios of financial assets.

- A treasurer who holds a fixed-income security and is forced to sell it prior to maturity will receive a lower than anticipated price if interest rates rise. In order to hedge this risk, the treasurer could sell a futures contract to offset the risk on the security. If interest rates rise, there will be a gain on the futures contract which will at least partially offset the loss on the security.

- A treasurer who anticipates having funds to invest in the future could buy a futures contract to lock in an investment rate. In this scenario, the treasurer would buy a futures contract to purchase T-Bills at a specified price at some time in the future. If interest rates were to drop, and current investment rates were down, the treasurer would realize a gain on the futures contract to offset the lower than anticipated investment yield on future cash investments.

- If the gain on the futures contract exactly offsets the loss on the security, it is a perfect hedge. For a perfect hedge to occur, the delivery date of the futures contract must coincide with the sale (purchase) date of the security, and the interest rate on the futures contract must move in exactly the same direction as the rate on the security.

- If there is not a perfect hedge, potential losses or gains on the security will not be matched exactly to the potential gains or losses on the futures contract.

3) Hedging Borrowing Risk: A treasurer can hedge borrowing risk by using a futures contract to lock in a borrowing rate. If short-term variable rates rise, more interest will be paid on the loan, but the gain on the futures contract will (at least partially) offset the higher interest.

c. Interest Rate Swaps: An interest rate swap occurs when two parties agree to exchange interest obligations for a specified period of time or when the sale of a security is coupled with a simultaneous purchase of a similar security with a different coupon rate. This topic is covered in detail later in this chapter and also in Chapter 2.

B. Management of Short-Term Borrowing

- This section covers short-term corporate borrowing from commercial banks and other financing sources. These borrowing arrangements do not include deferred payments, such as accounts payable and accrued expenses.

- In addition to discussing sources of funds, this section addresses the method of calculating the effective cost of borrowing, so that comparisons can be made between alternative sources of funds and short-term investment options. A method for breaking down the cost of borrowing into individual components is also explained.

- Short-term borrowing can serve as an important source for financing working capital requirements and provides interim financing between long-term debt or equity issues.

- Unused short-term borrowing capacity serves as a source of backup liquidity. The treasurer generally has the responsibility for determining the amount and source of short-term financing and for maintaining relations with the providers of that financing.

1. The Role of Short-Term Borrowing: Short-term borrowing is an important source of financing for most firms for a number of reasons:

- Because short-term borrowing is more flexible and easier to initiate in small increments than longer-term financing, it is used in incremental amounts until refinancing for a longer term is economically justified.

- Short-term borrowing is used to provide a temporary source of financing to support a temporary need for funds, such as a seasonal peak in accounts receivable or a buildup in inventory.

- In addition, short-term borrowing generally carries a lower interest rate than long-term financing and is often used on a continuing basis as a source of lower cost debt. However, in times of distress, its availability and cost are not as reliable as long-term debt.

- That distress could be caused by any of the following: (1) deterioration of the borrowing firm's financial condition, (2) credit rationing on the part of the lenders, (3) change in bank lending policies, or (4) general reduction in the availability of credit in the economy.

- Another important consideration is the use of maturity matching for the firm's short-term debt. In general, this entails matching the maturity of the debt to specific financing needs of the firm. An example would be a firm that borrows to purchase inventory, then pays off the loan as the inventory is sold. The concept of maturity matching in long-term debt is discussed in greater detail in Chapter 4, Cost of Capital and Capital Structure.

- Short-term borrowing can carry either a fixed or variable interest rate. The choice is influenced by the spread between the fixed and variable rates, expected future changes in interest rates, and the effect of changes in interest rates on the firm's cash flows.

a. Planning Borrowing Requirements: Short-term borrowing is an important part of the overall strategic financial plan. Failure to incorporate short-term borrowing into long-range strategic planning may result in inappropriate levels or types of borrowing.

1) Overall Strategic Financial Plan: The firm's management must determine and plan for the level of debt, as well as the proper mix of debt among short-, intermediate- and long-term sources. The debt decision is very critical to the firm's continuing success.

2) Strategic Objectives of the Firm: The strategic objectives must be defined by management. They will determine future courses of action and will have an impact on borrowing requirements.

3) Short-Term Requirements: The use of short-term sources of funds will often be determined by the firm's type of business as well as its strategic objectives.

- Factors such as seasonality of sales, timing of collections and disbursements, and economic conditions and trends can affect both use and cost of short-term borrowing.

- In addition, many firms (and state and local governments) use short-term borrowing as a temporary source of funds until they can roll over such short-term obligations into a long-term bond, term loan or another form of long-term debt or equity.

b. Steps to Successful Borrowing: In order to implement a short-term borrowing plan successfully, a treasurer must understand the basic concept of debt, the lender's perspective and the credit process. In addition, a treasurer must be aware of the advantages and disadvantages of using short-term borrowing.

1) The Basic Concept of Debt: The use of debt is a common practice for most firms.

- From the borrower's point of view, the use of debt (also known as leverage) involves receiving funds today in return for the borrower's promise to repay the funds, plus interest, at some time in the future.

- This repayment is not necessarily linked to the ability of the firm to generate positive net income, but to its ability to generate free net cash flows. The repayment schedule is agreed upon by both the borrower and the lender before the loan is made.

- It is important to note that many factors are considered in determining the payment schedule for a loan. These include: anticipated cash flows and their timing, existing covenants in other agreements, financial strength, collateral, etc. The key point is that there exists a reasonable expectation by both the borrower and the lender that the repayment schedule will be met.

- If a firm is profitable, borrowing represents an attractive source of funds, as the payments are limited to principal and interest, and the profits after deducting the principal and interest expense can be distributed to the firm's owners.

- Debt use, however, carries the risk that the firm's cash flows may not always be sufficient to service the debt, raising the possibility of default or bankruptcy.

- Another consideration in borrowing funds is the intended use of the funds. A very common and important reason for borrowing is to pay expenses that become due when other funds are not available. In this case, it may be a receipts and disbursements timing problem or may be due to the seasonal need of the business.

- If the borrowed funds are used to purchase an asset or to buy a security, the major justification for the borrowing should be that the asset or other investment will help generate funds for repayment of the loan.

- Finally, it is important to consider the maturities of assets versus those of the liabilities funding those assets. Although matching the duration of the assets to the liabilities is a common practice, there are other approaches used by treasurers. These include both aggressive and conservative working capital strategies and are discussed in detail in Chapter 7.

2) The Lender and Credit Process: The relationship between the borrower and the lender is intended to be mutually beneficial to both parties.

- To the lender, the loan is an investment, with an expected return in the form of interest and fees. The lender wants to be certain that both the principal of the loan and the interest can be repaid by the borrower as agreed.

- To the borrower, the loan allows immediate access to funds that can be repaid in the future. The interest and fees paid represent the cost of using the funds. In the credit process, the borrower usually develops a business plan that demonstrates the firm's capability to repay the loan according to the terms of the loan agreement.

c. Preparing the Financing Proposal Package: This package is prepared by the borrower and usually includes a term sheet, outlining the proposed terms of the loan, financial statements of the firm to indicate its current financial condition, and a brief overview of the business plan. These items, usually accompanied by cash flow projections to demonstrate the firm's capability to repay the loan, help the lender evaluate the borrower and make a decision on the loan request. Based on this information, the bank prepares its version of the loan term sheet and submits it to the firm as a proposal.

2. Borrowing from Commercial Banks: Although the credit role of commercial banks has declined over the last two decades, they still represent the largest single source of financing for short-term corporate needs.

- For many small- to medium-size firms, banks are often the primary source of short-term credit. Banks may be the alternative lender selected by larger corporations unable to borrow in the commercial paper market.

- Traditionally, banks have viewed lending as a part of the overall banking relationship with a client.

- Treasurers must be concerned with problems relating to the capital adequacy of banks. Capital adequacy is a regulatory issue that deals with the level of equity that a bank must have relative to its loan and deposit base. Recently, the regulations in this area have changed dramatically as the Federal Reserve and other bank regulatory agencies have significantly tightened bank capital requirements, resulting in fewer funds available for loans.

- Banks with capital adequacy problems may be restricted by the Federal Reserve or other regulatory agencies in the types and amounts of loans they can grant. In addition, most of the bank regulatory agencies have mandated broad increases in the quality of loans in financial institutions' portfolios, further restricting bank lending.

a. Bank Credit Arrangements: Commercial banks make a wide variety of loans, from working capital loans for small businesses (with inventory and/or equipment as collateral) to unsecured bridge loans to support tender offers for acquisitions. Regardless of the purpose of the loan, commercial banks generally make loans based on an analysis of the borrower's overall financial condition. Because banks offer a wide variety of loan products, a lending arrangement tailored to the borrower's needs can usually be negotiated. Banks also provide a range of maturities for their lending arrangements: short-term, intermediate-term, and long-term. Although this chapter is primarily devoted to short-term financial management, several of the longer-term bank loan products will also be discussed.

1) Single Payment Loans

- This type of loan is usually granted for a short period of time for a specific purpose, with both interest and principal paid at maturity.

- Single payment loans may be either coupon loans (face value of the loan is advanced and face value plus interest is repaid at maturity) or discount loans (face value less interest is advanced and face value is repaid at maturity).

- Often, the interest rate is fixed for the term of a single payment loan. Frequently a single payment note is used as the vehicle for the actual borrowings against a line of credit.

2) Line of Credit

- This is an agreement to borrow up to a specified maximum during a year.

- When a line of credit is used to cover a seasonal or short-term financing need, a bank may require a clean-up period (a period of 30–60 days during which no loan is outstanding under the line) to ensure the seasonal nature of the credit. In essence, this is done to prove that the borrower is not using the loan as a permanent source of financing, but only as a seasonal source.

- A line of credit may be committed (the bank is obligated to provide financing up to the agreed limit if all credit conditions are met and none of the covenants are in violation) or uncommitted (the bank can unilaterally cancel the line at its discretion, at any time). Generally, committed lines of credit are multi-year revolving credit arrangements (discussed below).

- A line of credit may also be used to provide a backup to support commercial paper issuance.

- To provide a committed line of credit, banks usually require compensation for the line, either in the form of commitment fees or compensating balances, in addition to the interest charges on the amounts borrowed. These fees and/or balances may be based on either the full amount of the line or the unused portion.

- It is important to note that if the firm compensates the bank in some manner, the bank has a contractual obligation to fulfill the line of credit commitment. Even committed lines of credit, however, can be revoked if the borrowing firm undergoes "material adverse changes" in its financial or operating condition. In addition, most bank lines of credit require the borrower to "re-represent and re-warrant" the condition of the firm on a regular basis as required in the loan agreement. This action may be required at each rollover of the loan, at covenant compliance, or at any other period required by the lender. Essentially, this process requires the management of the firm to guarantee to the bank that nothing has changed in either the financial or operational condition of the firm that may have an impact on the loan and/or repayment.

- Most lines of credit provide for borrowing at variable interest rates tied to some base rate, such as the prime rate or the LIBOR. The rate paid on the loan is generally the rate base plus some premium required by the lender (i.e., LIBOR + 1%, or prime + 0.75%). There are other base rates available in the market, and they are discussed in more detail in Chapter 3, Capital Market Relations.

3) Revolving Credit Agreement (Revolvers)

- This is defined as a line of credit, or credit facility, extended to a business that is good for a stated period of time, but does not have a fixed repayment schedule.

The borrower may draw down the line at any time or repay it in full without penalty. The borrower usually pays a commitment fee that secures the line of credit and commits the bank to lend as long as specified conditions are met.

- This type of bank lending is similar to a line of credit, but the agreement extends for more than a year (usually 3–5 years). Frequently, a revolver can be converted into a term loan, or, in some cases, may start as a term loan and later convert into a revolver.

- Revolving credit agreements can be classified as long-term on the firm's balance sheet. Generally, this requires that there be more than one year remaining on the agreement at the time of the financial statements.

- Revolver pricing is similar to that of a line of credit with a commitment fee or balance requirement (usually based on the unused portion of the credit line) and variable interest rates. This type of arrangement uses the various base rates discussed above.

4) Term Loan

- A term loan is a loan with a fixed maturity, usually greater than one year, which is typically repaid in installments of both interest and principal (amortized). This type of loan may also be structured in a "bullet" form where the interest payments are made on a regular basis (usually quarterly), but the principal is not repaid until maturity.

- Frequently, a term loan is issued for a specific financing need such the purchase of a piece of equipment, building, or other facility. Interest is usually paid at periodic intervals (typically quarterly) and may be fixed or variable.

5) Letter of Credit (LC)

- This is a commitment from a bank or other financial institution stating that payment for a firm's liability will be made by the bank under specified conditions.

- A letter of credit allows a substitution of the bank's credit rating for the purchaser's and is also known as a "credit enhancement." There is an important distinction between a trade LC and a standby LC, which may be used to back up commercial paper issues.

  - Trade LCs are essentially linked to a specific transaction (or transactions) and serve as a means of financing and a guarantee of payment.

  - Standby LCs are essentially a backup form of credit for a firm issuing commercial paper, and are used to guarantee insurance liabilities or back up general credit terms. This type of LC indicates that a bank is willing to provide funding to the firm in the event the commercial paper issue cannot be rolled over when it matures. It may be used for companies that are perceived as a potential credit risk by creditors. If the customer does not pay, the supplier can draft (draw) on the LC for payment.

- Letters of credit can also be used for guaranteeing issues of Industrial Revenue Bonds (IRBs) or in lieu of cash deposits.

6) Banker's Acceptance (BA): This is a time draft issued for a commercial transaction (usually drawn on a documentary LC) and accepted by the bank. Acceptance by the issuing bank indicates that all of the conditions of the underlying LC have been met, and the bank is now making an unconditional promise to pay the stated amount at some date in the future. Firms holding BAs can either wait for the BA to mature or, if they need funds immediately, they can sell the BA at a discount to the bank or on the secondary market. The rate used to value (or discount) BAs is the rate paid on other short-term obligations of the bank, such as CDs. Though BAs are typically related to international trade due to its heavy reliance on documentary LCs, there is also a substantial market in domestic BAs. The issuance of domestic BAs is regulated by the Federal Reserve and other U.S. bank regulatory agencies.

7) Reverse Repurchase Agreement (Reverse Repo): This is the other side of a repurchase agreement. A firm with a security sells it to the bank with an agreement to buy it back in the future. It is essentially similar to a loan with the security offered as collateral.

b. Unsecured Loans: These loans are made on the general credit standing and financial strength of the borrower. The bank is in the same position as any other general creditor in case of default.

c. Secured Loans: These loans generally have a specific asset(s) pledged as collateral, but may include blanket liens on all assets of the borrowing company. In case of default, the lender has first claim on the assets as a potential source of repayment.

1) Collateralized Loans

- These are secured loans based primarily on the financial strength of the borrower, but where the risk of repayment is judged to be higher than acceptable for an unsecured loan.

- An asset is pledged as security for the loan, with a Uniform Commercial Code-1 (UCC-1) filing used to perfect the lien on the assets. Advances are made up to a percentage of the value of the collateral based on three factors: (1) the condition, (2) the liquidity and (3) the cost to dispose of the asset. The asset is viewed as a means to reduce losses in case of a default rather than as a repayment source. This topic is covered in detail in Chapter 3, Capital Market Relations.

2) Asset-Based Loans

- Asset-based loans are secured loans made primarily on the value of certain assets (usually receivables and inventory). Liquidation of the asset, such as collection of an account receivable or sale of inventory, may be viewed as the primary repayment source.

- The pricing of asset-based loans reflects both the higher credit risk of the borrower and the costs of closely monitoring the asset. Asset-based loans are usually revolving loans with maximum advances based on formulas of value on the eligible assets in question; typically, 75–85% for accounts receivable (higher rates are for quality short-term receivables) and 40–75% for inventories (higher rates are for liquid, commodity-type inventories). In dealing with asset-based loans, it is important to determine which assets will be considered eligible by the lender for backing the loan. For example, the following categories of assets may be considered ineligible (excluded) by a lender: accounts receivable older than 90 days, excessive receivables from one customer, receivables from related companies, work-in-process inventory, etc.

d. Loan Agreements

- A loan agreement is a contract between the borrower and the lender specifying all of the conditions and terms of the loan. It is important to understand that many of the provisions in these agreements are fully negotiable. Successful negotiation may significantly reduce the firm's cost of borrowing and increase its borrowing capacity.

- In addition to general terms (amount, interest rate, timing of repayments, etc.), there are usually many covenants, representations and warranties included in a loan agreement. A listing of common items included in a standard loan agreement is provided at the end of this chapter.

- The covenants may require the firm regularly to provide financial statements and other information to the lender or, perhaps, restrict the firm's future actions in order to protect the lender's interests (i.e., limit additional debt, dividend payments, limited sale of assets, or pledge of assets for another loan). Covenants may specify that a company is in violation if it is in default on any covenants of other loans (known as a "cross default").

- Representations and warranties are usually related to claims on the firm's assets, other outstanding lending agreements, validity of current financial statements, or any other item which may be considered material to the borrowing agreement. As stated earlier, many agreements require the company to re-represent and re-warrant on a regular basis. This is generally a significant reporting burden for firms with outstanding loan agreements.

- If the firm violates any of the covenants or makes false representations or warranties, the lender usually has the right to declare the loan in default and, therefore, immediately due and payable in full. In some cases, the management and/or directors of the firm may be held personally liable for misrepresentations of the financial condition of the firm.

e. Troubled Loans

- Even the most carefully planned borrowing arrangement can run into trouble when the borrower can no longer meet the original terms and conditions of the loan.

- In this case, the loan is usually turned over to the workout department of the bank to try to salvage the loan. As long as the bank feels that there is a chance to get repayment, it may be willing to work with the borrower to reschedule or restructure the loan.

- If the workout department feels that all alternatives have been exhausted, it will call the loan (i.e., principal plus unpaid interest is immediately due and payable) and try to collect the money owed. If the loan is a secured loan, the bank may seize any associated collateral. The collateral ordinarily would be sold, with the proceeds being applied to the loan balance.

- One downside of tight credit periods is that banks with a large number of troubled loans usually are less willing to "work" with troubled clients. Banks in this situation often prefer a quick resolution of troubled loans, even if it means receiving less than full value for the loan, because they may have many such loans in their portfolio. This may mean forcing a firm into bankruptcy rather than allowing it to work itself out of its problems over time.

f. Lender Liability: Banks must consider the issue of lender liability, which can occur when a bank causes serious financial consequences by prematurely pulling a loan from a firm. In such a case, the bank could be held liable for damages by other creditors or owners of the firm.

3. Non-Bank Sources of Funds

a. Internal Sources of Funds: Once a firm has identified its needs for funds, the financial manager should determine the extent to which the firm would be able to raise the funds internally rather than to borrow.

- Some internal sources include: net income, depreciation allowance (essentially a result of accounting conventions and the tax shield provided by accelerated depreciation), accelerating collection of accounts receivable, expanding accounts payable, reducing inventory levels, reducing expenses and selling assets.

- These sources may be especially attractive to smaller firms, which usually have limited access to low-cost sources of short-term funds.

b. Commercial Paper: This is an organization's (firm or bank holding company) unsecured note issued directly to the supplier of funds.

- While commercial paper was originally issued only by large firms, the expansion of the market has increased its use among smaller companies.

- Commercial paper is a discount loan with interest rate dependent upon the market and the credit rating assigned to an individual issuer by the rating agencies. Most commercial paper has a backup credit arrangement (backup line of credit or standby LC), either partial or full, covering the outstanding liabilities. The purpose of the LC is to pay off the paper if it cannot be rolled over or otherwise paid off at maturity. The paper may be sold directly to the investor or through dealers.

c. Commercial Finance Companies: These are private companies that make commercial loans.

- Originally, commercial finance companies concentrated primarily on asset-based loans to businesses that were too risky to get loans from commercial banks.

- In recent years, they have expanded their lending into a wide variety of loans and borrowers and are often in direct competition with banks providing both private placements and innovative types of loans.

d. Factoring: This is the sale of accounts receivable to a financial institution or another third party, known as the factor. In many cases, the receivables are sold without recourse, which means that the factor cannot come back to the company which sold the receivable in the event that it is uncollectible.

- Factoring can be the sale of a specific set of receivables, or it can be an ongoing arrangement. In the latter case, the factor essentially runs the clients credit operation and makes all credit acceptance and rejection decisions.

- The factoring can be maturity factoring (the payment is made on the average collection date of the receivables) or discount factoring (funds are advanced, at a discount from face value, prior to the average maturity date).

- Factoring is most common in clothing and apparel-related industries.

- Factoring of highly risky receivables may be done on a "with recourse" basis, allowing the factor to return the uncollectible receivables back to the selling company, or simply to subtract the amounts owed from future payments (advances).

e. Captive Finance Companies: These companies are usually wholly owned subsidiaries that provide financing for the parent company's products.

- Because their assets consist primarily of receivables, many have high credit ratings and are very active sellers of commercial paper.

- Originally they financed only the accounts receivable of their own parent companies or their distributors, but many have expanded to serve as general commercial finance companies.

f. Off-Balance-Sheet Financing: This is the use of financing arrangements that do not appear on the balance sheet. Off-balance-sheet financing is advantageous for two reasons:

1. Removing debt financing from the balance sheet improves leverage ratios and protects borrowing capacity.

2. Securitized financing with a specific source of repayment, such as accounts receivable, may command a better borrowing rate than financing based on the company's balance sheet.

Some of the more common types of off-balance-sheet financing are as follows:

- Leasing (covered in Chapter 12) is a potential source of long-term off-balance-sheet financing.

- On a short-term basis, inventory may be purchased, financed and stored by a third party. This is usually done on a consignment basis or may be set up as a supplier-managed replenishment system. Another option for financing inventory is to utilize a "paid-on-production" arrangement with suppliers, where the inventory is paid for as it is utilized on the production floor. These types of arrangements will be explained in greater detail in Chapter 13, Electronic Commerce.

- The contract price includes storage and financing costs. The purchaser pays the same price, or perhaps more, for the goods, but the inventory and the related financing do not appear on the balance sheet.

- The securitization of assets such as receivables may be considered a source of off-balance-sheet financing. Securitization is a financing technique in which a company issues securities backed by selected financial assets, in this case accounts receivable. Debt service for the securities is supported by the cash flow from these assets, and neither the financing nor the assets appear on the company's balance sheet.

g. Short-Term Euromarket Financing: As the trend toward globalization of financial markets continues, more and more firms are regularly raising short-term funds in the Eurodollar markets. For a U.S. firm, this involves borrowing dollars from a bank (or syndicate of banks) located outside the U.S. These markets provide financing in foreign currencies, or in "basket" currencies such as the European Currency Unit (ECU).

4. Comparing the Effective Cost of Loans:

- The cost of short-term borrowing alternatives must be calculated on a consistent, effective interest rate basis so comparisons can be made among them.

- By analyzing components of the borrowing costs, the borrower can better negotiate the terms of the agreement with the lender.

- The effective cost calculation includes all costs, including interest, commitment fees, loan origination fees and asset management costs for any collateral required (costs over and above normal costs of asset management).

a. Fixed- versus Variable-Rate Financing: The effective interest cost of fixed-rate financing can be calculated in advance of the financing.

- The cost of variable-rate financing can only be an estimate based on an assumption of interest rate levels during the loan period.

- Consistent interest rate assumptions are required to compare variable-rate alternatives, and sensitivity analysis is required to compare variable- and fixed-rate alternatives.

b. Single-Payment Loans: The effective bond equivalent yield for a single payment loan is calculated as:

$$i = \frac{\text{Total Financing Costs}}{\text{Loan Proceeds}} \times \frac{365}{\text{Term of Loan}}$$

- The total financing costs include interest payments, commitment fees, loan origination fees, opportunity costs of any required compensating balances and any asset management costs for the collateral.

- The loan proceeds are the total amount of usable funds from the loan arrangement. This is the face value less any up-front fees, such as commitment fees, loan origination fees or discount interest. Examples of these calculations are provided at the end of this chapter.

  1) Coupon Interest Loan: For a coupon interest loan, the interest is added on and paid at maturity. The interest payment plus any other financing costs are the total financing costs. The loan proceeds are the face value of the loan less any up-front fees.

  2) Discount Loan: For a discount loan, the interest is deducted from the face value of the loan (i.e., paid in advance).

- The total financing costs include the amount of the interest plus any other financing costs. The proceeds for a discount loan are less than the face value of the loan by the amount of the interest plus any other up-front fees.

- Because the interest is calculated on the face value, but the proceeds are less than the face value by at least the amount of the interest, the effective rate on a discount loan is higher than the stated interest rate.

c. Credit Line Borrowing: Calculation of the effective rate on a line of credit is complicated by three factors:

1. The interest rate is usually variable.

2. The amount of the borrowing varies over the term of the agreement.

3. The commitment fee (or balance requirements) may be a function of the amount of the line, or the unused portion of the line, and not necessarily based on the amount borrowed under the line.

The first factor is handled by sensitivity analysis and the second and third by calculating an average cost for the year based on borrowing plans.

Average Effective Cost:

- The amount of the credit line required or requested is determined by the maximum estimated cash flow requirement, the compensating balance arrangements (if any) and any additional amount (buffer) to cover unexpected cash needs or unusually high peak periods. In today's cash management environment where banks usually charge explicit fees for both credit and non-credit services, the use of compensating balances in loan agreements is rare.

- The total interest and commitment fees for the year are determined for the planned borrowing schedule. The average effective cost is calculated by dividing the total finance costs for the year by the average loan amount used over the year.

- Therefore, the average effective cost can be determined as:

$$i = \frac{\text{Total Financing Costs}}{\text{Average Usable Loan}}$$

Breakdown of Component Costs:

- The components of the average effective cost are: (1) the stated interest rate, (2) the compensating balance or commitment fees, and (3) the buffer.

- The cost of the buffer is determined by recalculating the average effective cost assuming there is no buffer. The difference between this cost and the average effective cost is the cost of the buffer.

- These component costs can be used to assess the benefit of attempting to change some of the terms or conditions of the line-of-credit arrangement.

- Another approach to the measurement of borrowing costs is to calculate a daily, monthly and year-to-date weighted cost of funds for each bank used for credit purposes. The figures for each bank can be compared with an average overall cost of credit arrangements in order to rank the relative cost of funds.

d. Commercial Paper (From the Borrower's Viewpoint):

- This is essentially a discounted single payment loan. As such, its proceeds are the face value less the discount, which includes the interest and any dealer's fees. Dealer's fees are normally not identified separately.

- Calculation of the total financing cost includes the cost of any backup credit arrangement (such as commitment fees on a bank line of credit) necessary to sell the paper or to receive the desired rating.

- The portion of the cost of the backup credit arrangement to be included in the calculation of the cost depends upon whether the paper will be rolled over at maturity (which would be twelve 30-day loans per annum) or whether it is a single issue of paper for 30 days on one occasion during the year.

- For example, if 30-day paper is being issued and is planned to be rolled over on a continuing basis, only one-twelfth of the backup credit costs is included in the calculation of the effective cost for the one 30-day period. A refinement of this calculation would include the cost of rating-agency fees.

- The formula for determining the cost of commercial paper is as follows (an example is provided at the end of this chapter):

Effective Annual Interest Cost for Commercial Paper

$= (\text{Total Issue Cost}/\text{Proceeds}) \times (365/M)$

Where:

Total Issue Cost	=	Interest + Dealer Cost + Backup Line Cost
Interest	=	FV – Proceeds
FV	=	Face Value
Proceeds	=	$FV \times (1 - [\text{Discount Rate} \times (M/360)])$
M	=	Days to Maturity
Dealer Cost	=	Annual Rate for Dealer Cost $\times FV \times (M/360)$
Backup Line Cost	=	Annual Rate for Backup Line $\times FV \times (M/360)$

Note: Due to the fact that commercial paper is issued on a discount basis, 360 days rather than 365 are used to determine the interest and proceeds from the issue.

Similarly, the dealer cost and the backup line cost are also calculated on a 360-day basis and prorated for the actual maturity of the issue. The effective annual interest cost is usually computed on a 365-day basis.

e. Asset-Based Loans: The effective rate for asset-based loans is calculated in the same manner as for other loans.

- The financing cost includes all costs associated with maintaining the collateral that would not be incurred were it not used as security. For example, costs of bonding an employee and securing a storage area are included in the cost of an asset-based loan on inventory that requires storage under a field warehouse arrangement.

- In calculating the cost of a factoring arrangement, one must recognize the unique credit analysis and collection activities performed by the factor. To the extent that a firm's credit department costs are reduced because the factor is performing that function, the estimated amount saved by the firm is deducted from the factor's fee.

f. Interest Rate Protection: Interest rate protection can be provided by several different methods.

- Many banks will provide, for a price, caps or upper limits on the interest rates that can be charged on a variable-rate loan. These caps may be used in conjunction with floors or lower limits on interest rates to provide a narrow range of interest rate movement through a collar arrangement. These items are covered in greater detail in Chapter 2, which also discusses other types of hybrid and synthetic instruments used to raise capital for companies.

- Another option that can have the same effect is to utilize the futures markets to provide interest rate hedging. This technique requires constant monitoring of the financial markets and readjustment of the futures portfolio.

- A third approach to interest rate protection is the use of interest rate swaps where two firms essentially swap payments on their respective loans. The purpose and use of swaps are outlined below:

1) Purpose of Interest Rate Swaps

- The purpose of an interest rate swap between two parties is usually for one party to convert a fixed-interest-rate payment into a variable-rate payment while the other party takes the opposite position.

- An interest rate swap involving different securities is done to change the cash flow stream or the price sensitivity of the portfolio.

2) Use of Swaps

- Interest rate swaps exist because of differences in financial markets and in debt issuers and investors, such as different risk premiums between markets. For example, the risk premium may be different in a short-term variable rate market from what it is in a long-term fixed-rate market.

- There may be an opportunity to sell a low-coupon security and simultaneously buy a similar high-coupon security, thus generating a larger interest cash flow while receiving a similar overall return. A swap is used to exploit these differences at a profit.

- Similarly, cross-currency interest rate swaps can be used to change the currency denomination of the borrowings. These types of swaps are also called CIRCUS (currency–interest rate–currency swap) and involve the exchange between two parties of fixed- and floating-rate obligations in different currencies. In effect, the swap is made either because the two parties have diametrically opposed opinions of currency and interest rate trends, or because they may simply have different future currency or business needs that need to be hedged.

- Treasurers must consider the risk involved if the counterparties to the swap arrangement fail to meet their obligations or if the swap must be unwound. One party may go bankrupt or fail to fulfill its obligations, or a treasurer may find that the firm would incur substantial losses if the swap were continued. In either case, the cost to unwind the transaction may be significant and may put the firm at risk.

- A treasurer needs to consider the accounting aspects of using swaps. A discussion of the accounting issues related to swaps is provided at the end of this chapter.

C. Receivables and Payables Management

- Accounts receivable and payable arise out of the normal sales and purchasing activities of a business. In most companies, receivables and payables represent, respectively, a significant inflow and outflow of funds that affect a treasurer's actions.

- Accounts payable are a major source of funds for many firms. Similarly, accounts receivable are the major working capital source (as well as the primary form of security for short-term borrowing) for the majority of smaller firms.

- The treasurer, however, is often not consulted until the marketing and purchasing decisions have already been made. Furthermore, marketing and purchasing personnel may not adequately understand and include financial considerations in their negotiations with customers and vendors.

- In most situations, the non-financial dimensions of the sales and purchasing decisions (competitive pricing, delivery, product quality, etc.) are most important. However, normal financial procedures and concepts should also play a role in these decisions.

1. Introduction to Credit and Collections

- In most firms, credit policy is viewed as a marketing tool, and decisions are dominated by the competitive situation and by marketing personnel. Collection and monitoring of the resulting accounts receivable are the function of the credit manager. The treasurer should interact with these and other appropriate individuals to forecast cash inflows from accounts receivable and to obtain the financing necessary to support the resulting level of accounts receivable.

- Understanding how decisions in other areas of the company affect the financial position will enhance the treasurer's ability to include financial considerations in policy decisions.
- Issues in credit and collections include: policy decisions, implementation of credit decisions, monitoring the accounts receivable for compliance with credit terms, financing the accounts receivable and forecasting the future level of accounts receivable.

a. Credit Policy Issues

- The first, most basic issue is whether or not the firm will sell on credit. Most frequently, in the United States, the norm is to sell on credit with specific terms determined by the competitive situation or regulatory decisions in a given industry.
- Additional factors must be considered, such as: the credit terms to be offered, the level of risk to be accepted, the related impact on sales, the type of collection effort to be pursued, market conditions, industry norms, individual corporate and management directives, how to monitor the receivables and how to finance the receivables.

1) Credit Policy Decisions

- Credit policy is a marketing tool that may increase sales from the level that would be achieved without offering credit (or with a less liberal credit policy). The buyer likes to buy on credit because it allows an inspection period, provides financing by delaying the payment, and may reduce the costs of obtaining other sources of financing.
- Policy decisions include:
  1. Whether to offer credit
  2. The credit terms to offer
  3. The level of risk to accept
  4. The procedures to monitor the receivables
  5. The sources to finance the receivables
  6. Collection procedures to follow if payment is not made on time
- These decisions are interrelated. For example, the decision to use stringent standards for the extension of credit may allow the use of less harsh collection procedures.
- In considering these decisions, the usual objective is to maximize the value of total net collections (defined as sales less bad debt costs, administrative and other costs, and time value costs from delayed receipt of funds). An example of this type of calculation is provided at the end of this chapter.

2) Credit Policy and the Cash Flow Timeline

- Credit sales lead to an extension of the cash inflow timeline. However, in most industries, credit is necessary to make the sale in the first place.

- The existence of accounts receivable simply recognizes that a sale has occurred but the associated cash flow has not yet been realized.

- The total time delay extends from the date the sale is generated until the date funds are available in a bank account of the firm. This cash flow timeline may be different from the actual time the account receivable is outstanding.

- On the front end, this may be due to a date different (for services rendered or goods sent) from the date the receivable is recorded. On the back end, there may be a difference between the date the payment is applied to the account receivable and the date funds availability is granted by the bank.

3) Policy and Management Implementation Issues

a) Implementation of Credit Policies: Once credit policies have been determined, procedures are established to implement them. Two important implementation procedures are: (1) determining whether a credit applicant meets the acceptable risk level and (2) initiating specific collection procedures. Different levels of management approval are often required depending on the dollar amount.

b) Monitoring and Revising Credit Policies: Procedures are established for monitoring the success of credit and collections activities in achieving the desired goals. If the results are unsatisfactory, the monitoring system should provide information to determine whether the policies or their implementation should be revised.

c) Credit Department Management: It is critical that the management of the firm be provided with written credit policies that define the role of the firm's credit department. Also, the appropriate structure for the credit department must be determined with respect to physical operation, internal reporting and level of authority.

b. Credit Terms: Whether a matter of convention, or formally stated on the invoice or contract, credit terms are effectively an adjustment to the sales price.

- Terms vary by industry, by markets within the same industry and by lines of business. In some cases they can be a sales incentive or a competitive advantage.

- There may also be legal issues to consider, such as Robinson-Patman or Fair Lending legislation which are discussed later in this chapter. Terms are often established through negotiation, with factors such as the size of the order and the relative bargaining strength of the two parties having an influence.

- Examples of common terms are: open account, revolving credit, seasonal dating and C.O.D. In addition, a vendor may require some type of credit enhancement, such as a promissory note or a letter of credit, before making a sale.

c. Evaluating Credit Applicants: Credit policy establishes the level of acceptable risk. Implementation of that policy requires assessing whether a credit applicant's risk profile is acceptable and establishing a credit limit.

1) Types of Evaluation Errors

- Two types of errors can be made in evaluating credit applicants: (1) extending credit to a substandard customer, thus incurring higher-than-anticipated collection, monitoring and/or bad debt costs; and (2) rejecting a good credit risk, thus losing the profits from a potentially good customer.

- In addition, there is the risk of extending either too much credit or insufficient credit to a given customer. Extending too much credit may encourage a customer to buy more than can be repaid, while granting insufficient credit may result in lost sales.

- The objective in managing receivables is to minimize the overall level of all these risks. This is a difficult process because both customers and standards change over time, and reducing one type of risk generally results in increasing the other. For many credit managers, it is a trial-and-error process to determine the best credit evaluation strategy.

2) Credit Information Sources: To make credit decisions, a manager obtains information from internal sources, credit agencies (such as Dun & Bradstreet), credit references (such as present suppliers and banks) and directly from the applicant (in the form of credit applications, financial statements, and face-to-face customer visits).

3) Analysis of Information: Credit information can be analyzed qualitatively or quantitatively.

- Qualitative credit analysis may include classifying the information in convenient categories (sometimes called the five Cs of credit: character, capacity, capital, collateral and conditions) for judgmental analysis.

- Quantitative credit analysis could include financial statement analysis or a credit scoring system. A credit scoring system is a systematic, quantitative combining of credit information in a single index that helps discriminate between good and bad credit risks.

- These types of models are used extensively in consumer credit and are beginning to gain wider acceptance for use in corporate credit analysis.

d. Financing Related to Accounts Receivable (A/R): The funds necessary to support credit and collections can be obtained from the firm's general financial sources or from specific direct or indirect sources.

1) Direct Financing: In direct financing of receivables, the selling firm retains primary control over all aspects of credit and collections and obtains the financing necessary to support the receivables. Financing may be by a specific pledge of receivables on a secured loan or by the sale of receivables to a captive finance company or to another lender.

2) Indirect Financing: In indirect financing, the firm obtains outside financing and usually surrenders at least some control over credit and collections. There are several types of indirect financing:

a) Third-Party Tie-In: Credit information is collected by the seller and forwarded to a financial institution. The credit decision is made and the receivables are carried by the financial institution.

b) Factoring: The factor performs all the credit functions of the firm and will, on a discounted basis, advance funds upon an agreed date (see the section on Short-Term Borrowing earlier in this chapter).

c) Collection Agencies: The receivables may be collected for a fee or be purchased at a substantial discount.

d) Private Label Financing: This is similar to third-party tie-ins and factoring. A third party performs the firm's entire credit operation and carries the receivables. The operation is conducted so that the company appears to be running its own credit and collections.

e) Working Capital Financing: This is obtained for general corporate purposes (i.e., accounts receivable) on the general strength of the balance sheet.

e. Legal Issues: Many legal issues impact the credit decision.

- The primary concern is that discriminatory pricing and terms may be in violation of the Robinson-Patman Act, which prohibits different terms to customers unless they can be cost-justified.

- In addition, the credit manager must contend with laws covering usury and consumer and commercial credit, as well as with customers undergoing bankruptcy or reorganization.

- The major act relating to consumers is the Fair Credit Reporting Act (1971), and the principal act on commercial transactions is the Fair Credit Billing Act (1975).

2. Managing Credit Policy and Receivables: Once credit policies have been established or initiated, proper credit management and consideration of policy changes will each influence the amount of funds tied up in accounts receivable.

a. Collection Procedures: These are the systematic actions taken by a seller to encourage payment according to the agreed-upon credit terms.

- The procedures employed can have a major effect on the time it takes to receive the cash inflow from a sale.

- It is important to realize that, in most cases, a firm will be dealing with its customers on an ongoing basis. The desire to collect owed money quickly must be tempered by the consideration of future sales to the customer.

- Overly aggressive collection practices may force customers to purchase from other suppliers, but overly permissive practices may result in excessive bad-debt loss.

- There is a definite trade-off that must be considered in establishing and maintaining collection procedures.

1) Objective:

- The goal of collection procedures is the same as that of overall credit policy: to maximize the value of the total collection cash flows, not merely to minimize bad debts.

- Consideration must be given to the trade-off between the favorable impact on the profitability of sales and the expense of administrative, time value and other costs of bad debts.

- Another consideration is the influence of collection practices on future sales.

2) Billing: This is the initiation of the collection portion of the cash flow timeline. Prompt, correct billing is the first step in effective collection.

3) Enforcement of Terms: The primary function of collection procedures is to enforce the terms of sale properly. The steps include: determining when a payment is considered late, communicating this to customers, following up with direct collection actions, and initiating legal actions such as: referring the account for collection to a collection agency or having an attorney file suit against the debtor.

b. Monitoring Accounts Receivable: Proper monitoring of accounts receivable is necessary to:

1. Ensure that the firm is employing sound collection procedures
2. Determine how well customers are adhering to the intended terms
3. Make certain that the credit function is contributing to the financial objectives of the firm
4. Ensure that the receivables portfolio is liquid and that the risks being taken by the credit department are commensurate with the firm's profitability goals
5. Alert management to developing trouble.

Monitoring occurs on two levels: individual accounts and the aggregate level of accounts receivable.

1) Individual Accounts: Each account should be monitored to ensure that customers adhere to the credit terms and to determine when to initiate the next collection procedure. Monitoring procedures include preparing individual customer aging schedules (a listing of the amounts unpaid from prior reporting periods for each customer), calculating the average collection time (a weighted average of the number of days from the invoice date to the date of posting to accounts receivable) and flagging past-due or over-limit accounts for action. Frequently, this information is automatically generated by accounts receivable systems based on historical payment data.

2) Aggregate Level of Accounts Receivable: The firm must monitor the aggregate level of accounts receivable to:

1. Identify potential problems in its collection practices
2. Identify a widespread shift in payment patterns by customers
3. Assist in forecasting future financing requirements

- Effective receivables monitoring provides negative signals when collection times slow down, positive signals when they speed up and neutral signals when they remain stable.

- Aging schedules and average days outstanding (ADO) (total receivables divided by average daily credit sales) are both sensitive to sales patterns (possibly related to product and customer mix) as well as to changes in collection times. ADO is also known as days sales outstanding (DSO) and average collection period (ACP).

- Methods such as the payments pattern analysis usually offer a better approach to the analysis of the aggregate quality of receivables than do the more traditional measures discussed above.

- This approach examines the receipt of payments relative to the initial sale date (i.e., the percentage of a month's sales collected in the same month, one month later, two months later, etc.). These percentages are referred to as cash flow fractions.

- Seasonal sales patterns or changing sales levels will not affect the viability of this approach in monitoring the overall quality of the accounts receivable.

- Another approach to monitoring the quality of a firm's receivables is to use the Last-In First-Out (LIFO) DSO method. This approach differs significantly from the traditional calculation of DSO or ACP which use the average level of sales over a period. The LIFO DSO method assigns sales days outstanding in 30-day increments to end-of-period accounts receivable by subtracting current and prior months' sales in successive 30-day layers until the accounts receivable balance is netted to zero. This method provides a more precise measure of the quality of accounts receivable than the traditional calculation of DSO.[3]

c. Forecasting Accounts Receivable

- There is a difference between forecasting and monitoring accounts receivable. While some of the approaches may seem similar, monitoring examines past sales to see if payments are being made on time.

- Forecasting tries to predict both the collections from and the ending level of accounts receivable so that the firm can determine the amount of financing required to support the credit function. Another function of forecasting is estimating the firm's future financial condition, given some new sales level.

- A popular method used in this type of forecasting is the percent of sales approach. This is outlined and examples are provided in Chapter 11.

- The first step in percent of sales forecasting is to estimate sales for the period under consideration.

- Assuming that receivables are a stable percentage of sales, the level of receivables for the future period can be estimated. This is acceptable for long-range forecasts for firms with steady or slowly growing sales and a stable collection experience.

- Using receivable balance fractions is useful for creating forecasts for firms with seasonal or other fluctuations in sales, or with changing collection patterns.[4]
- Firms may utilize distribution analysis for forecasting receivables. This process involves tracking a batch of invoices for a set of customers and determining the general distribution of payment receipts. This type of analysis generally works best for high volumes of low-cost items.

d. Evaluating Credit Policy Alternatives: In evaluating its alternatives, the firm should identify the value of the cash flow pattern associated with each. A planning or evaluation horizon is chosen for comparing the value of alternatives. An example of this type of evaluation is provided at the end of this chapter.

1) Relevant Cash Flows: Costs and benefits are represented by cash flows with the appropriate sign. Some of the cash flows considered are: the invoiced amount, credit evaluation costs, collection costs, administrative costs, sales support costs (such as inventory or variable overhead costs) and bad debts. The cash flows vary in ease of measurement.

2) Timing and Uncertainty of Cash Flows: The timing of cash flows is important for determining time value costs. Uncertainty affects the appropriate opportunity cost rate to be used in determining the time value costs. Opportunity cost rate is the price or rate of return that the best alternative course of action would provide. The uncertainty may be either in the amount of the cash flow or in its timing.

3) Cash Flow Timeline and Present Values: Once the amount and timing of the cash flows have been estimated and the appropriate opportunity cost rate has been chosen, the present value of each alternative is calculated. A common evaluation date, such as the date of the sale, is used as an anchor for the present value of each.

3. Management of Payables and Accruals: Accounts payable and accrued expenses arise from delayed payments.

- Accounts payable come from the purchase of materials on credit. Accrued expenses come from the use of other production inputs, such as labor, raw materials and administrative costs, for which the payment is delayed.
- The total amount of financing provided by these sources is a function of the level of activity, over which the financial manager may have little influence, and the length of the time deferral on the payment.

a. Spontaneous Sources of Financing:

- Payables and accruals, generated through the normal operating activities of a firm, spontaneously rise and fall with the level of sales.
- As the amount of materials and inventory used in production increases or inventories increase, the financing provided by payables and accruals increases in the short term.

- This reduces the need for external financing as long as the inventory holding period does not substantially exceed payment terms.

b. Accounts Payable Decisions: These decisions include: specifying the credit terms (where negotiation with the seller or vendor is possible) and determining when to pay (when multiple payment options exist).

1) Negotiating Payment Terms: If the buyer is an important customer, the seller may be willing to negotiate payment terms. The terms may be affected by the quantity or frequency of purchase and the form of payment (e.g., electronic versus paper check).

2) Payment Options: Some payment terms contain options for different payment amounts (discounts) conditional upon when the payment is made.

- Typical discount terms might be: 2/10, net 30 (a 2% discount may be taken if payment is made in 10 days, otherwise the full amount is due in 30 days).

- The payor should take the payment option that minimizes the net present value cost of the payment. Any direct and indirect penalty costs that may result from delaying the payables beyond the due date should be considered.

- Direct penalty costs include explicit charges for delayed payment. Indirect penalty costs include damaging the firm's credit rating, damaging supplier relationships and employee time and effort in managing the past-due payables problem.

- Many small companies may have no choice other than taking the credit terms offered as they have no access to other sources of capital.

c. Accrued Expenses: These expenses are a function of the payment deferral period and the level of activity.

- For a given level of activity, the longer the deferral period (say, a monthly payroll period instead of a two-week payroll period) the larger the amount of financing provided.

- The present value benefit from deferral is compared to the costs of deferral, which may be intangible, such as employee relations.

d. Effect on Liquidity: A longer deferral time for payables and accruals results in:

1. A larger amount of spontaneous financing

2. A reduction in the external need for capital to provide liquidity

3. An extension of the time horizon of the cash forecast.

IV. Chapter Checklists

A. Listing of Federal Treasury and Agency Obligations[5]

Government Securities (Treasuries):

All treasuries are backed by the full faith and credit of the U.S. Government and most new issues are in "book-entry" form, existing as computer entries only, with no paper securities issued. Book-entry obligations are transferable only pursuant to regulations prescribed by the Secretary of the Treasury.

Treasury Bill: A "risk-free" U.S. Government security issued with a maturity between 91 days and one year. The bills are issued at a discount and sold to the public each week. The securities yield a return based upon the holding period rather than a stated amount of interest. They are redeemable in denominations between $10,000 and $1 million.

Treasury Note: A "risk-free" coupon-bearing U.S. Government security which matures between one and 10 years. It has a fixed rate of interest paid semiannually and can trade at a premium or discount.

Treasury Bond: A "risk free" coupon-bearing, long-term U.S. Government security which matures between five and 35 years. The bonds have a fixed rate of interest paid semiannually and can trade at a premium or discount. They have face values between $1,000 and $1 million.

Treasury STRIPS: Since October 1984, new issues of Treasury marketable securities maturing in 10 years or more may be "stripped" (i.e., the coupons and principal are separated), and the components may be traded in book-entry form under the Treasury STRIPS (Separate Trading of Registered Interest and Principal Securities) program. Reconstituting STRIPS components into the original note or bond is also permitted.

Government Agency and Government-Sponsored Enterprise Securities:

Export-Import Bank (Eximbank): This organization provides financing and grants loans for exporting and importing businesses and provides insurance to overseas companies. Minimum $5,000.

Farm Credit System: The Farm Credit System is a cooperatively owned nationwide system of banks and associations that provides mortgage loans, short- and intermediate-term credit and related services to farmers, ranchers, producers, or harvesters of aquatic products, rural homeowners and agricultural and rural cooperatives. The Farm Credit System issues both notes and bonds to finance its operations. These items are not guaranteed by the full faith and credit of the U.S. Government.

Federal Financing Bank (FFB): This government enterprise is under the general supervision of the Secretary of the Treasury and is authorized to purchase any obligation that is issued, sold or guaranteed by a federal agency. The FFB finances its operations by issuing obligations to both the public and the Secretary of the Treasury, and these obligations are backed by the full faith and credit of the U.S. Government.

Federal Home Loan Mortgage Corporation (FHLMC or Freddie Mac): This is a government-sponsored enterprise which was established to increase the availability of mortgage credit for residential housing, primarily through developing and maintaining an active, nationwide secondary market in conventional residential mortgages. Freddie Mac accomplishes this mission by purchasing residential mortgages from individual lenders, grouping the purchased mortgages into pools, and subsequently selling mortgage-backed pass-through securities backed by such mortgages. These obligations are not backed by the full faith and credit of the U.S. Government.

Federal National Mortgage Association (FNMA or Fannie Mae): This is a private corporation that issues fixed-income mortgage-backed securities. The mortgages are purchased from banks, insurance companies, mortgage companies, savings and loan associations, and trust companies. FNMA issues short-term notes and debentures which are not backed by the full faith and credit of the U.S. Government.

Government National Mortgage Association (GNMA or Ginnie Mae): This is a U.S. Government corporation within the Department of Housing and Urban Development (HUD) which issues mortgage-backed securities backed by the full faith and credit of the U.S. Government.

Small Business Association (SBA): Issues tax-exempt bonds (state and local) to help finance its lending programs. This organization grants loans or buys convertible debentures or stocks in small businesses, and it also provides counseling services. To qualify, an organization must have net income for the last two years of $250,000, net worth of less than $2.5 million, and assets of less than $5 million. These obligations are backed by the full faith and credit of the U.S. Government.

B.   Sample Listing of Typical Investment Guidelines[6]

This is a sample investment policy provided by the Treasury Management Association for the hypothetical XYZ Corporation. It is provided only as a sample, not as a recommendation or endorsement.

Short-Term Investment Policy

The Chief Financial Officer (CFO), Treasurer and any Assistant Treasurer are authorized to invest surplus cash of the XYZ Company in approved money market instruments for short-term periods under the guidelines shown below. "Surplus cash" is defined as cash in the XYZ Company's Treasurer's Accounts which is not required at that point in time to maintain adequate bank balances or to meet outstanding financial obligations.

Investment Objectives

The primary objectives for investing in interest-bearing instruments are safety and liquidity. The secondary consideration is yield.

Approved Investments

Investments are to be made only in the name of the XYZ Company. Investments must have a maturity of 45 days or less, consistent with projected cash needs. Investments are to be made only through approved banks and through recognized dealers whose Commercial Paper is rated A-1, P-1. Approved banks are defined as domestic banks with a minimum rating of B by Keefe, Bruyette and Woods. Specifically, investments are to be made only in the following instruments:

1.   United States Treasury Securities
2.   Financial Agency Securities other than Federal Farm Credit Debentures
3.   Repurchase Agreements against above-listed securities. The securities backing the agreement must be valued at market and must be at least 100% of the amount of the Repurchase Agreement.

4. Commercial Paper with rating of A-1, P-1
5. Bankers' Acceptances written by approved banks
6. Certificates of Deposit issued by approved banks

Investment Restrictions

Investments at any point in time are restricted to a limit of $10 million in any one bank, and a limit of $5 million in any one Commercial Paper instrument or in any one bank's Certificate of Deposit. Only the following banks are approved for the above investment limits: Bank ABC, Bank DEF, Bank LMN, Bank QRS, and Bank XYZ. All other approved banks are restricted to investments of less than $5 million.

Investment Safekeeping

All Repurchase Agreements can be place in safekeeping with the respective investment institutions. All investments which involve the direct purchase from a non-bank dealer of an obligation will be delivered to the company, or to any of the following: Bank ABC, Bank DEF, Bank LMN, Bank QRS, or Bank XYZ for safekeeping, or settled by direct book entries.

Responsibility

Implementation of this investment policy and day-to-day monitoring is the responsibility of the XYZ Company's Treasurer.

C. Accounting Principles for Swaps[7]

The following is an excerpt from a 1994 Government Accounting Office (GAO) position paper on financial derivatives.

"Generally Acceptable Accounting Principles (GAAP) are not adequate to ensure reliable and consistent financial reporting of derivatives activities. In particular, accounting rules for hedging activities are incomplete and inconsistent. Thus, investors, market participants, and regulators may lack reliable information on which to base investment and business decisions and regulatory actions. In the absence of accounting rules for certain derivatives, accounting practices of derivatives market participants have been shaped by common industry practice and the adaptation of existing rules for similar products. This approach to accounting for derivatives is likely to result in inappropriate and inconsistent financial reporting of derivatives activities, especially reporting of hedging activities by end-users.

"To address concerns about the extent and nature of the use of derivatives and other financial instruments, the Financial Accounting Standards Board (FASB) issued two disclosure standards. These standards require disclosure of certain risks involved in holding financial instruments and the fair value of these instruments. Because of the limitations of the existing standards, FASB recently proposed a third standard, which is intended to require more specific and comprehensive disclosures about derivatives activities. This proposed standard is an improvement over existing disclosure requirements. However, additional disclosures would provide financial statement users a more complete understanding of derivatives activities. While disclosure does provide important information about derivatives activities and associated risks, it is no substitute for accounting standards that promote reliable and consistent financial reporting.

"FASB recognizes the need for comprehensive accounting standards for derivatives and other financial instruments. FASB began work in 1986 to provide comprehensive accounting standards for the recognition and measurement of these instruments and has made progress in developing standards for certain financial instruments. However, progress on the development of proposed standards for derivatives has been slow, in part, because of the complexity and diversity of some derivative products and particularly because of controversy over how to account for products used for hedging purposes. FASB has been unable to reach agreement on basic accounting questions that must be resolved before meaningful progress can be made to develop accounting rules for derivatives.

"FASB has discussed market value account as a means to resolve many of the derivatives hedge accounting issues it faces. While GAO believes that market value accounting is ultimately the best solution to accounting for all financial instruments, including derivatives, GAO recognizes that the adoption of a new accounting model such as this is likely to take some time. Because time is critical for providing authoritative accounting rules for derivatives, it may not be feasible to strive toward a comprehensive market value accounting in the short-term. However, market value accounting should be FASB's ultimate objective."

Current FASB Rulings Concerning Swaps

While there have been no specific FASB rulings concerning the accounting for swap transactions, these arrangements have been covered in other rulings. The primary ruling is FAS 105, which requires full disclosure about financial instruments with off-balance-sheet risk and concentrations of credit risk. This would include disclosure of all interest rate and currency swaps that would materially affect the firm's financial statements and risk profile. FAS 107, which concerns the determination and disclosure of the fair market value of financial instruments held by a corporation, may also have some impact on the accounting for swap arrangements. Finally, the Emerging Issues Task Force (EITF) of the FASB has issued several publications on these topics including: Foreign Currency Swaps (EITF:86-25), Foreign Debt-for-Equity Swaps (EITF:87-12), and Interest Rate Swap Transactions (EITF:84-36 and EITF: 88-8).[8]

D. Sample Loan Term Sheet

The following listing of terms in a sample loan agreement is provided as a basic guideline for the reader. Actual term sheets will vary significantly from bank to bank. The term sheet is generally accompanied by a letter summarizing the bank's willingness to lend to the firm according the terms outlined.

Parties: This portion of the term sheet names the parties to the loan. The borrower, agent, and lender(s) are identified.

The Credit Facility: This portion of the term sheet covers the following items:

- **Closing Date:** This is the final possible ("no later than") closing date for the loan agreement.

- **Commitment Amount:** This is the maximum amount of the loan to be provided to the borrower. It usually includes all loans under the agreement, including letters of credit.

- **Facilities:** This section outlines the specific facilities (loans and/or letters of credit) or lending that will be provided to the borrower. The total of each of these facilities will equal the total commitment amount listed previously.

- **Availability:** This section outlines any availability restrictions on the facilities such as borrowing base as a percentage of accounts receivables and/or inventory.

- **Commitment Termination Date:** This is the normal termination date of the loan agreement, often expressed as an anniversary of the closing date (i.e., three years or five years).

- **Use of Proceeds:** This section outlines the primary use for the funds borrowed.

Common Terms: This portion of the term sheet covers the following:

- **Interest Rate:** This section specifies the interest rate, including the base rate to be used, and the spread or premium above the base rate. The interest rate may also fluctuate based on usage of the line, type of security, or on the firm's performance on key financial ratios.

- **Interest Payment Date:** This section states the timing or due dates of payments on the loan, which may vary depending on the base rate used.

- **Prepayments:** This section lists the optional (at the borrower's discretion) prepayment terms and any penalties involved. It also specifies certain mandatory prepayment terms, such as change of control of the firm or in the event of default.

- **Letter of Credit Fee:** This section states any charges for documentary and/or standby letters of credit issued under the credit facility.

- **Commitment Fee:** This section outlines the cost of any commitment fees on the loan and the basis for the fees (i.e., on the unused portion or on the total line).

- **Security:** This section details the security required for the loan agreement. The security may include: accounts receivable, inventory, marketable securities, or plant and equipment.

- **Guarantees:** This section lists any guarantees required on the loan. These guarantees may be required from a parent corporation, its subsidiaries, or in the case of smaller companies, personal guarantees of owners and/or managers.

- **Conditions Precedent:** This section lists the conditions that must be satisfied prior to the granting of the loan agreement. This list may include the following items:
  - Delivery of satisfactory credit, security, guarantee and other documentation
  - Termination or modification of existing debt covenants
  - Listing of commitments to other lenders
  - All liens on secured assets shall be perfected
  - No material adverse changes
  - Disclosure of any pending and threatened litigation
  - Payment of all costs, fees and expenses

- **Representations and Warranties:** This section outlines the required representations and warranties for the loan agreement.

- **Negative Covenants:** This section lists the restrictions on the actions of the borrower required to remain in good standing on the credit agreement. These may include the following:
  - Restrictions on additional debt or contingent liabilities
  - Restrictions on payment of dividends unless certain coverage ratios are met

- Restrictions on prepayment of other debt prior to prepayment of the agreement
- Restrictions on additional liens on pledged assets
- Restrictions on mergers where there would be a change of control
- Restrictions on investments, acquisitions or capital expenditures
- Restrictions on off-balance-sheet financing such as leases

- **Financial Covenants:** This section lists the financial covenants or ratio restrictions the firm must meet during the agreement period. The financial requirements and ratios are generally defined in a specific manner and may include:
  - Maintenance of minimum net worth figure
  - Maintenance of interest coverage ratios
  - Maintenance of leverage ratios
  - Maintenance of cash flow coverage ratios
  - Maintenance of working capital to sales ratios

- **Events of Default:** This section covers the general events of default, such as: violation of covenants, misrepresentation of current conditions, material adverse changes, cross-default to other indebtedness, or change of control of the borrower.

- **Miscellaneous:** This section lists any other terms that may be applied to the borrowing agreement. These may include certain terms the lender agrees to meet, such as: capital adequacy requirements, indemnity agreements, ability to assign and participate loans or commitments. This section also includes any general terms relevant to the agreement, such as: required indemnifications, payment of agent fees or expenses, and legal jurisdiction of the agreement.

V. Calculation Examples

A. T-Bill Pricing and Yield Calculations

Determine the purchase price of a 182 day $100,000 T-Bill sold at a 6.95% discount rate.

$$\text{Dollar Discount} = (\text{DR} \times \text{FV}) \times (\text{DM}/360)$$

Where: DR = Discount Rate = .0695
FV = Future Value = $100,000
DM = Days remaining to maturity = 182

Note: Be sure to use the actual number of days to maturity for outstanding issues, not the original days to maturity at the time of issue. Also use 360 days for computing dollar discount.

Dollar Discount = (.0695 × $100,000) × (182/360) = $3,513.61
Purchase Price = FV − Dollar Discount = $100,000 − $3,513.61 = $96,486.39

Using this information, determine the holding period yield (HPY).
HPY = (End of period cashflow Investment amount) / Investment amount
= ($100,000 − $96,486.39) / $96,486.39 = 3.64%

This information can also be used to determine the money market yield (MMY).

$$MMY = (D/PP) \times (360/DM)$$

Where: D = Dollar Discount   = $ 3,513.61
        PP = Purchase Price   = $96,486.39
        DM = Days to Maturity   = 182 days

$$MMY = (\$3,513.61/\$96,486.39) \times (360/182) = 7.20\%$$

Finally, the bond-equivalent yield (BEY) of the T-Bill can be determined in order to compare this investment with other types of investments. Note that for bond-equivalent yield, 365 days are used in the calculation.

$$BEY = (D/PP) \times (365/DM)$$
$$= (\$3,513.61/\$96,486.39) \times (365/182) = 7.30\%$$
OR
$$BEY = MMY \times (365/360) = 7.20\% \times (365/360) = 7.30\%$$

B. Tax-Exempt versus Taxable Yield Calculation

Assuming a marginal corporate tax rate of 34%, determine the taxable equivalent yield on a tax-exempt bond yielding 5.5%.

$$\text{Taxable Equivalent Yield} = 100 \times [\, r\,(1 - T)]$$

Where: r = the tax-exempt return = .055
        T = the marginal tax rate for the investor = .34

$$\text{Taxable Equivalent Yield} = 100 \times [\,.055\,(1 - .34)] = 8.33\%$$

C. Yield Curve Example

Assume a firm has a cash need in 30 days. The discount rate is 8.0% on T-Bills with 30 days to maturity and 8.5% on T-Bills with 60 days to maturity. The bond equivalent yield on matching strategy is:

$$r = (365 \times .08)/(360 - [.08 \times 30]) = .082 = 8.2\%$$

The bond equivalent yield from riding the yield curve (buying the 60-day bill and selling it after 30 days) is shown below. Note that while price calculations are done on a 360-day basis, yield is computed on a 365-day basis.

Price Paid: P = $100 \times \{\, 1 - [(.085 \times 60)/360]\} = 98.58$

Sale Price: S = $100 \times \{\, 1 - [(.080 \times 30)/360]\} = 99.33$

Yield: r = $[(99.33 - 98.58) \times 365]/[98.58 \times 30] = 9.26\%$

Note that the yield has improved by 110 basis points. While no additional default risk has been incurred, reinvestment or interest rate risk has. If the yield curve does not shift over the investment horizon, the firm realizes a higher yield than that afforded by other strategies. On the other hand, riding the yield curve can provide lower yields than under a matching strategy if market rates change during the investment horizon. For example, if interest rates rose during the 30-day investment period in the above example, so that when the 60-day bill was sold the 30-day discount rate was 9.5%, the yield would be below the yield for the matching strategy. The new sales price and yield are:

Sale Price: $S = 100 \times \{1 - [(.095 \times 30)/360]\} = 99.2$

Yield: $r = [(99.2 - 98.58) \times 365]/[98.58 \times 30] = 7.65\%$

D. Average Effective Cost Calculation on Line of Credit

Assume a firm has an average loan outstanding of $2,200,000 (including compensating balance) on a committed line of credit of $5,000,000. A compensating balance of 10% of the used line is required as is a commitment fee of .5% (.005) on the unused line. The stated interest rate is 8.0%. Determine the effective annual interest rate on this line of credit.

$$\text{Effective Rate} = [(I + F)/L] \times (365/t)$$

I = Total Interest Paid = $.08 \times (\$2,200,000) = \$176,000$

F = Dollar Amount of Fees = % Commitment Fee × Unused Portion of Line
    = $.005 \times (2,800,000) = \$14,000$

L = Usable Loan = Borrowed Amount × (1 − Comp. Bal. %)
    = $\$2,200,000 \times (1 - .10) = \$1,980,000$

t= days the loan is outstanding = 365

Effective Rate(i) = $[(\$176,000 + \$14,000)/\$1,980,000] \times (365/365) = 9.6\%$

E. Effective Interest Cost for Commercial Paper Calculation

Assume a company is issuing $60,000,000 (Face Value) in commercial paper with a 60-day maturity (M) at a discount rate of 6.5%. The paper is sold through a dealer who charges an annual rate of 0.25% and the backup line has an annual commitment fee of 0.5% on the line. Determine the effective annual cost and the investor yield on this issue. Note: dealer and backup credit line costs are calculated on a 360-day basis and pro-rated for the maturity of the issue. Effective annual cost and yield are calculated on a 365-day basis.

Proceeds   = FV × (1 − [discount × (M/360)])
          = $\$60,000,000 \times (1 - [.065 \times (60/360)]) = \$59,350,000$

Where: FV = Face Value, and M = Days to Maturity

Interest = FV − Proceeds = $\$60,000,000 - \$59,350,000 = \$650,000$

Dealer Cost   = (Rate × FV) × (M/360)
             = $(.0025 \times \$60,000,000) \times (60/360) = \$25,000$

Cost of Backup
Line of Credit = Rate × FV = $.005 \times \$60,000,000 = \$300,000$

Assuming continuing issues,
2 months of backup line cost = $\$300,000 \times (60/360)$
                             = $\$50,000$

$$\text{Total Issue Costs} = \text{Interest} + \text{Dealer Cost} + \text{Backup Line Cost}$$
$$= \$650,000 + \$25,000 + \$50,000 = \$725,000$$

$$\text{Eff. Annual Cost} = (\text{Total Issue Cost}/\text{Proceeds}) \times (365/M)$$
$$= (\$725,000/\$59,350,000) \times (365/60)$$
$$= 7.43\%$$

$$\text{Investor}/\text{Yield} = (\text{Interest}/\text{Proceeds}) \times (365/M)$$
$$= (\$650,000 \ \$59,350,000) \times (365/60)$$
$$= 6.66\%$$

F. Credit Policy Evaluation Calculation

Assume your company has $4,500,000 in annual sales and can generate a 5% increase in sales by changing its credit terms from Net 30 to Net 45. The actual collection period is expected to increase from 36 days to 52 days and the marginal profitability of the additional sales is assumed to be 30%. The appropriate cost of funds is 15%, and the additional bad-debt loss is assumed to be 4% of the marginal sales. Determine the costs and benefits of this proposed change in credit policy.

A.   Additional Sales $= \%$ increase $\times$ present sales $= .05 \times \$4.5$ Million
$$= \$225,000$$

Marginal Profit $=$ Profit Cont. $\% \times$ Add. Sales $= .30 \times \$225,000$
$$= \$67,500$$

B.   Add. Invest. in AR $=$ New Avg. Balance Present Avg. Balance
$= [\text{New Ann. Sales}/365 \times \text{New ACP}] - [\text{Pres. Ann Sales}/365 \times \text{Pres. ACP}]$
$= [\$4,725,000/365 \times 52] - [\$4,500,000/365 \times 36]$
$= [\$12,945.21 \times 52] - [\$12,328.77 \times 36] = \$673,151 - \$443,836$
$= \$229,315$

Cost of Add. Invest. in AR $=$ Add. Invest. in AR $\times$ WACC
$$= \$229,315 \times .15 = \$34,397$$

C.   Add. Bad-Debt Loss $=$ BDL Ratio $\times$ Add. Sales
$$= .04 \times \$225,000 = \$9,000$$

D.   Net Change in Pre-Tax Profits $=$ Marginal Returns $-$ Marginal Costs
$=$ Marginal Profitability $-$ (Cost of Add. AR $+$ Add. Bad-Debt Loss)
$= \$67,500 - (\$34,397 + \$9,000) = \$67,500 - \$43,397$
$= \$24,103$

The firm should implement the change in credit terms as the overall net impact will be positive.

G. DSO (Days Sales Outstanding) Calculation

Assume that end-of-first-quarter receivables are $675,000 and credit terms are Net 45. Sales history for the quarter is as follows:

January $225,000
February $375,000
March $550,000

Average Daily Sales = [$225,000 + $375,000 + $550,000]/90 = $12,778

Days Sales Outstanding = DSO = [End of Period AR]/Avg. Daily Sales
$$= \$675{,}000/\$12{,}778 = 52.8 \text{ Days}$$

The LIFO DSO can also be determined using the above information.[9] The basic concept is to work backwards from the most recent month's sales in determining DSO, rather than from the average sales over the period. In the above case, the LIFO DSO would be calculated as follows:

1. Subtract the most recent month's sales from period ending accounts receivable.

    $675,000 – $550,000 = $125,000

    a. If this number is positive, but less than the sales for the prior month, then LIFO DSO will be the number of days in the month (31 for March) plus a percentage of the number of days in the prior month.

        LIFO DSO = 31 + [(125,000/375,000) × 28] = 31 + 9.3 = 40.3 days

    b. If this number is positive, but more than the sales for the prior month, then LIFO DSO will be the sum of the number of days in the most recent and prior month, plus a percentage of the number of days in earlier months. Repeat this process for as many months as necessary to bring the balance to zero.

        Assume: period-ending accounts receivable = $1,000,000

March:	$1,000,000 – $550,000 = $450,000	31 days
February:	$450,000 – 375,000 = $75,000	28 days
April:	($75,000/$225,000) × 30 =	10 days

        Total LIFO DSO = 69 days

    c. If this number is negative, then the LIFO DSO is less than the number of days in the most recent month, and the percentage of accounts receivable to the month's sales multiplied by the number of days in the month.

        Assume: end-of-period accounts receivable = $400,000

        LIFO DSO = ($400,000/$550,000) × 31 = 22.5 days

H. Forecasting Accounts Receivable Calculation

Assume that a company's typical accounts receivable pattern is shown in the table below. At the end of June, 90% of June's sales, 40% of May's sales, and 15% of April's sales are still uncollected (in accounts receivable). Assuming the pattern remains stable, estimate the cash inflows for July.

Month	Sales	End of Month AR	AR as % of Sales	Difference
April	$560	$ 84	15%	25%
May	$450	$180	40%	50%
June	$300	$270	90%	10%
July	$400			

Or: In a given month the firm will collect 10% of the current month's sales, 50% of the previous month's sales, 25% of 2-month-old sales, and the remaining 15% of 3-month-old sales. For this example:

Cash Inflows for July = 10% of July Sales + 50% of June Sales
+ 25% of May Sales + 15% of April Sales

Cash Inflows for July = .10($400) + .50($300) + .25($450) + .15($560)
= $40.00 + $150.00 + $112.50 + $84.00 = $386.50

VI. Endnotes

1. See: *The Money Market: Myth, Reality, and Practice, 3rd Edition,* Marcia Stigum, Dow Jones-Irwin Publishers, Homewood, IL, 1990.

2. For a detailed discussion of yield calculations see the most current edition of *Essentials of Cash Management.*

3. The method of LIFO DSO is covered in detail in *Cash Flow, Credit, and Collection,* Basil Mavrovitis, pp. 147–157, Probus Publishing Company, Chicago, IL, 1990.

4. See: "A Better Way to Track Accounts Receivable" by D.J. Masson, *Corporate Cashflow,* August 1988, pp. 46–49.

5. For detailed information on all U.S. Government and Federal Agency Securities, see: *Handbook of U.S. Government and Federal Agency Securities and Related Money Market Instruments, 34th Edition,* The First Boston Corporation, Probus Publishing Company, Chicago, IL, 1990.

6. See: *Journal of Cash Management,* Treasury Management Association, November/December 1993, p. 52.

7. See: GAO/GGD-94-133, Financial Derivatives, pp. 12–13, Government Accounting Office, 1994.

8. Copies of *EITF Abstracts,* EITF Issue Summary packages and other FASB-related information can be obtained from the Financial Accounting Standards Board, 203-847-0700, ext. 555.

9. The concept of LIFO DSO and related calculations is covered in detail in: Chapter 5, *Cashflow, Credit and Collection,* Basil P. Mavrovitis, Probus Publishing Company, Chicago, IL, 1990.

9 Managing and Financing Inventories

I. Outline of the Chapter

A. Elements of Basic Inventory Policy
1. Why Hold Inventories?
   a. Transactions Motive
   b. Precautionary Motive
   c. Speculative/Hedge Motive
   d. Contractual Requirements
   e. Smoothing Production Rates
2. Types of Inventories
   a. Raw Materials Inventory
   b. Work-in-Process (WIP) Inventory
   c. Finished Goods Inventory
   d. Scrap and Obsolete Inventory
   e. Stores and Supplies Inventories
3. Cost/Benefit Tradeoffs

B. Economic Order Quantity (EOQ) Models

C. Just-in-Time (JIT) Method
1. Supplier Relationships
2. Transaction Costs
3. Planning Requirements
4. Recent Developments
5. Impact of JIT on Treasury Function

D. Inventory Financing
1. Accounts Payable

2. Collateralized Loans

3. Asset-Based Loans

4. Floor Planning

Calculations and Examples

A. Example of EOQ Calculations

II. Introduction

Although inventory management is generally the direct responsibility of the marketing or manufacturing managers, the treasurer of a firm is usually responsible for the financing of the inventory. The way that inventory is managed will determine the amount of inventory that is carried by the firm and, therefore, the amount of financing that is provided. The ability to use inventory as collateral for a loan is directly related to the type of the inventory and how it is managed.

The inventory carried by the firm is tied into its production and sales activities, which are responsible, in turn, for the majority of the firm's cash flows. How inventory is managed will affect the length of the firm's cash flow cycle and the estimation of cash flows. This, in turn, has an impact on both the type of cash flow forecasting that the firm can employ and its accuracy. The timing and uncertainty of cash flows also affects the firm's liquidity needs and, potentially, how that liquidity is maintained.

III. Coverage of the Chapter Material

A. Elements of Basic Inventory Policy

1. Why Hold Inventories? Some functions of a business, such as materials purchases and product manufacture, have a sequential, physical dependency. The use of inventories allows a firm to separate these activities so that each can be scheduled and performed independently. Within this general reason for holding inventory, there are several specific motives that affect the size of inventories maintained.

a. Transactions Motive

- The goal is to provide the goods required for the expected level of the firm's sales activities during its normal operating and production cycle.

- Inventory may be held because it is not possible to receive delivery during certain periods of production, such as nighttime manufacturing or weekend shifts.

- Inventory may be held because it is uneconomical to have materials delivered in very small quantities at very frequent intervals or because suppliers may not agree to deliver small quantities.

- The economics of the manufacturing process may require large production runs, such as the manufacturing of film or printing of books. Such runs may require substantial on-hand inventory to insure that the full run is completed without material shortages.

b. Precautionary Motive

- The purpose is to provide a cushion if actual demand is greater than anticipated demand. Therefore, most firms maintain excess inventory so that they can provide service levels desired by their customers.

- While there is some similarity to the transactions motive, the latter obliges the firm to carry only the inventory necessary to meet anticipated demand.

c. Speculative/Hedge Motive

- A firm may adjust its material purchases in anticipation of price or product changes.

- This is most likely to occur in firms whose materials are commodities undergoing rapid increases, or wide fluctuations, in market price. The downside is that commodity prices may drop, as in the case of the high technology industry's experience with memory chips. If old, higher-priced chips are held in stock too long, the company will suffer due to the cost of carrying the inventory. Another danger is that part of the inventory could become obsolete or lose significant value while held in stock.

d. Contractual Requirements: A supplier may require a dealer or franchisee to carry a certain level of inventory in order to maintain an exclusive right to handle the product.

e. Smoothing Production Rates: Another reason to hold inventory is to allow production rates to be level-loaded, using inventory as a buffer. Level-loading (or linearity) is extremely important in all Just-In-Time (JIT) installations. In a level loading environment, a firm plans to build the same product mix every single day during a given month. The production level and product mix can vary from month to month to meet changing customer demands but will flow smoothly and evenly each day within a month.[1]

2. Types of Inventories: Most inventories are connected with some part of the firm's production process. Furthermore, any item held in stock to link two or more production processes can be thought of as an inventory.

a. Raw Materials Inventory

- This type of inventory allows the arrival of the basic inputs to be separated from production scheduling.

- Separate purchasing and production decisions can be made without being tied to scheduling that is unique to the other elements in the production process.

- Partially completed components (such as sub-assemblies) also fall into this category, and they give the firm more flexibility in the production process. For example, a generic widget could be used in the production of several similar products, each of which could be quickly completed upon customer demand. The end result would be improved customer service.

b. Work-in-Process (WIP) Inventory

- This type of inventory allows different phases of the production process to be separated.

- The use and amount of work-in-process inventory are a function, in part, of the production process required for the product.

- A short, continuous process, such as chemical production, may have very little work in process, whereas a long batch-production process, such as furniture manufacturing, has a large work-in-process inventory.

- Different production processes for the same product may allow different firms to have different amounts of work-in-process inventory. Also, WIP inventories may be held as a buffer between production stages having different processing speeds.

- In an early JIT implementation, small quantities of raw materials inventory may be held on the production floor rather than in the stockroom, and they may mistakenly be counted as work-in-process inventory.

- In a true JIT implementation, raw materials are delivered only as needed, and WIP inventory consists only of products going through the production process, as explained later in this chapter.

c. Finished Goods Inventory

- This type of inventory allows a firm to fill orders as they are received rather than depending upon the completion of production to satisfy customer demands.

- This allows a separation of production from demand enabling a firm to maintain a steady production rate while facing highly variable or unpredictable demand. This type of inventory is very valuable for retail operations, as it allows the retailer to have a wide variety of goods always available for customers.

- It is important to note a significant difference in the management of finished goods inventory for generic products versus customized products. Due to their limited resale value, customized product inventories must be managed much more tightly than those of more generic, and easily saleable goods.

d. Scrap and Obsolete Inventory

- In some industries, such as steel or aluminum manufacturing, scrap from production can be easily reused in later batches or sold to recyclers.

- Some portion of a firm's inventories may become obsolete or damaged. This is especially true in environments where there are rapid changes in existing products or introductions of new products.

- Obsolete or scrap inventories need to be identified and dealt with separately from other inventories. They may be turned into cash through sales to scrap dealers or by taking tax deductions through the writeoffs. The firm may also be able to barter obsolete inventory for items it can use through a barter agent.

e. Stores and Supplies Inventories: These are inventories of items indirectly used in the production process, such as lubricating oils or maintenance materials for production machinery, or paper and office supplies in a service business.

3. Cost/Benefit Tradeoffs: Inventories provide some benefits by uncoupling elements of the purchasing, production and shipment processes.

- A primary benefit of holding sufficient inventory is in the reduction of stockout costs, that is, reducing the lost sales and margins as well as the number of "lost customers" due to stockouts.

- In a more positive sense, inventory (especially of finished goods) may provide a competitive advantage over other firms and result in increased customer goodwill and higher service levels, and therefore increased sales and profits.

- Stockout costs may arise from a disruption in production, from lost sales, from higher costs in producing a rush order, from poor forecasting of inventory needs or from shortage of raw materials in the marketplace.

- There are costs involved in maintaining varying levels of inventory. These are usually seen as consisting of set-up (or order) costs and holding costs. Set-up costs are transaction costs for obtaining a new batch of inventory, such as new supplies or setting up for a new production run. There are also costs involved in disposing of or writing off excess or obsolete inventories.

- Holding costs are the costs for carrying the inventory, such as physical storage and handling costs, insurance, taxes and the opportunity cost of funds invested in inventory. When inadequately monitored or planned, inventory can cause increased shelf life and scrap or waste problems.

- Benefits (reduced stockout costs) and transaction costs are a decreasing function of the amount of inventory held, whereas holding costs are an increasing function of the amount of inventory.

- The objective of inventory management is to minimize the total net costs associated with the inventory while meeting a desired level of production and/or customer service. The objective is served optimally by finding the level of inventory that minimizes the costs of holding higher inventory levels while maximizing sales and profit margins resulting from the inventory.

- This is done either in a opportunity cost approach, where the financing cost is explicitly recognized as one of the carrying costs, or in a present value approach, where the financing cost rate is used as the discount rate rather than being included in the carrying cost. There is definite tradeoff between the costs of maintaining and financing a firm's inventories and the costs of not having items on hand when needed.

B. Economic Order Quantity (EOQ) Models

Economic order quantity models generally assume a batch ordering or production process in which all of the costs of managing inventory are set. Minimizing the cost function consists of determining:

1. The average level of inventory to hold
2. The size of the order (production)
3. The frequency of orders

In the simplest version of the model, the stockout costs are not explicitly recognized. This is the same as assuming that stockout costs are very high, and stockouts are not allowed. The model balances the set-up costs with the carrying costs. The total costs are minimized by setting the order quantity to:

$$EOQ = \sqrt{\frac{2SR}{h + Ckt_m}}$$

Where: EOQ = the Economic Order Quantity.
        S   = the set-up (order) costs per set-up.
        R   = the total number of units required.
        h   = the physical storage and handling costs per unit in inventory.
        C   = the cost per unit.
        k   = the daily opportunity cost rate.
        t_m = the number of days in the time period.

- Extensions of this basic model include the incorporation of a safety stock and uncertainty of demand or delivery (production) time.

- The economic effects of quantity discounts can be considered by using the model twice: once at the undiscounted price and once at the discounted price. Inventory management costs can then be added to production costs in both to determine the option having the lower total costs.

- It is important to realize that the EOQ model has some severe problems in application and is not widely utilized in inventory management. The EOQ model does not handle very well volume discounts, blanket purchase orders with schedule of receipts or other real-world factors. An example of the basic EOQ calculations is provided at the end of this chapter.

C. Just-in-Time (JIT) Method[2]

Economic order quantity (EOQ) models assume that various cost elements are predetermined and treat the average inventory level, as determined from the optimal order quantity, as the decision variable. The JIT method (also known as zero inventory or materials-as-needed) attempts to minimize the level of inventory (an optimal order quantity as close to one unit as possible) by altering the costs or uncertainties that underlie the motives for holding inventories.

Closely related to the use of JIT is Material Planning Systems (MPS). MPS brings together long-range production planning with planning for the flow of materials through the production process. A firm can negotiate arrangements with suppliers to provide a continuous supply of production materials on short notice, resulting in reduced carrying costs for the raw materials used to generate finished goods. MPS and JIT methods allow better, time-phased methods of planning, which facilitate adjustment to changing costs.

- It is important for top managers to understand that JIT is not merely an inventory management system, but a production/business philosophy that treats inventory as: (1) undesirable, (2) a cover-up for poor planning, or for inventory location and accuracy problems, (3) poor supplier quality, or (4) unbalanced production processes.

- The JIT philosophy recognizes that inventory turns from an asset to a liability fairly quickly. The three basic goals of a JIT system are: (1) elimination of waste, (2) standardization of the production process and (3) continuous improvement in quality.

- In addition, the use of JIT can result in: (1) reduced cycle time, (2) quality improvements, (3) floor space requirement reduction and (4) productivity improvements (higher throughput in units per employee).

In general, JIT offers benefits to firms using it in the following categories:

1. Supplier Relationships

- A key issue in JIT inventory is the development of suppliers as "strategic partners" in the production of a product. Closely tied to this concept is the practice of having suppliers make more frequent delivery of small quantities of materials (which are immediately put into the production process). To do this successfully requires coordinating the arrival of high-quality materials (with a very low defect rate) as well as efficient communications between manufacturer and supplier. This type of relationship may require that suppliers be located nearby.

- In many cases, the quality of the supplies may be even more critical than the delivery of small quantities, as this will result in reducing the inspection required for incoming goods. The only way that this can be achieved is to plan and communicate effectively with suppliers so that the proper quantity and quality of materials are available as needed.

- The emergence of electronic data interchange (EDI) systems is making such communications feasible as well as economical. One of the terms used in EDI is "trading partners," which indicates a close, mutually beneficial relationship between supplier and manufacturer or manufacturer and customer. Electronic data interchange and electronic commerce are covered in Chapter 13.

- MPS requires that a manufacturer keep in close contact with its suppliers and is often implemented in an EDI environment in order to provide a faster, more orderly material release process.

- In order to make a JIT system work effectively, the manufacturer must share sales forecasts, production schedules and problems, and planned material requirements with its suppliers, again reinforcing the concept of strategic partnerships.

2. Transaction Costs

- A primary aim of JIT models is to redesign the ordering, set-up or production process (or in some cases the product itself) and to streamline or simplify them in order to reduce transaction costs.

- Lower transaction costs make more frequent and smaller batches economical.

3. Planning Requirements

- Through better planning, the reduction of inventories recouples the separate elements of the production-sales function.
- This recoupling requires coordinated planning of the elements of the process to work around potential problems in one element that would disrupt another. Essentially, this means that the manufacturer times the use of vendor materials in making goods to order in direct response to customer demand.

4. Recent Developments:[3] Two new inventory management techniques have recently emerged as refinement of the JIT philosophy. The first technique is "supplier-managed replenishment programs" and the second is "paid-on production."

- In supplier-managed replenishment programs, the supplier maintains and tracks the inventory of the materials it provides to a customer. As the inventory is used, the supplier replenishes it and bills the customer for the items. The rationale of this system is that the supplier is better able to track trends in inventory usage and manage the levels of inventory more efficiently, thus reducing costs for both the supplier and the customer.
- The paid-on production process is similar to supplier-managed replenishment programs, but has some specific implications for financial managers. Paid-on production is the process by which a payment record is created for goods and/or services based on a usage record rather than on shipping records. It is similar to consignment sales in retail, but is based on usage within a manufacturing environment. Typically there is only one supplier, and title to the product (supply item) is transferred somewhere during the manufacturing process rather than at the shipping dock. This process is outlined in greater detail in Chapter 13, Electronic Commerce.

5. Impact of JIT on Treasury Function:[4] The unique demand of the JIT manufacturing environment has a major impact on the treasury and reporting functions of a firm, especially with respect to its financial management information system (FMIS). JIT implementations will generally require changes in the accounting methods used for inventory and impact the timing of purchases. Firms using JIT will purchase more frequently and in smaller amounts, which could increase the number of transactions which need to be monitored and recorded. The process of costing the inventory has become more difficult for companies using JIT. Rather than using traditional "last-in-first-out" (LIFO) or "first-in-first-out" (FIFO) methods, proper costing of JIT inventories requires using a rolling average of actual costs. This approach provides a better tool for evaluating whether continuing improvement is being achieved.

D. Inventory Financing

While inventory can be financed as part of the general working capital requirements, some financing alternatives may be tied directly to the amount of inventory. These financing alternatives are likely to be used by firms experiencing rapid growth, firms with very seasonal operations, or by companies that are less financially secure. The amount of credit available, as a percentage of the value of the inventory, depends upon the nature of the inventory, its location, when and where transfer of title occurs, and the existence of a secondary market. Financing is usually not available for work-in-process inventory, but only for raw materials or finished goods.

1. Accounts Payable

- These represent the credit granted by suppliers (trade credit) for the purchase of inventory.

- They provide a spontaneous source of financing, increasing as the amount of inventory increases with a higher level of operations, and decreasing as the inventory declines with a lower level of operations.

- The amount of financing provided can sometimes be extended by delaying payments to suppliers. The opportunity cost for this form of financing is the cost of lost cash discounts, as well as lost goodwill with suppliers and potentially delayed shipments. For example, if the terms are 2/10, net 30, paying after 10 days will cause the loss of the 2% cash discount offered for early payment. If payment is further delayed beyond the 30-day net period (sometimes referred to as "stretching payables") the buyer runs the risk of damaging supplier relations and perhaps the firm's credit rating. In many cases, suppliers will refuse to ship additional products unless outstanding invoices are paid promptly, which could result in production and sales problems.

2. Collateralized Loans

- These may be arranged using the inventory as the collateral for the loan, with the lender providing financing for some predetermined percentage of the inventory value (usually based on liquidity and type of inventory). The company's cash flows are viewed as the primary repayment source for this loan. The inventory is viewed as a secondary repayment source or a means of reducing the amount of the loss in the event of a default.

- The claim against the inventory is usually perfected (i.e., necessary steps are taken to ensure that the lien against the asset is legally enforceable) by verification of the inventory's value and by filing the appropriate legal documents. This is usually accomplished by filing a UCC-1 statement to perfect the lien on the assets. Also, if the borrower is operating in a rented facility, in order to ensure clear claim on the assets, the lender may require the landlord to provide waivers of any rights to the inventory.

- The cost may be higher than that of an unsecured loan because of the additional expense incurred by the lending institution in perfecting and monitoring the claim.

3. Asset-Based Loans

- These are loans that are made primarily on the value of the inventory, rather than on the general financial strength of the borrower. To strengthen the claim on the inventory, the lender typically takes physical possession of it in the event of the firm's default or bankruptcy. As in the case of a collateralized loan, the lien on the inventory is perfected by the filing of a UCC-1 statement.

- The lender may store the inventory at a public warehouse or through a field warehouse arrangement. These warehouses are generally bonded storage facilities where commodities, finished goods, or works in process are held until a warehouse receipt is presented. In most normal arrangements firms have ready access to the inventory for manufacturing or sales purposes. In some cases, if the firm is in danger of default, the release of inventory may be allowed only with the consent of the lending institution. A warehousing arrangement may be useful for a firm that must produce in advance to meet a highly seasonal demand.

- In some cases, where the inventory is directly supporting a loan, the lending institution will release the materials only after that portion of the loan supported by the inventory has been paid.

- In estimating the effective financing cost of an asset-based loan, the manager should include the cost of managing the collateral in the all-in cost.

4. Floor Planning: This is a type of asset-based lending used for very high-value items, such as automobiles, trucks or heavy equipment. Loans are made against each individual item, and recorded by serial number. The loan is repayable when the item is sold.

IV. Calculations and Examples

A. Example of EOQ Calculations

A firm orders inventory with the following assumptions:

1. Orders must be placed in multiples of 25
2. Annual sales are 2,000,000
3. The purchase price of the inventory is $3
4. Carrying cost is 20% of the purchase price of inventory
5. Cost per order placed is $25

The EOQ is calculated as follows:

$$EOQ = \sqrt{\frac{2SR}{h + Ck}}$$

Where: EOQ = the Economic Order Quantity
S = the set-up (order) costs per set-up = $25
R = the total number of units required = 2,000,000 units
h = the physical storage and handling costs per unit in inventory = $0
C = the cost per unit = $3
k = the annual opportunity cost rate = 20%

$$EOQ = \sqrt{\frac{2SR}{h + Ck}} = \sqrt{\frac{2 \times 25 \times 2,000,000}{0 + .20 \times 3}} = 12,909.94$$

Note: Since you cannot order 94% of an item, you must round up to the next whole number. This would mean ordering 12,910 units, but since the order amount must be a multiple of 25, you must order 12,925 units per order.

V. Endnotes

1. See: *Just-In-Time for America,* Kenneth A. Wantuck, The Forum, Ltd., Milwaukee, WI, 1989.

2. Additional information on the implementation of JIT can be found in: "What's Your Excuse for Not Using JIT?", by Richard Walligh, *Harvard Business Review,* Mar./Apr. 1986, pp. 3–8.

3. See: "A Tonic for the Business Cycle," *Business Week,* April 4, 1994, p. 57.

4. Information in this section is taken from: *World-Class Accounting and Finance,* C.J. McNair, p. 16, Business One Irwin Publishers, 1993.

10 Financial Analysis

I. Outline of the Chapter

A. Role of the Treasurer in Financial Planning and Analysis
1. Relative to Treasury Management
2. Relative to Cash Management
3. Why Firms Need This Process
4. Who Participates in This Process

B. Financial Statement Analysis
1. Financial Statements and Reports
   a. Income Statement
   b. Balance Sheet
   c. Some Important Points on Financial Statements
   d. Statement of Cash Flows
   e. Concept of "Free Cash Flow"
   f. Earnings and Dividends
2. Ratio Analysis
   a. Liquidity Ratios
   b. Asset Management Ratios
   c. Debt Management Ratios
   d. Profitability Ratios
   e. Market Value Ratios
3. Common-Size Financial Statements
4. Comparative Ratios
5. Trend Analysis

Chapter Checklists

Calculations and Examples

II. Introduction

This chapter and the next (Chapter 11) present the topics of financial statement analysis and financial planning and control. The use of financial analysis and ratio analysis of the firm's internal financial statements helps the financial manager to properly manage and control its financial operations. Analysis of other financial statements is an essential element of the treasurer's credit granting and investment decisions, as well as for mergers and acquisitions. Also, through forecasting and financial planning the treasurer should be able to ensure that the company will be in compliance with present and anticipated covenants. Finally, proper planning and forecasting can help to determine the required size of any credit lines before they are actually needed.

Financial planning and control are an integral part of the treasury function because they involve forecasting future needs of the firm and are generally part of its strategic plan. These forecasts include sales forecasts, required asset investment to support sales, sources of funds for acquiring the assets, estimated need for external funds, and the firm's ability to sustain growth or to be properly sized. Financial planning needs to be a repetitive process, continuously revised as needs dictate. Financial planning may be under the direction of the controller rather than the treasurer, or a separate function reporting directly to the Chief Executive Officer (CEO) or Chief Financial Officer (CFO).

Although the material covered here is generally applicable to almost any organization (public, private, not-for-profit, etc.), the main focus is on publicly held corporations. In fact, in many cases the only real differences are the impact of taxes and the types of financing used for the company. Overall, the coverage in this section is broad-based and general.

This chapter provides a starting point for the financial management material covered in succeeding chapters. Treasury professionals need to comprehend the important elements of the various financial statements, both to manage their own firms and to analyze others. Moreover, financial planning and forecasting are important to the long-term success of the company.

III. Coverage of the Chapter Material

A. Role of the Treasurer in Financial Planning and Analysis

1. Relative to Treasury Management: Financial planning and budgeting are crucial to the long-term success of any company or organization. A key difference between the accounting and finance disciplines is that traditional accounting focuses on determining a company's past condition, while finance is more concerned with where it is going and how it is going to get there. This is why planning and budgeting for the future of a firm are so very important.

In many firms, the treasurer is responsible for many portions of the planning and budgeting process; if not directly, then by providing support for this process to other areas of the firm. Irrespective of any responsibility for the development of plans and budgets, the treasurer is often responsible for managing the impact on cash flow. As plans and budgets change the cash flow stream, the treasurer must manage short-term assets and liabilities to ensure that the company has adequate funds and liquidity. For the longer term, the treasurer must manage the financing of the firm's long-term assets with long-term debt and equity issues.

In the past, much of the planning and budgeting process has been driven by the operating areas of the firm (marketing, sales, purchasing, production, logistics, etc.). Recently, however, many treasurers have begun to take a more active role in this process, especially because they often deal with the consequences of the plans and budgets, and as the roles of finance and treasury professionals become more operational in nature.

Financial analysis is a major part of the treasury management function. Externally, financial analysis can be used in credit-granting and management decisions, as well as for assessing competitors' strengths and weaknesses. Internally, financial analysis can be used for both planning and control purposes. The key question in these times of corporate restructuring is: "What can the treasurer do to contribute to the firm's bottom line?" Closely related to financial analysis is the use of valuation procedures (both internal and external) to determine the changes in the value of the firm under different decision paths and possibilities of outcome.

2. Relative to Cash Management: Traditionally, the cash manager works under the authority of the treasurer and deals with the management of short-term assets and liabilities. Although the specific responsibilities of a cash manager vary from firm to firm (or organization), many are either involved in or affected by the financial planning and budgeting process. At a minimum, the cash manager must deal with the short-term impact of the financial plans and budgets as well as daily cash flows. At a higher level, the cash manager may be involved in providing support for other areas of the firm in forecasting cash flow streams, or providing expertise in the development of spreadsheet based models of cash flow streams resulting from various financial plans.

Financial analysis is important to cash managers, especially those who are responsible for any decisions concerning the granting or management of credit to customers. Financial analysis can be used to determine the financial strength of banks or companies in which the cash manager is making investments or utilizing operational services.

3. Why Firms Need This Process: For any firm (or organization) to be successful over the long term, it must make the right decisions concerning the acquisition and financing of assets and in the management of its operations. The financial planning and budgeting process is critical to this success. Firms that have no established procedures for planning and budgeting will be unable to consistently make the appropriate decisions necessary for financial success.

Financial analysis is critical to proper financial management and can be used for both external analysis (of customers, suppliers, banks, competitors, etc.) and for internal analysis and control.

4. Who Participates in This Process: One of the more significant benefits (and consequently, one of the major problems) of the financial planning and budgeting process is that it involves most areas of the firm or organization. Each area should be involved in the development of plans and budgets; otherwise, the latter may not contain the information needed to make proper decisions, and the uninvolved areas may not "buy into" the overall plan.

The problem stems from the fact that different areas of the firm often use very different sets of assumptions in developing their particular part of the plan; and in some cases, certain areas will develop their portion in complete isolation from the others. This means that the final consolidation of the various parts of the planning process may be rendered useless by those differing assumptions. One of the treasury area's critical tasks in financial planning, therefore, is to provide common assumptions for the plan to all groups. These assumptions may include GNP growth, inflation, interest rates, currency rates, etc.

Firms and organizations successful in the planning and budgeting process are those that can overcome the inherent problems of communication between different areas and can focus on developing consolidated plans and budgets. Participation from the different areas is critical to obtaining the best possible information for development of the plan, as well as gaining their agreement on the result.

B. Financial Statement Analysis

▪ Analysis of financial statements allows management to determine the strengths and weaknesses of its own firm and in others (customers, competitors or potential merger candidates).

▪ The firm's liquidity, leverage and profitability can be determined by analyzing its financial statements.

▪ In traditional accounting and financial analysis, the primary focus is on accrual-based accounting profits rather than cash flows.

▪ In the very long run, these accounting profits generally tend to track with cash flows, but there may be significant differences in the short run. The primary exceptions occur when the firm makes long-term adjustments to its financial statements as a result of pension funding, health care benefits for retired workers, goodwill, or changes in real estate values.

1. Financial Statements and Reports: The main sources of information on a firm are its annual report and SEC filings (if it is publicly listed in the U.S.), which contain the information listed below. The information released in these statements is also a function of the disclosure requirements of the country where issued. Generally, disclosure rules are most stringent in the United States, but are beginning to become more stringent in other industrialized countries.

The primary components of the reports are:

1. The management discussion and analysis, a written statement describing the past year's activities and plans for the future

2. The firm's basic financial statements. These contain important information that shareholders and analysts utilize to form their expectations about the firm's future prospects. In addition, financial information can be obtained from the firm's 10-K and 10-Q reports to the SEC, as well as through third-party sources, such as analysts and rating agencies. Any firm with assets over $1 million and publicly traded debt or equity must register and file with the SEC. Firms must file quarterly financial reports (10-Q), annual reports with audited financial statements (10-K), and reports of certain material events (8-K). In addition, statements may be either audited or unaudited. Audited statements are prepared and/or reviewed by an independent public accounting firm.

a. Income Statement:

- This shows the sales and expenses of the firm over the period reviewed. The bottom line of the report is net profit or loss for the period.

- In the U.S., the primary focus of most financial analysis is on the bottom line figure of net profits, or, more specifically, on earnings per share to stockholders.

- Stock prices will often react quite violently to unexpected changes in a firm's quarterly earnings reports. This short-run focus on the income statement is a major contributing factor to stock price volatility.

b. Balance Sheet:

- This shows the levels of the assets and claims on those assets (equity and liabilities) at the end of the accounting period.

- The assets are traditionally listed in the order of their liquidity, and the claims are generally listed in the order of their priority in liquidation (debt first, then equity).

- Some organizations (i.e., not-for-profit, hospitals, foundations, insurance companies and banks) use non-standard formats for published financial statements, so the analyst should read such statements carefully.

c. Some Important Points on Financial Statements: Several other important points concerning income statements and balance sheets are as follows:

1) Cash versus other assets: Although all of the assets are listed in terms of dollars, only cash and equivalents (marketable securities) represent actual money.

Note: Not all cash on the balance sheet is available due to float in the banking system or other factors related to international operations.

2) Cash flows: For many firms, the primary source of liquidity is the ability to generate cash flows through operations. One of the most common approaches to determining cash flows from financial statements is to add depreciation to net income.

Another popular cash flow measure (especially with bankers) is known as "free cash flow" which starts with net income, adds back depreciation, and then subtracts dividends and capital investments. Finally, cash can also be generated from changes in balance sheet accounts, such as the purchase or sale of assets or changes in capital.

3) Liabilities versus stockholders' equity: The two basic claims on the assets of the firm are debt owed by the company represented by liabilities and the ownership of the firm represented by equity. It is important to note the holders of that liability and equityholders have certain claims on the firm's earnings stream.

Debt generally has a fixed payment claim on the earnings stream that occurs prior to the payment of taxes, and such payments to debt holders are tax deductible. In addition, debtholders have a prior claim on the assets of the firm in the event of its dissolution.

The equityholders in the firm have the last claim on any of the firm's assets, as well as on any of its earnings; however, the return (cash flows) to the shareholders is potentially unlimited. Any earnings remaining after all other claims are satisfied (debt, taxes, sinking funds, etc.) are the property of the holders of the firm's equity.

4) Breakdown of the common equity: There are several considerations regarding the common equity accounts of a firm:

- First, the equity account may be broken up into several categories: preferred stock, common stock, additional paid-in capital, and retained earnings, to name a few.

- Preferred stock may be voting or non-voting, generally pays a fixed dividend, and has prior claims on earnings and assets over common stock.

- The common stock account generally refers to the par value of the stock, while additional paid-in capital represents the excess value (above par) of common stock issued after the formation of the company. Treasury stock (the firm's stock held by itself) will be accounted for in the common equity section of the balance sheet.

- The total value of the stockholders' equity account is the sum of par value, additional paid-in capital and retained earnings, minus treasury stock and adjusted for foreign currency translation gains or losses.

- In recent years, various "derivative" or "synthetic" securities have been developed, based on equity or debt claims combined with options and/or futures.

Unless these form a substantial portion of the firm's capital structure, they may only be noted in a footnote to the financial statements.

5) Inventory accounting: The methods used for inventory accounting will impact the value of the inventory and thus the overall level of company assets. The degree of impact of accounting methods generally depends on whether costs of replacing inventory are increasing or decreasing and general rates of inflation. The annual report of the firm will contain information on the methods used for the valuation of inventory. The basic types of inventory accounting are First-In-First-Out (FIFO) and Last-In-First-Out (LIFO). When inflation is high, FIFO accounting will tend to understate the true value of the inventory for income statement purposes, while LIFO will track more closely to the true value (but not for balance sheet purposes). An example of the impact of LIFO and FIFO inventory accounting on financial statements is provided at the end of this chapter.

6) Depreciation methods: The methods used for depreciation will impact the rate at which a firm "expenses" its capitalized assets (property, plant and equipment) over time.

- Accelerated depreciation will "write off" an asset faster, and therefore will result in lower net income in the earlier years of the asset's life and higher net income in the later years. It is generally permissible to use different depreciation methods for tax purposes versus public accounting (book) purposes.

- Since depreciation is used to reduce taxes and is added back to net income to determine cash flows, the primary impact on cash flows from accelerated depreciation is to increase them in the early years and decrease them in the later years. The net effect is to increase the Net Present Value (NPV) of the asset (and thus the value of the company).

7) The time dimension: The balance sheet of a firm represents the value of assets and claims on those assets at some specific point in time, while the income statement represents the flows of income and expenses through the firm over a period of time.

8) Intangible assets: These are assets that lack physical substance (goodwill) or represent a right granted by a government (patent, trademark or mineral rights), or by another company (franchise). Intangibles have a life in excess of one year and are amortized into expense over the period benefited, up to 40 years.

- As more and more companies either spin off divisions or acquire other companies, the problem of accounting for intangible assets, especially goodwill, becomes more significant.

- Goodwill represents the historical value of a firm as a "going concern," or the value of the firm over and above the market value of the assets of the firm. It can only be recorded in a business combination (merger or acquisition) accounted for under the purchase accounting method.

- Goodwill equals the purchase price less the book value of the acquired company's net assets less the amount by which the acquired company's depreciable assets are written up to their fair market value. The fair market value of the total going concern should be equal to the purchase price. For example, if XYZ Company paid $3 million for the net assets of ABC Company having a fair market value of $2.8 million, the excess of $200,000 represents goodwill. This accounting process is very critical in leveraged or management buy-outs (LBOs and MBOs) and is covered in greater detail in Chapter 6.

9) Accounting changes: In the last few years, many firms have had to recognize significant liabilities related to funding of pension accounts and providing health benefits for retirees. Accepted guidelines for this type of accounting are covered in FASB Statement 87 on pension fund accounting. As in the case of accounting for intangible assets, these changes will have a significant impact on the future balance sheets of some firms.

10) Retained earnings: It is important to realize that retained earnings are only an accounting concept, and not a pool of funds residing in the firm. Technically, they represent shareholder earnings that have been reinvested in the firm rather than paid to the shareholders in the form of dividends. Retained earnings are thus the accounting for the increased claims of the shareholders in the firm as a result of reinvested earnings.

11) International differences: Firms operating in several countries must manage the problems of differences in accounting conventions, or GAAP, from country to country. In addition, for companies based in the U.S., there must be a consolidation of foreign financial statements into a single set of U.S.-dollar-denominated statements according to guidelines issued by the FASB.

d. Statement of Cash Flows:

- This shows the funds obtained by the firm over the period as well as how it utilized those funds; in addition, it shows how the overall liquidity of the firm has changed.

- This statement has been known as the Sources and Uses of Funds Statement, and has been referred to more recently as the Statement of Working Capital Position or Statement of Changes in Financial Position.

- The most current version of this statement has been defined in FASB Statement 95.

- This statement is unique because the cash flow impacts from depreciation are recognized and incorporated into the statement, and it is prepared by combining information from both the income statement and the balance sheet.

- Balance sheets from the beginning and end of the period (either actual or pro forma) are required, as well as income statements for the same period.

- The steps in preparing the Statement of Cash Flows are as follows:

    1) Analyze the change in each balance sheet account to determine if it is a **source** or a **use** of funds.

    - **Source of funds:** An increase in a claim on assets (debt or equity account) or a decrease in an asset account. Sources of funds provide cash to the company.

For example, if a firm were to borrow $100,000 from the bank, that would represent a funds inflow to the firm. Likewise, if a firm were to sell off an asset for $25,000, that would also represent an inflow of funds.

- **Use of funds:** An increase in an asset account or a decrease in a claim on an asset. Use of funds means utilizing cash to invest in assets, pay off obligations or produce goods or services. Using the example above, when the firm pays off the $100,000 bank loan, that represents an outflow of funds. Purchasing a new asset to replace one that was sold would also represent an outflow of funds.

2) Analyze income statement to determine other funds generated from operations, as well as other uses of funds.

3) Combine information into the Statement of Cash Flows. An example of the calculations involved in the determination of sources and uses of funds is provided in the case example at the end of this chapter.

e. Concept of "Free Cash Flow": A primary use of the Statement of Cash Flows is the determination of a firm's "free cash flow."

- Essentially, the Statement of Cash Flows examines the impact of changes in balance sheet accounts and the cash flows from operations to determine the net change in the firm's cash account.

- This change, as represented by the net increase (or decrease) in cash and cash equivalents, is the cash flow that remains after considering all cash inflows and outflows (including capital asset sales or purchases) over the period in question.

- The free cash flow calculation is often used by bankers as a loan covenant, and may be defined as net income plus depreciation less cash dividends and capital expenditures.

f. Earnings and Dividends: This information may be included in the income statements and/or provided as a separate statement. If a separate statement is provided, it usually furnishes more years of earnings and dividend information than are given in the income statement.

2. Ratio Analysis: The real value of ratio analysis is that it allows an investor or a manager to summarize quickly the complex relationships between income statement items and balance sheet items relating to the firm's liquidity, viability, leverage, financial strength and profitability. An investor or a firm's credit manager can thus quickly and easily decide whether or not the firm is a good investment opportunity or an acceptable credit risk, and a financial manager can determine if the firm is meeting financial management goals.

In forecasting, the treasurer can determine how projected changes in financial variables, as measured by financial ratios, will affect the health of the firm, as well as the impact on compliance with any covenants. Another useful form of ratio analysis is to examine the changes in the ratios over several time periods; this is known as trend analysis.

The financial manager can use industry average ratios for comparative purposes and for developing pro forma financial statements for new ventures or expansion into new areas. The various types of financial ratios are discussed below. In addition, case examples later in this chapter present some sample financial statements and ratio analysis to illustrate the practical applications of the ratios presented below.

a. Liquidity Ratios:

- These indicate the firm's ability to meet its maturing obligations and are generally of greatest interest to creditors (or financial managers who are considering the granting of credit to a customer).

- There are many sources of liquidity for a firm other than current assets. These include funds from operations and short-term borrowing arrangements.

- These ratios can be easily manipulated by moving assets and liabilities around at year's end (window dressing). This means that the traditional liquidity measures may not really provide financial managers with the information they need.

1) Current ratio:

$$\frac{\text{Current assets}}{\text{Current liabilities}}$$

The current ratio is often used by creditors as a measure of the firm's ability to meet current obligations with current assets. In addition, restrictions on the current ratio are a popular form of constraint used in debt covenants. A current ratio of 1.50, for example, would indicate that the firm in question has $1.50 of current assets for every $1.00 of current liabilities. The assumption is that in the event of financial downturn, the current assets could be sold off or liquidated in order to pay off the current liabilities. There is really no "proper" level for this ratio and, in fact, excess liquidity may be a very inefficient use of the firm's limited resources. Appropriate levels for this ratio will vary widely from industry to industry. However, the ratio can be easily affected by accounting manipulations designed to make the end-of-period statements for the firm appear more attractive.

2) Quick or acid test ratio:

$$\frac{\text{Cash} + \text{Marketable Securities} + \text{Accounts Receivable}}{\text{Current liabilities}}$$

The key difference between the current ratio and the quick ratio is the removal of inventories (known as "stock" outside of North America) as well as any pre-paid assets from the current assets. The rationale for removing these items in the calculation of the quick ratio is that they are traditionally the least liquid of the current assets. This ratio, therefore, gives an indication of the firm's ability to meet its current obligations (liabilities), utilizing only the most liquid of the current assets: cash, marketable securities and accounts receivable. As in the case of the current ratio, this figure can be manipulated by end-of-period accounting changes intended to show the firm in a better light.

Examples of the calculations involved in both the current and quick ratios are presented in a case example later in this chapter.

b. Asset Management Ratios:

- These measure how effectively the firm utilizes its assets, and are often called turnover or utilization ratios.
- For the turnover ratios, the higher the turnover, the higher level of sales the firm is able to support with a given level of assets.
- For the average collection period, the lower this measure is, the faster the firm is able to turn sales into collections and, therefore, usable cash.

1) Inventory turnover:

$$\frac{\text{Annualized Cost of Goods Sold}}{\text{End of Period Inventory}}$$

Generally, the idea behind inventory turnover is to determine how fast the firm utilizes its inventory in order to generate sales. For example, an inventory turnover of 2.00 would indicate that the firm in question is turning its inventory twice a year, or approximately every six months. Higher inventory turnover indicates faster usage, while lower turnover represents lower usage. Inventory can be related to the required investment to finance the inventory. All else equal, firms with lower inventory turnover generally require additional capital in order to finance their inventory levels.

There are several different definitions of inventory turnover, but the one provided above is the most accurate. Another definition of this ratio is given as revenues (or sales) divided by ending inventory (Note that outside of North America sales may be referred to as "turnover," which may cause some confusion; this definition recognizes that most inventory is carried at cost and is more comparable to cost of goods sold than sales at market value).

Another approach is to use an average inventory figure rather than the period-ending figure, as this may reduce the probability of over- or understating the inventory levels because of end-of-period fluctuations. Also, it is important to realize that a higher inventory turnover (relative to industry averages) may actually be bad. This is true if the faster inventory turnover translates into a high percentage of stockouts and back orders.

There is a problem in deciding what figure to use for inventory. In addition to the approaches detailed above, the firm may use a net investment in inventory figure, which is typically net of reserves, slow-moving items, and returns and adjustments. Other considerations are whether to include only finished product inventory, or work-in-process and raw materials as well. The correct approach will vary widely from industry to industry.

In a customer service context, it could also be argued that having a low inventory turnover simply means that the firm carries sufficient safety stock to ensure that customers are always able to get what they need without waiting. In short, this (and most of the other ratios) must be interpreted with some degree of caution. The general idea is to find the turnover ratio which is "optimal" for the firm.

2) Average collection period:

$$\frac{\text{Year–end accounts receivable}}{\text{Annual revenues}/365}$$

The general purpose of this ratio (also known as Days Sales Outstanding or DSO) is to measure the time it takes (in days) to collect an average credit sale. For example, a firm with an average collection period of 35.0 would have to wait an average of 35 days to collect cash on a credit sale. The average collection period is generally driven by a firm's stated credit period, but may extend significantly beyond that period if the quality of receivables is not properly monitored. As the average collection period increases, so does the investment in accounts receivable and the associated capital requirements.

In many definitions of this ratio, 360 days are used rather than 365 days for annual calculations. For monthly or quarterly periods, 30 or 90 days are generally used in the calculation. This is another case where it is difficult to determine whether a given ratio is good or bad. The proper comparison is with industry averages.

Generally, a lower DSO indicates aggressive collection of receivables and can be interpreted positively. A low average collection period, on the other hand, could indicate a very tight credit policy on the part of the firm, which could mean that possible sales are being lost as marginal (but ultimately creditworthy) customers are turned away.

As in the case of the inventory turnover ratio, it may be preferable to use average accounts receivable (if available) rather than ending receivables, in order to prevent end-of-period accounting adjustments that affect the measurement.

The average collection period is of critical interest to cash managers because it provides an indication of the length of time a company must wait for collections on sales. The number of Days Sales Outstanding is the time between the recording of the sale and ultimate collection based on those sales. It represents a major portion of the firm's cash flow timeline.

3) Fixed assets turnover:

$$\frac{\text{Revenues}}{\text{Net fixed assets}}$$

The fixed assets turnover should be calculated as revenues (sales) divided by net fixed assets. The purpose of this ratio is to measure the earning power of the company, especially in relation to other corporations in the same industry. As in the case of the inventory turnover, the higher this figure, the faster the firm is turning over its fixed assets and thus making more efficient use of its fixed asset base. Therefore, the fixed asset turnover ratio can be thought of as a measure of a firm's operating leverage, a measure of efficiency in the use of fixed assets, or as a "yield" measurement of dollar sales per dollar of assets.

As in many other ratios, the firm's analyst should have a target or "optimal" level for this ratio. In addition, the proper level will be significantly affected by the industry to which the firm belongs. Firms in industries with high levels of capital intensity (heavy manufacturing) will have much lower fixed asset turnover than those in industries with low levels of fixed asset investment (such as services). The ratio analyst should take care to compare a firm's ratio with other firms in the same industry or with appropriate industry averages.

4) Total asset turnover:

$$\frac{\text{Revenues}}{\text{Total assets}}$$

The total asset turnover measures the efficiency with which the firm utilizes its total asset base in generating revenues. As in the case of the fixed asset turnover ratio, the proper level for this ratio is significantly affected by the industry to which the firm belongs.

For both the fixed asset turnover and total asset turnover ratios, the real measure is the level of revenues (sales) supported by a given level of assets. One problem with these ratios is that they can be significantly affected by the acquisition or sell-off of assets. If a firm were to buy a large quantity of inventory at the end of the year (possibly because of very attractive prices), that would adversely impact the total asset turnover ratio. Similarly, if a firm were to dispose of a large fixed asset at the end of a year, both the fixed asset and total asset turnover would be affected positively. In neither example would the true state of the firm's sales-to-assets relationships be shown by the ratios.

Again, the solution for end-of-period adjustment problems is to use an average figure (i.e., month-end asset levels averaged over the year) in computing the ratio. The only danger in this approach is that it may not be the calculation convention used by several of the ratio reporting services (covered later in this chapter). Be sure in using these ratios for comparison purposes that you are indeed comparing "apples with apples."

c. Debt Management Ratios:

- These ratios monitor the use of debt (also known as leverage) by the firm, either by determining the ratio of debt levels to asset levels or by analyzing the ratio of various indicators of profitability to debt service.

- Like the liquidity ratios, these are of great interest to creditors in analyzing the financial health of a firm.

- It is important to note that use of debt is desirable (at least to a point) because of both its tax deductibility and the fixed payment associated with debt.

- The downside of using debt is the accompanying restrictions and covenants that are placed on the firm by lenders trying to protect their interests in its earnings stream and assets.

- The financial analyst should note that in most cases long-term lease arrangements (also referred to as capitalized leases) are generally considered to be a direct substitute for debt on a firm's balance sheet.

Typical debt management ratios include:

1) Total debt to total assets:

$$\frac{\text{Total debt}}{\text{Total assets}}$$

This measure shows the relative importance of total debt in the capital structure and is used as a general measure of the creditworthiness and financial risk of the company. The real problem with this ratio is in determining exactly what is meant by "total debt." Traditionally, total debt includes all short- and long-term liabilities of the firm; but sometimes the ratio is calculated using only the long-term portion of the debt. In international circles, this ratio is sometimes referred to as a "gearing" ratio.

Be careful about which definition you use when comparing this ratio to that of other firms or to standard industry ratios. In addition, many firms may have debt covenants that use the total debt ratio to restrict the firm's ability to issue additional debt. In that case, be sure to utilize the formula described in the bank covenants to compute this particular ratio.

2) Times interest earned (TIE):

$$\frac{\text{EBIT}}{\text{Interest charges}}$$

This ratio is defined as earnings before interest and tax (EBIT) divided by interest charges, and is generally referred to as a coverage ratio. It indicates how many times the earnings before interest and tax could decline before the firm is unable to meet (or "cover") its interest obligations. For example, a TIE of 3.0 means that the firm's EBIT could decline by as much as three times before the firm would be unable to cover its interest charges. This ratio is similar to some of the coverage ratios discussed below, in that it utilizes a measure of income (or earnings) to determine the ability of the firm to meet some fixed obligation. An alternative calculation of this ratio uses EBITDA (earnings before interest and taxes, plus depreciation and amortization charges) in place of EBIT.

3) Bank Debt to Cash Flow:

$$\frac{\text{Cash Flow Measure}}{\text{Bank Debt}}$$

This ratio (or some variation) is often included as a part of bank loan covenant agreements or as a performance measurement for highly leveraged firms. The cash flow measure may be defined as EBIT plus depreciation and amortization (EBITDA). In some forms of the ratio, the cash flow portion may be defined as net income plus depreciation minus dividends. The credit agreement with the bank will typically define the exact form to be used in meeting the covenant. The cash flow measure may be calculated on a 12-month rolling basis.

4) Debt-to-equity ratio:

$$\frac{\text{Debt (Total or Long–Term)}}{\text{TotalEquity}}$$

This ratio shows the relative importance of long-term debt in the capital structure and is used to compare the ratio over time for the same corporation and for similar corporations. This ratio may be defined in two ways: Some analysts calculate it as total debt (current liabilities plus long-term debt) divided by equity, while others feel that only long-term debt should be compared to equity.

Deciding which ratio to use depends on the firm and the industry conventions for ratios. In most cases, firms that utilize a significant amount of short-term debt on a regular basis (i.e., use short-term debt for permanent financing) should generally use total debt in the ratio. Firms that use small amounts of short-term debt, or utilize it only on a seasonal basis, should generally use long-term debt.

For this ratio, total equity is usually defined as the sum of all items in the equity account (par value, paid-in capital in excess of par and retained earnings). For firms that have a substantial amount of goodwill in their equity accounts, however, a better measure might be tangible net worth, defined as total equity minus intangibles (such as goodwill, patents, etc.).

In the case of multinational corporations, there is another factor to consider in the determination of equity. Such firms generally utilize a special equity account to reflect the changes in foreign subsidiary balance sheets resulting from translation gains and losses. The requirements for foreign balance sheet accounting are outlined in FASB Ruling 52. These translation changes result from converting foreign-currency-denominated balance sheets into the consolidated balance sheet of the U.S. parent. Since this currency translation account can fluctuate widely with exchange rate changes, it is generally best to exclude it from equity in calculating this ratio.

5) Fixed-charge coverage: This is similar to the TIE ratio, but it includes the long-term lease obligations of the firm. It is calculated as:

$$\frac{\text{EBIT} + \text{Lease Obligations}}{\text{Interest Charges} + \text{Lease Obligations}}$$

This ratio is used to relate the financial charges of a company to its ability to service those obligations. As in the case of the TIE ratio, this ratio measures the ability of the firm to meet fixed payment obligations with its earnings. Since lease payments are deducted in the determination of EBIT (earnings before interest and taxes), they must be added back in the numerator of the ratio to accurately measure the cash flows available to meet both interest and lease obligations.

6) Cash flow coverage: This ratio takes into account all of the fixed financial flows of the firm, as well as the cash flows from depreciation, and is calculated as:

$$\frac{\text{EBIT} + \text{Lease Obligations} + \text{Depreciation}}{\text{Interest} + \text{Lease Obl.} + \text{Preferred Stock Divs.}/(1-T) + \text{Principal Repmts.}/(1-T)}$$

Where: T is the firm's marginal income tax rate

In order to obtain the correct level of cash flows to meet obligations, lease payments and depreciation are added back into EBIT. In some versions of this ratio, amortization may be included in the determination of cash flows. This provides the total amount of earnings that can be used to satisfy the various fixed outflows in the denominator of the ratio.

As preferred stock dividends and principal repayments on debt are not tax-deductible items, they must be "grossed-up" to determine the amount of cash needed before tax, to meet the required after-tax obligations. The adjustment here is made by dividing these items by 1-minus-the-tax-rate to convert the after-tax obligations to required before-tax cash flows.

This ratio provides the financial analyst with a good measure of a firm's ability to meet most of its fixed-charge obligations with cash flows generated by earnings and depreciation.

d. Profitability Ratios:

- These ratios show the combined effects of liquidity and asset and debt management on operating results. As was discussed earlier with regard to liquidity ratios, the current assets and liabilities of the firm can be easily manipulated. Liquidity does not just "happen." Liquidity management is the essence of working capital management, and it is obvious that high levels of liquidity are not necessarily the desired goal of the financial manager, though some desired level of liquidity is important.

- There is a potential problem, however, in the calculation of the return on investment ratios, such as return on assets and return on equity. This problem involves choosing which profit indicator to use in the calculations.

- As with other ratios, the most widely accepted approach for the given industry should prevail. If used for industry comparisons, a consistent calculation is obviously needed.

- The various profitability ratios include:

1) Profit Margin on Sales:

$$\frac{\text{NPAT}}{\text{Sales}}$$

This ratio determines the ratio of net profit after tax (NPAT) divided by sales, and is a measure of the general profitability of the firm. For the equityholders (shareholders) of the firm a better version of this ratio may be defined as net income available to common stockholders divided by sales. In this case, any sinking-fund payments and/or preferred stock dividends are deducted from NPAT to determine the amount of income available to the common shareholders for either payment of dividends or reinvestment in the firm.

There are several other profit margin ratios, the most popular being gross profit margin, which is calculated as gross profit (sales – variable costs of goods sold) divided by sales. This ratio provides a measure of the general operating profitability of the firm.

2) Basic earnings power:

$$\frac{EBIT}{Total\ assets}$$

This ratio shows the earnings power on total assets, and is sometimes computed on total tangible assets to show the operating profit rate of return. Another way to interpret this ratio is to think of it as a measure of the pre-tax profitability of the firm's assets, or as a measure of the ability of assets to generate profits. This is a useful measure of comparison between different firms because is does not include the impact of taxes or debt structure (leverage) which may vary greatly from firm to firm.

The analyst should also be aware that accounting conventions or major changes in asset accounts (purchases or sales of assets) can have a significant impact on this (and other) ratios. In order to adjust for these items, it may be necessary to average assets over the year (average of quarterly asset balances or average of beginning and ending), or to remove intangible assets, such as goodwill, in computing the total assets figure. In analyzing companies in highly seasonal businesses it is desirable to average assets over the year in order to smooth out fluctuations.

3) Return on total assets (ROA):

$$\frac{Net\ income}{Total\ assets}$$

The return on assets after taxes shows the net operating profit rate of return. Both the ROA and basic earnings power calculations give an indication of the company's efficiency of operations, as well as the ability of the firm's asset base to generate profits. In the case of ROA, the ability of the assets to generate after-tax profits is measured, thus reflecting the impact of both taxes and use of debt (leverage).

In this ratio, the term "net income" could refer to net profit after taxes (NPAT) or could be a more restrictive measure, such as earnings available to common shareholders. The ratio analyst must have a clear definition of all components utilized in the ratio; this is especially important if industry average or comparative ratios are being used. Most sources of industry or comparative ratios will provide the formulas they use to determine them. The same formula should be used in calculating ratios for the firm being analyzed if comparisons are to be made.

4) Return on common equity (ROE):

$$\frac{\text{Net income available common shareholders}}{\text{Common equity}}$$

This widely used ratio tells the earning power on shareholder investment and is frequently used in comparing two or more firms in an industry. This ratio focuses on the returns or earnings available to common share holders and measures the returns to these owners of the firm. Since the dividends paid to preferred shareholders and sinking fund payments are generally regarded as fixed payment obligations, they are deducted from NPAT to determine income available to the common shareholders.

e. Market Value Ratios:

- These provide an indication of how investors feel about the firm's past history and future prospects.

- To this end, they differ from the previous ratios in that they are based primarily on the current market value (share price) for the firm being analyzed.

- These ratios include:

1) **Price/earnings (P/E) ratio:** tells how much investors are willing to pay per dollar of reported profits.

It is calculated as:

$$\frac{\text{Price per share}}{\text{Earnings per share}}$$

For any publicly traded firm, both of these figures are generally available from public sources of financial information such as *The Wall Street Journal,* market reporting services or on-line stock market quotation services. Historical information on P/E ratios is also available from these sources.

Generally, P/E ratios are higher for firms with good growth prospects and lower for those deemed to be riskier; but it must be remembered that because this ratio is based on market prices, it may fluctuate widely due to speculation and other non-operational factors.

If a firm has securities outstanding that can be converted or exchanged into shares of common stock (i.e., convertible bonds or stock options), it may be required to disclose a "fully-diluted" earnings-per-share figure (EPS). This figure will be lower than the regular EPS because of the possible "dilution" of earnings if the convertible items are exchanged for common stock.

2) Market/book ratio:

$$\frac{\text{Market price per share}}{\text{Book value per share}}$$

Where: Book value per share = Common Equity/Shares outstanding

This ratio provides a general indication of how investors in the market value the company relative to its book value. Firms with high rates of return on equity generally will have high multiples of share price relative to book value. This recognizes the value of the firm as a going concern with respect to the value of the underlying assets.

The one caveat for this ratio is in the determination of book value per share. As has been discussed before, there are several ways to calculate the equity value for a given company, especially if goodwill is involved or when dealing with a multinational firm. Generally, the analyst should be consistent in the definition of equity, choosing one that is most representative of the value of the company to the common shareholders.

The other problem in determining book value per share is what figure to use for the number of shares. A firm's corporate charter will determine the total number of shares which the firm is authorized to issue, but most firms will not have that total outstanding at any given time.

The preferred figure to use in this calculation is the current number of outstanding shares, which is usually listed on the firm's balance sheet. In some cases, the analyst may want to use fully diluted shares or a number which has been adjusted for outstanding options and/or warrants. Treasury stock is stock which the firm has repurchased and is not currently outstanding; therefore, it should not be included in the calculations.

3) Dividend Yield:

$$\frac{\text{Annual dividends per share}}{\text{Market price per share}}$$

This measure is generally used by investors to determine annual yield from dividends only (income yield) on a share of common stock in a given firm. The total yield to the investor would include both the dividend yield and the growth yield from appreciation of the stock's price. For some institutional investors (such as pension funds), income or dividend yield, rather than possible price appreciation, is the primary factor in choosing stocks.

3. Common-Size Financial Statements:

- These statements are developed by expressing each item as a percentage of either total assets (for common-size balance sheets) or gross revenues (for common-size income statements).
- The advantages of these statements are:
1) It is easier to compare statements from firms of different sizes
2) They facilitate comparison of a firm's financial statements over time.

4. Comparative Ratios:

- A problem in ratio analysis is that an individual ratio means very little without something against which it can be compared.

- One approach is to use trend analysis as described below; another is to compare the firm's ratios with those of other firms in the industry or with industry averages.
- Unfortunately, many ratios do not have standard, universally accepted definitions. Be certain that you apply the same formulas when making comparisons.
- There are several sources of data to utilize in ratio comparison.
  - The Dun & Bradstreet Corporation produces ratios based on data from its listings of financial and credit information about public and private firms.
  - Robert Morris Associates produces industry ratio figures sorted by standard industrial classification (SIC) codes, based on data received from bank loan officers and other commercial lenders.
  - The federal government and many state governments produce various forms of industry data.
  - Many of these sources provide breakdowns of industry ratios by firm size and provide the first quartile, median and the third quartile of the distribution of the ratio to help assess the significance of ratio deviations from industry norms.

5. Trend Analysis:

- This involves tracking the value of a given ratio over time.
- It is important for control purposes because it helps the manager determine when a particular area of the firm is having problems.
- Trend analysis can also be helpful in forecasting, as it provides an indication of future changes in the ratio variables.
- This is one area where the use computer-based spreadsheets has made this task much easier for the financial manager.

6. Uses and Limitations of Ratio Analysis: The three main users of financial ratios are:

1. Corporate managers, who use ratios to manage, control and improve their firm;
2. Credit analysts, who use ratios to determine the creditworthiness of a firm;
3. Security analysts or investors, who use ratios to determine which securities to recommend or purchase, or what a firm's securities ratings should be.

a. Primary Problems: There are four primary problems or limitations in the use of ratio analysis in corporate finance. These are:

1. Ratios look primarily at past performance and may not be an accurate indicator of future performance. They only represent one point in time; conditions could change the next day.
2. Ratios only point to potential problem areas and do not always identify the specific problem.
3. It is not always easy to distinguish between good and bad values for ratios. Also, what is good for one firm may be bad for another.

4. By itself a ratio is of little value; the user must have something to which it can be compared, such as a past value for the same firm, a comparison with other firms in the industry, or industry averages.

b. How to Use Ratios: The best analogy in speaking of ratios is to consider them similar to "warning lights" on a car. If used properly, they will generally indicate a problem in some area of a firm, either by comparing with past values or with industry averages. They will not, however, tell exactly what the problem is or how to solve it. The analyst must probe to find the reason. For example, a firm may have a low current ratio relative to the industry average, but additional analysis would be needed to determine why the current ratio is low. It could be a shortage of current assets, or an over-abundance of current liabilities, or even a result of some end-of-period adjustment on the part of the accountants. The important thing is to recognize that the ratio only gives us an indicator of where there may be a problem requiring additional investigation.

c. Additional Considerations: In addition to the basic limitations discussed above, there are several other problems or limitations which the user of ratio analysis must recognize:

1) Analysis of large multidivisional or geographically diversified firms is difficult. This is especially true for firms that are widely diversified in many different business areas. Analyzing the ratios for the overall firm would be of little value due to the diversification effects of the various divisions. The analyst may have to analyze each division of the company separately and compare the ratios for each division with those of related industries.

2) Most firms would rather compare favorably with above-average ratios than with merely average ones. This is generally so if the ratio analysis is being done internally, or by an investor looking for a good investment opportunity. Most of the sources of comparative ratios provide listings for the upper and lower portions of a given industry. Alternatively, the analyst could compare the firm in question to the industry leaders.

3) Inflation may distort financial statements.[1] In periods of high inflation, the value of asset accounts is generally understated, as is the value of long-term debt. Also, the value of the firm's inventory will be affected by the accounting method used for valuation (LIFO versus FIFO). Generally, the analyst should restate the financial statements on some common basis, but the problem cannot be completely eliminated.

At the time of writing, inflation in the U.S. is at historic low levels, but this has not always been the case. Also, companies with international operations may have to deal with hyper-inflationary environments. Accordingly, treasurers need to understand the impact of inflation on financial statements.

- First, inflation can affect the cost of fixed assets and the depreciation charges on those assets. Firms with newer assets will show higher depreciation charges and therefore lower profits. Using replacement cost accounting can help to offset these problems.

- Second, profits can be affected by the method of accounting. If a firm uses LIFO, it will show lower profits in times of rising prices than a firm using FIFO.

4) Seasonal factors may distort ratio analysis. Depending on when the end of the accounting period comes, the value of many of the accounts of firms in seasonal industries may not be representative of the true value of the company. The best approach to resolving this problem is to use average levels for the financial statement items rather than the year-end figures.

5) Firms may employ "window dressing" to make their financial statements look better than they really are. Most publicly traded firms attempt to place their financial statements (and therefore many key ratios) in the best possible light. Since generally accepted accounting principles (GAAP) allow a significant amount of leeway in interpretation, this means that the year-end financials may not be truly representative of the firm's financial position during and throughout the year. Firms may utilize different accounting conventions for GAAP versus tax accounting.

For the external analyst, the best solution may be to use the average of quarterly financials, which are generally less subject to window dressing. For the internal analyst, the best approach is to remove the window dressing adjustments wherever possible. A checklist of different types of accounting adjustments is provided at the end of this chapter.

6) Different accounting and operating practices may distort the analysis (especially true when comparing firms among industries and countries). Often, different industries use special conventions in accounting for certain assets and liabilities on their financial statements. This makes comparisons with firms in other industries difficult. The only solution is to recognize the special conventions and adjust for them where possible. The problems involved in the analysis of multinational firms are discussed below.

7) Analysis of multinational firms (MNFs) may be difficult. One of the primary problems of MNF analysis is that their U.S. financial statements are consolidated from their various foreign subsidiaries, according to FASB 52 guidelines. In this consolidation process, adjustments are made for:

a) Changes in exchange rates over the accounting period

b) Intra-company trade between subsidiaries

c) Different accounting conventions and practices used in foreign countries

All of these adjustments mean that it is generally very difficult to use ratio analysis on the total MNF. The problem is that the information needed may only be available to internal management and not to external analysts. Some possible solutions are:

a) Perform analysis only on the domestic portion of the company

   b) Analyze the foreign subsidiaries as separate entities

   c) For non-U.S. based MNFs, utilize the home country financial statements and accounting conventions.

8) A firm may give mixed readings with some ratios being good and others bad. Remember that ratios are only indicators of potential problems in certain areas. There may be good explanations for the "bad" ratios or special circumstances for the "good" ratios. If the analysis is being done internally, the analyst may be able to obtain the additional information necessary to properly interpret the ratios.

For the external analyst, the written statement accompanying the financial statements often contains explanations of any unusual events which may have affected the financial statements or certain ratios.

9) Many ratios do not have standard definitions, and wide variations persist in the ways ratios are calculated. The solution for this problem is to be certain of the definition of the ratios you are using. Sources of industry data generally provide the formula used in the calculation of their ratios, so be sure to use the same formula if you expect to make accurate comparisons.

7. Use of Computer Spreadsheets and Databases: There are many computerized sources of financial data available to the financial manager or analyst.[2] ValueLine and Compustat offer data in both an on-line format and a tape format for mainframes. The Treasury Management Association also offers an on-line database covering treasury management topics, known as TMA Online. In addition, financial and economic data are available through on-line computer services such as Compuserve and Western Union, and PC-based information from companies such as Micro-Disclosure and Gold Data Services. Many of these services allow the user to obtain data (or convert it) in a format that can be read into a PC-based spreadsheet program such as Lotus 1-2-3, Quattro or Excel.[3] Using such a program, the financial manager or analyst can then build a spreadsheet that will allow easier analysis of the financial data.

Another useful PC-based package is Monarch, which was developed by the Personics Company. This program allows the spreadsheet user to easily download information from mainframe-based information systems into a format that can be quickly translated into an analysis or planning spreadsheet.

IV. Chapter Checklists

A. Accounting Adjustments (Window Dressing)

1. Adding back outstanding checks to cash to eliminate "negative" checkbook (cash) balances.

This adjustment helps to eliminate negative cash positions on balance sheets caused by a firm's running a negative balance in its checking account in order to take advantage of disbursement float. By adding the amount of outstanding checks back to cash, and creating an offsetting current liability account called "drafts payable," the negative cash balance can often be eliminated.

2. Borrowing funds on the last day of the year to eliminate "negative" book balances or to meet loan covenants.

This approach to eliminating negative cash balances involves borrowing money for a short period of time (only a day or two) at the end of the year and holding it in cash in order to increase the cash account on the balance sheet. Sometimes this is necessary to meet liquidity restrictions on loan covenants. The money may be borrowed under a multi-year revolving credit agreement, which is considered long-term borrowing in many cases. This will further increase the apparent liquidity of the firm.

3. Recording significant sales at the end of the year in order to meet planned revenue targets.

Often a firm has some discretion over when sales are "booked" or recorded. If this is the case, by recording a large sales figure at the end of a firm's fiscal year, both revenue and profit figures can be improved.

4. Pushing payables out of the period into the next period (or generally delaying payments), in order to increase cash flows in the current period.

While this may not have much impact on the income statement of a firm, it will serve to increase the cash flows for the current period. It may also leave the firm with a higher level of cash on its balance sheet than had the payments been made on time.

5. Re-evaluating inventory or accounting reserves, which may make the end-of-period financial statements appear in a more favorable light.

These balance sheet accounts can be adjusted (i.e., inventory sold at the end of the year will increase the quick ratio) to make the financial statements appear more favorable.

6. Readjusting accruals or allowance for pension funding.

Accounting conventions allow some leeway in determining accruals or pension funding. These accounts can also be readjusted to make the financial statements appear more favorable.

7. Use of off-balance-sheet transactions such as leasing.

In some cases, leases need not be disclosed on financial statements, thus "hiding" the financing of the firm's assets. Lease payments will always appear on the income statement, however, and any significant lease arrangements must be disclosed in footnotes.

8. Cashing out certain favorable derivative transactions, such as selling currency swaps just prior to statement day.

By cashing out a currency swap position just prior to the date of financial statements, the firm can include the gains or losses on its position on the statements.

B. Checklist of Financial Ratios

Liquidity Ratios:

1) Current ratio:

$$\frac{\text{Current assets}}{\text{Current liabilities}}$$

2) Quick or acid test ratio:

$$\frac{\text{Cash} + \text{Marketable securities} + \text{Accounts receivable}}{\text{Current liabilities}}$$

Asset Management Ratios:

1) Inventory turnover:

$$\frac{\text{Annualized Cost of Goods Sold}}{\text{End--of--Period Inventory}}$$

2) Average collection period:

$$\frac{\text{Year--end Accounts receivable}}{\text{Annual revenues}/365}$$

3) Fixed assets turnover:

$$\frac{\text{Revenues}}{\text{Net fixed assets}}$$

4) Total asset turnover:

$$\frac{\text{Revenues}}{\text{Total assets}}$$

Debt Management Ratios:

1) Total debt to total assets:

$$\frac{\text{Total debt}}{\text{Total assets}}$$

2) Times interest earned (TIE):

$$\frac{\text{EBIT}}{\text{Interest charges}}$$

3) Bank Debt to Cash Flow:

$$\frac{\text{Cash Flow Measure}}{\text{Bank Debt}}$$

4) Debt-to-equity ratio:

$$\frac{\text{Debt (Total or Long–Term)}}{\text{Total Equity}}$$

5) Fixed charge coverage:

$$\frac{\text{EBIT + Lease obligations}}{\text{Interest charges + Lease obligations}}$$

6) Cash flow coverage:

$$\frac{\text{EBIT + Lease Obligations + Depreciation}}{\text{Interest + Lease Obl. + Preferred Stock Divs.}/(1-T) + \text{Principal Repmts.}/(1-T)}$$

Profitability Ratios:

1) Profit Margin on Sales:

$$\frac{\text{Net Profit after Tax}}{\text{Sales}}$$

2) Basic earnings power:

$$\frac{\text{EBIT}}{\text{Total assets}}$$

3) Return on total assets (ROA):

$$\frac{\text{Net income}}{\text{Total assets}}$$

4) Return on common equity (ROE):

$$\frac{\text{Net income available to common shareholders}}{\text{Common equity}}$$

Market Value Ratios:

1) Price/earnings (P/E) ratio:

$$\frac{\text{Price per share}}{\text{Earnings per share}}$$

2) Market/book ratio:

$$\frac{\text{Market price per share}}{\text{Book value per share}}$$

Where: Book value per share = Common Equity/Shares outstanding

3) Dividend Yield:

$$\frac{\text{Annual dividends per share}}{\text{Market price per share}}$$

V. Calculations and Examples

A. Financial Analysis Case Example

THE GERSIN MANUFACTURING CORPORATION

1. Analysis of the Current Situation

The Gersin Manufacturing Corporation is currently going through the development of its three-year plan and, as the Treasurer, you have been put in charge of this process. Figure 10.1 provides the year-end balance sheets for both last year and this year, including the change from year to year and the common-size percentages for the balance sheet items. Figure 10.2 provides two years of income statements and computation of key ratios for the two years, and also includes the income statement items expressed as a percentage of sales. Figure 10.3 shows the changes in balance sheet accounts and the statement of cash flows for the current year's financial statements.

Figure 10.1
Financial Statements – Gersin Manufacturing Company

BALANCE SHEET (Thousands of Dollars)

ASSETS	Previous Year	Current Year	Change	Prior Year % of Sales	Current Year % of Sales
Cash	$ 2,120	$ 2,450	$ 330	0.9%	1.0%
Accounts Receivable	17,850	18,500	650	7.6%	7.5%
Inventory	19,750	21,060	1,310	8.4%	8.5%
Total Current Assets	39,720	42,010	2,290	16.9%	17.0%
Plant and Equipment	148,430	155,490	7,060	63.0%	62.9%
Less: Accumulated Depreciation	(37,340)	(42,240)	(4,900)	15.8%	17.1%
Net Plant and Equipment	111,090	113,250	2,160	47.1%	45.8%
Other Long-Term Assets	25,370	23,950	(1,420)	10.8%	9.7%
Total Long-Term Assets	136,460	137,200	740	57.9%	55.5%
TOTAL ASSETS	$176,180	$179,210	$3,030	74.8%	72.5%
LIABILITIES AND EQUITY					
Notes Payable	$ 11,600	$ 13,536	$1,936	4.9%	5.5%
Accounts Payable	10,500	8,100	(2,400)	4.5%	3.3%
Accrued Wages	4,800	5,800	1,000	2.0%	2.3%
Accrued Taxes	5,000	7,700	2,700	2.1%	3.1%
Total Current Liabilities	31,900	35,136	3,236	13.5%	14.2%
Long-Term Debt	75,000	72,000	(3,000)	31.8%	29.1%
Long-Term Lease	9,750	10,800	1,050	4.1%	4.4%
Total L-T Debt/Lease	84,750	82,800	(1,950)	36.0%	33.5%
Par Value: Common Stock (10,000 Shares @ $1)	10,000	10,000	0	4.2%	4.0%
Paid-In Capital	17,050	17,050	0	7.2%	6.9%
Preferred Stock (15%)	5,000	5,000	0	2.1%	2.0%
Retained Earnings	27,480	29,224	1,744	11.7%	11.8%
Total Equity	59,530	61,274	1,744	25.3%	24.8%
TOTAL LIABILITIES AND EQUITY	$176,180	$179,210	$3,030	74.8%	72.5%

Figure 10.2
Financial Statements – Gersin Manufacturing Company

INCOME STATEMENT (Thousands of Dollars)

ASSETS	Prior Year	Current Year	Change	Prior Year % of Sales	Current Year % of Sales
Sales	$235,678	$247,113	$11,435	100.0%	100.0%
Less: Cost of Goods Sold	(110,125)	(116,143)	(6,018)	46.7%	47.0%
Gross Profit	125,553	130,970	5,417	53.3%	53.0%
General Operating Expense	56,780	57,110	330	24.1%	23.1%
Administrative Expense	23,540	25,460	1,920	10.0%	10.3%
Rents	14,700	15,700	1,000	6.2%	6.4%
Insurance	3,540	3,250	(290)	1.5%	.3%
Depreciation	4,750	4,900	150	2.0%	2.0%
Lease Expense	1,550	1,750	200	0.7%	0.7%
Total Admin. and Operating Costs	104,860	108,170	3,310	44.5%	43.8%
EBIT (Earnings Before Int. & Taxes)	20,693	22,800	2,107	8.8%	9.2%
Less: Interest Expense	(6,550)	(6,900)	(350)	2.8%	2.8%
EBT (Earnings Before Taxes)	14,143	15,900	1,757	6.4%	6.4%
Less: Provision for Taxes (34%)	(4,809)	(5,406)	(597)	2.0%	2.2%
NPAT (Net Profit After Tax)	$ 9,334	$ 10,494	$ 1,160	4.0%	4.2%
Less: Sinking Fund Obligations	(2,000)	(2,000)	0	0.8%	0.8%
Less: Preferred Stock Dividends	(750)	(750)	0	0.3%	0.3%
Earnings Available to Common Share Holders	$ 6,584	$ 7,744	$ 1,160	2.8%	3.1%
Less: Common Stock Dividends ($.60/sh) (10M shares outstanding)	(6,000)	(6,000)	0	2.5%	2.4%
Retained Earnings	$ 584	$ 1,744	$ 1,160	0.2%	0.7%

The Figures Below are in actual dollars

Earnings per Share	$0.66	$ 0.77
Stock Price	$8.66	$10.05

Figure 10.2 (Continued)
Financial Statements – Gersin Manufacturing Company

RATIO ANALYSIS: for Gersin Manufacturing

	Prior Year	Current Year	
Current Ratio	1.25	1.20	Current Assets/Current Liabilities
Quick Ratio	0.63	0.60	(Cash + Mkt. Securities + Accounts Receivable)/Current Liabilities
Avg Collection Period	27.64	27.33	Accounts Receivable/(Sales/365)
Fixed Asset Turnover	1.73	1.80	Sales/Net Fixed Assets
Total Asset Turnover	1.34	1.38	Sales/Total Assets
Total Debt to Total Assets	66.2%	65.8%	Total Debt/Total Assets
Times Interest Earned	3.16	3.30	EBIT/Interest Charges
Total Debt to Equity	1.96	1.92	Total Debt/Total Equity
Fixed Charge Coverage	2.75	2.84	(EBIT + Lease Payments)/(Interest Charge + Lease Payments)
Cash Flow Coverage	2.20	2.30	$\dfrac{\text{(EBIT + Lease Pmts. + Depreciation)}}{\text{(Interest + Lease Pmts. + Pref. Stk. Div.}/(1-T) + \text{Sinking Fund Pmts.}/(1-T))}$
Gross Profit Margin	53.3%	53.0%	Gross Profit/Sales
Net Profit Margin	4.0%	4.2%	Net Profit After Tax/Sales
Basic Earnings Power	11.7%	12.7%	EBIT/Total Assets
Return on Assets	5.3%	5.9%	Net Profit After Tax/Total Assets
Return on Equity	12.1%	13.8%	Earnings Available To Common Shareholders/Common Equity
Price/Earnings Ratio	13.15	12.98	Price Per Share/Earnings Per Share
Book Value per Share	$5.45	$5.63	Common Equity/Shares Outstanding
Market/Book Ratio	1.59	1.79	Market Price/Book Value

Figure 10.3
Financial Statements – Gersin Manufacturing Company

CHANGES IN BALANCE SHEET ACCOUNTS

	Prior Year	Current Year	Change	Source	Use
Cash	$ 2,120	$ 2,450	$ 330	$ 0	$ 330
Accounts Receivable	17,850	18,500	650	0	650
Inventory	19,750	21,060	1,310	0	1,310
Gross Plant and Equipment	148,430	155,490	7,060	0	7,060
Accumulated Depreciation	37,340	42,240	4,900	4,900	0
Other Long-Term Assets	25,370	23,950	(1,420)	1,420	0
Notes Payable	$ 11,600	$ 13,536	$1,936	$1,936	$ 0
Accounts Payable	10,500	8,100	(2,400)	0	2,400
Accrued Wages	4,800	5,800	1,000	1,000	0
Accrued Taxes	5,000	7,700	2,700	2,700	0
Long-Term Debt	75,000	72,000	(3,000)	0	3,000
Long-Term Lease	9,750	10,800	1,050	1,050	0
Common Stock	10,000	10,000	0	0	0
Paid-In Capital	17,050	17,050	0	0	0
Preferred Stock	5,000	5,000	0	0	0
Retained Earnings	27,480	29,224	1,744	1,744	0

Figure 10.3 (Continued)
Financial Statements – Gersin Manufacturing Company

STATEMENT OF CASH FLOWS (Thousands of Dollars)

CASH FLOW FROM OPERATING ACTIVITIES

Net Income	$10,494
Additions (sources of cash)	
Depreciation	4,900
Increase in Accrued Wages	1,000
Increase in Accrued Taxes	2,700
Subtractions (uses of cash)	
Increase in Accounts Receivable	(650)
Increase in Inventory	(1,310)
Decrease in Accounts Payable	(2,400)
NET CASH FLOW FROM OPERATIONS	$ 14,734
CASH FLOW FROM INVESTING ACTIVITIES	
Acquisition of Gross Plant and Equipment	$ (7,060)
Sale of Other Fixed Assets	1,420
NET CASH FLOW FROM INVESTING ACTIVITIES	$ (5,640)
CASH FLOW FROM FINANCING ACTIVITIES	
Increase in Notes Payable	$ 1,936
Repayment of Long-term Debt	(3,000)
Sinking Fund Obligation	(2,000)
Increase in Long-term Lease	1,050
Preferred Dividends Paid	(750)
Common Dividends Paid	(6,000)
NET CASH FLOW FROM FINANCING ACTIVITIES	$(8,764)
NET INCREASE (DECREASE) IN CASH & EQUIVALENTS	$330
CASH AND EQUIVALENTS AT START OF YEAR	$2,120
CASH AND EQUIVALENTS AT END OF YEAR	$2,450

Some observations and comments on the sample financial statements:

1. Most asset accounts increased over the last year, with the exception of the Other Fixed Asset Account. Total assets increased by approximately $3 million.

2. Notes payable were increased by almost $2 million over the past year to cover a reduction in accounts payable, a result of a major supplier tightening its credit terms.

3. The firm retired $3 million in long-term debt during the year, and added an additional long-term lease for approximately $1 million.

4. With the exception of the $1.7 million increase in retained earnings, there were no changes in the equity accounts for the firm over the year.

5. There was little change in cost of goods sold on a percentage basis, but administrative and operating costs increased by over $3 million, primarily due to the implementation of a new customer service division.

6. Lease and interest expense were up only slightly and preferred stock dividends and common stock dividends remained constant.

7. Liquidity as measured by the current ratio and the quick ratio has decreased slightly, mainly due to the increase in notes payable. The current ratio declined from 1.25 to 1.20, while the quick ratio declined from 0.63 to 0.60.

8. The average collection period (also known as days sales outstanding) is slightly better at 27.3 days compared to 27.6 days for the previous year.

9. Both the fixed asset turnover and total asset turnover ratios show a little improvement, indicating that the firm is using its assets at a slightly higher level of efficiency. Fixed asset turnover increased from 1.73 to 1.80, while total asset turnover increased from 1.34 to 1.38.

10. The debt ratios and coverage ratios all indicate that the firm is in better shape than the previous year in its use of debt. Levels of debt relative to assets and equity have declined (total debt to equity declined from 1.96 to 1.92) and coverage ratios (the ability to make the debt and other fixed charge payments) have increased over the past year (TIE increased from 3.16 to 3.30 and Fixed Charge Coverage increased from 2.75 to 2.84).

11. The gross profit margin is relatively unchanged, but other profitability measures are all up from the previous year, Return on Equity has increased from 17.1% to 18.6%.

12. The stock market viewed the past year's performance favorably, with an increase in the stock price from $8.66 to $10.05 on an increase in earnings per share from $0.66 to $0.77.

13. Analysis of the Statement of Cash Flows indicates that the firm generated $14.7 million of cash flows from operations, while spending $5.6 million for the net acquisition of new assets. The firm decreased debt by $3 million, increased capitalized leases by $1 million and contributed $2 million towards future debt retirement (sinking fund payment). Finally, the total amount of dividends paid the preferred and common shareholders was $6.75 million. The net change in the cash position of the firm was an increase in cash and cash equivalents of $330,000.

B. Example of Inventory Accounting

The example below provides an illustration of the impact of LIFO versus FIFO accounting for inventory on the income statements of a firm.

XYZ, Inc.
Inventory Information

Beginning Inventory, January 1	1,500 units	@ $7.00 per unit =	$10,500
Purchase, March 15	750 units	@ $7.50 per unit =	5,625
Purchase, September 14	1,000 units	@ $7.75 per unit =	7,750
	3,250 units		$ 23,875

| Sales during the year | 2,500 units |
| Ending Inventory, December 31 | 750 units |

XYZ, Inc.
Inventory Information using FIFO

Sales (2,500 units)

1,500 units @ $7.00 per unit (Beginning Inventory)	=	$10,500.00
750 units @ 7.50 per unit (Purchase, March 15)	=	5,625.00
250 units @ 7.75 per unit (Purchase, September 14)	=	1,937.50
2,500	**Cost of Goods Sold**	$18,062.50

XYZ, Inc.
Inventory Information using LIFO

Sales (2,500 units)

1,000 units @ $7.75 per unit (Purchase, September 14)	=	$ 7,750
750 units @ 7.50 per unit (Purchase, March 15)	=	5,625
750 units @ 7.00 per unit (Beginning Inventory)	=	5,250
2,500	**Cost of Goods Sold**	$18,625

The LIFO ($18,625) method shows Cost of Goods Sold higher then the FIFO ($18,062.50) method. The result on the income statement shows that by using the LIFO method the Gross Profit will be lower, and therefore the taxes paid will be lower, than using the FIFO method.

In the example above, the ending inventory for the LIFO method would include a lower inventory balance on the balance sheet than if the FIFO method were used. This is because, when using the LIFO method, the ending inventory is calculated with the smallest per-unit cost.

This example shows an increase in per-unit cost over the year; if, instead, per-unit cost had declined, the situation would be reversed. This means that the LIFO method would have lower Cost of Goods Sold and a higher balance in the ending inventory account compared with the FIFO method.

According to FASB principles, the basis for stating inventories should be applied consistently and disclosed clearly in the financial statements. Whenever a significant change is made, there must be a full disclosure of the nature of the change and its impact on the firm's income statements and balance sheets. Firms are allowed to use different accounting conventions for tax purposes versus public statement purposes.

VI. Endnotes

1. See: FASB 33, *Financial Reporting and Changing Prices* (September 1979), for a discussion of the effects of inflation on financial statements. This ruling by the Financial Accounting Standards Board outlines the various approaches used by the accounting profession to provide more accurate and useful financial statements during periods of high inflation. More recent FASB rulings, 82 and 89, also cover inflation adjustments for financial statements.

2. Several of the more popular or widely available software packages and databases are mentioned in this section. This list is not meant to be exhaustive, nor is any endorsement implied.

3. Several of the listed services (specifically, Compustat and Micro-Disclosure) offer publicly available financial information such as SEC 10-K and 10-Q reports on compact disks (CD-ROM), which can be read by equipment linked to a PC.

11 Financial Planning and Control

I. Outline of the Chapter

A. Strategic Plans
   1. Corporate Purpose
   2. Corporate Scope
   3. Corporate Objectives
   4. Corporate Strategies
   5. Corporate Directives

B. Operating Plans

C. The Financial Plan
   1. Basic Steps in Developing the Financial Plan
   2. Basic Components of the Financial Plan

D. Revenue (Sales) Forecast
   1. Develop a Pricing Strategy
   2. Divide Revenues into Major Groups
   3. Forecast the Level of Business Activity in Each Market Area
   4. Forecast the Firm's Market Share for Each Market Area
   5. Determine the Impact of Any Other Factors
   6. Complete Forecasts for Each Product Group Both in Aggregate and on an Individual Product Basis

E. Forecasting Financial Requirements: Percentage-of-Sales Method
   1. Projected Financial Statements

Chapter Checklist

Calculations and Example

II. Introduction

This chapter is primarily concerned with developing *pro forma* financial statements and projecting the future funding requirements of the firm. The financial manager typically uses these pro forma statements for long-range forecasting of capital budgets, determination of covenant compliance and determining the need for different sources of long-term financing of the corporation.

III. Coverage of Chapter Material

A. Strategic Plans

- These are the overall long-run plans for the firm's future, often done on a three-to-five-year basis and revised annually. Some treasurers, however, argue that in these rapidly changing times, any forecasting or planning beyond a one-year time horizon is "blue-sky" planning.

- The basic purpose of the strategic plan is to chart a course for the firm over the long term and, more specifically, what it needs to do in the next few years in order to achieve its long-term objectives. This may involve the determination of the progression of debt and equity over the upcoming periods and their impact on the firm's financial structure. Once the plan has been set, it can become a "road map" for the firm to follow.

- For the financial planner, strategic plans are important because they establish the basic assumptions necessary for developing more detailed financial plans.

  1. Corporate Purpose: This is a general statement that defines the overall purpose of the firm. Usually it includes a "mission statement" that indicates the firm's future direction. The purpose can be defined in either general or specific terms. For example, for many years the General Motors statement of corporate purpose was: "GM is in the business of providing transportation for people." Although this statement was rather broad, it did state the reason for GM's existence.

  Some firms state their corporate purpose in terms of what they will do for their shareholders ("maximize the value of shareholder wealth"); others may take a customer-oriented approach ("provide our customers with state-of-the-art communication systems at the best available prices").

  It is important to remember that the company must consider both its customers and its shareholders (the owners and other stakeholders) in setting its corporate purpose. It is also important to note that things change over time, and the corporate purpose that is valid today may not be valid in the future.

  2. Corporate Scope: This defines the corporation's lines of business and geographic areas of operation. As in the case of the corporate purpose, this may be either general or specific. It is very useful for clarifying exactly what portion of the market the firm plans to occupy for distinguishing itself from other firms in its industry.

  A good example is found in the steel industry. Many large steel companies, such as USX Corporation are diversifying widely, while others are sticking to their basic business. Nucor, a specialty steel manufacturer, is an example of a firm that has decided to concentrate on its basic line of business, as this statement of corporate scope reveals:

  > "We are a manufacturing company producing primarily steel products. The major strength of our company is constructing plants economically and operating them efficiently."

  3. Corporate Objectives: These provide managers with specific goals. They usually tend to be quantitative in nature and should be challenging yet realistically achievable. These objectives can be stated in quantitative terms, such as target returns, profit margins, earnings per share, etc., or they can be stated in qualitative terms such as "maintaining the highest levels of customer service and satisfaction." To be measurable and achievable, objectives should be stated in quantitative terms whenever possible.

  Firms often will establish multiple goals, and these goals will change as market and economic conditions change. In order to properly motivate managers, their compensation may be linked to the achievement of those objectives.

4. Corporate Strategies: These are the approaches used to realize the corporate objectives within the framework of the corporate purpose and scope. These strategies provide the detailed "blueprints" showing how the managers of the firm will achieve its stated objectives. Specifically, these strategies address questions such as: what products will be sold in which markets, how will they be priced, what marketing approaches will be used, etc.

5. Corporate Directives: These directives set up the basic set of assumptions concerning overall growth, the economy, inflation, etc. that will be used by different areas of the firm in developing their plans and forecasts for the future. This ensures that all areas will be "in sync" with each other as their plans are developed.

B. Operating Plans

- The most important task in developing any operating plan is obtaining an accurate forecast of sales. Since the sales forecast drives so many variables in the operating and financial plans, its accuracy is critical to building a realistic plan.

- There are two basic approaches to developing operating plans, the "bottoms-up" approach and the "top-down" approach.

- In the "bottoms-up" approach, the operating plan is developed from the lowest operating levels of the company, using uniform assumptions concerning production volumes, sales, economic factors, etc. The plans from each of the operating areas are then consolidated into a firm-wide operating plan. This approach requires substantial effort and coordination of different areas of the firm, but generally results in a more realistic and achievable plan.

- In the "top-down" approach, the basic goals and even the desired results of the plan are specified at the highest level of management. The operating areas must then figure out what they need to do to meet these goals. In some corporate environments, especially when major change is required, this approach can achieve excellent results. If, however, the goals are unrealistic or the operating divisions do not "buy into" the plan, it may not yield the desired results.

- In many companies, operating plans are typically developed for a three-to-five-year horizon, with the first year being very detailed (i.e., broken out by quarter or month) and the following years more general. Due to rapid changes in the financial and economic arenas, long-term projections are usually difficult to make. These plans, therefore, are usually updated yearly.

- While this three-to-five-year time frame is typical for U.S. companies, those in other countries may take a much longer view. For example, some Japanese companies have 100-year strategic plans, which chart where the company wants to be at that far-distant time. Many European companies regularly use a 10–20-year planning horizon. Some of these differences are cultural in nature and some result from different methods of accounting. The short-term view in the U.S. is due in great part to the emphasis on quarterly earnings by owners of U.S. companies (versus those of foreign companies), and the readiness of those investors to quickly sell off the stock of any company that shows poor short-term performance.

- The operating plan provides the detailed implementation of the corporate strategies. The operating plan is usually constructed at the department level and first consolidated into organizational units, such as divisions and/or operating subsidiaries of the firm, and then into the total consolidated plan for the overall firm.

- Firms in seasonal industries may "calendarize" their projections by producing monthly forecasts based on past seasonality trends.

C. The Financial Plan

- The financial plan is an important part of the firm's overall operating plan. While the general operating plan has some financial aspects, the financial plan goes into much greater detail.

- The purpose of the financial plan is to take the information provided by sales and production forecasts, as well as from capital budgets, to determine what the future financial statements of the firm will look like.

- On a more detailed level, this plan determines how the company will raise the funds it needs to pay for all the things it wants to do.

- The cash flows from operations will be computed, as will the projected outflows of cash for the purchase of new assets.

- Also in the plan are the sources of funds that will be needed to finance the company over the life of the plan.

- The plan helps management to answer questions such as: how much profit will be generated, how much will be paid in shareholder dividends, what will be the available retained earnings, will new debt need to be issued, and should it be short-term or long-term debt, etc.

- The process of developing the financial plan can be broken down either by basic steps to implementation or by basic components.

  ### 1. Basic Steps in Developing the Financial Plan:

  a. Set up a system of pro forma financial statements to analyze and monitor the effects of the operating plan on projected profits and other indicators of financial condition. This basically entails determining the required investment in assets necessary to support the projected sales level, as well as liability and equity accounts that can be forecast as a variable of the projected revenues.

  b. Determine the specific financial requirements needed to support the company's plan. In most cases, net revenues from operations and other sources tied to revenues will not be sufficient to fund the necessary asset investment; therefore, the financial manager will need to look elsewhere for capital.

  c. Forecast the financing sources, both internal and external, to be used over the planning horizon. Some internal sources (retained earnings and some liability accounts) will be forecast during the previous steps, and the financial manager must determine what additional internal sources can be utilized. The major portion of this step, however, is determining the external sources that will be required to fund the plan. These include new borrowing (short and long-term), sale of assets, leasing arrangements, reduction in dividends or the sale of new equity.

It should be noted that one option may be to reduce the projected growth in the plan so as to minimize dependency on external sources of funding. This concept has been referred to as "sustainable growth," or the growth rate that a firm can achieve without having to rely "too much" on external sources of funding.

d. Establish and maintain a system of controls to ensure that the plan is properly carried out. Planning or forecasting for the future does a firm little good if the plan is filed away and never referred to again. The primary purpose of the financial plan is to provide a "road map" showing where the firm will be going during the next few years. Maintaining a system of controls ensure that the "road map" is checked on a periodic basis. This results in better overall financial management and also provides the additional benefit of controlling unplanned expenditures.

e. Develop procedures for adjusting the basic plan as economic and other conditions change. Regardless of how well-developed a financial plan may be, things change over time and the planner must be flexible enough to adjust the forecast to reflect new economic and market realities as they arise. The procedures for a regular review and "reality check" of the financial plan are essential if it is to be used by the firm as a true planning tool. The plan's projections must also be compared with actual results on a monthly or quarterly basis to see how well they are tracking with reality.

2. Basic Components of the Financial Plan: This section outlines the various components of the financial plan:

a. Analysis of the firm's current financial condition: The best place to start the financial plan is to determine the current condition of the firm. This involves the preparation and analysis of the current financial statements to determine its strengths and weaknesses.

b. Revenue forecast over the planning period: As will be discussed below, the revenue or sales forecast is a critical part of developing the overall financial plan, as many other variables are forecast as a function of sales. In many companies, the revenue forecast becomes the basis for the monthly cash budget and forecast.

c. Capital expenditure budget for the planning period: This portion of the financial plan outlines the planned expenditures for new assets and projects in which the firm will be investing over the planning period. The information will often come from many different areas of the firm, especially if the capital budgeting process is decentralized.

d. Cash budget or forecast for the planning period: The cash budget for the planning period allows the treasurer to determine when the firm will need to obtain funds from external sources and when it will have surplus funds to invest. The cash budget is an essential forecasting tool for the cash manager, who needs to determine the timing of the cash inflows and outflows over the planning period.

e. *Pro forma* financial statements: The *pro forma* financial statements allow the treasurer to determine the impact of capital expenditures and financing on the firm's future income statements and balance sheets. It is useful to perform financial analysis (ratio analysis) on the pro forma statements to determine the impact on the firm's key ratios over the planning period and for covenant compliance.

f. Listing of planning assumptions: This portion of the financial plan outlines the key assumptions used in the development of the forecast. These assumptions include the overall market for the firm's products and services, the general economy, inflation forecasts and expected trends over the planning horizon.

g. External financing plan: The final portion of the financial plan outlines where the firm will obtain the necessary external funds over the forecast period. Specifically this indicates when the firm will issue additional debt or equity to support the needs of the financial plan.

D. Revenue (Sales) Forecast

- This is the most important part of the financial plan because many other variables are forecast as a function of the projected revenue or sales levels. It is also, typically, the portion of the forecast over which the firm has the least direct control.

- The revenue forecast for each market area of the firm can be determined by estimating total business activity for that area, and then analyzing the probable market share achievable. Other factors, such as advertising, promotions, backlogs, recent trends, etc., should be taken into account.

- Because of the importance of the revenue forecast, the firm should make every effort to generate one that is realistic.

- In essence the revenue forecast should determine how the overall market is growing (or shrinking) as well as how the firm's "share of the pie" is changing.

- It is important to note that this forecast is the least likely to be predicted correctly and that it is usually outside of the treasurer's control. The best approach to ensure that it is not being built on fallacious assumptions is to force the marketing or sales department. which often develop the forecast, to fully outline and defend all of the assumptions used in its development. Outside data, such as industry studies or projections, can also be used to support the plan.

- It is usually useful to generate several versions of the financial plan for various levels of sales. Utilizing computer-based spreadsheets will greatly simplify the process of creating several financial plan scenarios.

- An alternative approach to the basic revenue forecasting described here is to use a "bottom-up" method. In this methodology, monthly *pro forma* financial statements are developed for each product or line and then summed up in an overall forecast for the company.

- The process of developing the revenue forecast is generally as follows:

    1. Develop a Pricing Strategy: The first step is to develop a strategy for pricing or at least a range of appropriate prices for all of the major products or services.

2. Divide Revenues into Major Groups: Because different products or services will be competing in different markets, it is best to forecast each major product or service separately.

3. Forecast the Level of Business Activity in Each Market Area: This portion of the forecast determines the overall size of the market for each of the product or service groups in which the firm competes.

4. Forecast the Firm's Market Share for Each Market Area: This portion of the forecast determines how much of each market the firm will obtain over the planning period. This involves analyzing both the firm's products and services and those of the competition. The forecast may cover various price/volume scenarios. Part of this process should be a determination of where any growth will come from: Is it a function of general market growth or coming from an increase in market share (the latter being more difficult to manage because you are "taking it away" from a competitor)?

5. Determine the Impact of Any Other Factors: These include considering the impact of items such as advertising campaigns, promotional discounts, credit terms, order backlogs and recent trends in new orders. The interrelationships with other variables should also be considered in this phase of the forecast. For example, higher sales may result in additional required investment in inventory and/or receivables, which the firm will have to finance.

6. Complete Forecasts for Each Product Group Both in Aggregate and on an Individual Product Basis: In this portion of the forecast, the individual sales forecasts are summed and then compared with the aggregate product/service group forecast. Any differences are then reconciled, and the end result is an overall sales forecast for the firm, with breakdowns by major divisions and product/service lines.

E. Forecasting Financial Requirements: Percentage-of-Sales Method:

- This is a simple yet effective forecasting method that allows the manager to estimate the future financial needs of the firm quickly. It is based on two assumptions:

    1. Most balance sheet accounts are tied directly to sales.

    2. The current levels of all assets are optimal for the current sales level (or the existing ratio of assets to sales will continue).

- These are critical assumptions and the successful use of this method is highly dependent upon accurate sales forecasts. The steps in the process are detailed below and the financial planning example using the percentage-of-sales forecasting method is provided at the end of this section. Some of the problems with this method and how to manage them are covered in Section F below.

- This is another area where a "bottom-up" forecasting approach can be used. In this instance, key ratios are developed for each product or area of the firm. These ratios are used to develop *pro forma* financial statements for the various areas, which are then consolidated into the overall forecast.

- The steps in developing the percentage-of-sales forecast are:

1. Determine which balance sheet items will vary directly with sales and calculate the percentages of sales for those items for the current year based on actual and historical levels.

2. Use these percentages multiplied by the sales forecast to determine the balance sheet levels for the following year. While depreciation does not seem to be explicitly considered as a source of funds, the current year's depreciation charges are included in the determination of retained earnings.

3. Insert previous levels for balance sheet accounts that cannot be forecasted as a percentage of sales (notes payable, long-term debt and equity). At least one of these will be changed in the final version of the balance sheet.

4. Add the expected increase in retained earnings to the previous year's equity level to obtain the forecast for the equity account.

5. Determine the level of external funds needed to balance the accounts; this amount will have to be added to the various external fund accounts.

6. Determine the projected allocation of additional funds needed for the debt and equity accounts, adjusting for any restrictions on the firm's debt or liquidity, or any other restriction. This allocation should be consistent with the firm's capital structure policy.

- Some of the major features of the percentage-of-sales method are:

1. Projected Financial Statements: Given the steps outlined above, the firm can construct a set of pro forma financial statements for the planning period. These pro forma statements then can be analyzed to determine the financial impact on the firm over the planning horizon.

2. Analysis of Projected Ratios: Once the projected financial statements are completed, financial ratio analysis can be performed to determine the impact of strategies and other assumptions on the future of the firm. These ratios can be compared either to past values for the firm or to industry averages or competitors' ratios.

3. Relationship between Growth and Financial Requirements: There are relationships between the growth rate in sales and other factors in the forecasting approach that will ultimately affect the overall financial requirements of the firm. Those relationships will affect the ability of the firm to sustain growth over time without excessive reliance on external sources of financing.

This concept of "sustainable growth" basically attempts to find a growth rate which the firm can sustain over time without having to raise new capital in the external markets. This means that growth must be "financed" by cash flows from operations and other sources tied directly to sales increases (i.e., increases in accounts payable and accrual items).

Some of the considerations concerning growth and financial requirements are:

a. Growth and Financial Planning: At low growth rates, the firm may find that it can generate all the funds it needs through internal sources (retained earnings and spontaneous increases in certain liabilities, such as accounts payable and accrual items).

b. Effect of Dividend Policy on Financing Needs: Dividend policy will have a major impact on the ability of the firm to grow over time. Essentially, dividends are earnings of the firm which are diverted to the shareholders rather than reinvested to fund the acquisition of new assets. Dividend policy is covered in detail in Chapter 5, but here it is sufficient to understand that most firms will pay some level of dividends and this will have an impact of the need for external funding.

In general, if a firm wishes to sustain a high growth rate, its directors may decide to pay low dividends or none at all, thus increasing the level of retained earnings and reducing the need for external funds. This is often the case for new or start-up firms in high growth industries.

c. Capital Intensity: As the capital intensity of the firm increases, more assets are required to support a given level of sales. Alternatively, if the firm can increase its productivity (reduce capital intensity) it will also reduce its need for external funding for a given revenue stream. As will be discussed below, this kind of productivity increase is often seen in firms that are growing and can realize economies of scale in their production processes.

d. Profit Margin: As the firm increases its profit margin it will decrease its need for external funding, all other variables being constant. Again, as will be discussed below, as a firm grows and begins to realize economies of scale it may be able to reduce its per-unit costs of production, resulting in increased profit margins. In addition, some costs may be relatively fixed, which offers the firm some operating leverage as the revenue levels increase.

F. Forecasting with Changing Balance Sheet Ratios

- The percentage-of-sales forecasting method makes some critical assumptions in the development of the pro forma financial statements for the planning period.

- In many cases these assumptions may not fit a "real-world" context, thus making the model more difficult to use. Fortunately, many planners utilize computer-based spreadsheets to develop these models, which makes the adjustments for changing assumptions much easier.

- Some of the most common problems, together with suggested solutions, are listed below.

  1. Economies of Scale: When these are present, the firm's effective productivity will increase over time as the size of the firm increases. This generally results in a reduction in the ratio of assets to sales, lower per-unit production costs, and higher profit margins due to greater operating leverage from fixed production costs. In order to accommodate these changes in the forecast, the financial planner must forecast new ratios for each of the above items over the planning horizon and use the new ratios rather than constant ratios.

  2. Lumpy Assets: For many firms, assets cannot be added in small continuing amounts but must be added in large discrete lumps. This is usually the case with fixed assets, where we tend to see a step function in the relationship between increasing fixed assets and sales. In managing this change in the assumptions, the planner must forecast the level of assets (usually only the fixed assets) needed for each year of the planning horizon in order to support the estimated level of revenues.

3. Cyclical Changes: Unforeseen changes in the economic environment may significantly affect the accuracy of the forecast. As the economy changes, the stream of revenues forecast and/or expenses may change, resulting in an inaccurate set of pro forma statements. The best way to adjust for this problem is to develop several sets of pro forma statements for different economic scenarios. This is especially easy if the forecast is developed in a spreadsheet.

4. Seasonal Industries: In industries with strong seasonality, firms must either make substantial investments in plant and equipment to produce at a high rate during a short period, or they must build up high levels of inventories and/or receivables to meet demand. These factors make forecasting in seasonal industries more difficult. Typically, companies in those industries use seasonal dating on invoices. For example, toy manufacturers may ship much of their merchandise to retailers in late summer or early fall in anticipation of the heavy Christmas season. The invoices for the toys, however, would usually be dated for some time after the selling season starts, allowing the retailers to generate the revenues to pay them off.

This factor can be adjusted in much the same way that it is adjusted for lumpy assets. The planner must determine the level of assets needed to support the projected sales level during the heaviest production season for each year of the planning horizon. These assets levels can then be used to develop the forecast.

5. Strategic Changes: If a company changes its strategy by acquiring or divesting a business, or if it changes its debt structure, forecasting becomes difficult, as historical financial statement relationships will change. In the case of a major strategic change, the current financial plan may have to be scrapped and a new one developed. In the event of a divestiture, if the original plan was broken out by division, the remaining divisions could be recombined to create a new forecast. Again, this is a case where it is very helpful to develop the model on a computer-based spreadsheet.

G. Other Forecasting Approaches

- Generally, a planner would use other methods to forecast certain items that cannot be reliably forecast using ratios or percentage of sales.

Some of these forecasting approaches are:

1. Regression Analysis: This approach may be useful where there is a general trend in the relationship between sales and the variable in question. The most simple of these methods is a single variable linear regression, where one variable is determined as a function of another.

More complex techniques such as multiple linear regression (multiple input variables) or curvilinear regression (non-linear relationship) may be useful for certain types of forecasting. Caution should be exercised in using these approaches, however, as they are difficult to use and can be easily misinterpreted.

Often factors such as day-of-the-week or day-of-the-month effects that are difficult to determine can have an impact on the variable being forecast. In addition, sometimes the explanatory variables used in a regression analysis may themselves be correlated (this is known as multicolinearity), which would producing spurious correlation indicators in the regression.

For variables such as interest rates and foreign exchange rates, sophisticated time-series regression techniques exist (e.g., Box-Jenkins) which can be very accurate under certain conditions.

2. Specific Item Forecasting: Some balance sheet items, especially where there is no relationship to sales, need to be forecast separately, based on historical trends and other factors impacting projected levels. Some of these have already been discussed above, e.g., dealing with lumpy assets. In these cases, primitive methods such as intuition or educated guessing may sometimes be used, or some combination of methods. In any case, this is one area where forecasters should be certain to make a "reality check" to determine if their estimates are reasonable given the circumstances.

3. Cash Flow Statement: Another approach, similar to the percent of sales, focuses primarily on a projected or pro forma cash flow statement. This approach determines the firm's need for cash in the future, but is generally most appropriate only for periods of less than one year.

One of the best kinds of forecasting within a year's time frame is the receipts and disbursements forecast (essentially a cash budget). This forecast takes the relationships between accounting and other information to determine the timing of cash inflows and outflows for horizons as short as a single day up to a year in the future.

Another approach is the adjusted net income forecast, which uses accrual based income information and makes certain adjustments (usually for depreciation and accrual items) to arrive at an estimate of cash flows.[1]

H. Financial Controls

- One of the greatest problems in financial planning is that although firms may spend many dollars and people-days creating elaborate financial plans, they often fail to use them properly for control purposes.

- To become more successful in the planning process, the financial manager must review past forecasts to see how accurate they were. This provides two benefits:

    1. From a control aspect, checking actual performance against the forecast may prevent misappropriation of funds.

    2. The only way to improve the future forecasts is to determine what was "right" or "wrong" with the prior forecasts.

- As discussed earlier in this section, the purpose of any plan should be to provide a "road map" to figure out where the company is going, as well as a guide to how well it is doing.

- Variance analysis should be used as a financial control. This involves comparing actual with planned results on a continuing basis. The basic question to ask is: "How are we doing with respect to the plan?"

I.   Computerized Financial Planning Models

- One advance in the financial planning area is the use of computer-based spreadsheet programs, such as Lotus 1-2-3, EXCEL and Quattro.

- When forecasts are made in the spreadsheet format, it becomes much easier to determine the impact of changes in the underlying assumptions of the forecast.

- The forecaster can perform multiple sensitivity and scenario analyses in order to pinpoint how changes in the assumptions affect other variables in the forecast.

- Some of the newer versions of the spreadsheets allow "goal seeking," where one variable is set at a "goal value" and the other variables are automatically adjusted until the goal is reached.

- Another option is "Monte Carlo" simulation analysis, where several input variables are changed according to predetermined distributions, and the results on the output variables are recorded for many simulations. For example, the important input variables for the forecast may be sales revenues and the interest rate paid on short-term debt, while the output variable of interest is net profit after tax (NPAT). In a Monte Carlo simulation, the forecaster would specify a distribution for each of these variables as part of the input process. Sales could be normally distributed with a mean of $10 million and a standard deviation of $2 million. Interest rates, on the other hand, may have a uniform distribution between 5.0% and 7.5%. The Monte Carlo simulation would randomly choose input values for sales and interest rates based on these specified distributions, and run the forecast model many times (sometimes thousands of times). The results of each run of the model and the resulting output of NPAT are recorded and then displayed as the distribution of the output variable. This process allows the forecaster to better determine the potential distribution of the output variable.

- There is, however, a potential problem in the use of computer spreadsheets. Their use may make the propagation of false or inaccurate assumptions easier and more acceptable. Results of any computer-based projections need to be given a very careful "reality check" in order to make sure that the results are acceptable, i.e., beware of the "garbage-in, garbage-out" problem, and check for problems in the model design.

IV. Chapter Checklist

A.   Methods of Forecasting and Planning

1. **Strategic Plan:** This is primarily a long-term, fully developed plan for determining the future direction of a firm. The method consists of developing the purpose, scope, objectives, strategies and directives that the firm will employ over the next 3 to 5 years.

2. **Operating Plan:** This can be developed in either a "top-down" or "bottom-up" approach and provide more detailed directions for the firm's management over the succeeding 12 months.

3. Financial Plan: This is part of the firm's overall operating plan and focuses on the projected *(pro forma)* financial statements.

4. Revenue Forecast: This is the most important part of the financial plan, because many of the variables in the financial plan are determined as a function of revenues (sales).

5. Percentage-of-Sales Forecasting Method: This is a simple forecasting method that allows management to estimate the future financial needs of a firm, based on the relationship of many financial variables to sales or revenue projections.

6. Regression Analysis: This statistical forecasting approach is most often used where one variable can be determined as a function of another. It is more useful for forecasting individual variables than to groups of variables.

7. Specific Item Forecasting: Some items in a forecast may be best determined as a function of historical trends or other functional relationships.

8. Cash Flow Statement: This approach involves developing a pro forma cash flow statement (receipts and disbursements) for the firm.

9. Computerized Financial Planning Models: Most of the methods discussed above can be easily developed in spreadsheets or other computer-based models.

V. Calculations and Example

A. Financial Planning Case Example

Note: This example is a continuation of the example in Chapter 10.

THE GERSIN MANUFACTURING CORPORATION

1. Analysis of the Current Situation

The Gersin Manufacturing Corporation is currently going through the development of its three-year plan and, as the Treasurer, you have been put in charge of this process. In Chapter 10, an analysis of the current state of the firm was provided, together with current and historical financial statements.

2. Developing the Three-Year Financial Plan

In developing its three-year plan (Figures 11.1, 11.2, and 11.3), the Gersin Corporation has made the following key assumptions:

1. All of the asset accounts are assumed to vary directly with sales according to the current asset to sales ratio. These ratios will remain constant over the forecasting period.

2. On the liabilities and equity side, only the accounts payable, accrued wages and accrued taxes accounts will vary directly with sales.

3. The level of long-term leases will remain at the current level and will not change over the forecast period.

4. No changes in the common stock, paid-in capital or preferred stock accounts will be made over the planning period.

5. Any amount of external financing needed will be initially allocated 50% to additional notes payable and 50% to additional long-term debt. The average cost of funds for this additional debt is 7.5% for the short-term portion of the debt and 12.5% for the long-term portion.

6. Preferred stock and common stock dividends will remain constant at current levels over the forecast period.

7. Cost of goods sold, general operating expense, administrative expenses and depreciation are assumed to vary directly with sales over the planning period, while rents, insurance and lease expense are assumed to remain constant.

8. Interest expense will increase as additional external financing is obtained. As noted above the average cost of this financing is 10%.[2]

9. The marginal tax rate will remain constant at 34%.

10. Sinking fund obligations will remain at $2 million per year.

11. Projected revenues (sales) are expected to grow at an annual rate of 7.5% over the planning period.

3. Observations on the Financial Plan

1. The firm will need to raise approximately $22.5 million in order to support its planned level of revenues over the next three years. The current version of the plan calls for increasing notes payable and long-term debt in order to finance the expansion.

2. Analysis of the pro forma ratios for the firm shows decreasing liquidity due to the increase in notes payable. Potentially, this can cause problems with lenders. On the plus side, however, debt as a percentage of total assets is generally stable, as is debt to equity.

3. The current plan does not assume any increase in productivity or increased efficiency in the use of assets. If either of these can be achieved, the firm may be able to reduce the level of external funding needed.

4. Even though liquidity is decreasing (note decreasing current and quick ratios in Figure 11.3), the coverage ratios appear to be improving over the forecast period. This indicates that the firm should have no problem covering the payments on the additional debt.

5. Due to both operating and financial leverage, return on assets and return on equity are increasing over the planning horizon.

6. The current plan calls for common stock dividends to remain constant over the planning period. Given the increased earnings of the firm, the stockholders may expect their per-share dividends to go up. This would reduce the amount of retained earnings, and increase the need for external funding. Also, the firm's management may want to consider raising additional capital by issuing additional preferred or common stock.

Figure 11.1

Sample Financial Statements – Treasury Management Handbook

PRO FORMA BALANCE SHEET (Thousands of Dollars)

	Current Year	% Growth	YEAR 1	YEAR 2	YEAR 3
PROJECTED REVENUES	$247,113	7.5%	$265,646	$285,570	$306,988
ASSETS	Current Year	% of Sales	YEAR 1	YEAR 2	YEAR 3
Cash	$ 2,450	1.0%	$ 2,634	$ 2,831	$ 3,044
Accounts Receivable	18,500	7.5%	19,888	21,379	22,982
Inventory	21,060	8.5%	22,640	24,337	26,163
Total Current Assets	42,010	17.0%	45,162	48,547	52,189
Plant and Equipment	155,490	62.9%	167,152	179,688	193,165
Less: Accumulated Depreciation	(42,240)	17.1%	(45,408)	(48,814)	(52,475)
Net Plant and Equipment	113,250	45.8%	121,744	130,874	140,690
Other Long-Term Assets	23,950	9.7%	25,746	27,679	29,754
Total Long-Term Assets	137,200	55.5%	147,490	158,553	170,444
TOTAL ASSETS	$179,210	72.5%	$192,652	$ 207,100	$222,633
LIABILITIES AND EQUITY	Current Year	% of Sales	YEAR 1	YEAR 2	YEAR 3
Notes Payable	$ 13,536		$ 17,778	$ 21,555	$ 24,777
Accounts Payable	8,100	3.3%	8,708	9,361	10,063
Accrued Wages	5,800	2.3%	6,235	6,703	7,205
Accrued Taxes	7,700	3.1%	8,278	8,898	9,566
Total Current Liabilities	35,136		40,999	46,517	51,611
Long-Term Debt	72,000		76,242	80,019	83,241
Long-Term Lease	10,800		10,800	10,800	10,800
Total L-T Debt/Lease	82,800		87,042	90,819	94,041
Par Value: Common Stock (10,000 Shares @ $1)	10,000		10,000	10,000	10,000
Paid-In Capital	17,050		17,050	17,050	17,050
Preferred Stock (15%)	5,000		5,000	5,000	5,000
Retained Earnings	29,224		32,561	37,714	44,931
Total Equity	61,274		64,611	69,764	76,981
TOTAL LIABILITIES AND EQUITY	$179,210		$192,652	$207,100	$222,633
ESTIMATED EXTERNAL FINANCING NEEDED (1/2 Notes Payable, ½ L-T Debt)			$ 8,484	$ 16,037	$ 22,481

Figure 11.2

Sample Financial Statements – Treasury Management Handbook

PRO FORMA INCOME STATEMENT (Thousands of Dollars)

	Current Year	% of Sales	YEAR 1	YEAR 2	YEAR 3
Sales/Revenues	247,113	100.0%	265,646	285,570	306,988
Less: Cost of Goods Sold	(116,143)	47.0%	(124,854)	(134,218)	(144,284)
Gross Profit	130,970	53.0%	140,792	151,352	162,704
General Operating Expense	57,110	23.1%	61,393	65,998	70,948
Administrative Expense	25,460	10.3%	27,370	29,422	31,629
Rents	15,700		15,700	15,700	15,700
Insurance	3,250		3,250	3,250	3,250
Depreciation	4,900	2.0%	5,268	5,663	6,087
Lease Expense	1,750		1,750	1,750	1,750
Total Administrative & Operating Costs	108,170		114,731	121,783	129,364
EBIT (Earnings before Interest & Taxes)	22,800		26,061	29,569	33,340
Less: Interest Expense	(6,900)		(7,748)	(8,504)	(9,148)
EBT (Earnings before Taxes)	15,900		18,313	21,065	24,192
Less: Provision for Taxes (34%)	(5,406)		(6,226)	(7,162)	(8,225)
NPAT (Net Profit after Tax)	$ 10,494		$ 12,087	$ 13,903	$ 15,967
Less: Sinking Fund Obligations	(2,000)		(2,000)	(2,000)	(2,000)
Less: Preferred Stock Dividends	(750)		(750)	(750)	(750)
Earnings Available to Common Shareholders	$ 7,744		$ 9,337	$ 11,153	$ 13,217
Less: Common Stock Dividends (.60/sh) (10M shares outstanding)	(6,000)		(6,000)	(6,000)	(6,000)
Retained Earnings	$ 1,744		$ 3,337	$ 5,153	$ 7,217
Earnings per Share (in Actual Dollars)	$ 0.77		$ 0.93	$ 1.12	$ 1.32

Figure 11.3

Sample Financial Statements – Treasury Management Handbook

RATIO ANALYSIS FOR COMPANY

	Current Year	YEAR 1	YEAR 2	YEAR 3
Current Ratio	1.20	1.10	1.04	1.01
Quick Ratio	0.60	0.55	0.52	0.50
Avg. Collection Period	27.30	27.30	27.30	27.30
Fixed Asset Turnover	1.80	1.80	1.80	1.80
Total Asset Turnover	1.38	1.38	1.38	1.38
Total Debt to Total Assets	65.8%	66.5%	66.3%	65.4%
Times Interest Earned	3.30	3.36	3.48	3.64
Total Debt to Equity	1.92	1.98	1.97	1.89
Fixed Charge Coverage	2.84	2.93	3.05	3.22
Cash Flow Coverage	2.30	2.42	2.56	2.73
Gross Profit Margin	53.0%	53.0%	53.0%	53.0%
Net Profit Margin	4.2%	4.6%	4.9%	5.2%
Basic Earnings Power	12.7%	13.5%	14.3%	15.0%
Return on Assets	5.9%	6.3%	6.7%	7.2%
Return on Equity	13.8%	15.7%	17.2%	18.4%

VI. Endnotes

1. Cash flow forecasting is covered in detail in the current edition of *Essentials of Cash Management*.

2. Note for spreadsheet users: Making interest expense a function of external funding required usually results in a circular reference in the spreadsheet. Setting the iteration feature on a high number generally will allow the spreadsheet to resolve the circular formula and balance out the balance sheet.

12 Capital Budgeting and Leasing

I. Outline of the Chapter

        b.   Sale of Valuable Asset

        c.   Loss Minimization

        d.   Fixed versus Variable Costs

        e.   Shut-Down (Exit) Costs

    6. Inflation in Capital Budgeting

    7. Adjusting for Unequal Project Lives

    8. Dealing with Foreign Investments

    9. Cash Flow Estimation Bias

  10. Managerial Options

C. Considering Risk in Capital Budgeting

    1. Measuring Project Risk

        a.   Stand-Alone Risk

        b.   Market (Portfolio) Risk

    2. Use of Risk-Adjusted Discount Rates

    3. Capital Rationing

    4. Optimal Capital Budget

        a.   Investment Opportunity Schedule (IOS)

        b.   Marginal Cost of Capital (MCC) Schedule

        c.   Combining the IOS and MCC Schedules

    5. Hurdle Rate

    6. Feedback Loop

D. Leasing Decisions

    1. Types of Leases

        a.   Sale and Leaseback

        b.   Operating Leases

        c.   Financial (Capital) Leases

        d.   Combination Leases

        e.   Cross-Border Leases

    2. Tax Considerations

    3. Financial Statement Effects

    4. Evaluation by the Lessee

    5. Evaluation by the Lessor

    6. Leveraged Lease Analysis

    7. Other Issues in Lease Analysis

      a.   Estimated Residual Value

      b.   Increased Credit Availability

      c.   Depreciation Tax Savings

      d.   Computer Model

      e.   Leasing under the 1986 Tax Act

   8. Why Do Firms Use Leasing?

Chapter Checklists

A. Listing of Lease Components

Calculations and Examples

A. Capital Budgeting Example

B. Leasing Example

II. Introduction

Capital budgets are established to plan and control a firm's investment in capital assets, for example: the replacement of existing equipment, the expansion of existing facilities, the purchase of new equipment and the introduction of new product lines. Because such projects involve a substantial capital investment by the firm, it is important that the decision-maker use sound decision rules and guidelines.

This chapter describes several decision-making models and rules to aid in the capital budgeting process. These models will be fully explained, as well as the strengths and weaknesses associated with each. The chapter also describes the process of identifying the appropriate cash flows for evaluation, and the decision-making process for leasing assets included in the project instead of purchasing them directly.

Also covered here are decision-making rules used to evaluate a firm's capital budgeting projects. The weighted average cost of capital developed in Chapter 4 (Cost of Capital and Capital Structure) is used as the required rate of return for those capital projects. Finally, this chapter explains how the appropriate use of these decision-making rules enhances the firm's value to investors. The proper analysis of projects will aid the firm in making cash flow projections, which has important implications for many of the working capital analyses described in Chapters 7–9.

III. Coverage of the Chapter Material

A. Basics of Capital Budgeting

- Capital budgeting is an ongoing process used to improve decision-making when evaluating proposed capital projects. These projects usually require significant investment of capital and represent a large portion of the company's asset base.

- Capital projects tend to have lives that extend beyond one year, meaning that the time element should be included in the analysis.

- Capital budget decision-making is a form of cost/benefit analysis in which the investment required for the project (the initial cash outflows) is compared with the benefits (the ongoing net cash inflows generated). In most cases, the benefit must outweigh the investment cost if the project is to be approved.

- There are some examples of firms accepting projects with negative NPVs; these are usually related to regulatory compliance (OSHA, EPA, etc.), goodwill, or safety and security. This is only done in a very narrow sense. In a general, broad view, if a firm regularly accepts negative NPV projects, eventually it will go out of business.

- Since the benefits of capital projects are typically spread across time, the time element should be included in the analysis. In most of the decision models discussed, this is done by discounting the estimated cash flows to be generated by the project. The decision-maker must take into account the riskiness of the cash flows. Future cash flows are not guaranteed to the company, so there is an uncertainty associated with the analysis.

- A final important point is that the decision-maker must be able to arrive at consistent, rational decisions. The goal should be to enhance the firm's value (and hence its value to the common shareholders). Models used to make capital budgeting decisions must have decision rules consistent with the overriding goal of maximizing shareholder value (wealth).

- The models used in this section are described fully and are evaluated with the above considerations in mind. Relative strengths and weaknesses are also discussed.

1. Capital Budgeting Decision Models: Four decision models are outlined:

1. Payback Period
2. Net Present Value (NPV)
3. Internal Rate of Return (IRR)
4. Profitability Index (PI)

Following this outline, one can do an evaluation of the decision models to determine which contributes most to the goal of enhancing the firm's value.

a. Payback Period:

- This decision model determines the number of years it takes for the project's cash flows to return the firm's initial investment in the project.

- The most basic form of this model does not take into account the timing of cash flows. In other words, the cash flows from period to period are added up until they equal the initial investment.

- In a simple example, if a project has an initial cash investment (outlay) of −$1,000 and a six-year cash flow stream of $200, $300, $500, $500, $500 and $500, then the payback period of the project is three years. In most cases, the payback will occur sometime during the year instead of at the end of the year as in this simple example. It is usually correct to assume that the cash flows occur in a linear fashion during the year, so determining the fractional period is a simple matter.

- The decision rule for the payback model is to compare this calculated payback for the project with a firm's maximum or required payback period. For example, if the firm evaluating the simple project outlined above requires that projects have a payback of four years, the project under analysis is acceptable. On the other hand, if company policy states that projects must repay within two years, the project is unacceptable.

- One of the key problems with the payback method is that the decision criteria (maximum years to payback) generally tend to be somewhat arbitrary. They may be a function of what the lenders are willing to accept, a function of the last person to review the decision, or a function of the rapid pace of change in the particular industry involved.

- This form of the payback method ignores the timing of the cash flows and gives each year's cash flow equal weight. This is one of its major drawbacks, since the model ignores the opportunity cost of the funds invested in the project.

- A second form of the payback model adjusts the cash flows before determining the payback period. The adjustment is discounting the cash flows by the firm's incremental cost of capital (see Chapter 4). This adjustment corrects the problem described above and takes into account the time value of money.

- Both forms of payback method ignore the cash flows that occur after the calculated payback period, and this can result in significant errors. For example, assume a decision maker is evaluating projects A and B, using the first form of the payback method:

Cash Flows	Project A	Project B
Year 0	($1,000)	($1,000)
Year 1	$ 300	$ 300
Year 2	$ 300	$ 300
Year 3	$ 400	$ 400
Year 4	$ 100	$1,000
Year 5	$ 100	$1,000

- According to the payback period, the two projects are equally acceptable (given a required payback of three years). The payback method, therefore, cannot distinguish between the two projects. Both have the same acceptability, yet project B is clearly preferable due to its significantly higher cash flows in years 4 and 5 (given the same risk, etc.). This inability to distinguish between the two projects exists because the model ignores the cash flows occurring after the payback period.

- A second problem associated with both forms of the payback model is that it is not clear whether, by following the recommendations of the model, the value of the firm (to the shareholders) will be maximized.

- This model does not establish the value of the project itself and does not allow us to determine whether accepting a project will increase the firm's value (or whether rejecting it will reduce the firm's value). Projects that may enhance firm value by generating substantial cash flows several years in the future may be rejected by the model. This decision model may lead the firm's decision makers to be shortsighted in terms of capital projects.

- The payback model does, however, provide a measure of liquidity. This feature leads many firms to use it as a measure of risk when evaluating a project. Firms may use the payback model as one of a set of multiple hurdles, or in conjunction with the discounted cash flow model described below.

- In fact, many firms do use the payback model extensively in their capital budgeting process. It is easy to calculate and may be an easy way to justify the "rationing" of a limited amount of capital available for new projects. In addition, firms operating in rapidly changing industries or environments may need to utilize short payback periods in order to stay competitive.

b. Net Present Value (NPV): The Net Present Value model corrects most of the problems associated with the payback method. To calculate the NPV:

1. The decision-maker calculates the present value of the cash flows (both inflows and outflows) associated with the project, using the firm's marginal (or incremental) cost of capital as the discount rate. In practice, many firms use a hurdle rate to determine whether or not to invest in a given project. This will be covered in more detail later in this chapter.

2. The decision-maker then adds up the discounted values of the cash flows. This summation of the discounted values is known as the NPV of the project.

The decision rule for the NPV model is that if the NPV is greater than or equal to zero, the project is acceptable; if the NPV is negative, the project should be rejected.

Mathematically, NPV is expressed as:

$$NPV = \sum CF_t/(1+k)^t$$

Where: CF_t = the expected cash flow for period t.
  t = the period.
  k = the firm's cost of capital.

For example, if we were to calculate the net present value (NPV) of projects A and B in the previous chart at a 10% cost of capital, the following would result:

NPV_A = −$1,000 + $300/(1.10) + $300/(1.10)^2 + $400/(1.10)^3
  + $100/(1.10)^4 + $100/(1.10)^5
  = −$48.42

NPV_B = −$1,000 + $300/(1.10) + $300/(1.10)^2 + $400/(1.10)^3
  + $1,000/(1.10)^4 + $1,000/(1.10)^5
  = $1,125.12

Note that NPV may have either a positive or negative value. This value has a specific meaning in the evaluation of the project. If the NPV is equal to zero, the project will earn exactly the required rate of return. If the NPV is positive, the project will earn an excess return relative to the required return, and the value of the firm will increase by the amount of the positive NPV.

Using the firm's weighted average cost of capital (WACC) as the discount rate assumes that the project in question carries the same basic risk as the firm. If this is not the case, a risk-adjusted discount rate should be used. In most cases, firms assign a discount rate higher than the WACC in evaluating risky projects. The topic of adjusting discount rates for project riskiness is covered later in this section.

A negative NPV signifies that the project will not earn the required rate of return, and, if the firm were to take on the project, its value would decline by the amount of the negative NPV. The NPV model allows us to determine the impact of the project on the firm's value. Properly implemented, the model will enable the user to further the overriding goal of maximizing the firm's value.

As mentioned earlier, sometimes a firm will use NPV to evaluate projects that have negative NPVs, but in which investment may be required by legislation or regulation (pollution controls, environmental clean-ups, etc.). In such cases, the proper decision is to compare the different alternatives and choose the one having the least negative NPV within the regulatory guidelines.

Some of the concerns discussed in relation to the payback method do not apply in the NPV model. The NPV takes into account all of the cash flows related to the project. Also, the time value of money is explicitly considered by the decision model, as is risk, by using a risk-adjusted discount rate.

c. Internal Rate of Return (IRR): The Internal Rate of Return is defined as that discount rate, r, which equates the present value of a project's expected cash inflows to the present value of the project's expected costs:

$$\text{PV inflows} = \text{PV investment costs (outflows)}$$

This is equivalent to:

$$\Sigma \, CF_t/(1+r)^t = 0$$

Where: CF_t = the expected cash flow for period t.

 t = the period.

 r = the IRR, or the discount rate that equates the left-hand side of the equation to 0.

Notice that this equation is the same as the NPV equation, except that in this case the NPV is equal to zero, and the equation is solved for the discount rate. The decision rule for this model is that if the IRR is greater than or equal to the required rate of return for the project, the project is acceptable. If the IRR is less than the required rate, the project is unacceptable.

For example, if we were to calculate the IRRs for Projects A and B from the previous table, we would solve for r in the following equations:

Project A: $\$1,000 = \$300/(1 + r) + \$300/(1 + r)^2 + \$400/(1 + r)^3 + \$100/(1 + r)^4 + \$100/(1 + r)^5$

Solving for r: r = 7.7%

Project B: $1,000 $= \$300/(1 + r) + \$300/(1 + r)^2 + \$400/(1 + r)^3$
$+ \$1,000/(1 + r)^4 + \$1,000/(1 + r)^5$

Solving for r: r = 38.1%

In the case of independent projects, the IRR decision rule will give the decision maker the same recommendation as NPV in terms of acceptability of the project. All of the advantages that the NPV model exhibits are present in IRR. As will be discussed later, however, the IRR and NPV methods may conflict in ranking mutually exclusive projects.

Mechanically calculating the IRR can be somewhat tedious, as it involves using a trial-and-error process (attempting different discount rates until the conditions of the IRR model are met). A financial calculator or a computer spreadsheet program is often used to calculate the IRR.

d. Profitability Index (PI): This model is virtually identical to the NPV and IRR models. The only real difference is that NPV and IRR are sums, but the profitability index is a ratio. To calculate the PI, the decision-maker calculates:

PI = PV benefits/PV costs or PI = PV inflows/PV outflows

Where: PV = Present Value

The PI shows the relative profitability of any project or the present value of benefits per dollar of costs. The discount rate used to calculate the present value of the benefits and costs is the relevant cost of capital. The decision rule is that if the PI is greater than or equal to one, the project is acceptable.

If the PI is less than one, the project is rejected. This decision rule conforms exactly to the decision rule for NPV or IRR. The PI model has the same advantages as both the NPV and IRR.

In the case of projects A and B, the profitability index (PI) for each is calculated as follows:

PI_A = [($\$300/(1.10)^1 + \$300/(1.10)^2 + \$400/(1.10)^3 + \$100/(1.10)^4 +$
$\$100/(1.10)^5$] / \$1,000

PI_A = 0.95

PI_B = [($\$300/(1.10)^1 + \$300/(1.10)^2 + \$400/(1.10)^3 + \$1,000/(1.10)^4 +$
$\$1,000/(1.10)^5$] / \$1,000

PI_B = 2.13

2. Decision Rule Evaluation: The decision-maker should use the appropriate model to make decisions consistent with the overriding goal of firm value maximization. For a model to meet this goal, it must exhibit three properties:

1.   The model must consider all cash flows throughout the entire life of a project.

2.   The model must consider the time value of money (adjusted for relevant risk), reflecting the fact that dollars that come in sooner are less risky (more certain and can be invested sooner) and therefore more valuable than distant dollars (with higher risk).

3. When the model is used to select from a set of mutually exclusive projects, it must choose the project that maximizes the firm's stock price and/or shareholder value.

Using these three properties, how well do the four models discussed stack up against each other? The payback method, in either form, violates the first of the three properties. The non-adjusted payback method also violates the second property. The NPV, IRR and PI methods all conform to the first two properties; however, only NPV consistently will choose the appropriate project when selecting from mutually exclusive projects and under unlimited capital budgets. The PI method is useful for ranking projects when the firm has a limited amount of capital to invest. The IRR models may rank highly some projects that may not maximize the firm's value. Comparing the NPV and IRR models is the topic of the next section.

The reason for ranking projects is generally due to a firm's capital rationing (constraints). If it has only a limited amount of capital for investment purposes, it may have to decide how best to invest that capital so as to maximize its overall value. The PI provides a measure of present value of benefits per present value of costs, and thus allows a firm to determine which projects have the greatest potential benefit for the firm.

3. NPV and IRR Comparisons: Since both the NPV and IRR models are common to business decision makers, it is important to understand why NPV is preferred over IRR when evaluating mutually exclusive projects. Mutually exclusive project decisions require that only one of the competing projects can be chosen. For example, if a firm were considering buying either a Brand X or Brand Y delivery van, it would have to choose either one or the other; buying both would not be acceptable.

a. NPV Profiles: An NPV profile graph shows how NPV changes when the discount rate changes. Two projects can have different rankings, according to NPV, depending on the discount rate used. The profile graph also shows the IRR for the project at the intersection of the profile with the horizontal (X) axis. The data on the cash flows for the projects appear in the table below and the graph of the NPV profile appears in Figure 12.1. Modified Internal Rate of Return (MIRR) is discussed later in this chapter.

Cash Flows	Project S	Project L
Year 0	($1,000)	($1,000)
Year 1	$ 550	$ 100
Year 2	$ 450	$ 300
Year 3	$ 350	$ 450
Year 4	$ 250	$ 550
Year 5	$ 150	$ 700
NPV @10%	$ 399	$ 487
IRR	28.5%	23.4%
PI	1.40	1.49
Payback	2.00 YRS	3.27 YRS
MIRR @ 10%	17.6%	19.1%

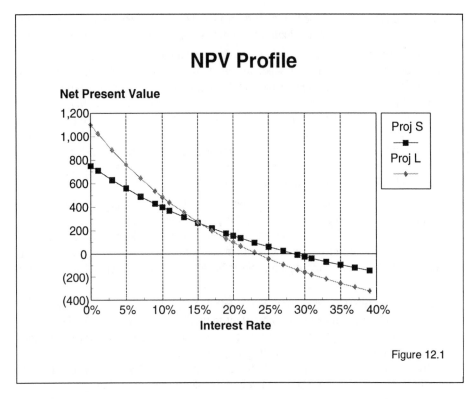

Figure 12.1

b. NPV Rankings:

- In the NPV profile graph (Figure 12.1) note that NPV will rank the projects differently, depending on the discount rate used.
- At a discount rate of 10%, the graph indicates project L is the preferred project.
- At a discount rate of 20%, the graph indicates project S is preferred.
- Also, note that at the required rate of 10%, the NPV ranking differs from the ranking provided by the project's IRR. Therefore, it is important to know which model is preferable when these rankings are different.
- The "crossover rate," or the rate at which the two projects have approximately the same NPV, is 15%. At any discount rate less than 15%, Project L will be preferred; at any discount rate above 15%, Project S will be preferred.

c. Independent Projects:

- If two or more projects are independent, this means that they are acceptable or unacceptable on their own merits.
- Under these conditions, NPV and IRR will give an identical accept/reject recommendation.
- If a project is acceptable (positive NPV or IRR greater than required rate of return), the project should be implemented. NPV and IRR are consistent in this case.

d. Mutually Exclusive Projects:

- If projects are mutually exclusive, the choice of one project from those evaluated rules out investing in the others. In this case, it is important that the decision maker be able to evaluate the projects properly and choose the one that will maximize firm value.

- Implicit in each of the two decision models under evaluation is an assumption that cash flows of the project will be reinvested.

- The preferred assumption lies with the NPV model, which assumes cash flows are reinvested at the project's required rate of return. This assumption is more realistic than one that uses a high IRR as a reinvestment rate.

- The IRR model implicitly assumes reinvestment at the project's IRR, which may not be realistic. This feature of the IRR model may be a problem when evaluating projects with very high IRRs.

- It is generally preferable for the decision maker to use the NPV model to rank mutually exclusive projects. Choosing the project with the highest NPV will maximize the firm's value.

- An alternative approach for mutually exclusive projects is the adjusted IRR model, which includes a specific assumption about the reinvestment rate on periodic cash flows from the project. Once a specific reinvestment rate is assumed, the resulting IRRs can be compared on an equal basis.

e. Other Problems with IRR:

- In evaluating some projects, there will be a conflict between IRR and NPV decision rules. This usually occurs only with mutually exclusive projects or when ranking projects under capital rationing. As explained above in the discussion of reinvestment rate assumptions of the IRR and NPV models, the NPV approach is generally the more acceptable in such cases.

- The basic conditions under which there will be conflicts between the IRR and NPV rankings occur when:

  1. The projects are of different size or scale (one is significantly larger than the other).

  2. The projects have significant differences in timing (one has major cash flows early in its life, while the other has the majority of its cash flows later). The examples of Project S (sooner) and Project L (later) show this type of conflict. Projects in conflict will generally have crossing NPV profiles.

- The best way to resolve NPV/IRR conflicts is to use the NPV profile and determine where the crossover rate (the interest rate at which the two projects have equivalent NPVs) between the two projects is attained. Then determine what the most likely distribution is for interest rates, and make your decision based on the highest probability for maximum NPV.

- In some projects, there is the possibility of obtaining multiple IRRs as a solution. This is especially a problem with projects in which there are both positive and negative cash flows over their lifetimes. Whenever the cash flows "change signs," there is a mathematical possibility of an additional solution to the IRR. This may cause some calculators or spreadsheets to give you an error message in the calculation of certain IRRs. In evaluating projects with multiple IRRs, the general rule is to use the IRR closest to the project's NPV in the project investment decision.

- One way to resolve the problems with IRR is to adjust IRR for its unrealistic reinvestment rate assumption. This is important, because even though NPV is theoretically superior, the IRR is more generally accepted in corporate financial circles. Managers seem to prefer to analyze investments in terms of percentage rates of return than dollars of net present value. For this reason, the Modified IRR (MIRR) offers an acceptable alternative to the NPV analysis.

- The MIRR method determines the rate of return that equates the present value of the project cost with the present value of the terminal value of the project. The terminal value of the project is calculated as the future value of the yearly cash flows at a pre-determined reinvestment rate (usually the firm's cost of capital). This approach yields a more consistent estimate of rate of return.

- The Modified IRR (MIRR) can be calculated as follows:

PV(Costs) = PV(Terminal Value)

Where:

$$PV(Costs) = \sum_{t=0}^{n} \frac{COF_t}{(1+k)^t} \text{ and}$$

$$PV(Terminal\ Value) = \sum_{t=0}^{n} \frac{CIF_t (1+K)^{n-t}}{(1+MIRR)^n}$$

COF_t = Cash Outflow in period t
CIF_t = Cash Inflow in period t
TV = Terminal (future) Value of cash inflows, reinvested at k
K = Firm's Cost of Capital or Reinvestment rate
MIRR = Modified IRR (Solve for this rate)

In this example, the present value of the costs is easy to determine because all of the outflows occur in the initial outlay (at time = 0). In a more complicated example, the present value of the costs would be determined as the present value at time = 0 of all cash outflows associated with the project.

The determination of the terminal value is a bit more difficult, because it requires assuming that any cash flows generated from the project will be reinvested at some specifically assumed reinvestment rate. In most cases, this rate is equal to the firm's cost of capital, but in practice any rate can be used. For project S for example, the terminal value of the cash inflows is calculated as follows:

Cash Flow Year 1
(reinvested for 4 years @ 10%): $550(1.10)^4 = \$805.26$

Cash Flow Year 2
(reinvested for 3 years @ 10%): $450(1.10)^3 = \$598.95$

Cash Flow Year 3
(reinvested for 2 years @ 10%): $350(1.10)^2 = \$423.50$

Cash Flow Year 4
(reinvested for 1 year @ 10%): $250(1.10)^1 = \$275.00$

Cash Flow Year 5
(no reinvestment possible) $150(1.10)^0 = \$150.00$

For the purposes of matching up to the formula, the cash flow in year 5 is shown as being multiplied by $(1.10)^0$. Mathematical rules for handling exponents hold that any value taken to the zero exponential power is equal to 1.

Thus, the total terminal value for Project S is equal to the sum of the reinvested cash flows or $2,253. Following a similar procedure for Project L would result in a terminal value for that project of $2,395. The final step in the process is to the determine the interest rate that makes the present value of the outflows equal to the terminal value of the reinvested inflows. Thus, the MIRRs for the two projects are:

$MIRR_S$ @10% = 17.6% $MIRR_L$ @10% = 19.1%

- As can be seen from the above example, project L is the preferred project when the IRR is adjusted.

- One of the last steps in the capital budget (and often the least followed) is the post-audit. Since capital budgeting involves the forecasting of cash flows, the best way to determine whether the forecast was correct is to compare the actual cash flows with those that were projected. This process allows for increased control and improvement of the capital budgeting process in the future, and enables the analyst to modify the assumptions of future analysis to mirror the reality actually achieved.

B. Estimation of Cash Flows

The most difficult task in capital budgeting is estimating cash flows. The decision maker must realize that any estimate of cash flows is going to have some error in measurement. Consequently, the decision maker must have a thorough understanding of how cash flows are measured.

1. Identifying Relevant Cash Flows: The basic calculation of cash flows from a new project determines the changes in the cash inflows and outflows of the firm in each period t, as a result of taking on the project, or:

Project $CF_t = CF_t$ with project – CF_t without project

The only impact included in the analysis is the impact of the project itself. The remainder of this section details the evaluation of a project's cash flow.

a. Cash Flow versus Accounting Income: Accounting information about a firm's performance during any period includes, by necessity, both revenues and expenses that are neither cash inflows nor cash outflows. Credit sales and depreciation represent common examples of this process. However, the firm needs to evaluate the cash flow impact of the project in order to determine its acceptability. These adjustments are necessary due to the differences between accrual-based accounting of income and expenses and cash flows.

The general method used to determine the cash flow associated with a project from period to period based on accounting data is as follows:

$$CF_t = [(RP_t - R_t) - (OCP_t - OC_t) - (DP_t - D_t)](1 - T) + (DP_t - D_t)$$

Where: CF_t = the cash flow generated by the project during period t.
R = the revenues generated without the project.
RP = the revenues generated with the project.
OC = the cash operating costs without the project.
OCP = the cash operating costs with the project.
D = the depreciation (for tax purposes) without the project.
DP = the depreciation (for tax purposes) with the project.
T = the firm's marginal tax rate.

- Allowable depreciation is determined by the current IRS code, and will change as the code changes over time.

- At a basic level, this equation represents the after-tax operating income from the project, plus the depreciation generated by the project. The depreciation is added back to the after-tax operating income because it represents a non-cash expense.

- Since the non-cash expense is subtracted from the cash flows before taxes are taken into account, it shelters cash flow from the effect of taxes. Therefore, to measure cash flow accurately, it is necessary to add the depreciation back into the equation, not accounting income.

- If other non-cash expenses are allowed for tax purposes, they must be taken into account. Typically, items such as goodwill would be included in capital budgeting analyses of mergers and acquisitions.

b. Timing of Cash Flows: In a perfect world, the analyst would take the cash flows into account at the moment they were either received by or disbursed from the firm. However, for simplicity, we normally assume that the cash flows occur at the end of an annual period. If more accuracy is needed or considered vital by the decision maker, steps can be taken to convert the cash flows to a semi-annual or quarterly basis. The increased use of computers in the analysis makes such adjustments viable, even in projects that cover many years. In fact, as many firms use increasingly shorter investment horizons, the use of quarterly cash flow estimation is becoming ever more common in analyzing capital investments.

c. Incremental Cash Flows: As discussed above, the decision maker should evaluate the cash flows only on an incremental basis, meaning that the decision is made based only on the impact that the project has on the firm's cash flows. There are several other factors that the decision maker must take into consideration in evaluating the project's cash flows:

1) Sunk Costs: Sunk costs are not incremental costs, but costs that have already been incurred or committed. Therefore, the decision as to whether a project is acceptable or unacceptable is not affected by sunk costs. A good example is the cost of a marketing feasibility study. Once that expenditure has been made, it is no longer a factor in any future capital budgeting analysis and should therefore be excluded from the analysis.

2) Opportunity Costs: The cost of resources used in the project must be measured at the opportunity cost of the resources.

- An excellent example is a firm's use of land for a new plant. If the land has been owned by the firm for a period of time, it is likely to have appreciated in value. The decision maker should include in the cost of the project the appreciated value of the land, not its historical cost, because an alternative is to sell the land.

- This type of measurement will be needed whenever the accounting book value differs from the market value of the resource. When these values differ, the market value of the resource is the cost that should be included in the analysis.

- Another approach is to determine the next best use for the asset in question. The value to the firm from this next best use would be an appropriate value for the opportunity costs. In some cases, the opportunity cost may be zero, as in the case of using land that had no other value, either for sale to someone else or for some other use by the company itself.

3) Effects on Other Parts of the Firm (Externalities):

- It is vital for the decision maker to include in the analysis all of the incremental effects that the project will have on the firm. This includes the incremental effect that the project may have on other parts or projects of the firm.

- An example would be a brewery evaluating the introduction of a light beer. The firm must include in the analysis the possibility that the new product will capture some of its consumer base from the firm's existing consumers. Part of the revenues generated by the new product will come from reduced revenues in the existing product line. In marketing terms, this is called "cannibalizing." Overlooking this aspect in the analysis can cause the decision maker to make a fundamental mistake and cause great harm to the firm.

4) Actions by Competitors:

- No organization exists in a vacuum, so the future actions that may be taken by competitors must be considered.

- A classic example of ignoring the competition is the U.S. steel industry in the post-World War II period. The industry analyzed the purchase of new, more efficient production equipment and determined that the NPV was negative. Therefore, the new investment was not made.

- The U.S. steel companies failed to consider that their Japanese and European competitors were investing in those more efficient production techniques, and, in due course, the U.S. steel industry found that it was no longer competitive in the world market. Perhaps the steel companies did not fully understand the capital budgeting process, or the time horizons they used were not long enough. Generally, however, the failure to take into account actions by competitors was a key element in the ultimate decline of the U.S. steel industry.

2. Tax Effects:

- Tax effects can have a major impact on the viability of the project. This is especially true where investment tax credits or accelerated depreciation are concerned. Also of importance are tax incentives for investment in certain areas or countries (e.g. drug company subsidiaries in Puerto Rico).

- One area in which the impact can be greatest is the project's depreciation effect. The use of accelerated depreciation versus straight-line depreciation will have a major impact because of the time value of money.

- It is vital that the decision maker use the correct estimated future tax rate in the analysis. It is also important that the decision maker use the same depreciation in the analysis that the firm will use in its tax preparation.

- The impact of future changes in the tax code should be weighed in the capital budgeting analysis.

3. Salvage Value:

- When evaluating the cash flows of a project, one of the most important components is the salvage value, or residual value, of the equipment purchased. When the life of the project has expired, it is very rare that the assets used in the project have no remaining value. This would be especially true of real estate.

- The decision maker must take into account not only the residual value of the assets but the tax effect from the sale of the asset. If the asset is sold for a taxable gain, the decision maker must take into account the taxes that must be paid. In some industries (for example, leasing companies) the estimate of the residual value can be critical in the evaluation of the project's acceptability.

4. Working Capital Investment:

- In many types of projects, it is necessary to invest in short-term assets (working capital) in order for the project to begin. As one good example, in either an expansion of existing facilities or a new product introduction the firm will need to invest in additional inventories to facilitate the process.

- While some of these current assets will be financed with current liabilities, others will require a cash investment. The net amount of assets that need to be purchased with cash should be included as part of the investment or cash outflows associated with the project evaluation.

- It is also important to take this investment into account at the end of the project's life, when the investment will be reconverted into cash.

5. Project Abandonment: Occasionally, a project will be more valuable if discontinued rather than continued. Also, in some cases equipment requires replacement before it wears out. This section discusses the analysis used in making these important decisions.

a. Economic Life: The economic life of an asset can differ significantly from its actual physical life. A good example is computer equipment, which frequently becomes obsolete long before it wears out. The decision maker should evaluate the equipment over its expected economic life, not its physical life.

b. Sale of Valuable Asset: As mentioned above, the market value of the equipment is almost always positive during its economic life. NPVs can be significantly affected by the residual value of the equipment. During the life of the project, occasionally the market value of the asset may be so high that the best way to maximize the firm's value is to sell the asset on the market instead of continuing the project. The firm should adopt a policy that projects must be constantly monitored to determine whether this is the case. This would involve a normal NPV calculation, where the firm accepts the alternative with the highest NPV.

c. Loss Minimization: In another scenario, occasionally conditions will change in such a way that a project becomes unprofitable to the firm. Projects should be monitored to ensure that, should they become unacceptable, the firm is notified and the projects are abandoned. This has been the experience of many utility firms in the construction of nuclear-powered generating plants. Projects that were initially considered acceptable have become unacceptable because of changing conditions. Such projects must be identified by the firm, and steps must be taken to minimize losses.

d. Fixed versus Variable Costs: At a minimum, the firm should evaluate ongoing projects to be certain that they are at least covering variable costs of production and operation. A project may ultimately be profitable for the firm, even if over a short period of time it does not generate enough cash flows to cover fixed overhead costs. For many such projects, cash flows may be sufficient to cover variable costs, but not the occasional sunk overhead that may have been assigned to the project. If, for some short period, the project does not cover the overhead, abandoning it may not be in the best long-term interests of the firm. Rather, the firm should consider the project viable as long as variable costs are being covered.

e. Shut-Down (Exit) Costs: In evaluating the abandonment of any project, the estimated shut-down or exit costs must also be considered. These may include plant closing laws or union contracts that require significant termination benefits for employees, or costly environmental clean-up operations. Substantial exit costs may force a firm to run a project at a loss if the present value of this ongoing loss is less than the present value costs for closing down the project.

6. Inflation in Capital Budgeting:

- Though inflation in the United States is currently at record low levels, this has not always been the case, and many countries are now experiencing high rates of inflation. For this reason, the financial manager needs to understand the impact of inflation on the capital budgeting process.[1]

- In general, most interest rates used in the evaluation of capital budgets include an adjustment for inflation, and inflation expectations are "built into" almost all long-term rates.

- If the cash flows used in the capital budget projections do not include an inflation adjustment, the calculated NPV will be biased downward as a result.

- The most common form of adjustment is to take inflation specifically into account by using the expected inflation rate in determining the annual cash flows from a project. For example, if a 10% inflation has been implicitly assumed in the determination of the discount rate, this same 10% inflation rate should also be applied to the cash flows of the project in question. This involves increasing the projected cash flows by the anticipated inflation rate over each year of the project. In this way, both the cash flow and the discount rate will be utilizing the same inflation adjustment assumptions.

- The adjustment for inflation will add some additional uncertainty in the capital budgeting process, especially for longer-duration projects where the inflation rates may be more difficult to estimate.

7. Adjusting for Unequal Project Lives:

- In the case where a firm is evaluating mutually exclusive alternatives that require ongoing replacement, an adjustment may have to be made for unequal project lives.

- An example might be a sign-service firm contemplating the purchase of a new service truck. One model is less expensive, but only has a three-year useful life, while another model might be more expensive, with a six-year useful life. Since the firm must replace whichever truck it buys with a new one at the end of its useful life, it cannot directly compare the NPVs of the two alternatives.

- One approach for the adjustment process is to determine common-life replacement chains for the two alternatives. In the example above, it would involve comparing two consecutive purchases of the three-year trucks with a single purchase of the six-year truck. Thus, the comparison would be between two common-life chains of six years each. The problem with this approach is that trying to find a common life for some sets of alternatives can be unwieldy, especially if there are more than two alternatives.

- The preferred approach is to use the equivalent annual annuity. In this method, the NPV for each alternative is divided by a present value annuity factor for the cost of capital for the useful life of the alternative. Thus, in the example above, the three-year model's NPV would be divided by a three-year annuity factor, while the six-year model's NPV would be divided by a six-year annuity factor. The result is the equivalent annuity cash flow for each project which would result if the alternative were to be replicated over an infinite horizon.

- An annuity factor is simply a sum of present value factors over a period of years. It assumes that a continuous payment stream of a single payment of $1 is being made over some series of periods. Thus, multiplying an annuity factor by the amount of a periodic payment would yield the present value of this payment stream. For example, the present value factor for three years at 10% is 2.487. If the annual payment were $5,000, the present value of this three-year annuity would be $12,435.

- The decision after applying the equivalent annuity approach calls for choosing the project with the highest equivalent annuity payment. Adjustment for the difference in project lives is made by assuming infinite replacement.

8. Dealing with Foreign Investments:

- Foreign projects add additional complexity to the capital budgeting process. First, the firm must evaluate the project from both the subsidiary's and the parent's point of view. The cash flow stream into the subsidiary may be very different from that into the parent due to foreign exchange differentials, restrictions on profit transfers, tax laws, or obligatory reinvestment in the foreign country. Although the parent viewpoint will usually take precedence, both viewpoints should be evaluated to ensure that all options have been considered.

- Evaluating foreign projects from the subsidiary's point of view is a straightforward application of capital budgeting. The return on the project can be compared with returns on comparable investments in the foreign country concerned.

- In analyzing foreign projects from the headquarters viewpoint, a U.S. parent must make an additional adjustment for the fact that the cash flows will be denominated in foreign currencies that may fluctuate in value relative to the dollar over time. Multiple points of view may be required in the analysis. The firm's headquarters may view the foreign investment from one perspective, while the management of the foreign operation may view it very differently.

- One approach to adjusting foreign cash flows is to include an adjustment for the expected exchange rate changes for the discount rate. This adjustment process will be covered in greater detail in a later section on risk-adjusted discount rates. Due to the greater uncertainties in international capital budgeting, however, this approach is not recommended.

- A better approach is to adjust each of the cash flows attributable to the foreign project for expected changes in the exchange rates over the life of the project. This cash-flow adjustment approach is considered more accurate for international capital budgeting than risk-adjusted discount rates.

- The foreign investment decision may require the financial manager to "take a stand" on the movement of foreign exchange rates. A decision must be made on when to hedge foreign cash flows and when to remain exposed.

- Other factors, such as foreign taxes, restrictions on export of funds from foreign countries, hyper-inflation, mandatory reinvestment in the foreign country and possible seizure of foreign assets, must also be taken into consideration in evaluating foreign projects, especially with respect to determining the riskiness of the cash flow stream.

- Another consideration in the foreign investment arena is the possibility of special project financing. Many foreign governments offer substantial incentives (special financing, tax holidays or provision of infrastructure) which make an otherwise unprofitable investment attractive.

9. Cash Flow Estimation Bias:

- Cash flow estimation is both the most critical and the most difficult part of the capital budgeting process. Cash flows must be forecast well into the future, and estimation errors are bound to occur.

- Several studies have shown that managers making cash flow estimations for capital budgets generally tend to overestimate revenues, while at the same time underestimating costs. This managerial optimism causes overall cash flows to be severely overstated in many cases.

- The first step in uncovering cash estimation biases (especially for highly profitable projects) is to ask: "What is the basic reason for this project's profitability?" In some cases, such as unique products or services, patent or copyright protection or well-known brand names, the projected excess profits may be justifiable.

- In the long term, however, competition or loss of patent/copyright protection will result in a more normal profit stream for the capital budget. For the cash flow estimation to be accurate, such factors must be taken into account. Wherever possible, therefore, unit sales and profits per unit should be estimated separately.

- It is also well to remember that higher returns are often accompanied by higher risk, which may significantly increase the variability of the cash flows.

10. Managerial Options:

- Traditional cash flow estimation, which does not consider managerial options, may cause the value of the project to be understated. Managerial options refers to the many investment projects that may lead to other valuable investment opportunities for the firm.

- These additional opportunities or options could include:
  - The opportunity to develop follow-up products
  - The opportunity to expand into new markets/products
  - The opportunity to expand or retool plants
  - Synergistic benefits from combining projects

- If any of these options are truly viable, the firm should reflect their value in the capital budgeting analysis. Generally, this is accomplished by adding the estimated value (adjusted for risk) of the managerial options to the value of the traditional NPV. These options may be re-evaluated on an annual basis as the firm's situation and the general business environment change.

C. Considering Risk in Capital Budgeting

It is vital for the decision maker to evaluate accurately the risk of the project to be undertaken. The models in the sections above used the firm's cost of capital as the estimate of the project's required rate of return. This is the appropriate required rate of return only when the firm is investing in projects that have risk similar to that of its existing assets. The projects would be the firm's standard day-to-day or "bread-and-butter" types of investment. New projects, or investments in new areas of business, will almost always require a higher rate of return. This section describes several ways to adjust the discount rate when the cost of capital is not the appropriate required rate of return.

1. Measuring Project Risk: Project risk can be evaluated in two different ways. The first is to evaluate the project on a stand-alone basis. In this case, the total risk of the project must be considered and adjustments must be made. The second method is to view the project in a market or portfolio context. In this case, it is necessary to evaluate only the portfolio (market) risk of the project.

a. Stand-Alone Risk: There are several reasons for taking stand-alone risk into account.

1. It is much easier to estimate a project's stand-alone risk than to measure other types of risk.
2. Stand-alone risk is usually highly correlated with the more theoretically correct portfolio risk. This means that even though portfolio risk is hard to measure, stand-alone risk is a good proxy for it.

Understanding the evaluation of stand-alone risk is important for the decision maker. The best way to begin the analysis is by attempting to measure the uncertainty in the project's cash flows. There are many types of statistical techniques for measuring this uncertainty.

1) Sensitivity Analysis:

- The first technique for measuring project uncertainty is known as sensitivity analysis.
- This procedure indicates exactly how much the NPV will change in response to a given change in an input variable, other variables being held constant.
- Many computer applications will allow the decision maker to change some of the assumptions made in the initial analysis.
- For example, if revenues were to increase more slowly than original projections, the impact on the project's acceptability could be analyzed. Increases in operating costs can also be evaluated. This type of analysis can improve the decision maker's understanding of the project.
- In sensitivity analysis, therefore, the analyst will usually vary one of the input variables in a systematic manner to determine the impact on the output variable of interest (usually NPV or IRR in capital budgeting analysis).

2) Scenario Analysis:

- This technique usually generates reports for best-case, most-likely-case and worst-case analyses of the project's performance. The usual result is a range of possible outcomes.
- Once these have been generated, we can assign probabilities to them, develop an expected NPV and, perhaps more important, develop a standard deviation of the NPV outcomes.
- The decision maker then uses the standard deviation as a measure of project risk. Scenario analysis can also be thought of as using a set of input variables to

determine their combined impact on the output variable being examined (in this case NPV).

- The development of scenarios depends upon the different types of risk or the different possible outcomes for the project(s) being analyzed. While the sensitivity analysis changes only one variable at a time, this approach changes a full set of input variables simultaneously to see how the project would perform under such assumptions.

- This type of "what-if" (sometimes referred to as "if-then") analysis can be easily done if a firm has developed its capital budgets on a computer-based spreadsheet. The key is to determine what would happen to a capital budget under different economic and/or business conditions.

3) Monte Carlo Simulation:

- A variation on the scenario analysis approach is the Monte Carlo Simulation, wherein input variables are assigned specific distributions and values.

- In the next step of the simulation, values from these distributions are chosen at random and used to compute the desired output values.

- If enough scenarios are run (several thousand in some cases), the user can usually determine the approximate distribution of the output variable (NPV or IRR) for the project in question.

- Some spreadsheet programs include this type of analysis, while others require "add-in" supplements. There are also some stand-alone packages that offer this type of simulation analysis.

4) Goal Seeking:

- This technique allows you to specify the value for the output variable you want to achieve (i.e., an IRR of 20% or greater) and determine the input variables needed to reach this goal. Most popular spreadsheet packages offer this option.

b. Market (Portfolio) Risk:

- Another approach to project-risk measurement is to determine the impact that a project will have on the firm's market risk.

- The general theory is that the firm can be viewed as a portfolio of assets, each contributing to its overall market risk.

- Developments in the investment area of finance have provided many ways of measuring the risk of asset investments. One of these is the Capital Asset Pricing Model (CAPM). This model allows the decision maker to evaluate the assets' portfolio risk.

- Portfolio risk is the risk inherent in the market system or risk that is not diversifiable by further investment. This form of risk is also known as market risk and can be measured by the beta of the asset. This topic is covered in detail in Chapter 4.

The required rate of return, as developed by the CAPM, is:

$$k_s = k_{RF} + (k_M - k_{RF})b_i$$

Where: k_s = the required rate of return.

k_{RF} = the risk-free rate of return.

k_M = the expected return on the market portfolio.

b_i = the beta of the asset.

- The beta of an asset is generally defined as the riskiness of an asset relative the market as a whole. Thus, if an asset were to have a beta of 2.0, one could say that this asset was approximately twice as risky as the overall market. The riskiness of the overall market is generally determined by the movement on a broad-based index, such as the S&P 500.

- Generally, proxies are needed for the various components of this model. The return on Treasury securities could be used for the risk-free return.

- The return on a securities index such as the S&P 500 is used for the market portfolio. The difficulty comes in developing a proxy for the beta of the asset. The best technique is known as the "pure-play" method. The decision maker attempts to find an existing firm whose sole line of business is the same as that of the project. The decision maker then uses that firm's beta as the project's beta in order to calculate a required rate of return.

- For example, if the stock of the ABC corporation has a beta of 1.5, and if we use a T-Bill rate of 4.0% as an indicator of the risk-free rate and 8.3% as the average market premium over the risk-free rate,[2] then the required rate of return (k_s) for the firm would be calculated as:

$$k_s(ABC) = 4.0\% + 1.5(8.3\%) = 16.5\%$$

2. Use of Risk-Adjusted Discount Rates:

- Once the required rate of return has been established using the CAPM, the decision maker would then use it in calculating the project's NPV.

- The decision maker then evaluates the project's acceptability under the changed conditions (higher or lower required rate). This analysis should not be considered the final analysis needed, but it will improve the information available to the decision maker.

- Using the CAPM is only one approach to adjusting discount rates for risk. Many firms may use a more informal approach that groups projects into one of several risk classes.

- For example, projects might be classified as below-average risk, average risk or above-average risk. Those of average risk would be assigned a cost of capital equal to the firm's weighted average cost of capital (WACC), while those of below-average risk would be evaluated at the WACC minus 3% and those of above-average risk at the WACC plus 3%.

- In order to manage its overall mix of risky projects, the firm could mandate that only a certain portion of the total capital budget may be allocated to below-average or above-average projects. This approach is tied to the concept of capital rationing covered next.

3. Capital Rationing:

- In many firms there may be a significant number of positive NPV investment projects, but only a limited amount of capital available for investment. This is known as "capital rationing."

- One approach to this problem is to rank the projects by profitability index, invest in the highest PI projects first, and continue down the rankings until the funds run out. In most cases (but not all) this approach will maximize the NPV for the amount of dollars invested.

- Another approach for managing capital rationing is to determine the "optimal capital budget." This method is discussed below.

4. Optimal Capital Budget:

- This is mainly a theoretical discussion of microeconomic concepts applied to capital budgeting. It is important to understand these concepts as they aid in the development of an overall financial theory for the firm.

- From the economic perspective, the capital budgeting process can be summarized as follows: Potential projects are developed and evaluated using the project's risk adjusted cost of capital. Those that have a return higher than the required rate of return are acceptable. Those not meeting this criterion are not acceptable. This is summarized graphically as follows:

  a. Investment Opportunity Schedule (IOS): Figure 12.2 shows the projects that have been evaluated and their relative returns plotted along the IOS line. This schedule ranks the projects and establishes the necessary investment required for each.

  b. Marginal Cost of Capital (MCC) Schedule: The basic premise of the marginal cost of capital schedule is that the cost of funds increases as the firm attempts to raise larger amounts. In reality, for most large firms, the MCC curve is fairly flat for most levels of capital that they raise. A rising MCC schedule curve would probably be more applicable to smaller firms with less advantageous access to the capital markets or to highly leveraged companies. This schedule is also shown in Figure 4.2.

  c. Combining the IOS and MCC Schedules: The final step in the process is to examine the combination of the two schedules above. Those projects having returns above the MCC will be acceptable to the firm. Once we have established the acceptable projects, we know how much we will need in the next period to fund them. This is the information that the firm expects from the capital budgeting process.

5. Hurdle Rate:

- In most companies, the internal rate of return method is used in combination with a hurdle rate for a given type of investment.

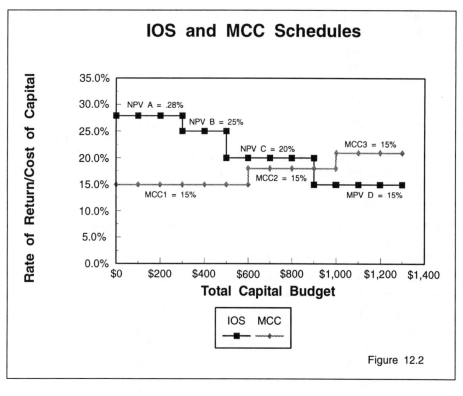

Figure 12.2

- Each class of project is assigned a minimum rate of return, or hurdle rate, which must be earned for the project to be accepted.

- The hurdle rate is typically based on the firm's cost of capital, with adjustments made for the type and overall riskiness of the project.

- Adjustments may also be made for projects required for safety, security or regulatory reasons.

- A firm may have different hurdle rates for its various divisions. Typically, a project will be assigned a hurdle rate; then the internal rate of return (IRR) for the project will be compared with this rate. If the IRR for the project is above the hurdle rate, the firm will undertake the project.

- In order to resolve some of the problems of using the IRR discussed earlier, a firm could utilize the Modified IRR instead. This approach provides a more realistic assumption concerning the reinvestment rate used in the analysis.

6. Feedback Loop:

- An important part of any analysis is the feedback loop. This involves comparing the actual cash flows associated with the capital project with the cash flows projected in the capital budget.

- The reason for this comparison is to determine how the forecasting process can be improved. Finding out why a projection was incorrect is often more important than finding out why it was correct. Many firms neglect this analysis, and often they find that the same capital budgeting errors are repeated.

- Unfortunately, this is the part of the capital budgeting process to which most firms devote the least amount of time.

D. Leasing Decisions

- Sometimes it is in a firm's best interests to lease the equipment used in a project rather than to purchase it outright. There may be an advantage to using leasing as a source of "off-balance-sheet" financing, or for certain tax incentives. This section describes different types of leases and provides the analysis techniques used to evaluate the relative benefits of leasing. The analysis techniques will aid the decision maker in determining whether leasing is preferable to outright purchase.

- It should be noted that in most cases long-term lease arrangements are considered a direct substitute for debt in the firm's capital structure. Also, loan and debt covenants may dictate the form and structure of leases for many corporations.

- In leasing, the owner of the asset is called the lessor, and receives lease payments from the lessee who has use of the asset.

1. Types of Leases: There are several types of leases. The differences are primarily length of lease period, which party is responsible for maintenance and upkeep of the asset, how much the residual value of the asset will be, what the relevant tax treatment will be, and who will get the assets at the end of the lease and under what terms.

a. Sale and Leaseback:

- Under this type of lease arrangement, equipment owned by a firm is sold to another party (the lessor) and then immediately leased back by the original owner (lessee).

- This type of lease arrangement aids firms that need a cash infusion or that cannot take full advantage of the tax advantages from depreciation due to excessive operating losses.

- This type of lease arrangement can move the cash flow stream (income or costs) to different periods. For example, a short-term gain could be created by stepping up the basis (original amount of the lease) and putting the cost in future periods through higher lease payments.

- The lessor also benefits from the depreciation tax shield provided by the lease.

- In this type of arrangement, there is generally no residual value (or perhaps a token $1) and the payments made on the lease are just sufficient to return the full purchase price to the investor, plus a stated return on the lessor's investment.

- High-value, fully depreciated assets can also be used as a basis for a sale-leaseback arrangement. This is an especially attractive option for firms needing a cash infusion.

b. Operating Leases:

- These are also known as service leases and are established in such a way that the lessor provides maintenance for the equipment and retains ownership of the equipment at the end of the lease. These are often done on an "off-balance-sheet" basis, meaning that the lease payments are reflected only on the income statement, but neither the assets nor the lease appear on the balance sheet.

- These leases usually run for periods substantially shorter than the life of the equipment and may be either on or off the balance sheet of the firm. This means that the lease payments usually are not sufficient to amortize the equipment but the lessor intends to make up the full value of the equipment upon releasing it or selling it at the end of the lease contract.

- This type of lease usually includes a provision allowing the lessee to cancel the lease prior to the expiration of the original contract (cancellation clause). This provides flexibility to the lessee if the equipment becomes obsolete or the business of the lessee declines in such a way that the equipment is no longer needed.

- This type of leasing arrangement is especially popular for large computer systems, where there is substantial risk of technological obsolescence.

- This arrangement is also used by manufacturers who are pushing sales of equipment. The manufacturer is willing to take on the risk of a short-term operating lease because the risk is more than offset by the profit from the sale of the equipment.

- Many manufacturers may have other reasons for extensive leasing of their products, rather than selling them. Some are able to re-market the used equipment in other markets, such as developing countries. Others want to control the re-marketing of their equipment in order to maintain high values for new equipment.

c. Financial (Capital) Leases:

- Financial leases, also known as capital leases, have terms different from those of operating leases.

  1. Usually, the lessor does not provide maintenance for the equipment.

  2. The lease agreement is not cancelable.

  3. The lease appears on the balance sheet as a capitalized lease.

  4. The payments are set up to fully amortize the cost of the equipment.

- The lease usually runs for the life of the asset, and the lessee has the option to renew the contract or purchase the asset at the end of the original lease contract for an agreed-upon residual value.

- The residual value for this type of lease is generally the estimated value of the asset at the end of the lease. The amortization of the asset's value will take this residual value into account in the computation of the lease payments.

- The lessee is generally responsible for maintaining the asset and must pay any applicable taxes and insurance.

- Since the lessor receives payment after these expenses are paid, a financial lease is sometimes referred to as a "net, net lease." This type of lease is really just an alternative to borrowing funds to finance the acquisition of an asset.

d. Combination Leases:

- As with any financial instrument, combinations of the various types of lease will always be available. An example would be a financial lease that includes a cancellation provision.

- Usually the terms of a lease include some type of penalty associated with cancellation, so this represents a departure from the pure financial lease. These types of adjustments are negotiated at the implementation of the lease.

e. Cross-Border Leases: These leases are set up to take advantage of tax benefits in two countries: the country where the asset is located and the home country of the parent company.

2. Tax Considerations:

- The full amount of the annual lease payment is a tax-deductible expense for the lessee, provided that the IRS agrees that a particular contract is a genuine lease, and not simply an installment loan in the guise of a lease.

- The primary provisions of the IRS guidelines are as follows:

1. The lease term must not exceed 80% of the leased asset's estimated useful life (Note: useful life is usually much longer than depreciable life).

2. The leased asset's estimated residual value at the expiration of the lease must equal at least 20% of its value at the start of the lease.

3. The only option for lessee purchase of the asset at the end of the lease is for the fair market value of the asset.

4. The only investment the lessee can have in the leased assets is the lease payments.

5. "Limited use" clauses, which permit the lessee exclusive use of the asset at the end of lease, are not allowed.

  - The primary reason for the IRS restrictions on lease terms is to prevent a company from setting up a lease arrangement which allow for more rapid write-off of an asset than that allowed by MACRS depreciation schedules. MACRS is the IRS designation for its Modified Accelerated Cost Recovery Schedule. This depreciation schedule provides a listing of how much can be depreciated annually for various types of assets.

  - Even with the IRS restrictions, many firms use leases for obtaining tax advantages that otherwise may be unavailable. An example would be a firm which, due to other losses, has no tax liability currently or in the near future. If this firm were to borrow money to buy an asset, it would probably not receive any tax benefits from either the interest or depreciation deductions. If, however, it were to lease the asset from a firm able to take advantage of the tax benefits, some of those benefits could be passed along to the lessee. The net result is that the cash outflows from the leasing arrangement will be less than the cash outflows from borrowing and purchasing the asset.

3. Financial Statement Effects:

- Under certain conditions, leases may be considered a source of off-balance-sheet financing, thus avoiding the appearance of additional debt on the firm's balance sheet, as well as increasing return on assets.

- To correct this problem, the Financial Accounting Standards Board issued FASB Statement 13. This requires firms that enter into financial (or capital) leases to "capitalize the lease." This process restates the firm's balance sheet in order to show the leased asset as a fixed asset and the present value of the lease payments as a liability.[3]

- The logic behind the FASB requirement is that when a firm signs a financial lease agreement, its obligation to make the lease payments is just as binding as it would be in a long-term loan agreement. Thus, for most purposes, capitalized leases are a direct substitute for a firm's long-term debt financing.

- Significant operating lease arrangements must be reported in a footnote to the financial statements, further ensuring that no investor or lender will be "fooled" by leasing arrangements.

4. Evaluation by the Lessee:

- The lessee must determine whether it is in the firm's best interests to lease or to purchase the equipment to be used in a project.

- The logical way to make this determination is to calculate the costs and benefits associated with each alternative and chose the one with the lower net cost. The basic analysis is similar to the NPV decision model discussed earlier in this chapter under capital budgeting. In analyzing operating leases, be certain to consider carefully the flexibility of cancellation they offer.

- The leasing decision process has three stages:

1. **Acquisition Decision:** The firm decides to acquire a particular building or asset; this decision is based on regular capital budgeting procedures. The decision to acquire the asset is not the issue of the following analysis—the decision to go ahead with the project has already been made.

2. **Financing Decision:** Financing the project is the next step. Even most well-run firms do not keep idle cash available for project expansion; therefore, capital must be raised from other sources.

3. **Lease versus Purchase Decision:** Funds to purchase the asset could be obtained by borrowing, using invested funds or cash generated over the next period, or issuing new equity (or some combination of sources). Leasing normally has the same effect on capital structure as borrowing, so the cash flows from leasing are usually compared with the cash flows from borrowing and using the funds to purchase the asset.

- Since the acquisition of the asset has already been justified, the analysis focuses on the differential cash flows between the two financing alternatives.

- When an asset is leased, the lessee typically must pay for maintenance; also, the lessee is not entitled to deductions for either interest or depreciation (Note, however, that this is not the case in capital leases). Furthermore, at the end of the lease, the lessee must either return the asset to the lessor or purchase it for the residual value.

- If the asset is purchased with borrowed funds, the purchaser is entitled to deductions for interest and depreciation, and also retains ownership of the asset at the end of the loan period.

- The analysis technique essentially involves comparing the present value of the cash flows associated with lease financing of the asset with the present value of the cash flows associated with borrowing funds to purchase the asset. It is important to take into consideration any differences in the cash flows for the two financing methods. Any cash flows that are not affected by the method of financing are not relevant to the decision process.

- Since leasing is essentially a direct substitute for debt, the appropriate discount rate for the analysis is the after-tax cost of debt.

- Any tax considerations must be taken into account. Some of the more obvious tax implications have already been covered above. One of the less obvious considerations involves property taxes that may apply to purchased assets. Also, depending upon the then-prevailing version of the tax codes, investment tax credits may have an impact on the lease-versus-purchase decision. Section 861 of the Internal Revenue Service Code covers most of the relevant tax issues for leasing, such as deductibility of interest for multinational firms.

5. Evaluation by the Lessor:

- It is important for the lessor to evaluate the lease arrangement to determine whether required rate of return on the lease is being earned.

- The lessor must:

1. Determine the cash outflow associated with the contract (the purchase price of the asset less any lease payments received at the initiation of the contract).

2. Determine the periodic cash inflows (lease payments less taxes and maintenance costs).

3. Determine the after-tax salvage value of the equipment.

4. Determine whether the arrangement is an acceptable investment using the NPV method as the appropriate form of analysis.

- In large leases, as a general rule, the two parties will negotiate the size of the payment and terms of the lease. In smaller leases, the lessor will generally offer the lessee terms on a "take-it-or-leave-it" basis, but competitive pressures will usually cause lease payments to be set at a fair level.

6. Leveraged Lease Analysis:

- Sometimes lessors may decide to finance part of the purchase price of the equipment instead of making the purchase with their own funds.

- If part of the purchase price is financed, the lease is known as a leveraged lease. The presence of leverage does not change the analysis from the standpoint of the lessee, but it does modify the analysis from the lessor's standpoint.
- While leverage may increase the potential return on the lease to the lessor, it will also increase the riskiness of the lease due to the use of debt.

7. Other Issues in Lease Analysis:

a. Estimated Residual Value: The lessor owns the property upon expiration of the lease and thus has a primary claim on the asset's residual value. In most cases, the estimated residual values are built into the leasing arrangements. Assets with potentially high residual values will generally have lower lease payments than similar assets with lower residual values. The setting of the residual value may also have an impact on the tax status of the lease, as well as on requirements for listing the lease as an on- or off-balance-sheet item. It is critical in lease analysis to know the asset's assumed residual value in order to avoid surprises at the end of the lease.

b. Increased Credit Availability: Leasing arrangements may allow smaller firms to finance a larger portion of their assets than if they were to borrow the funds for purchase (in effect, a secured loan). For larger firms, however, leasing arrangements will show up in financial statements, and in most cases will be considered a direct substitute for other sources of long-term debt.

c. Depreciation Tax Savings: If a firm is unprofitable, or currently has very high levels of depreciation, it may find it worthwhile to consider a lease. A lessor in a high tax bracket may be willing to pass along some of the tax benefits from a lease in the form of lower lease payments.

d. Computer Model: As in the case of capital budgeting analysis, it may be helpful to use a computer-based spreadsheet model, or some other type of lease-analysis software, to compare different types of lease arrangements and terms.

e. Leasing under the 1986 Tax Act:

- This act contains several provisions that have reduced the potential advantages of leasing arrangements:
  1. The investment tax credit was eliminated.
  2. Depreciation tax rates were lowered.
  3. Maximum tax rates for corporations and individuals were lowered.
- In most types of lease arrangements, there are fewer advantages under the new tax codes than under the old ones.
- One provision of the new tax code, the Alternative Minimum Tax (AMT), did provide some advantages to leasing. Because many firms utilize accelerated depreciation and similar techniques to minimize taxes, but then use longer depreciation schedule for determining earnings for shareholders, the AMT was established to ensure that some level of taxes be paid. AMT requires firms to compute a minimum tax based on "reported profits" (approximately 20%) as an alternative to paying no taxes due to high levels of depreciation for tax purposes.

- Many companies determined that they might be exposed to significant tax liabilities under AMT, and were considering using leases as a means to reduce their overall reported income. These were typically short-term, high payment leases which would result in lower reported profits. The fact that these leases might not qualify for tax-deductibility was not an issue, because companies were simply trying to reduce reported income and thus reduce their AMT liabilities.

8. Why Firms Use Leasing

- A key reason for leasing is the existence of tax or other differentials that make it attractive to both the lessee and the lessor. Related to this is the benefit of keeping leases "off balance sheet" in some instances, thereby potentially increasing the debt capacity of the firm. The lease versus buy decision is one of the most important types of analysis for firms acquiring capital assets.

- Leasing is an appealing choice for assets that have high potential for technological obsolescence, such as many types of electronic devices, medical equipment and communications technology.

- Leasing may be attractive to start-up firms or firms beginning sales in a new area where there is a high level of uncertainty about future demand. The cancellation provisions of an operating lease may offer substantial protection in business ventures of this kind.

- Firms may choose to lease assets that are used in their business, but fall outside their area of expertise. For example, a food wholesaler may choose to lease its fleet of delivery trucks rather than purchase them. The lessor takes care of the financing and maintenance of the fleet, while the wholesaler focuses its efforts on what it knows best.

- Leasing may be offered at the same time as the acquisition of the asset, making it an easy "one-stop shopping" arrangement.

IV. Chapter Checklists

A. Listing of Lease Components

1. **Type of Lease:** A lease is generally one of four basic types: (1) sale-leaseback, (2) operating lease, (3) financial or capital lease, or (4) combination lease.

2. **Tax Impact of Lease:** Leases must meet certain IRS criteria in order to be considered leases for tax purposes. Leases that do not qualify under IRS guidelines are treated as a type of loan financing.

3. **Impact of Leases on Financial Statements:** Leases are generally regarded as a substitute for debt, but some leases can be classified as "off balance sheet," which may distort the firm's true debt structure.

4. **Analysis of Leases:** Generally, leases are compared with borrowing funds to purchase the asset in question. Whether or not the firm can justify the acquisition of the asset is not the issue; how to finance the asset is the issue.

5. **Terminal or Residual Value of Lease:** A key factor affecting the ultimate value of the lease is the value placed on the asset at the end of the lease, as well as disposition of the asset at the end its useful life. In most types of leases, there is some residual or terminal value for the asset at the end of the lease, to which the lessor is usually entitled. The lessee may be able to purchase the asset for the terminal value, or in some cases may be required to make up the difference between the assumed terminal value and the actual market value of the asset at the end of the lease (known as residual value risk). These issues are normally stated in the lease agreement.

6. **Lease Payment:** The lease payment will be a function of the asset's initial and terminal values, the term of the lease, any capital reduction at lease inception and the interest rate associated with the lease.

7. **Why Leases Are Attractive:** Leasing is generally motivated by differentials between lessees and lessors. Some of the more common reasons for leasing are: (1) tax rate differentials, (2) situations where the lessee faces alternative minimum tax (AMT), and (3) cases where the lessor is better able to bear the residual value risk than the lessee.

V. Calculations and Examples

A. Example #1—Capital Budgeting

Fred's Downhill Ski Shop is contemplating replacing its equipment for injecting foam into the linings of downhill ski boots to provide a custom fit. The foaming machine currently in use was purchased eight years ago for $24,000, has been completely depreciated, and has a current market value of $4,200.

Fred estimates his cost of capital at 12%, uses straight-line depreciation on all his equipment, and faces a marginal tax rate of 40% for the foreseeable future. The 40% tax rate applies to all taxable income, including any gain from selling the old foaming machine.

Fred is considering the following two mutually exclusive alternative replacements:

Alternative 1:

A similar but larger-capacity machine costing $30,000 is available. Fred estimates that this machine will increase annual revenues by $15,000 and increase annual non-depreciation expenses by $6,500 over its estimated 15-year life. It is expected that the new machine will have an actual after-tax salvage value of $2,000 at the end of 15 years. The machine will be depreciated for tax purposes on a straight-line basis over 15 years (assume a zero salvage value for computing depreciation).

Alternative 2:

The latest in boot-foaming technology is available (a high-pressure machine capable of injecting a new ultralight foam with exceptional insulating characteristics and high resistance to breakdown). Since ultralight foam represents the frontier in ski boot technology, Fred anticipates that this process will provide an increase in annual revenues of $34,000 and an increase in annual non-depreciation expenses of $15,500 over the 15-year life of the process. This alternative requires an initial outlay of $75,000 for equipment. The machine will be depreciated on a straight-line basis to a zero salvage value over its 15-year life.

The primary issue in this analysis is the difference in scale between the two alternatives and the decision will hinge on whether or not the additional cash flows generated under Alternative 2 will be great enough to justify the additional investment.

Solution to Example #1

The first step in the analysis is to determine what the initial outlay would be for each alternative. The initial cash flow consists of the sale of the old equipment (plus or minus any tax effects) and the outlay for the purchase of the new equipment. For our purposes here, cash inflows to the firm are signified by positive numbers and cash outflows by negative numbers. The initial cash flows for each alternative are as follows:

Initial Cash Flows for Alternatives (Dollars)		
Type of Cash Flow	Alternative 1	Alternative 2
Sell Old Equipment	4,200	4,200
Tax Effects from Sale	$-4,200 \times .40 = (1,680)$	$-4,200 \times .40 = (1,680)$
Buy New Equipment	(30,000)	(75,000)
Net Outlay @ Purchase	(27,480)	(72,480)

The next step in the analysis is to determine the change in the cash flows to the firm for each alternative. Each alternative has a different impact on income, expenses and depreciation resulting in a different impact on the cash flows. The calculation of the cash flows is provided in the table below:

Annual Cash Flows For Alternatives (Dollars)		
Impact on Cash Flow	Alternative 1	Alternative 2
Added Income	15,000	34,000
Added Expense	(6,500)	(15,500)
Added Depreciation	$30,000/15 = (2,000)$	$75,000/15 = (5,000)$
Before-Tax Profit Change	6,500	13,500
Income Taxes (.40)	(2,600)	(5,400)
After-Tax Profit Change	3,900	8,100
Add Back Depreciation	2,000	5,000
Incremental Net Cash Flow (Years 1–14)	5,900	13,100
Add Back Salvage Value	2,000	0
Incremental Net Cash Flow (Year 15)	7,900	13,100

The next step in the analysis is to examine the cash flows and determine the NPV, IRR, and payback period for each of the alternatives. The results of this analysis are contained in the table below:

Decision Criteria for Alternatives		
Decision Criteria	Alternative 1	Alternative 2
Net Present Value (NPV) @ 12%	$13,069	$16,742
Internal Rate of Return (IRR)	20.2%	16.2%
Payback Period	4.7 Years	5.5 Years

The final step in the analysis process is to choose one of the alternatives based on the decision criteria in the preceding table. Unfortunately, the various methods do not agree about which project is better for the company. Alternative 2 has the higher NPV (almost $3,700 higher), but Alternative 1 has the higher IRR at 20.2% versus 16.2%, and a shorter payback by almost a year. The best choice in this case, is Alternative 2 because of its higher NPV and its greater increase in the value of the firm. The primary reason that Alternative 1 has a higher IRR and a shorter payback is its smaller scale, not that it is inherently more profitable.

B. Example #2—Leasing

The Gulf Coast Off-Shore Supply Company provides supplies and transportation of crews for off-shore oil rigs near the coast of Louisiana. The company is currently considering the addition of another supply boat to its fleet and is examining several ways to finance this acquisition. Some of the information relevant to the decision is as follows:

- The boat costs $55,000, and the company plans to hold it for eight years, at which time it will be sold at an expected residual value (book value) of $15,000.
- The company is in the 40% tax bracket, and would depreciate the boat on a straight-line basis over the full eight years if it were to borrow funds for the purchase.
- The annual maintenance costs are estimated at $5,000, and annual operating costs (gas, food, water, etc.) are estimated at $15,000.
- Initially, the company intended to buy the boat outright with no financing involved; but the current low prices on oil have eroded profits and forced the firm to consider other financing options. The treasurer of the firm has narrowed the options down to two:

1. The first option is to borrow the funds needed from a commercial bank at a rate of 14% on an eight-year fully amortized loan with equal annual payments.

2. The other alternative is to lease the boat from ABC Marine for $13,500 per year, payable at the *beginning* of each of the eight years. If the boat is leased, the lessor will take care of maintenance (but not operating expenses) and will, of course, be entitled to all tax benefits as well as any salvage value at the end of the eight years. These lease payments will be fully deductible for tax purposes.

- Under the leasing option, the lease would be treated as a direct substitute for debt and therefore would appear on the balance sheet of the firm as a capitalized lease. If the firm were to borrow funds and purchase the boat, the loan would be reported on the balance sheet as a long-term liability.

Based on this information, should the firm borrow the funds to purchase the boat or lease it from ABC Marine?

Solution for Leasing Example (Dollars)

Borrow Option	Yr 0	Yr 1	Yr 2	Yr 3	Yr 4	Yr 5	Yr 6	Yr 7	Yr 8
Loan Amount	55,000	50,844	46,105	40,704	34,546	27,526	19,523	10,400	0
Loan Payment		11,856	11,856	11,856	11,856	11,856	11,856	11,856	11,856
Interest		7,700	7,118	6,455	5,699	4,836	3,854	2,733	1,456
Principal Repayment		4,156	4,638	5,402	6,158	7,020	8,003	9,123	10,400
Loan Payment		(11,856)	(11,856)	(11,856)	(11,856)	(11,856)	(11,856)	(11,856)	(11,856)
Tax Shield from Interest		3,080	2,847	2,582	2,279	1,936	1,541	1,093	582
Tax Shield from Depreciation		2,000	2,000	2,000	2,000	2,000	2,000	2,000	2,000
A/T Maintenance		(3,000)	(3,000)	(3,000)	(3,000)	(3,000)	(3,000)	(3,000)	(3,000)
Salvage Value									15,000
Net Outflow		(9,776)	(10,009)	(10,274)	(10,577)	10,922	(11,315)	(11,763)	2,726
PV of Payments	(44,047)								
Lease Option	**Yr 0**	**Yr 1**	**Yr 2**	**Yr 3**	**Yr 4**	**Yr 5**	**Yr 6**	**Yr 7**	**Yr 8**
Lease Payment	(13,500)	(13,500)	(13,500)	(13,500)	(13,500)	(13,500)	(13,500)	(13,500)	0
Tax Benefit	5,400	5,400	5,400	5,400	5,400	5,400	5,400	5,400	0
Net Outflow	(8,100)	(8,100)	(8,100)	(8,100)	(8,100)	(8,100)	(8,100)	(8,100)	0
PV of Payments	(42,835)								

Borrow and Purchase Option

The first step in analyzing the borrow and purchase option is to construct an amortization table for the loan. This is necessary because only the interest portion of the loan is tax-deductible, and since this is a fully amortized loan, the amount of interest in each year of the loan will be different. Thus, the net cash outflow for the borrow and purchase option will also be different for each year.

- The basic approach in the analysis is to determine the net cash outflow for each year for the borrow and purchase option and compute its NPV, and compare it with the NPV from a similar analysis of the leasing option.

- Based on the information for the case, a $55,000, eight-year, fully amortized loan would have an annual payment of $11,856 at the end of each year. The top four lines of the solution table show the amortization schedule for the loan, with the amount of interest and principal repayment determined for each of the eight payments.

- The basic purpose of the amortization schedule is to determine the interest and principal components of each loan payment. This is necessary because only the interest portion of the payment is tax-deductible. In the early years of a loan, the payments are primarily interest, while in the later years they are mostly principal.

- The next six lines of the solution table show the calculation of the net outflow for each year of the loan. The primary outflow is for the loan payment, with offsetting cashflows from the tax deductions (shield) on the interest and the depreciation. An additional outflow is the after-tax amount for maintenance of the boat.

- Note that the amount of the interest portion of the payment declines each year, as does the tax shield it provides. Also note that the expected salvage value is deducted from the purchase price in determining the basis of depreciating the boat. Thus, annual depreciation is only $5,000.

- In the final year of the loan term, the salvage value of the boat is recognized as a cash inflow. Since the estimation is that the boat will be sold for book value, there are no tax consequences at the time of the sale.

- The present value of the outflows associated with the borrow and purchase option is calculated at 14% (the cost of borrowing funds), which is appropriate for this type of analysis and is determined to be $44,047 (shown as negative because it is the NPV of outflows).

Lease Option

The calculation of the outflows for the leasing option is somewhat easier than for the borrow and purchase option because no amortization calculations are needed.

- The lease payment is given as $13,500, and after the deduction for taxes, results in an after-tax outflow of $8,100 per year.

- The lease terms specify that the payment must be made at the beginning of the year rather than the end of the year as in the borrow and purchase option. This is typical of lease arrangements.

- The cash flow at the end of year eight is zero, because the lessor is entitled to any salvage value from the boat.
- Note that under the lease option you do not pay separately for the maintenance of the boat as this is included in the lease payment.
- Note that the $15,000 annual operating costs are not considered in either option. These costs would be the same whether the boat is leased or owned, and thus are not relevant to the lease-versus-purchase decision.
- The present value of the outflows associated with the leasing option is calculated at 14%, and determined to be $42,835 (again, shown as negative in the solution table because it is the NPV of outflows).

The Decision

In this case, the lease option appears to be better than the borrow and purchase option. The present value of the outflows is about $1,200 lower in leasing. However, leasing is usually done for other than purely financial reasons. Some other factors that favor leasing are:

- The company may find it easier to qualify for a lease than for a loan to purchase the boat.
- The accounting for the lease may be easier for the firm than for the borrow and purchase option.
- The company's primary line of business is providing services to off-shore oil rigs, not owning a fleet of boats. It may be able to provide better service to its customers if it concentrates on its primary business, letting an experienced marine leasing company manage the financing and maintenance of the boats.

VI. Endnotes

1. See: "Capital Budgeting Procedures under Inflation" by Cooley, Roenfeldt and Chew, *Financial Management,* Winter 1975, pp. 18–27.
2. In a 50-year study of returns on common stock versus the T-Bill rate, the average premium was determined to be 8.3%; *Stocks, Bonds, Bills and Inflation: The Past and the Future,* 1982, by R.G. Ibbotson and R.A. Sinquefield.
3. FASB Statement 13, "Accounting for Leases," provides complete detail about the conditions under which a lease must be capitalized and the procedures involved.

13 Electronic Commerce

I. Outline of the Chapter

A. Basics of Electronic Commerce (ECOM)
   1. Definitions
      a. Electronic Commerce (ECOM)
      b. Electronic Messaging
      c. Electronic Data Interchange (EDI)
      d. Electronic Funds Transfer (EFT) and Financial EDI (FEDI)
   2. Types of EFT Systems
      a. Fedwire
      b. Automated Clearing House (ACH) Transfers
      c. Other EFT Systems
   3. Relationship between EDI, EFT and FEDI

B. Benefits and Costs of ECOM and EDI
   1. Benefits of ECOM and EDI
      a. Less Labor Intensive
      b. Faster
      c. Lower Error Rates
      d. Certainty
      e. Acknowledgment
   2. Costs of ECOM and EDI
      a. Software
      b. Communications
      c. Hardware
      d. Training
      e. Trading Partner Promotion
      f. Shortened Payment Times

    4. Negotiating Shared Benefits

        a. Price Changes (Discount)

        b. Payment Timing Changes

    5. Determination of Discount for Change in Payment Terms

        a. Timing Differences

        b. Opportunity Costs

        c. Transaction Costs

        d. Minimum Acceptable Discount

        e. Maximum Allowable Discount

        f. Discount Negotiating Range

F. Redesign of the Treasury Function

    1. Evaluated Receipts Settlement (ERS)

    2. Paid-on-Production (POP)

G. The Future of Electronic Commerce

Chapter Checklist

A. Checklist of EDI Costs and Benefits

Calculations and Examples

A. Example of Negotiating Credit Terms Calculation

II. Introduction

Information exchanged between firms includes requests for quotes, bids, purchase orders, order confirmations, shipping documents, invoices, remittance advices and payments. The last two usually fall under the responsibility of the treasurer.

This chapter introduces the basic concepts of Electronic Commerce (ECOM) and Electronic Data Interchange (EDI), and outlines some of the potential costs and benefits. The three key elements of the EDI infrastructure that make EDI implementation possible on a large scale will be covered: generic format standards for EDI messages, off-the-shelf software to use the standards more easily, and value-added communication networks for connecting trading partner computers. The chapter concludes by discussing the impact EDI is beginning to have on credit terms.

ECOM impacts all areas of the firm dealing with information exchanges with trading partners: marketing, production, transportation, purchasing and finance. Banks also provide some ECOM services, especially where they are critical for banking relations and providing services. ECOM also changes the cash flow time line, and therefore the level of current assets and working capital will be affected. When firms implement electronic payments, the typical cash management problems of collections, disbursements and concentration change considerably.

In fact, most of the treasurer's traditional cash management products (lockbox, controlled disbursing, etc.) become much less important in an electronic payment environment. ECOM enables firms to capture payment and other data electronically and, when this capability is combined with treasury management systems, the treasurer gains access to much more current information than is possible with paper-based systems. Finally, while ECOM brings many potential benefits, it introduces a new set of problems in the legal, audit and security areas. For centuries, policies, laws, procedures and practices have been in place for paper documents, but electronic information is much more recent and the business and social scaffolding is not yet complete.

III. Coverage of the Chapter Material

A. Basics of Electronic Commerce (ECOM)[1]

Currently the vast majority of documents and payments exchanged among firms in North America consist of paper carried by the postal system. Electronic commerce (ECOM) is the use of electronic means to send data from one organization to another. ECOM ranges from the use of unstructured electronic formats such as facsimile transmission (FAX) and electronic mail (E-mail) to more elaborate formats such as Electronic Data Interchange (EDI). In this context, the terms electronic commerce and electronic messaging have essentially the same meaning.

In a broader context, however, electronic commerce can be thought of as the ultimate culmination of the EDI development process.[2] ECOM is essentially the end-to-end connection of any person, application or computer to another using some accepted standard. Thus, true ECOM would be the ultimate in open systems communications, where business data could be moved easily from one place to another, from firm to firm, or from application to application. Broad-based adoption of ECOM would allow the creation of true "virtual corporations" (temporary business networks or small groups formed quickly to exploit opportunities). These networks or partnerships would be based on ECOM linkages, rather than on legal agreements or organizational structures.

ECOM and EDI require that suppliers and manufacturers work more closely with each other in their day-to-day relationships. This usually means that manufacturers will work with fewer suppliers and those remaining will become "strategic partners" who help the manufacturer to provide better products to its customers, more quickly and at a better price. In the ECOM arena, companies are usually referred to as trading partners, indicating the value of the strategic relationships outlined above.

EDI is a new technology application that promises eventually to replace paper documents with electronic communications. The impact of EDI on firms, particularly on the treasury function, will be significant: information and cash value can move more rapidly and with greater accuracy, overhead costs related to paper processing can be reduced and inventories may be lowered, and, most importantly, customer and supplier relationships can be strengthened. Further, many of the traditional organizational roles in the firm may have to be redefined. For example, treasurer's responsibilities, such as float management, may become unnecessary as payments become electronic and their value dates are negotiated more explicitly.

1. Definitions: The following definitions should be helpful in developing a basic understanding of ECOM, EDI and EFT:

a. Electronic Commerce (ECOM): In its broadest definition electronic commerce is the exchange of business information between one organization and another in some type of electronic format. At one end of the spectrum ECOM would include unstructured electronic messaging such as FAX or E-Mail, while at the other end it would include more sophisticated formats such as EDI. ECOM also has been more specifically defined as the end-to-end connection of any person, application or computer to another in some accepted standard. In the purest case, ECOM would essentially entail the establishment of true open systems where data could be easily moved from one place, system, or application to another.

b. Electronic Messaging: This is broadly defined as moving data electronically between two points. The various forms of electronic messaging may be arrayed along a continuum (see Figure 13.1). On the far left are totally unstructured messages such as Faxes and E-mail. On the far right are highly structured messages, including EDI.

c. Electronic Data Interchange (EDI): EDI is defined as the movement of business data electronically between or within firms (including their agents or intermediaries) in a structured, "computer processable" format that permits data to be transferred, without re-keying, from a computer-supported business application in one location to a computer-supported business application in another.

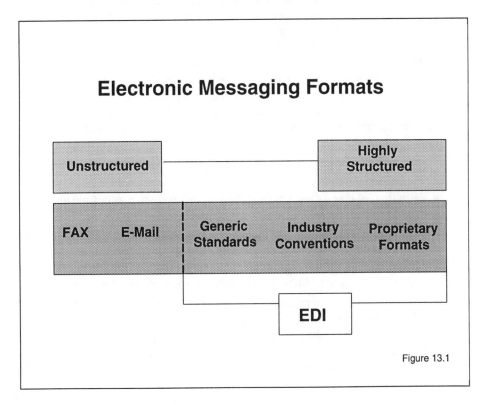

Figure 13.1

This definition of EDI excludes Fax, which requires the receiver to re-key the information into a business application. EDI also excludes E-mail, which moves business data electronically but generally uses a free format requiring editing before a document can enter a business application.

There are three basic types of EDI:

- **Generic EDI** refers to format standards that have been developed by one of the standards organizations (discussed later). The format for a generic purchase order, for example, is defined broadly in order to satisfy the needs of many different users in many industries. When a firm sends a generic EDI purchase order to another firm that subscribes to the same generic standard, the receiving firm can capture the data directly in a computer-supported business application without re-keying.

- **Industry Conventional EDI** is used by certain industries (including retail, chemical and electrical) that have developed standard formats and communications conventions based on a subset of the more generic EDI standards.

- **Proprietary EDI**, currently one of the most prevalent types of EDI, is developed by one firm for exclusive use by its trading partners. Many firms using proprietary formats, however, are moving toward the use of generic or industry conventional standards.

d. Electronic Funds Transfer (EFT) and Financial EDI (FEDI): These are subsets of electronic data interchange (EDI). The distinguishing feature of EFT is the exchange of value, which requires the involvement of financial intermediaries such as banks. Financial intermediaries must be included in the exchange of value among the parties. EFT refers to bank-to-bank electronic payment instructions. Examples of EFT include wire transfers, automated clearing house (ACH) payments and transfers and instructions via the Society for Worldwide Financial Telecommunications (SWIFT). FEDI refers to the exchange of electronic business information (non-value) between a firm and its bank or between banks. Examples of FEDI are electronic lockbox deposit reports and remittance information processed through a bank to a firm.

2. Types of EFT Systems: There are several types of EFT systems available in the U.S.:

a. Fedwire: Fedwire is a real-time method for transferring cash value from one bank to another using Federal Reserve account balances.

- With a Fedwire transaction, the payor's reserve account is debited and the payee's reserve account is credited on a real-time basis. Fedwire transactions are final and not reversible. UCC4-A is the Uniform Commercial Code section which deals with the legal responsibilities of both customers and banks in using wire transfers.

- Fedwire is both a communications and a transfer system. Besides transferring value through the use of simultaneous debits and credits, Fedwire can be used to send messages throughout the banking system. The payor can obtain a confirmation number that can help in tracking a transfer through the Fedwire network. The Federal Reserve guarantees that the receiving bank is credited with the funds and that instructions on the proper account to credit are transferred along with the funds. It does not, however, guarantee that the receiving bank will properly credit the payee's account.

- When a wire transfer is received at the payee's bank, the payee can be notified on a real-time basis through an intraday feature of the bank's balance reporting system. Wire transfers do not allow for extensive ancillary information to accompany payment.

b. Automated Clearing House (ACH) Transfers: The ACH system is a computer-based clearing and settlement facility for interchange of electronic debits and credits among financial institutions. Since the mid-1970s, the ACH system has functioned as a unified payment clearing system consisting of regional clearing house associations owned by financial institutions. The ACH, while used extensively in the early years as a payment system for fixed-amount recurring payments, is being used increasingly for business-to-business trade payments. Some of the features of the ACH system are as follows:

- The ACH system is designed for next-day settlement of large-volume, batch-processed payments. At each processing step in an ACH transfer, payment information is stored, sorted, and forwarded in batches to the next processor. Therefore, it is called a "store-and-forward" or "store-process-forward" system.

- The ACH system is a special-purpose EDI application that uses bank-specified information formats and a communication network to facilitate value transfer.

- The Fed operates most of the regional ACH associations. VISA is also one of the key ACH operators, especially in the western U.S., and several of the ACH associations are privately operated.

- Government-initiated transactions (primarily social security payments, payrolls and vendor payments) make up a significant portion of transactions in the ACH system. Corporate-to-household transactions (direct deposit of payroll, payment of bond coupons and dividend payments) and household- to-corporate payments (debits for mortgages, insurance premiums, utility payments, etc.) also account for a large volume of ACH transactions.

- In the corporate arena, the ACH is used extensively for the concentration of cash from remote deposit banks into concentration banks. The one area where ACH use is currently low (but does show signs of significant future growth) is in corporate-to-corporate trade payments.

- The National Automated Clearing House Association (NACHA) is the member-run organization that sets policies for the ACHs and performs other functions such as research, pilot programs and marketing.

c. Other EFT Systems:

- One of the major alternative large-dollar payments system is the Clearing House for Interbank Payment Systems (CHIPS). Located in New York City, CHIPS is a computerized netting system that handles an enormous volume of cash flow between local financial institutions. This system is primarily composed of large

New York City financial institutions and is operated by the New York Clearing House Association. Many other institutions have access to CHIPS through offices or correspondents in New York City.

- One of the primary international large-dollar payment systems is the Society for Worldwide Interbank Financial Telecommunications (SWIFT). This organization is actually a value-added communication networks (VAN) operated for more than 1,600 member banks in 54 countries and handling more than one million messages each day. Each message is sent in a proprietary SWIFT format designed to handle information relating to payment instructions, letters of credit, trade information, transaction confirmations, balance reports, deposit reports, etc.

3. Relationship between EDI, EFT and FEDI: Figure 13.2 shows the relationships between firms and banks. "Pure" EDI, EFTand FEDI are illustrated. For example, a firm sends an EDI invoice to a customer. The customer sends a FEDI payment instruction to its bank. The customer's bank and the seller's bank then exchange EFT instructions through the ACH system. The seller's bank notifies the seller of the received payment through an electronic deposit report.

This exhibit also shows the creation of a new entity, a Value-Added Bank or VAB. These VABs provide EDI services to their customers beyond the strict forms of payment-related, firm-bank-firm, FEDI transmissions. This type of bank will be covered in detail later in this chapter.

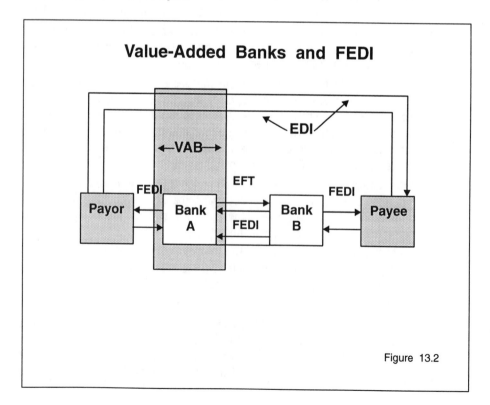

Value-Added Banks and FEDI

Figure 13.2

MODE	NAME	PARTIES	APPLICATIONS
EDI	Electronic Data Interchange	Firm-to-firm	Catalogs/Price Information Request for Quotes Purchase Orders Shipping Information Invoices Remittance Information
FEDI	Financial EDI	Firm-to-bank/ Bank-to-firm/ Bank-to-bank	Lockbox Information Balance Information Payment Initiation Reconciliation Information
EFT	Electronic Funds Transfer	Bank-to-bank (value transfer)	ACH Debits and Credits Fedwire Transfers CHIPS and SWIFT

B. Benefits and Costs of ECOM and EDI

There are many benefits and costs to consider in the implementation of ECOM and EDI in a firm. The most important are discussed below, and a checklist is provided at the end of this chapter.

1. Benefits of ECOM and EDI: The benefits of ECOM and EDI are:

a. Less Labor Intensive: Once data have been entered at the beginning of a transaction, they can be moved from one computer to another electronically without manual intervention. With EDI, filing, matching, sorting and retrieving are no longer manual processes; and stuffing, stamping, and mailing are eliminated.

b. Faster: With no mail-time delays and minimal processing delays, EDI transactions flow very rapidly. EDI enables firms to reduce safety stock and, for many, makes just-in-time inventory management possible. This enables them to achieve significant reductions in cycle times for many processes. Firms that use EDI have reported average cycle-time reductions of 44% in key functional processes.[3]

c. Lower Error Rates: Since data are not re-keyed, error rates can be greatly reduced by the implementation of EDI. EDI users have reported average error-rate reductions of 27% in key functional processes.

d. Certainty: Because: (1) mail time is eliminated, (2) processing is much faster and (3) payments become available in either one or two days with ACH and immediately with Fedwire, it is possible with EDI/EFT to completely eliminate, or greatly reduce, uncertainty in cash flow timing.

e. Acknowledgment: With EDI, it is possible to receive a functional acknowldgement that a message has been received by the other party. However, the details of acknowledging EFT messages need to be worked out, so for the time being a canceled check is still considered the best method for proof of payment.

2. Costs of ECOM and EDI: These costs need to be considered in the implementation of EDI:

a. Software: EDI requires the ability to retrieve data from existing databases. This may involve extensive modification of current business software applications. In addition, the retrieved data must be translated from the firm's current format into a recognized EDI format, and security features may be required. When generic EDI is used, there are off-the-shelf software packages that perform the translation process and help in data retrieval.

b. Communications: The firm must pay for transmission of the data to the recipient. The communication may be done directly (usually over telephone lines) or through a Value-Added Network (VAN—covered later in this chapter). Regardless of how the data are transmitted, the relevant costs must be attributed to the EDI implementation. The firm may need to consider the cost of communications software and hardware (modems) in this process.

c. Hardware: EDI may or may not require new computer equipment. As mentioned above, communications hardware, such as modems, may be needed for sending and receiving electronic data. Extra computer security hardware may be necessary to protect sensitive translation data.

d. Training: Since EDI is a new field, many of the firm's trading partners will not be knowledgeable about it. Firms pioneering EDI have had to spend substantial sums for internal and external training.

e. Trading Partner Promotion: Benefits of EDI accrue only when a significant number of transactions is converted from paper. This requires the firm to actively solicit trading partners willing to send and receive EDI messages.

f. Shortened Payment Times: Payors fear that EDI/EFT will result in faster payments, thereby reducing cash balances. While this result is possible, a later discussion will show that float can be negotiated so that neither payor nor payee is disadvantaged.

3. Additional Barriers to ECOM and EDI: Besides the perceived costs of using EDI, additional barriers to EDI implementation are the acknowledged benefits of the paper-based transaction system.

a. Convenience of Paper-Based System: The current paper system requires no sophisticated processing system by payor or payee. The U.S. Postal Service delivers to all addresses in the U.S. for a uniform postage fee and is quite efficient in low-cost delivery of paper-based messages and payments. Virtually every company and individual has access to the delivery system and has a bank account or check-cashing service to handle the clearing part of the cycle.

b. Versatility of Paper-Based System: The check-paper system is versatile in the way ancillary information can accompany the payment instrument. The check, for example, can be attached to any required documentation such as a copy of the invoice.

c. Tradition of Paper-Based System: Legal, audit and processing structures surrounding the check system have been built up for hundreds of years. Almost all of the Uniform Commercial Code, as well as most accounting and legal standards, are based on paper and signatures for reporting and control purposes. Though there has been some introduction of EDI into legal and audit systems, it is still in the early stages of adoption.

d. Dual Systems May Be Initially Required: Due to legal and auditing constraints, many firms implementing EDI find they must continue to run dual systems (both paper and EDI) for a significant time after EDI implementation. The same is true in the EFT payment area where the administrative tasks that accompany EFT payments, such as account verification, pre-notes, etc. for one-time payments, will necessitate a dual check/EFT transaction system for the foreseeable future.

C. EDI Standards and Software

A primary reason for the slow movement to an electronic environment in transaction processing has been the lack of a cost-effective infrastructure. Recently, however, the infrastructure has been developing rapidly. It includes four primary elements:

1. Accepted formatting standards for most business documents
2. Off-the-shelf software for translating internally stored data into standard formats
3. Communications networks and inter-networking communications standards
4. Low cost computer hardware

These four developments have lowered the barriers to EDI implementation. This section discusses only the first three as the last is already well understood by most readers.

1. National Standards: To send documents to each other electronically, firms must agree on a specific data format and technical environment. In the early days of EDI, large firms announced a proprietary format and communications interface, and either encouraged or mandated trading partner participation. Proprietary data formats and technical requirements are adequate when a firm deals with a small number of partners. But when it has multiple EDI partners, a common standard becomes a necessity.

a. Transportation Data Coordinating Committee (TDCC): The development of widely accepted standards for EDI has been formally under way since the formation of the Transportation Data Coordinating Committee (TDCC) in 1968. This non-profit organization set out to establish standards for communications between and within railroads, ocean carriers, air carriers and motor carriers. The first TDCC standard was published in 1975, and in 1991 TDCC standards came under the jurisdiction of the ANSI X12 Committee.

b. ANSI X12 Committee: In 1978, the Credit Research Foundation and TDCC formed the Business Applications Committee (BUSAP), which subsequently received a charter from the American National Standards Institute (ANSI) as the ANSI

X12 Committee. This committee's mandate is to develop EDI standards that will be acceptable across industry groups. In 1983, five standards were published by X12. The ANSI X12 committee has subsequently published standards for more than 20 documents including purchase orders, remittance advices, invoices, and requests for quote. Work is proceeding to define EDI formats for an additional 100 documents.

c. Uniform Communication Standard (UCS): In 1980, Arthur D. Little Consultants issued a report on the grocery industry suggesting that adoption of electronic communications would greatly facilitate movement toward greater use of EDI. The TDCC was asked to develop a set of standards applicable to that industry. The first such standard (Uniform Communication Standard or UCS) was applied to an actual transaction by the Quaker Oats company in 1981. UCS standards are now widely applied in the grocery and retail trades.

d. Toward Common Standards: In 1984, the ANSI X12 committee and other industry groups joined with Europe's Trade Data Interchange (TDI) to form the Joint EDI Committee (JEDI). Parallel efforts in standards development in Europe have led to the development of the EDIFACT standards (EDI for Administration, Commerce and Trade). The EDIFACT committee has produced a common data dictionary and rules of syntax that enable different industries and countries to develop standards using the same building blocks.

e. Industry Conventions of Generic Standards: Several industry groups (e.g., automotive, chemical, communications) have decided to adopt X-12 standards for their industries. Rather than developing them from the ground up, however, they often suggest subsets of generic X12 standards that fit the needs of their industries. The overall trend seems to be toward an ANSI X12 basis for future standards development in EDI.

f. EDI Format Standard Defined: An EDI format standard consists of rules for translating one or more business documents into electronic messages.

- UCS standards, for example, define a family of about 15 different types of electronic documents: purchase orders, promotional announcements, price changes, invoices, etc.

- A transaction set is the electronic analog of a paper business document or form. Transaction sets are formed using specific rules for formatting the information in the business document.

- Within a transaction set, related information, such as a line item in the purchase order, is called a data segment. A transaction set consists of at least three data segments and usually many more.

- Data segments consist of pieces of data called data elements, such as price, unit of measure and quantity. Data elements are defined in a data dictionary.

g. NACHA Standards Formats for ACH Payments: ACH transactions use standardized formats. There are currently several different formats for various ACH applications, and banks must have special computer software to process them. All are based on a basic fixed-length record containing 94 characters. The most commonly used ACH formats are:

1) Prearranged Payments and Deposits (PPD): This is the format used for direct deposit of payroll and government transfer payments.

2) Cash Concentration and Disbursement (CCD): This format is widely used for cash concentration purposes and there is some use of the format for corporate-to-corporate payments. It contains only limited space for ancillary payment information but can be processed by almost all banks.

3) CCD Plus Addenda (CCD+): The CCD+ format combines the widely used CCD record with an addenda record (also 94 characters) providing space to add a segment of an ANSI X12 820 remittance advice. The segment can identify, in standard format, the invoice being paid or give other reference information needed to apply the payment. The Federal government's Vendor Express initially used the CCD+ format, and has been recently expanded to also use the Corporate Trade Payments (CTP) and Corporate Trade Exchange (CTX) formats.

4) Tax Payment Format (TXP): This new format is still under development and is similar to a CCD+, but is specifically designed for the payment of taxes at the state and federal levels.

5) Corporate Trade Payments (CTP): Introduced in 1983, this format overcomes the restrictions created by limiting an ACH transfer to 94 characters. It permits up to 4,990 additional 94 character blocks of information to be included with the basic CCD record. It has limited use because: (a) few banks can process CTP records and (b) while the addenda records are rigid and fixed, there are no standards specifying how data in the addenda records are to be organized.

6) Corporate Trade Exchange (CTX): The CTX format is designed to overcome one of the main drawbacks of the CTP format by combining the record structure and enveloping required by the ACH system with flexible length standards of ANSI X12. Developed by NACHA in 1987, a CTX transfer is essentially an ANSI X12 820 (payment order/remittance advice) transmitted using ACH communications protocols. This is known as an "ANSI 820 in an ACH wrapper."

h. Changing Standards: As information needs change and firms gain experience in using EDI standards, the standards themselves evolve. Each year, most standards bodies publish revisions to the standards. While this process is necessary to adapt the standards to changing needs, it poses some problems for the EDI user's systems staff. Some of a firm's trading partners may be using one version of the standard, while others are still using an older version. Therefore, an EDI user must support multiple versions of the EDI standards.

2. Translation Software: Translation software is necessary to convert messages into standard formats and communicate messages between trading partners.

a. Steps Performed by EDI Translation Software: There are three basic steps in EDI translation. The order outlined below is for an outgoing EDI message; the order would be reversed for an incoming message.

1) File Conversion Software: This software extracts data stored in the firm's business application and reformats (maps) it for input into the formatting software. This portion of the software is generally referred to as the "mapper" or "mapping utilities."

2) Formatting Software: This software operates on the input data and translates it into the desired EDI standard format. Most software is capable of formatting data into any accepted generic standards and industry conventions.

3) Communications Software: This software dials the trading partner or communications network and sends (or receives) the EDI-formatted data to (or from) another party's computer using acceptable protocols.

b. Availability of Off-the-Shelf Software: Today, off-the-shelf EDI software packages with sophisticated mapping utilities is generally available for most computer platforms and operating systems. In addition, most EDI software is table-driven, meaning that by changing input tables the software can produce any desired transaction set and can be easily updated as standards evolve.

D. Value-Added Networks (VANs)

1. Need for VANs: When firms first began using EDI, most communications were directly between trading partners. This required that many difficult communications protocols be resolved before the computer of one firm could talk to the computers of others.

- Direct computer-to-computer communications with a trading partner require that both firms

  1. Use similar communication protocols
  2. Have the same transmission speed
  3. Have phone lines available at the same time
  4. Have compatible computer hardware

- If these conditions are not met, communications become difficult if not impossible.

- In recent years, third-party communications intermediaries known as Value-Added Networks (VANs) have been developed. They solve some of the problems of direct communications by providing services that enhance the basic phone network.

2. VAN Services: VANs offer many services to their customers. These include:

a. Mailboxing: This permits one trading partner to send transactions sets to the other's mailbox for storage. When the other trading partner is ready, it will retrieve the transactions sets. This solves the problem of setting a fixed time when both partners are able to communicate.

b. Protocol Conversion: This means that one partner can use a communications package with one transmission protocol to communicate with a partner that uses a different protocol.

c. Standards Conversion: Some VANs offer the ability to receive a document in one format and translate it into another before sending it to the customer.

d. Implementation Assistance: This is frequently offered in the form of consulting, software and training of trading partners.

e. Line Speed Conversion: This is provided so that messages may be received and sent at whatever line speed the user requires.

f. Gateway to Other VANs: Most VANs currently permit trading partners to communicate with other parties even though the other party uses a different VAN.

3. Banks That Provide VAN Services: Some banks provide VAN services for information relating to payments. They are called value-added banks (VABs). They solve the problem firms face when trading partners differ in their abilities to process the kind of electronic payment they want to send. VANs solve interface problems between two firms that have different computer systems, different format needs and different protocols. VABs solve the problem between two firms that have different requirements for payment information.

a. Example of Value-Added Bank (VAB) Payment Services:

- The payor sends payment instructions to the bank in proprietary format or X12 820 transaction set (ANSI X12 payment order/remittance advice). The bank then uses a cross reference table to determine how each payee wishes to receive remittance detail and payment.

- For some payees, a paper check is created and mailed along with a printout of the remittance detail. For some, a CTX transmission (containing the full 820 transaction set) is sent to the payee's bank and that bank then forwards 820 information to the payee. For others, a payment is sent via Fedwire and a paper remittance advice is mailed. For still others, an ACH CCD payment is made while remittance information is transmitted to the payee in Bank Administration Institute (BAI) lockbox format.

- The VAB handles the interface problems so the payor need only have one method of communicating with the bank.

b. Example of VAB Collection Services:

- At the other end, some banks are offering a collection service that performs the same function. Regardless of how they are received (paper check, ACH, wire), the payments are reformatted by the bank and transmitted to the firm in a proprietary format, in BAI lockbox format or in 820 format.

- This provides the firm with only one data stream from the bank. Unfortunately, this approach does not work as well as it might appear since some ACH and wire formats do not contain enough data to permit the payee to apply the payment.

There are still some problems in the use of BAI lockbox transmission formats as a vehicle for recording electronic payments. Banks have found that when they reformat an electronic payment (CTX for example) into the BAI lockbox format, there is inevitably a loss of data due to the relatively sparse nature of the BAI lockbox format.

To get around this problem, banks today commonly augment the electronic transmission from the lockbox area with a backup paper printout of the full electronic payment transaction details. Then, if there is insufficient data in the electronic transmission to enable the company to apply the payment automatically, the paper printout can be used to apply the payment manually. For the same reason, many banks have long needed to back up the check payment data included in the BAI transmission with check photocopies and paper remittance data.

E. Credit Terms and EDI Transactions

1. Current Credit Terms and Practices: Most credit terms used today assume a paper-based environment and are usually 30 days and rarely shorter than 10 days (except in perishable items). This permits time for paper-based processing. Firms often allow a "grace period" to accommodate mail and processing time delays.

2. Impact of EDI and EFT: EDI permits firms to complete paper processing more rapidly, and EFT removes much of the payment float due to mail, processing and availability delays. Therefore, many firms are re-examining conventional credit terms. Other things being equal, faster payments, however, would hurt buyers and help sellers. To compensate for changes in the cash flow time line, firms are beginning to negotiate new EDI-based credit terms.

3. Movement to EDI Is Not a Zero-Sum Game: Contrary to past cash management strategies where "my win is your loss," EDI can bring significant cost savings to both parties. Therefore, it should be possible to shift the timing and/or amount of cash flows so that both buyer and seller realize significant savings.

4. Negotiating Shared Benefits: There are several ways for buyers and sellers to transfer value by changing the terms of transactions. It is important to note that some firms will negotiate terms separately with each of their trading partners, while others may decide to unilaterally adjust terms for all of their partners. The two most popular approaches are:

a. Price Changes (Discount): The seller offers the buyer a cash discount to compensate for a reduction in collection float. For example, a large oil company offers a 1.5% discount for electronically debiting a customer's account on the day of product delivery. Credit and collection float under the paper system is normally 30–40 days.

b. Payment Timing Changes: The buyer initiates later payment (compared to when paper checks were sent) to compensate for shorter EFT collection float. For example, a manufacturer initiates an ACH-type payment to its suppliers three days later than a check payment would have been mailed out. This, in effect, preserves the float that would have been lost by the buyer due to the switch to EFT.

5. Determination of Discount for Change in Payment Terms: The amount of discount each party is willing to consider depends on several factors:

a. Timing Differences: The discount depends on the difference between the total time line when paper is used (n) and the total time line when electronics is used (m). The longer the time difference, the greater the discount.

b. Opportunity Costs: The discount depends on the opportunity costs as viewed by each party, and these are not necessarily the same. One party may have a higher or lower cost of funds than the other.

c. Transaction Costs: The discount demanded by the buyer or offered by the seller depends on transaction cost savings (or increases) incurred in moving from paper to electronics.

d. Minimum Acceptable Discount: To be as least as well off under the electronic system as under the paper system, the buyer would want the discount to be at least as large as the interest lost (or paid if funds are borrowed) due to the earlier payment. Transaction cost savings would also be factored into this equation. This minimum acceptable discount can be calculated as follows:

$$D_b >= k_b \times (n - m) - f_b$$

Where: D_b = Minimum acceptable discount for buyer.
  k_b = Daily opportunity cost for buyer.[4]
  f_b = Transaction cost savings/dollar value of the transaction for the buyer.
  n = Time delay under paper-based payment information system.
  m = Time delay under EDI/EFT system.

e. Maximum Allowable Discount: Similarly, the seller would be just as well off if the amount of the discount offered (a loss to the seller) were offset by the interest earned due to earlier receipt of payment, as well as by any transaction cost savings. This maximum allowable discount can be calculated as follows:

$$D_s <= k_s \times (n - m) + f_s$$

Where: D_s = Maximum allowable discount offered by seller.
  k_s = Daily opportunity cost for seller.[5]
  f_s = Transaction cost savings/dollar value of the transaction for the seller.
  n = Time delay under paper-based payment information system.
  m = Time delay under EDI/EFT system.

f. Discount Negotiating Range: This is defined as the difference between the maximum allowable discount from the seller's viewpoint and the minimum acceptable discount from the buyer's viewpoint:

$$R = D_s - D_b$$

If this number is positive, it is possible to find a discount that is better for both parties in terms of present value. In effect, this difference is the amount up for negotiation. An example of its calculation is presented at the end of this chapter.

F. Redesign of the Treasury Function

EDI and ECOM have played an important part in the redesign of functions or processes in the treasury area. Two primary examples are the implementation of evaluated receipts settlement (ERS) and paid-on-production (POP). These are discussed below:

1. **Evaluated Receipts Settlement (ERS):** ERS is a payment method designed to eliminate the need for a supplier to provide an invoice to a customer. The dollar amount for ERS payments is based not on an invoice but on a calculation of the quantity in the customer's receipt record multiplied by the price on the purchase order.

- In the ERS process (shown in Figure 13.3) the supplier sends the customer an advance ship notice one day prior to shipment specifying the items to be delivered as well as time of delivery and other shipping information.

- When the items are received at the customer's dock, the receiving clerk typically uses a bar code scanner to input the shipment code, which can then be matched to the information in the purchase order file and in the advance ship notice.

- The supplier does not send an invoice, but is simply paid by the customer on an agreed date after receipt of the shipment.

- The use of the ANSI 820 Payment Order and Remittance Advice allows customers to automate their payables process and suppliers to automate their receivables and payment application process.

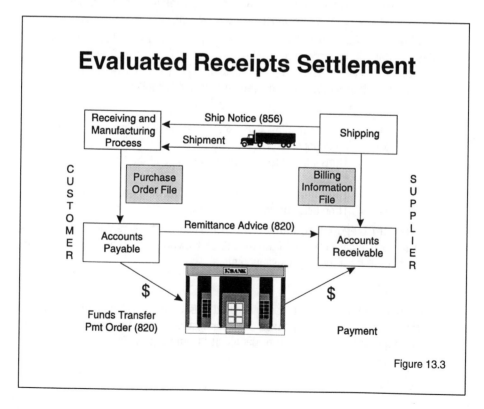

Figure 13.3

2. Paid-on-Production (POP): POP is the process by which a payment record is created for goods and/or services based on a usage record rather than on shipping records. It is similar to consignment sales in retail, but is based on usage within a manufacturing environment. Typically, there is only one supplier and title to the product (supply) transfers somewhere during the manufacturing process rather than at the shipping dock as in ERS. Because of legal concerns relating to liability, potential bankruptcy, and use of inventory assets for supporting loans, it is very important to determine exactly when and where the title to the inventory transfers. This process is outlined in Figure 13.4.

G. The Future of Electronic Commerce

The future of electronic commerce is undoubtedly very bright, but it is difficult to predict exactly what form it will take. Fax, E-mail and EDI have their individual strengths and weaknesses, and each has certain types of transactions to which it is best suited. In contrast, true electronic commerce transactions would provide the best means of transferring information from one application or database to another, regardless of individual formats. Moreover, in many cases EDI implementations are only utilizing electronic documents to replace paper documents and are not really redesigning the applications systems. True innovation in this area calls for complete processes to be redesigned and entire companies to be reengineered in order to take advantage of new communications methods and

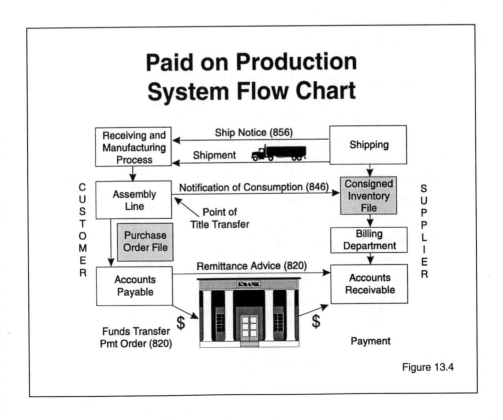

Figure 13.4

technologies. The future of electronic commerce, and how fast it is adopted, will rest on addressing these questions.

IV. Chapter Checklists

A. Checklist of EDI Costs and Benefits

This checklist can be used to identify the key costs and benefits in implementing an EDI system. The cost/benefit factors are only representative. A given firm's particular circumstances may involve more or fewer factors depending on the scope of the implementation.

Benefits of Eliminating Paper-Based Systems

1. Personnel

- Keying operations
- Reconciliation of payments with invoices, POs with invoices, etc.
- Filing
- Retrieval
- Preparation for mailing
- Reports
- Telephone costs
- Error resolution
- Overhead for personnel costs

2. Error Consequences

- Misdirected orders
- Loss of business due to errors
- Spoiled merchandise due to errors
- Costs of restocking merchandise

3. Sales Staff Effectiveness

- Preparation of purchase orders
- Following-up on order status, payments, etc.

4. Maintenance of Customer Base

- Faster service
- Customer locked into system
- Responding to customer request

5. Inventory Reduction

- Value of reduction in safety stock
- Value of reduction in storage costs

6. Assembly Line Efficiency

- Value of reduction in uncertainty of material arrival

7. Time Value Benefits

- Benefit of earlier payment

8. Mail, Paper, and Storage Costs

- Postage
- Envelopes/paper
- Storage of paper documents

Costs of Implementing an EDI System

1. Hardware

- Computer systems
- Communications hardware

2. Software

- File conversion
- Translation
- Communication
- Bridging

3. Personnel

- Addition, if any, to run EDI system

4. Training

- Internal: users in firm
- External: trading partners

5. Time Value Costs

- Costs of earlier payments to suppliers

6. Network or Other Third-Party Costs

- Costs for VAN or other communications services

Remember: Some costs are one-time only, while others are ongoing. Some costs are insensitive to transaction volume, others are sensitive. Determination of costs/benefits should be done over a multi-year horizon. Present value techniques work best for this type of analysis. Be sure to use after-tax costs and after-tax interest rates.

V. Calculations and Examples

A. Example of Negotiating Credit Terms Calculation

A large company approaches one of its major customers with a proposal. All future purchases by the customer of bulk tank loads of chemicals would be given a 1.5% discount if the customer agreed to a next-day settlement by ACH. That is, the oil company would electronically debit the customer's account through the ACH on the day following a delivery. The customer estimated that the average transaction was $200,000, and that the current payment system resulted in 41 days of total delay from delivery to check clearing. The customer's cost of capital is considered to be 13.5% and the seller's cost of capital is 15%. The transaction cost savings to the customer are estimated to be $10.00 per payment, while the seller has no transaction cost savings. What is the maximum discount the seller would offer and the minimum discount the customer would accept? Should the customer take the terms offered?

Solution:

1. Using the calculation below, the maximum discount offered by the buyer is determined to be .01644.

   Maximum Allowable = Cost of Capital × Time Savings + Transaction Costs
   Discount by Seller
   $$= 15.0\% \times [(41 - 1)/365]$$
   $$= .15 \times (.109589) = .01644$$

2. Using the calculation below, the minimum discount required by the buyer is determined to be .01475.

   Minimum Acceptable = Opportunity Cost × Time Savings − Transaction Costs
   Discount to Buyer
   $$= 13.5\% \times [(41 - 1)/365] - 10/200,000$$
   $$= .135 \times (.109589) - .00005$$
   $$= .0147945 - .00005 = .01475$$

3. The seller is willing to offer the 1.5% discount because it is below the maximum allowable discount and the customer should accept the new terms because the offered discount of 1.5% is above the minimum required discount.

VI. Endnotes

1. Additional information on EDI and Electronic Commerce in the treasury area can be found in the current edition of *Essentials of Cash Management*.

2. See: "Electronic Commerce: Toward the Virtual Corporation—Parts 1 and 2," Norman F. Barber, *EDI Forum*, 1994, Volume 6, No. 3 and No. 4.

3. Information on current usage of EDI was obtained from a 1993 survey of business managers about their EDI implementations conducted by The EDI Group, Ltd., Oak Park, IL.

4. This would be the appropriate opportunity cost or cost of funds for the buyer, divided by 365 to obtain a daily rate.

5. This would be the appropriate opportunity cost or cost of funds for the seller, divided by 365 to obtain a daily rate.

14 Insurance and Risk Management

I. Outline of the Chapter

A. Overview of Insurance and Risk Management
1. Types of Losses
2. Responsibilities of Treasurers in Risk Management
3. Basic Types of Business Insurance
   a. Liability
   b. Excess and Umbrella
   c. Property and Casualty
   d. Business Interruption
   e. Difference in Conditions
   f. Directors and Officers
   g. Fidelity and Crime
   h. Workers' Compensation
   i. Employee Benefits
   j. Other Types of Insurance

B. Steps in Risk Management
1. Identify Manageable Risks
   a. Types of Risk to Be Identified
   b. Methods of Identification
   c. Using a Risk Management Consultant
   d. Ongoing Information Needs
2. Measure Potential Losses and Financial Impact
3. Consider Available Control and Financing Techniques

    4.   Select Most Appropriate Techniques

    5.   Monitor the Results

C. Risk Control Techniques

    1.   Safety

    2.   Exposure Avoidance

    3.   Limiting Contractual Acceptance of Risk

    4.   Combination of Exposures

    5.   Separation of Exposures

D. Risk Financing Techniques

    1.   Risk Retention

        a.   Non-Insurance

        b.   Borrowing

        c.   Self-Insurance

        d.   Captives

    2.   Risk Transfer

        a.   Contractual Transfer

        b.   Additional Insured

        c.   Guaranteed Cost Insurance Program

        d.   Retrospectively (Retro) Rated Insurance Program

        e.   Cash Flow Casualty Retro Programs

        f.   Group Captive

        g.   Risk Retention Group

        h.   Alternative Risk Financing Facilities

E. Negotiating Insurance Programs

    1.   Insurance Providers

    2.   Dealing with Insurance Brokers

    3.   Selecting Insurance Coverage (Insurers)

    4.   Selecting a Deductible

    5.   Selecting a Liability Limit

    6.   Negotiating Techniques

F. Captives and Other Alternative Financing Techniques

    1.   Single-Parent Captive

    2.   Rent-a-Captive

G. Risk Management Services

Chapter Checklists

A. Source Documents for Risk Identification
B. Types of Liability Losses
C. Listing of Disclosure Information for Insurance Negotiation
D. Areas of Broker Services and Evaluation Criteria

II. Introduction

Every firm's assets and activities are subject to many types of accidental loss. The possibility of loss has three broad implications for the firm's financial management: (1) the threat of accidents, even if they do not occur, imposes a very real "cost of risk" on every firm, (2) the financial managers have responsibilities for controlling and limiting accidental losses that may strike the firm, and (3) any accidental losses require the firm to have resources available to finance a recovery.

Treasurers need to consider the risk management implications of all financial decisions. In many types of financial analysis, a "most-likely" or expected-value outcome is assumed, and risk from losses may be included in overhead rather than in the cash flow analysis. A thorough study of this chapter and other sources of information on this subject will help treasurers gain better understanding of the risk management implications of their decisions.[1]

III. Coverage of the Chapter Material[2]

A. Overview of Insurance and Risk Management

Accidental loss has broad implications for treasurers. Even if all losses can be covered by insurance, management will find that accidents generally tend to:

1. Reduce the firm's profitability
2. Increase its liquidity requirements
3. Impair its financial security

1. Types of Losses: Effective risk management will help control or prevent losses, and adequate insurance will help finance the firm's recovery.

First, with respect to actual accidents, any major loss incurred will almost surely disrupt a firm's operating and financial plans. These losses may include:

1. Property loss (including internal or external theft)
2. Business interruption or net income loss
3. Surety or breach of contract loss (such as a contractor's failure to perform)
4. Liability loss (e.g. lawsuits from injured customers)
5. Personnel loss (president or other "key person" and workers' compensation)

Damage to property lowers the projected rate of return on the impaired assets, even if insurance eventually pays to repair or replace them. Any substantial interruption of business is likely to lower profits, and, even if the firm has business interruption insurance, cash inflows will be slowed and there may be pressure on its ability to meet debt service obligations.

Even with insurance, not all damages are covered (such as the loss of market share). Liability losses can drain a firm's cash through payment of uninsured claims, legal defense costs, or expenditures in negotiating with the insurers involved. Similarly, contractors' failure to complete projects can deprive a firm of anticipated revenues and impede its growth—just as can the death, disability, or resignation of a valuable, hard-to-replace employee.

Beyond the economic losses from accidents that actually occur, the mere possibility of accidents has a second important implication for any firm's treasury management. Safeguarding against threatened accidents imposes added costs, such as outlays to prevent accidents or to reduce their severity, and may include expenditures for:

1. Fire detection and suppression ("sprinkler") systems
2. Maintaining production and sales records for potential recalls
3. Training drivers of the firm's vehicles to drive more safely
4. General worker safety training

Many firms seek to limit their risk by attaining Highly Protected Risk (HPR) status for their buildings and plants. This rating, which entails the installation of appropriate sprinklers, fire gear, safety equipment, etc., provides the firm with a preferred rating status for fire and hazard insurance, resulting in significantly lower insurance premiums.

Another major cost in anticipation of accidents is risk financing. This involves ensuring the availability of funds in the case of loss from accidents, either through insurance or the ability to obtain funds from other sources.

In addition to these loss prevention and risk financing costs, the possibility of accidental losses imposes administrative costs on the firm. Management must decide where and how to best apply loss prevention. It must select the proper types and amounts of insurance and collect the insurance reimbursement when a covered loss occurs.

The total of all these costs from both actual and potential losses constitutes a firm's "cost of risk" from losses. This cost is often difficult to estimate; however, there are experts in the area to assist the treasurer in this process.

The critical question is how much to spend on loss prevention. The firm should try to identify the location of the break-even point between costs of insurance and cost of uninsured losses.

2. Responsibilities of Treasurers in Risk Management: Treasurers often have diverse but important responsibilities related to the cost of risk.

- The primary decision is to identify the potential losses for which the firm should purchase insurance and those which it would pay for itself.

- The treasurer must also decide how much coverage the firm needs for the insured potential losses and how much money to retain for self-insurance purposes.

- Ultimately, the overall intent is to control the cost of risk from a given set of loss exposures.

- On a more analytical level, treasurers may be called upon to identify, measure and allocate the cost of each of the risk elements for a given project (or even for the entire firm) so that the risk factors are considered in management decisions.

- Treasurers often have direct responsibilities for managing exposures to accidental loss that arise from the assets or activities they manage.

Everything a firm owns or does is a source of potential loss; treasury management activities are no exception. Some of the many possible loss exposures related to treasury management are:

1. Loss, theft or destruction of cash or securities by a firm's employees or by others

2. Loss of the firm's accounts receivable records, which can cripple revenue collections for substantial periods

3. Improper procedures for collecting receivables, which may subject the firm to tort liability for defamation of customers or invasion of their privacy

4. Inability (or reduced ability) to raise needed capital due to financial or operating difficulties or loss of key officers.

For these and other exposures to accidental loss originating in the finance department, treasurers are most likely to be directly responsible for: (1) preventing the losses or controlling their size and (2) bearing the brunt of the losses in the form of allocated risk management costs charged against the department.

Directly or indirectly, the remainder of this chapter deals with the responsibilities of treasurers for dealing effectively with a firm's exposures to risk (and the associated costs) from accidental losses, whether or not covered by insurance. The treasurer should be aware that insurance is usually the risk management technique of last resort and works well only where loss frequency is low and loss severity is high.

3. Basic Types of Business Insurance: There are many types of business insurance available. The major types are discussed below.

a. Liability: There are many liabilities that a company may face and there are forms of insurance available to cover most of them. The liabilities could arise from product defects, business practices, accidents, actions of the firm's employees, officers or board of directors, and general negligence in the operation of the company. Types of liability insurance include business, automobile, business owner's liability, product liability, comprehensive general liability, and manufacturer's and contractor's liability.

b. Excess and Umbrella: This type of insurance is designed to supplement basic or primary liability coverage. These policies generally pay after the primary policy's limits have been exhausted. For example, if the primary insurance policy has a limit of $250,000 and claims exceed this amount, an umbrella or excess policy would then pay the excess claims up to the limit of the policy. Excess or umbrella policies can also be used to fill in gaps in coverage in basic liability policies.

c. Property and Casualty: This type of insurance provides for reimbursement in the event of loss of some type of asset, such as buildings, equipment or inventory. Insurance will often be for "replacement value" of the items in question, paying the cost to completely replace the item at current market prices, rather than the historical or book value of the asset.

d. Business Interruption: This insurance provides for payments to the firm in the event it is unable to pursue its normal line of business for some period of time due to some unforeseen event, such as fire.

- This type of insurance generally covers loss of profits and continuing fixed expenses (debt, lease, etc.) while the firm is temporarily out of business for various types of reasons. For example, if a firm were to suffer a fire at its main production facility, casualty insurance would pay for the rebuilding of the facility, and business interruption insurance would make payments to compensate the firm for lost profits and increased costs during the rebuilding process.

- Other types of business interruption insurance could cover: (1) failure of a contingent business (key supplier), (2) extra expenses due to basic loss (the firm can continue to operate, but only if extra costs are incurred), or (3) loss of profits and commissions due to the loss of inventory.

e. Difference in Conditions: The primary purpose of Difference in Conditions (DIC) insurance is to cover the insured's property for all of the perils that are not covered by the basic property insurance policies. It is usually used in conjunction with multiple basic policies to make them all uniform.

- It does not provide higher limits of coverage for these basic perils as does an umbrella policy; rather, it provides coverage for conditions and perils not included in the basic policy.

- DIC insurance is often purchased to insure property in transit and overseas property, and is used to fill voids in policies purchased overseas.

- DIC insurance is not typically standardized because: (1) the market for this type of insurance is limited and (2) it is generally written to cover special exposure and circumstances.

- DIC insurance often has exclusions for important perils such as fire, vandalism, employee dishonesty, machinery losses, etc., since it is assumed that an insured business already has coverage for these losses under its standard business property insurance.

f. Directors and Officers: This insurance provides coverage when a director or officer of a company commits a negligent act or omission, misstatement or misleading statement, and a successful libel suit is brought against the company as a result. The policy provides coverage (usually with a large deductible) for directors' and officers' liability exposure if they are sued as individuals. Coverage is also provided for the costs of defense, such as legal fees and other court costs.

g. Fidelity and Crime: Fidelity bonds provide coverage that guarantees payment for money or other property lost because of dishonest acts of bonded employees, either by name or by position. The bond generally covers all dishonest acts, such as larceny, theft, embezzlement, forgery, misappropriation, wrongful abstraction, or willful misapplication, whether employees act alone or in concert. Since a fidelity bond makes up only part of the protection against theft, other crime insurance is mandatory. A blanket bond could be used to cover all employees of the firm, while crime insurance provides specific coverage for the perils of burglary, theft, and robbery by external parties.

h. Workers' Compensation: This insurance provides coverage for the four basic types of benefits (medical care, death, disability, rehabilitation) for employee job-related injuries or diseases as a matter of right (without regard to fault). This insurance is usually purchased by the employer from an insurance company, although in a few states there are monopolistic state funds through which the insurance must be purchased. The premium rates are generally based on a percentage of the employer's payroll and vary according to the employee's occupation.

i. Employee Benefits: Many corporations provide certain types of insurance for the benefit of their employees. Most firms will pay for only a portion of the coverage, with the employees being asked to pay the balance. The most common type offered is medical or health insurance, which is covered in detail in Chapter 15. Disability insurance, which provides coverage for non-work-related disabilities, may be provided for all or some of the firm's employees. For corporations, life insurance coverage for key personnel can provide the firm with the resources it may need to replace them should they die. In some cases this is referred to as "key-man insurance." It is especially useful for smaller firms and partnerships.

j. Other Types of Insurance: There is a wide variety of other types of insurance for a firm's special needs. The most popular include:

- Ocean/marine policies to cover ships and their cargos.
- Special Multiperil Insurance (SMP), which covers special losses in four basic areas: property, liability, crime, and boilers and machinery. Endorsements can be added to cover almost any standard risk in these areas.
- Exclusions policies, which cover losses either not covered or excluded under other policies held by the firm. These policies are intended to "fill in the gaps" or to provide higher overall levels of coverage.

B. Steps in Risk Management

Every firm needs proper risk management due to the possibility of accidental loss (loss exposures) that may disrupt its operations and lower its efficiency and profitability. Risk management reduces the adverse effects of actual and potential accidental losses through cost-effective techniques for either preventing such losses from occurring (risk control) or financing recovery from those that do occur (risk financing). The goals of risk management are as follows:

1. Insure against catastrophic loss
2. Decide when and what to insure

3. Manage the purchase and use of insurance (including brokers)

4. Obtain efficient pricing for insurance needs

Risk management is a decision or problem-solving process where the "problem" is exposure to accidental losses. The steps a firm should follow in this process are outlined in the following sections.

1. Identify Manageable Risks: Manageable risks are defined as those that a company can control by managing the risk itself or its consequences.

a. Types of Risks to Be Identified: Risks or loss exposures are usually classified as: property risks, business interruption risks, workers' compensation risks, legal liability risks (including surety risks for failing to carry out contracts) and fidelity risks (from employee dishonesty). Personnel risks (from loss of the services of especially talented employees who resign, become disabled or retire) often are added as another risk category. In addition, the firm must often consider health care and medical insurance for its employees (covered in Chapter 15). Several of the more important risks are discussed in detail below.

- **Property Risks:** Property losses are generally characterized as either direct or indirect. Direct losses could include destruction of a facility by fire, theft of inventory, or damage to a delivery vehicle in a traffic accident. Indirect (or consequential) damages could include the costs of shifting production to another plant, restocking the inventory, or renting a replacement delivery vehicle while the damaged one is being repaired. To properly identify property risks, a treasurer needs to examine property schedules, appraisals, and the process flow of operations from raw materials receipt through delivery of finished goods. This will help to identify critical points in the process where property losses could slow down or stop production and delivery of products. As a general rule, property insurance policies should be written for replacement value rather than book value in order to protect the company fully in the event of loss. However, if an asset insured for replacement value is lost and not actually replaced, the insurance will typically only pay for its book value.

- **Workers' Compensation Risks:** This type of risk stems from potential losses in the form of medical expenses, disability wages and rehabilitation costs for injured workers. In most cases, the schedule of benefits is determined by state law, but may be open-ended, especially in the event of company negligence. To help identify this type of risk, management needs to evaluate safety practices and loss histories at all work locations, the types and distribution of jobs, general hiring practices, and the legal and legislative climate in states where the firm has employees.

- **Liability Risks:** These risks arise as a result of any obligations the firm may have for the cost of injuries to others. These obligations could arise from contracts entered into by the firm, accidents by the firm's employees or management, or from negligence on the part of the firm. A listing of the various types of liability losses is presented at the end of this chapter.

- **Fidelity Risks:** These risks arise from the theft of money, securities or property by employees, as well as from crime involving employees or outsiders to the company. To properly deal with these types of risk, management should examine amounts and locations of cash and securities holdings; maintain adequate control procedures for cash, securities, property and inventory; and implement proper screening and bonding procedures for all employees involved with handling cash, securities or inventory.

- **Surety Risks:** These risks are related to contractual obligations on the part of the firm that may not be fulfilled. To identify this type of risk, management should determine the total amount of outstanding surety bonds (or other similar instruments), plus any other guarantees that may be attached to contractual obligations.

b. Methods of Identification: As the first problem-solving step in identifying the kinds of losses (including liability claims and failure to fulfill contracts) that a firm may suffer, its treasurer needs to gather information from many areas of the firm. The treasurer may want to consider using a survey or guide in this stage of the process in order to ensure that all possible areas of potential risk are covered.[3] Many insurance companies and brokers require this type of survey on a regular basis. The documents required for this process may include property schedules, lists of employees, loss runs for expired insurance policies, flow charts, financial statements, etc. A more complete listing of the possible sources is included at the end of this chapter.

Once the information has been gathered, the treasurer needs to determine the probability of occurrence for each of the risks. One approach is to use a five-point scale, with the figure five indicating highly probable and the figure one indicating not at all probable. Using historical loss data, management can calculate loss or accident frequency rates and determine if there is any correlation with specific parts of the firm, plants, buildings, employees, etc.

c. Using a Risk Management Consultant: When a firm is first implementing an insurance and risk management process, or if major changes are being made in existing policies, the use of a risk management consultant may be appropriate. This type of consultant can help with interviews, inspections, analysis of risk, and in the design and selection of required plans.

d. Ongoing Information Needs: Proper risk management also requires that the identification of risk be kept as current as possible. This process entails the use of good communications with other areas of the company and the creation of awareness throughout the company of the importance of risk identification and control.

2. Measure Potential Losses and Financial Impact: The significance of any loss exposure depends on how often actual losses occur (loss frequency) and how large these actual losses are (loss severity). A series of individually small losses may be severe in the aggregate if they occur within a brief period. Proper risk management requires that a firm have sufficient resources available (cash, credit or insurance) to finance recovery from any foreseeable accidental loss or series of losses. Suggested methods for measuring some of the types of loss are:

- **Property Loss Measurement:** Estimate the replacement cost of properties and the resulting business interruption costs (including the costs of recovering lost customers) if the property is damaged, destroyed or stolen.

- **Workers' Compensation Loss Measurement:** Estimate the cost of disability payments, death benefits, and lost time, based on payroll, job descriptions and the potential injuries. A loss history report from the last three to five years is useful in developing this estimate.

- **Liability Loss Measurement:** Estimate the probability of loss from potential product liabilities, injuries to customers or visitors to company facilities, accidents, and general liability claims on the firm.

- **Fidelity Loss Measurement:** Estimate the potential losses from employee theft of cash, securities, company property or inventory.

- **General Loss Measurement:** Estimate the potential losses from any other source, including the impact on personnel, property, finances (administrative costs, taxes, or intangible costs) and the future of the company.

3. Consider Available Control and Financing Techniques: All risk management involves either risk control or risk financing, with the financing options entailing either retention (the firm relying on internal resources) or transfer (relying on insurance or other external resources). Although risk control is generally considered more important than risk financing, combining the techniques is the best approach. Risk control without risk financing may lead to bankruptcy if, despite the best safety measures, losses occur. Risk financing without risk control wastes money paying for losses that could have been prevented at little cost, and may lead to negligence claims. The firm may decide to self-insure small risks, but risks with large potential losses should be treated in a more systematic manner. The following steps should be taken for these larger risks:

- Develop an ongoing program to monitor and control large risks.

- Utilize deductibles or self-insurance for recurring losses (this will be covered later in this chapter).

- Establish a primary insurance layer with reasonable coverage terms and policy conditions.

- Purchase excess insurance for protection against large catastrophic losses not covered in the primary insurance layer.

- Determine the firm's policy with respect to the following factors:
  - Use of in-house control versus contracted service
  - Administrative impact of control and finance techniques
  - Estimated savings from establishment of loss control procedures
  - Tolerance for risk and for variability in risk over time
  - Impact on the firm's cash flows (operations, taxes, claims, etc.)
  - Insurance availability and current insurance market conditions
  - Ultimate cost of all estimated losses and control procedures

4. Select Most Appropriate Techniques: When a firm commits its resources to particular assets or activities, it becomes vulnerable to related loss exposures. By properly managing these exposures, the firm can maintain its profitability and efficiency at a high level despite threats of accidents. The firm should develop disaster contingency plans in the event of large losses, insurance cancellation or insurance company failure.

5. Monitor the Results: To assess the effectiveness of the risk management techniques it has chosen and to adjust to changing conditions, management should periodically review its entire risk management program. This process includes the regular generation of loss reports, the review of all losses over a period of time, and comparison of these losses with both historical data and losses by other firms in their industry. This information may be generated internally or may be obtained from the insurance company holding the firm's policies.

C. Risk Control Techniques

Several approaches can be used to reduce the frequency or severity of the accidental losses that may strike a firm. The most popular are:

1. Safety: Any action that reduces the frequency with which accidents occur, or the amount of harm done should an accident occur, is a safety measure. The focus of safety is not on the financial consequences of accidents but on the frequency or severity of the damage or injury they cause. Firms should review examples of accidents in their industry and provide employees with training on accident prevention and how to cope with accidents when they occur.

2. Exposure Avoidance: Avoidance involves refraining from taking on an asset or activity, or eliminating an existing one, when there is no combination of risk control or financing techniques that produces a projected risk-adjusted rate of return that is adequate. This may require a firm to reconsider its lines of business if a particular area is too risky from the standpoint of potential loss.

3. Limiting Contractual Acceptance of Risk: A firm may subcontract with other firms (not insurers) to perform certain activities and, thereby, take on the loss exposures those activities create. Another possibility is for a firm to require others to pay for, indemnify, or "hold it harmless" from losses for which it would otherwise have to pay. An example would be in the area of wire transfers done through banks. Banks are generally indemnified from any consequential damages to the company originating the wire from a wire which is either misdirected or not sent.

4. Combination of Exposures: Bringing together many isolated loss exposures and placing them under common control makes the aggregate losses more predictable and application of uniform safety measures more effective. An example would be the grouping of several diverse production facilities under a single joint risk management program, or risk pools formed by airlines to deal with suits from air crashes.

5. Separation of Exposures: Any single asset or activity concentrated at one location is subject to being destroyed in one accident. Physically spreading an asset or activity over two or more locations, or having an available backup, reduces the firm's vulnerability. The procedure of maintaining parallel facilities or assets to reduce exposure is usually known as "duplication."

D. Risk Financing Techniques

These techniques involve resources upon which a firm may draw to finance recovery from losses and liabilities for which it is held responsible. This is only one of the many competing uses to which a firm devotes its financial resources. Sound financial management requires integrating the firm's risk financing needs with all its other, more traditionally "productive" needs. This is necessary because, without proper risk financing, profit-generating activities and assets are almost certain to be impaired (or perhaps ruined) by accidents.

1. Risk Retention: Retention involves use of a firm's internal financial resources (including credit if appropriate) to provide funds to finance recovery from accidental losses. In other words, the firm retains the loss rather than paying someone else (an insurance company) to take it.

a. Non-Insurance: This technique involves relying on normal revenues to pay for small, "normal" losses as current expenses. Non-insurance is appropriate for losses a firm can readily absorb as "costs of doing business," but not for highly disruptive, potentially ruinous accidents. The proper cost of these funds is the rate of return the firm could have earned on them in their optimal alternative use.

b. Borrowing: A firm may draw upon short-term credit sources to pay for uninsured losses or funding delays in reimbursement. The cost of these funds is the effective interest rate charged for them. Relying on credit for risk financing may introduce new uncertainties, however, because some accidental losses may exceed the firm's available credit and because a serious loss may so weaken the firm's ability to repay debt that its credit risk may rise. This practice is not generally considered good risk management for large, high-dollar risks.

c. Self-Insurance: The term "self-insurance" is actually a misnomer. It generally denotes a retention program that is more formalized than non-insurance.

- Unlike non-insurance, self-insurance requires real efforts to forecast losses to be retained. In addition, the firm must systematically maintain resources from which to pay losses.

- Self-insurance is not really a form of insurance because it involves no transfer of risk to an insurer or other separate entity. Also, the term "self-insurance" is often used to describe any risk retention program, even highly informal, unfunded arrangements.

- Many firms that practice self-insurance set "cap limits" on their self-insurance exposure by purchasing excess coverage (i.e., "real insurance") for claims above some pre-determined limit. Any claims below this limit will be "self-insured," while amounts above the limit (i.e., excess losses) will by covered by the cap limit policy. For example, a firm may purchase an excess insurance policy for product liability that will only be available in the event of a settlement over $100,000. For any claims under this amount, the firm will pay the full amount of the claim. For any claims over this amount the firm will pay the first $100,000 and the insurance policy will pay the amount of the claim over $100,000. The insurance company may administer all of the claims for a fee or percentage, even though it only provides excess coverage.

d. Captives: A captive is a subsidiary through which a parent firm finances specified types and amounts of the parent's losses in a highly structured form of retention that often resembles insurance, but in reality is not. These are covered in detail later in this section.

2. Risk Transfer: As noted earlier, the essence of any risk transfer is a contract between a transfering firm (transferor) and another entity (the transferee), under which the transferee agrees to pay (within contractual limits) designated types of the transferor's losses. The transferor may have to pay the transferee a fee (such as an insurance premium) for this promise of indemnity, or the transferor may have the bargaining power to secure this promise as a condition for agreeing to do business with the transferee. Such risk transfer arrangements are often made for tax or regulatory reasons, and may be accomplished through the purchase of reinsurance either from a broker or directly from the market. It is important to note that the transfer of risk is only as good as the transferee's, or its insurance company's, ability to pay claims.

a. Contractual Transfer: Under these contracts, typified by "hold harmless" agreements, the transferee is not an insurer, and the transfer contract may take any form permitted by applicable law. Because most "hold harmless" transferees are not primarily in business to bear others' risk of loss, and because their contracts and business activities are not as strictly regulated as insurers', such contractual transfers may not provide transferors the degree of financial security they could obtain from a true insurer.

b. Additional Insured: In this case, one firm is listed as an additional insured on another firm's policy. In essence, the second party (the named insured) is covering the first party (the additional insured) through its own insurance policy, and will provide a certificate of insurance as proof of coverage. This is usually done to cover small distributors or franchisees under the policy of the larger manufacturer or parent company. Also, in many cases, this is less expensive than purchasing individual policies for the same amount of coverage.

c. Guaranteed Cost Insurance Program: For this type of insurance the insured pays a fixed premium at the beginning of the policy period. The insurer then takes the risk of paying all losses occurring during the policy period that fall within the scope and amount of the policy. The premium the insured pays cannot be changed until the next policy period, although either the insurer or the insured may be allowed to cancel the coverage in the middle of the policy period under certain conditions. If the insured cancels this type of policy mid-period, it may not be entitled to a refund of premiums paid.

d. Retrospectively (Retro) Rated Insurance Program: In these programs, the insured's cost of coverage for a policy period varies with the insured's losses during that period. Such programs are often used for workers' compensation plans and for product liability insurance.

- The insured pays a "standard," or "deposit" premium at the beginning of the coverage period. At the end of the period, the insurer computes a final premium based upon an agreed formula that varies with the insured's actual losses (subject to limits) for the policy period.

- If the covered losses are very large, the insured must pay some extra premium, up to a predetermined maximum for the period. For losses above this maximum, the risk rests with the insurer. Within the retro minimum-maximum range, there is no transfer of risk. For example, if the maximum premium is set at $10,000, but experience rating over the period indicates a premium of $12,000, the firm will only owe the predetermined maximum premium of $10,000.

- If the insured has experienced few or no losses, some of the standard premium is returned but the insurer keeps a minimum premium that it has earned for its services and for bearing the risk that the insured's losses might have been severe.

- The rating period may be defined as any period of time, and in some cases is actually a rolling, multi-year rating period.

e. Cash Flow Casualty Retro Programs: These are similar to the retrospective plans above but, in addition, provide a variety of ways for the insured to have limited access to (or credit for investment earnings from) funds the insured has paid the insurer.

f. Group Captive: A group captive, also known as an association captive, resembles a single-parent captive except that it provides risk financing for multiple owners instead of just one. The captive may be jointly owned by each of the individual parents or by an association that these parents have formed. This shared ownership makes the group captive arrangement a form of insurance by virtue of the transfer of risk. For example, the American Newspaper Publishers Association has established an association captive to provide libel insurance for member newspapers, and the American Bankers Association sponsors a captive that provides directors' and officers' liability insurance for member banks.

g. Risk Retention Group: A risk retention group is a special type of group captive formed under the terms of a federal law designed to more fully enable business firms to work together in jointly financing their product liability claims. To the extent that risks are shared, this is considered insurance.

- The Risk Retention Act of 1986 is composed of amendments to the Product Liability Risk Retention Act of 1981 and was enacted to make the procedures more efficient for creating risk retention groups (capitalized, member-owned insurance companies) and purchasing groups (insurance buyers' group formed to obtain coverage for homogenous liability risks for hard-to-insure companies or industries).

- These plans are often used in industries with high risk or with potential for catastrophic losses, such as the airline industry and certain professional occupations (doctors in high-risk practices, accountants, lawyers, etc.).

h. Alternative Risk Financing Facilities: In response to an absence of coverage for some types of risk, combinations of private insurers, agents and brokers typically offer excess property or liability coverage. Also, many firms may utilize letters of credit as a backup for self-insurance plans, for worker's compensation programs, or for paying large deductibles on other types of insurance policies.

E. Negotiating Insurance Programs

In dealing with insurers, many firms enter the marketplace not so much to buy coverage but, instead, to "sell" their overall risk management programs to insurance underwriters. To "sell" their programs in this way, treasurers need to be familiar with the structure of insurance markets and be equipped to make the rational decisions that transactions in these markets require.

1. Insurance Providers: Legally, most property and liability insurers do not offer insurance; rather, they accept offers to purchase insurance from applicants who make these offers to insurers' marketing representatives.

- These representatives may be the insurers' own salaried employees (if the insurer is a direct writer) or, as is more likely, they may be independent agents or brokers.

- Although agents and brokers both receive commissions rather than salaries from insurers, an independent agent is legally an agent of the insurer, while a broker is the legal agent of the applicant.

- Both agents and brokers, as well as employees of direct writers, compete for high quality accounts by offering many services to applicants and insureds without direct charge.

2. Dealing with Insurance Brokers: Insurance brokers present options to a company and then place that company's insurance business through an insurer. Brokers often do not have the authority to bind an insurer because they are only acting as agents for the insurer. In deciding whether to use a broker and choosing a particular broker, a firm should consider the broker's experience with the types of coverage needed by the firm, as well as access to special markets or insurers. A listing of the areas of service provided by brokers, and evaluation criteria, are provided at the end of this chapter.

3. Selecting Insurance Coverage (Insurers): When selecting among competing insurers, the crucial factors to consider are financial strength, business integrity, the extent of coverage offered, services available to insureds, claims facilities and cost. There are several points to consider in the selection of an insurer:

- **Long-Term Solvency of the Insurer:** The treasurer should investigate the financial solvency of all insurers for the firm. Generally, state guarantee funds provide only limited protection when an insurer fails, and the delay involved in settling claims may be significant. Insurance coverage is only as good as the ability of the insurance company to pay claims, especially for large losses. Finally, a firm's credit agreements or loan covenants may stipulate minimum ratings for insurance carriers.

- **Coverage:** In many cases, liability insurance is provided on a claims-occurrences basis, meaning that coverage is triggered by occurrences during the policy period, regardless of when they are reported.

Claims-occurrence is generally considered to be the preferred basis of claims. Policies could be written on a claims-made basis, which applies only to claims reported during the policy period, regardless of when the event causing the claim occurred. Uninsured gaps in coverage may occur if a firm switches from a claims-made policy to a claims-occurrences policy. For example, a firm was using a claims-made policy in 1993, but switched to a claims-occurrences policy in 1994. If a claim is made in 1994 for an event that occurred in 1993, the firm will not be covered under either policy. Also, it is very difficult to compare pricing for these two types of policies because of their differing time periods over which claims may be reported.

- **Service:** The ability of an insurer to provide good loss control and/or claims service may help to reduce the overall cost of an insurance program. Service considerations, and specialization or expertise in a particular area of insurance, should always be taken into account in selecting insurers.

- **Cost:** Cost should always be measured in relation to the financial stability, overall coverage and quality of services offered by the prospective insurers.

4. Selecting a Deductible: By selecting insurance (particularly property insurance) that has a deductible, an insured can save many premium dollars in comparison to the cost of "first-dollar" coverage. In essence, the deductible forces the insured to share some of the front-end risk from potential losses; the higher the deductible, the lower the cost of the premium for the insurance. However, it is important to weigh against these potential savings the costs of absorbing the many losses that could fall within the deductible and the managerial uncertainty that these deductible payments impose. Deductibles may also be on a per-occurrence basis (the deductible applies for each occurrence during the policy period) or on an aggregate basis (deductible is set on a per-period basis, regardless of the number of occurrences).

5. Selecting a Liability Limit: This challenging problem may be made more complex by the unavailability of the large amounts of excess liability insurance that some firms may wish to purchase. The firm's management must consider the following in determining overall limits for liability:

- **Catastrophic Event Exposure:** A company's total assets are only one measure of potential liability. A better measure may actually be the projected cash flow stream which these assets can produce over a reasonable horizon.

- **Other Catastrophic Exposure:** This type of risk may arise from product or service liability claims, suits by competitors, etc.

- **Cost versus Limits:** Purchasing standard policies with high liability limits may become very expensive. Therefore, firms may need to examine the use of excess coverage and self-insurance. Excess coverage can often be purchased in "layers" to provide better overall insurance coverage at a lower cost. For example, a firm's basic policy (Policy A) has a liability limit of $100,000. The firm then purchases an excess policy (Policy B) which adds $200,000 in coverage, but only pays in the event the coverage on Policy A is exhausted. Finally, the firm purchases another excess policy (Policy C), which adds $300,000 in coverage, paying only if limits on both Policies A and B have been exhausted. The firm has a total liability limit of $600,000 by combining the three policies. In some instances, a business firm cannot obtain the total coverage it requires from a single insurance company, or a single high-limit policy may be prohibitively expensive. Thus, the firm may buy several policies from different companies in order to acquire the total liability limit needed at an affordable price. Self-insurance can also be used to cover "pockets" or gaps between regular policy limits and excess coverage, or between layers of excess coverage if there is a gap.

- **Cost versus Exposure:** Regardless of the insurance cost, the exposure is present and must be managed. It may be more important for a firm to have catastrophic protection than primary insurance.

6. Negotiating Techniques: While effective techniques for negotiating with underwriters, agents and brokers are largely matters of individual style, in insurance dealings it is crucial to:

1. Disclose all information pertinent to the risk the insurer is being asked to undertake (full disclosure in the insurance application). A listing of the data required for disclosure is provided at the end of this chapter.

2. Refrain from changing insurers frequently for small potential gains.

3. Obtain coverage during off-periods if possible (i.e., directors' and officers' insurance is usually purchased at the end of the year, but purchasing off-cycle may yield a better rate).

4. Work with the insurers and their representatives in building a total risk management program, consisting of risk control and risk financing, in which insurance is a major, but probably not the most important, part.

5. Take advantage of a "good" loss history during a period of low claims and try to lock in a commitment for a low premium for future periods.

F. Captives and Other Alternative Financing Techniques

Using either single-parent or group captives, as well as other sophisticated risk financing techniques, has several potential advantages (usually tax related), as well as possible disadvantages, for most larger firms. Evaluating these factors is a very complicated task and many treasurers may wish to call upon the expertise of specialists.

Reasons for forming a captive insurance company include:

- Instances when insurance for a business risk cannot be purchased from commercial insurance companies. In many cases, companies within an industry form a joint or group captive insurance company for that reason.

- Premiums paid to a captive insurance company are generally deductible as a business expense for tax purposes according to the Internal Revenue Code. However, sums set aside for self-insurance programs are not usually deductible as a business expense.

- Insurance can be obtained through the international reinsurance market (covered below) at a more favorable premium, with higher limits of coverage.
- Investment returns can be obtained directly on the captive's invested capital.

However, competent personnel to manage and staff the company could be excessively expensive, and a catastrophic occurrence or series of occurrences could bankrupt the company.

Captive insurance companies make take several forms:

1. Single-Parent Captive: A captive is a subsidiary through which a parent firm finances specified types and amounts of the parent's losses in a highly structured form of retention that often resembles insurance, but in reality is not.

- The captive "insurer" may compute and collect from its single parent, payments that resemble insurance premiums. It may issue documents that look much like insurance policies and make payments to its parent when the parent suffers a "covered" loss.

- The real benefit to a parent firm from this type of arrangement is usually the development of a formalized and objective retention program. There are, however, two important exceptions to the standard single-parent captive.

  1. The first is in the case of "offshore" insurance captives, which may be determined to be truly separate entities. In this case, there may be risk transfer and the premiums are generally tax deductible.

  2. The other case is when the single-parent captive "lays off" (transfers) some of the risk through the reinsurance market. Reinsurance is a form of insurance that insurance companies buy for their own protection. Essentially, reinsurance enables an insurance company (captive or independent) to share its risks over a larger pool of insurers. By diversifying the risk over different industries, geographical areas, and time periods, all of the parties in the reinsurance market can benefit.

2. Rent-a-Captive: Many insurers and large insurance brokers operate captive-like risk financing arrangements whose administrative structure and personnel a client firm may contract to use (rent) for a specified period. This arrangement allows the client to test the feasibility of establishing its own captive and to obtain at least some benefits of a captive while experimenting. The tax treatment of these arrangements depends on the extent to which they involve risk transfer.

G. Risk Management Services

Most firms maintain an in-house risk-management information system and a complete set of internal records on insurance and losses. Additional expertise needed to make and carry out risk financing, management, and control decisions is available on a fee basis from a wide range of risk management consultants. Also, as discussed earlier, many insurers and brokers offer these services.[4] Some considerations regarding risk management services are as follows:

- Independent audits of the firm's risk-management program should be performed on a regular basis (every one to three years).

- Major program reviews of a firm's risk-management procedures should be performed at least every five years, and more often if the firm (or its risk structure) is changing rapidly.

- Claims administration (the investigation of losses when a claim is made) may either be done internally or outsourced as part of purchased risk-management services.

- Many firms utilize claims auditors, who are independent consultants retained to audit the work of claims administrators (internal or external).

- Loss-control and safety engineering consultants can help identify risks and ways to prevent or reduce losses, especially in areas such as fire protection, industrial safety, environmental risks, computer security, and general security concerns.

- Firms may utilize the services of actuaries who analyze aggregate loss experience (rather than individual claims) and project the ultimate cost of claims over a given period.

- Information systems consultants can help establish or upgrade loss-control and claims-handling reporting and record keeping systems.

IV. Chapter Checklists

A. Source Documents for Risk Identification

Some of the sources that can be used to help identify risks are the following:

1. Financial statements
2. 10K reports or stock registration statement
3. Property schedules and valuations
   - Real property: location, type, original cost, current replacement cost
   - Personal property: location, type, costs
   - Computers and media
   - Inventories
   - Vehicles
   - Equipment
4. Schedules of employees, by location and job classification
5. Organization charts
6. Operations flow charts
7. Current and expired insurance policies (minimum five years) and final premium adjustments
8. Insurance proposals
9. Loss runs and retrospective rating adjustments for all insurance policies (minimum five years)
10. Records of uninsured losses (or losses under insurance deductibles)
11. Procedure manuals for safety, claims or hazard control
12. Survey or inspection reports of buildings, processes, etc.

13. Budgets, financial or operational plans and projections

14. Product brochures or descriptions (current or discontinued products)

15. Schedules of all work or projects in progress

B. Types of Liability Losses

1. **Automotive Liability:** This involves the harming of people or property with a vehicle.

2. **General Liability:** This involves employees, premises, or practices that harm people or property.

3. **Product Liability:** This is a type of general liability and involves injuries or damages caused by any products manufactured or work performed by or on behalf of the firm.

4. **Directors' and Officers' Liability:** This is related to actions taken by directors and officers on behalf of the firm.

5. **Professional Liabilities:** These are related to actions of doctors, lawyers, accountants and other professionals and may include negligence, errors and omissions.

6. **Fidelity Liability:** This is related to loss of money or other property as a result of dishonest acts by employees, such as larceny, theft, embezzlement, forgery, misappropriation, wrongful abstraction or willful misapplication.

7. **Fiduciary Liability:** This is related to holding of property, or otherwise acting on behalf of another party, in trust. The fiduciary must exercise due care in safeguarding property left under corporate care, custody and control.

8. **Contingent Liability:** Although a business may not have any direct liability, it may incur a secondary or contingent liability, for example through the employment of an independent contractor.

9. **Workers' Compensation Liability:** This is related to potential claims by employees for work-related injuries or damages.

10. **Special Types of Liability:** These may include pollution, aircraft, watercraft and nuclear hazards.

C. Listing of Disclosure Information for Insurance Negotiation[5]

1. **Summary of Past Losses:** Updated summaries of losses by type of coverage, including all reserves for reported but unpaid claims. Loss data for three to five years is usually required.

2. **Financial Reports:** Annual financial report, Form 10-K, and other financial and operating statements.

3. **Business Affiliations and Subsidiaries:** List of names and descriptions of all subsidiaries or affiliates, including inactive entities.

4. **Employee Information:** Listing of payrolls and past workers' compensation claims by employee classification and by location.

5. **General Liability Data:** Information to provide a rating on general liability, such as sales, payrolls, types and location of facilities, types of products, hazardous materials handled, etc.

6. **Fidelity Bond Information:** Employee fidelity bond classifications, types and amounts of cash, securities or other items handled, locations and security procedures, etc.

7. **Schedules of Property:** Schedules and statements broken out by location and type of insurance (cost, replacement value, etc.) of property values for buildings and improvements, furniture, equipment, boilers and machinery, autos and trucks, business interruption values, etc.

8. **Other Information:** Any other information requested by the insurance company, broker or agent must be provided.

D. Areas of Broker Services and Evaluation Criteria[6]

Area/Criteria	Explanation
1. Marketing	
– Insurers Selected	Evaluate financial stability, claims-handling capabilities, and reputation.
– Coverage	Broad scope of coverage for all insurable risks should be provided, but with appropriate retentions or deductibles for eliminating small claims.
– Price	Competitive premiums reflecting scope of coverage should be offered.
2. Policy Review	
– Wording	Broker should obtain well-worded and easy-to-understand forms and endorsements.
– Organization	The number of endorsements and exclusions should not be excessive and the basic policy forms should be notated or cross-referenced to the endorsements and exclusions.
3. Loss Control Assistance	Either the broker or insurer should be capable of providing appropriate support on loss control, fire protection, employee safety, and OSHA.
4. Property Valuations	Where the insured does not have an established valuation method, the broker should help in providing property valuations (updated annually) and frequent reviews of business interruptions exposures.
5. Auditing Claims	The broker should audit the insurer's claim-handling and also assist in obtaining timely payment by the insurer on valid claims.
6. Verifying Rates and Premiums	The broker should verify the accuracy of the insurer's rates and experience-rating modifiers.
7. Risk Identification and Evaluation	Brokers should be thoroughly familiar with the client's exposures to loss for all major risks. Insurance (or non-insurance) recommendations should be offered, as appropriate, for all major risks.
8. Service	
– Communications	Transmittals, letters, or memos should document all transactions and present options to the insured.
– Timeliness	All responses to inquiries, telephone contacts, change requests, and renewals should be timely. Renewal policies should be in hand prior to expiration.
– Reliability	Performance promises should be realistic and action taken as promised.
– Accessibility	Broker and/or support personnel should be available when needed by phone or to respond to written requests.

Area/Criteria	Explanation
– Cost	Commissions or fees paid for brokerage services should be divulged, explicit, and reasonably related to the level of service required.
9. Reports to Management	
– Insurance Summaries	Insurance summaries should be provided at each renewal or whenever major changes in coverage are made.
– Loss Summaries	Either the broker or the insurer should regularly (at least quarterly) provide a summary of all losses reported under each policy.
– Problems or Action	Any problems encountered in any area should be communicated, together with action taken by the broker to correct them.

V. Endnotes

1. Suggested textbooks on the topics of risk management and insurance include: Neil A. Dougherty, *Risk Management: a Financial Exposition,* McGraw-Hill, New York, 1984; George L. Head and Steven Horn II, *Essentials of the Risk Management Process,* Insurance Institute of America, Malvern, PA, 1985; Robert I. Mehr and Bob A. Hedges, *Risk Management: Concepts and Applications,* Dow Jones, Irwin, Homewood, IL, 1976; and William C. Arthur and Richard M. Heins, *Risk Management and Insurance, 6th Ed.,* McGraw-Hill Book Company, New York, 1989. For current information regarding issues in risk management, the reader is directed to the Risk and Insurance Management Society, Inc. (RIMS), a non-profit association dedicated to advancing the practice of risk management.

2. See: *The Handbook of Cash Flow and Treasury Management,* Chapter 17, James A. Robertson, Probus Publishing, Chicago, IL., 1988

3. An example of such a guide is the *Fact-Finding Questionnaire for Risk Managers,* written by Bernard Daenzer and published by the Risk and Insurance Management Society, New York.

4. A source for information and listings of consultants and firms that provide services in this area is *Business Insurance,* a weekly news publication covering property, casualty and employee benefits insurance. This publication also provides special editions during the year that contain directories of consultants and other service firms.

5. See: James A. Robertson, *The Handbook of Cash Flow and Treasury Management,* Chapter 17, Probus Publishing, Chicago, IL.

6. Ibid.

15 Employee Pension Fund and Benefit Management

I. Outline of the Chapter

A. Employee Retirement Income Security Act (ERISA)
  1. Qualified Pension Plans
     a. Reporting and Disclosure
     b. Fiduciary Requirements
     c. Participation
     d. Vesting
     e. Benefits
     f. Funding
     g. Tax-Qualified Plans
     h. Plan Termination Insurance
  2. Non-Qualified Pension Plans

B. Types of Pension Plans
  1. Defined Contribution Plans
     a. Company Perspective
     b. Employee Perspective
  2. Defined Benefit Plans
     a. Company Perspective
     b. Employee Perspective
  3. Examples of Defined Contribution Pension Plans
     a. Profit-Sharing Plans
     b. 401(k) Plans
     c. Money-Purchase Pension Plans
     d. Stock Bonus Plans

Chapter Checklists

B. Factors to Consider in Selecting Defined Contribution versus Defined Benefit Pension Plans

C. Sample Guidelines for Asset Allocations in Investment Portfolios

D. Comparison of Non-Qualified and Qualified Deferred Compensation Plans

II. Introduction[1]

This chapter describes many of the regulations and necessary details related to the management of employee pension funds and benefit plans. The relevant costs and benefits need to be understood by the firm's decision maker. The pension fund and benefit plans can represent a major portion of employee compensation packages. They also represent a major cash flow for the firm and are an important fiduciary responsibility. There have been many changes in this area in recent years as firms try to hold down costs and as employees change employment more frequently.

This chapter is intended as a stand-alone discussion of the issues surrounding employee pension fund and benefit management. Many of the cost/benefit discussions associated with working capital management and the capital budgeting decision models are also pertinent. Liquidity, security and yield considerations for pension investments are similar to those for short-term investments.

The first part of this chapter describes the regulations and intricacies associated with the management of a firm's pension fund. Since the pension plan typically contains significant funds and involves large cash flows and expenses, it is important that a firm's decision-makers understand the management of the plan's funds and future funding obligations. Later sections of the chapter cover the management of employee benefit plans.

III. Coverage of the Chapter Material

A. Employee Retirement Income Security Act (ERISA)[2]

1. Qualified Pension Plans: The Employee Retirement Income Security Act (ERISA), passed in 1974, set the rules governing management of pension plans. For companies to have ERISA-qualified pension plans, they must, by law, follow these guidelines:

a. Reporting and Disclosure: Companies with ERISA-qualified plans (plan sponsors) are required to provide plan participants with summary plan descriptions, benefit statements and access to plan financial information. Plan sponsors file an annual financial report (Form 5500 series) with the IRS, which is made available to other government agencies.

b. Fiduciary Requirements: Plan sponsors are subject to an ERISA fiduciary standard mandating that the plan be operated solely for the benefit of plan participants. The fiduciary standard, or "prudent person standard," requires the plan fiduciary to perform duties solely in the interest of plan participants with the care a prudent person acting under like circumstances would use. The standard applies to plan sponsors, trustees, and to investment advisors with discretionary authority over the purchase and sale of plan securities. Both the IRS and the Department of Labor are responsible for enforcing the fiduciary standards. The Department of Labor may file charges on behalf of the participants if the fiduciary has breached or violated the standards imposed by ERISA. The IRS may fine the employer and revoke the plan's favorable tax treatment.

c. Participation: Although ERISA does not currently require every employer to set up an employee pension or welfare benefit plan, it does impose requirements on those who do. For employers that sponsor plans, the age of employee eligibility cannot be higher than 21. A maximum of one year of service and 1,000 hours of work may also be required for eligibility.

d. Vesting: Upon satisfying the participant requirements, further conditions must be met for the participant to become entitled to receive a benefit—that is, to have a vested right to the benefits. Vesting is covered in detail later in this chapter.

e. Benefits: Under ERISA, benefits generally must be earned in a uniform manner while the participant is employed. This does not affect the levels of benefits provided by the plan, only the rate at which the benefits are earned.

f. Funding: Minimum funding standards attempt to ensure that plans will have sufficient assets to pay benefits. This is especially an issue with defined benefit plans (covered later in this chapter) which guarantee employees a specified level of benefits at maturity.

g. Tax-Qualified Plans: In addition to meeting ERISA qualifications, plans must meet IRS criteria in order for the employer to deduct contributions from income and make investment earnings on plan assets that are exempt from current taxation.

h. Plan Termination Insurance: Most defined-benefit pension plans (those that provide a fixed monthly benefit at retirement) are required to pay premiums to the Pension Benefit Guaranty Corporation (PBGC). The PBGC is a governmental body that insures payment of plan benefits under certain circumstances.

The primary goals of ERISA are to protect employees, to govern every aspect of private pension and welfare plans, and to require the employers who sponsor plans to operate them in compliance with ERISA standards. Specific details of ERISA standards and other legislation are provided at the end of this chapter.

2. Non-Qualified Pension Plans: Employee pension plans that follow ERISA guidelines are considered to be tax-qualified plans by the Internal Revenue Code (IRC). Employee pension plans that do not satisfy the IRC requirements may be set up as either funded (employer contribution) or non-funded (no employer contribution). Most funded plans must satisfy ERISA, but unfunded plans must only meet ERISA's reporting and disclosure provisions. The primary disadvantages of utilizing non-qualified benefit plans are that current contributions may not be considered a tax-deductible expense of the employer, and the contributions to the plan made by the employer may be considered taxable income to the employee, even before the employees receive them.

The other types of non-ERISA pension plans are related to deferred compensation which allows employees to defer some salary to a later date when it may be (hopefully) taxed at a lower rate. These plans do carry significant tax benefits, but they must meet strict requirements as outlined in Section 401(a) of the IRC. A non-qualified deferred compensation plan does not have to meet these requirements and may include only selected employees, usually top-level management. The tradeoff is that these types of plans do not receive any immediate tax benefits and the company is allowed no deduction until the funds are actually received by the employee. These plans are covered in more detail later in this chapter.

B. Types of Pension Plans

There are two choices of pension plans available to a firm: a defined contribution plan or a defined benefit plan. A listing of factors that need to be considered in deciding between the two is provided at the end of this chapter. The firm must consider the three types of contributions that can be made to a pension plan: (1) contributions by the employee, (2) regular or matching contributions by the firm, and (3) contributions by the firm based on profits or earnings (profit sharing). The provisions of the plans are discussed first, followed by specific examples for each category.

1. Defined Contribution Plans: With this type of plan, the firm makes a specified contribution to the plan—for example, a contribution equal to 10% of the employee's salary. The contributions are allocated to individual employee accounts. The employee may be allowed to make contributions to this type of plan, but is not obligated to do so. The company's contributions may be in the form of cash, or non-cash such as company stock. The disbursements are then based on the accumulated account balance when the employee retires. This balance will be based on the contributions and the investment performance of the plan.

Some plans invest in only a single fund and all employees share in the aggregate gains and losses. It is more common, however, for employers to offer two or more investment funds and allow the employees to choose how the balances in their accounts are invested. Available choices typically include a money market fund, a fixed income fund (usually bonds or a guaranteed interest contract from an insurance company) and an equity fund. In the case of a profit-sharing plan, the employee might be given the option of investing in the stock of the employer, or may simply receive company stock as all or part of the company's contribution.

a. Company Perspective: From the company's point of view, these plans are always fully funded, and there are no investment objectives that must be met in order to provide benefits.

- The negative aspect is that the contribution to the plan may represent a relatively fixed cost to the firm, unless it is a profit-sharing plan.
- Another disadvantage is that this cost will increase if salaries increase over time and the plan's contributions are based on a percentage of salaries (a common practice).
- Also, the firm may have significant restrictions on how contributions can be made to the plan. For example, the plan may require that contributions be made in cash rather than stock.

- Many of the defined contribution plans are profit-sharing plans with the contributions based on the profitability of the company. A profit-sharing plan provides a greater degree of flexibility than a fixed contribution plan, because the firm must only make contributions if there are profits equal to or greater than a targeted amount set by the company or in the rules of the plan. Most plans specify contributions from profits or retained earnings that are determined yearly by the board of directors.

- The IRS has defined profit-sharing plans as follows:

  "A profit-sharing plan is a plan established and maintained by an employer to provide for the participation in his profits by his employees or their beneficiaries. The plan must provide a definite predetermined formula for allocating the contributions made to the plan among the participants and for distributing the funds accumulated under the plan after a fixed number of years, the attainment of a stated age, or upon the prior occurrence of some event such as layoff, illness, disability, retirement, death, or severance of employment."

- The plan can be used as an employee incentive program since the company can contribute from 0% to 15% of compensation each year, depending on its profitability.

- Regulations and restrictions on profit-sharing plan contributions are set forth in IRC Section 404(a)(3). For deferred profit-sharing plans, the employer's annual deductible contributions may not exceed "15% of compensation otherwise paid or accrued during the taxable year to all employees under the plan."

- The IRS requires "substantial and recurring contributions" in order for the plan to maintain qualified tax status. Qualified tax status means the firm may deduct the contributions as a business expense in the year they are made, while the employees are allowed to defer taxation until they receive disbursements from the plan. If the firm does not make contributions, it must show the IRS that they ceased due to "business necessity," usually lack of profitability.

- The company faces some disadvantages with a profit-sharing plan. A major drawback is that the plan cannot recognize past service by the employee.

- Additionally, tax deductions are usually limited to 15% of compensation, but under some circumstances they may exceed that figure. This can occur if an employer is providing both cash and deferred profit-sharing compensation plans. The IRS restriction of 15% applies only to the deferred compensation portion, not to the cash portion.

- This type of plan requires significant interaction between management and employees to be successful, since the employees now have a direct stake in the annual profitability of the firm.

- The major advantage for the firm is that profit-sharing plans are always considered fully funded because of the nature of the contributions and the fact that they are funded on a current basis.

b. Employee Perspective: For the employee, a defined contribution plan does not guarantee a fixed monthly benefit upon retirement. On the other hand, the employee can determine the balance in the plan at any time and does not have to worry about the plan being underfunded.

- The plan can be a financial asset to the employee before retirement through loan or withdrawal provisions. Under certain specified conditions (usually serious illness, hardship, emergencies, or education) employees may be allowed either to borrow against their pension fund balance or to withdraw it completely. The tax treatment for these loans and withdrawals varies depending on the reason for withdrawal.

- For the employee, the major disadvantage of this type of plan is that the retirement benefit is not fixed or guaranteed. The company's contributions are made from cash flows or profits, over which the employees do not have ultimate control. Further, there is usually no guarantee of the return on investment on the funds in the plan. Therefore, this type of plan may not provide enough funds for retirement.

- With respect to profit-sharing plans, the major benefit is that the employee is allowed to share in the profitability of the firm. Also, the employee may share in forfeited accounts, which, for long-service employees, can account for a substantial portion of their balances in the plan. Forfeitures arise when employees terminate employment without being fully vested (see later section on vesting) in their account balances. These non-vested amounts can be used to reduce employer contributions or they can be reallocated to employees in the same manner that the employer contributions were originally allocated.

- Another advantage for the employee is the portability of the accumulated value of the plan in the event that the employee leaves the company. Any contributions made by the employee (and resulting earnings) belong to the employee and are fully portable. Contributions made by the firm (and resulting earnings) may be portable if the employee has become vested through length of service or other criteria.

2. Defined Benefit Plans: These types of plans are set up so that the employees know what their retirement income will be.

- The benefits are typically defined by some formula utilizing average compensation and years of service for each particular employee. For example, in the U.S., the pension liabilities determined by this formula are usually funded by depositing funds in a trust.

- The funds are then invested, and the combination of contributions by the company and investment return provides the assets to cover the liabilities. Annuities may be purchased to fund the future liabilities, which shifts the investment management responsibility to cover the future obligation to the annuity seller.

- These plans have several advantages and disadvantages for both the employer and employee.

a. Company Perspective: A defined benefit plan can be useful in attracting and retaining employees and provides a consistent method for funding the desired retirement benefits. Also, it allows the firm to take into account prior service of the employee. Therefore, the plan can maximize tax benefits for contributions on the behalf of older, higher-paid key employees.

- There are some disadvantages in this type of plan.
  - The company must fund the plan regardless of profitability. Failure to make the required contribution, known as minimum funding standards, can cost the company a non-deductible tax penalty.
  - The company bears the investment risk associated with the investments made by the plan. If the fund fails to earn the rate in the actuarial evaluation, this will result in additional cost to the firm as it must make up the return shortfall.
  - The employer must pay termination insurance premiums to the Pension Benefit Guaranty Corporation (PBGC). If an underfunded plan is terminated, the firm is liable for up to 30% of its net worth for payment of benefits.
  - If investment results are substantially better than expected, the plan could become overfunded. These funds may not be immediately recoverable by the company, but the company does have the option of lowering future contributions to the plan to adjust for the overfunding.
  - As workers live longer, retire later, and earn higher salaries, companies using defined benefit plans run the risk of having to put additional funds into their plans to meet the higher benefit needs.

b. Employee Perspective: The plan provides a guaranteed retirement benefit for the employee.

- The defined benefit plan insulates employees from investment risk since the company guarantees payment of the defined benefits at retirement. Also, the longer an employee stays with a company, the more valuable the pension plan.
- Certain benefits levels may be guaranteed through the PBGC, a quasi-governmental agency that insures most plan benefits up to a certain limit if a company terminates an underfunded pension plan due to inability to make further contributions.
- This type of plan has some disadvantages for the employee.
  - The employee only receives benefits from the plan upon retirement.
  - If an employee retires early (at age 50 for example), the benefit (usually set at some percentage of the most recent salary history) may not be sufficient by the time the employee reaches age 65.
  - Unless the benefit payments are indexed to inflation, their real value may be inadequate to support the employee in the later years of retirement.
  - These types of plans are generally not portable, although employees can become vested. If non-vested employees leave, they forfeit all rights to the pension plan. If vested employees leave the company, they will be entitled to retirement

benefits, but the benefits will not start until normal retirement age and will be based on salary history prior to leaving. If a young employee leaves the firm and is vested, usually the benefit is fixed at the time of leaving. Due to inflation and lower wages and service levels early in a career, this retirement benefit may be minimal.

- There are several limitations imposed by the Internal Revenue Code (IRC) on defined benefit plans for highly paid employees. Under the Tax Reform Act of 1986 (effective in 1989), the maximum amount of pay that can be taken into account for most qualified plan purposes is $200,000. Also, under Section 415 of the IRC, a defined benefit plan cannot provide a benefit that exceeds $90,000 (or 100% of pay, if less) per year. This amount is indexed to increase with the Consumer Price Index (CPI).

3. Examples of Defined Contribution Pension Plans:

a. Profit-Sharing Plans: In these plans, the contributions are based on the profits of the firm. This type of plan was discussed in detail above as the primary example of a defined contribution plan.

b. 401(k) Plans: These are profit-sharing plans that allow employees to defer a percentage of their salary each year, up to a specified maximum, by making pre-tax contributions through payroll deduction.[3] In many instances, the employer will make a cash or stock contribution to the plan matching some or all of the participant's contribution. The employee's contribution and the employer's matching contribution may be invested in the stock of the employer's company or in a variety of other assets or mutual funds. In all cases, employees may direct their own contributions, but some plans may require that the employer be allowed to direct the employer's contribution to the plan. New regulations (404(c)) require firms to offer at least three basic options for investment of employee-directed funds. At a minimum, these options must include: (1) a money-market type fund, (2) an income (bond) fund, and (3) an equity (stock) fund.

c. Money-Purchase Pension Plans: This type of pension plan contains a formula that determines the amount of employer contributions to the plan. These contributions are not subject to the employer's discretion and may not be made a function of profits. Amounts contributed to the plan are allocated to participant accounts and no guaranteed benefits exist. Consequently, on retirement, participants will be entitled only to the benefit that can be purchased with the "money" in their accounts; hence, the term "money purchase." As a result of the Tax Reform Act of 1986, these types of plans are essentially treated the same as profit-sharing plans. Prior to this act, any forfeitures (funds forfeited due to employees leaving prior to vesting) in money-purchase plans were required to be used to reduce employer contributions, rather than being reallocated to the remaining participants. The major difference between these plans and profit-sharing plans is that employers utilizing money-purchase plans must make the contribution specified in the plan or face minimum funding penalties. This is not required of profit-sharing plans.

d. Stock Bonus Plans: Under these plans, which are similar to profit-sharing and money-purchase plans, the firm contributes stock in addition to or instead of cash. Up to 100% of the contribution can be made in stock. These types of plans increase employee stock ownership in the company, which could be an advantage or disadvantage depending on the fortunes of the company. Generally, the plans are for senior management and are tied to some performance measure, such as profits or earnings.

e. Employee Stock Ownership Plans (ESOPs): In this option, the plan invests primarily in the stock of the sponsoring employer. It is essentially a special kind of defined-contribution plan.

- The plan may be either leveraged or unleveraged. An unleveraged ESOP is essentially a stock bonus plan (or a combination of a stock bonus and money-purchase plan) that buys employer stock using money that was contributed by the employer. As outlined below, a leveraged ESOP is the only employee benefit plan that can use corporate credit to finance the purchase of company stock.

- Many tax incentives have been granted to ESOPs to promote their use as a means to allow employees to "buy out" their company. Tax laws allow the firm to deduct both principal and interest payments on the loans of a leveraged ESOP plan, therefore making it a very attractive vehicle for structuring an employee buy-out.

- In most cases, an ESOP is a financing device assisting the transfer of all or part of the ownership of a firm to the employees. Additional information on ESOPs (mainly as a source of long-term funds for a firm) can be found in Chapter 3.

f. Floor-Offset Arrangements: This is a hybrid plan, incorporating both defined benefit and defined contribution features.

- The defined benefit portion of the plan sets a floor level of pension benefit for the employee.

- The defined contribution portion of the plan (usually a profit-sharing arrangement) initially offsets the defined benefit portion of the plan, but may provide a significantly higher benefit overall.

- Therefore, the employee knows that there will be a minimum level of benefit available upon retirement, while the profit-sharing portion can raise the ultimate benefit level.

- There are, however, two major caveats in floor-offset arrangements:

  1. Accrued benefits under the floor-offset plan must be preserved under the "anti-cutback" rules of ERISA. In essence, this requires the employer to maintain the minimum "floor" level of accrued benefits regardless of the profit performance of the company.

  2. If the defined benefit plan terminates after a few years, it could be underfunded. If the plan is considered to be underfunded at termination, the firm could still have contingent liabilities under ERISA. A firm that terminates an underfunded plan must show long-term financial or cash flow problems which preclude further funding of the plan.

4. Vesting of Pension Plans: Vesting simply means that an employee is entitled to receive any accrued benefits from a pension or profit-sharing plan in the event of early retirement or leaving the company.

- Any tax-qualified pension or profit-sharing plan must provide full vesting of any employee contributions. The accrued benefits related to employer contributions must be vested either at normal retirement or after a reasonable length of service.

- Beginning in 1989, an employer could satisfy this requirement either by using a five-year "cliff" vesting (all accrued benefits fully vest after five years of service) or a graduated vesting schedule. The graduated schedule requires 20% vesting of accrued benefits after three years, increasing by 20% each year until full vesting after seven years or at retirement age, whichever comes first.

- The two exceptions to these rules are: (1) certain multi-employer plans (often used in mergers) may still use a 10-year "cliff" vesting, and (2) top-heavy plans for senior management must provide 100% cliff vesting after three years or provide for a graduated vesting with 100% achieved after six years.

C. Determining Funding of the Pension Plan

There are three concepts related to pension funds that affect the company's costs in providing defined benefit plans. These are:

1. Annuity Purchase Rates: The annuity purchase rate is the amount needed to purchase an annuity providing a payment of $1 per month for the actuarially determined lifespan of the employee after retirement.

- For example, assuming a 5% interest rate, for an employee retiring at age 65 the cost of the $1 per month annuity is $120.43 (assuming the annuity is purchased at age 65). This calculation uses a unisex post-retirement mortality table called UP-1984, which assumes a 10-year guaranteed annuity for a single individual. There are many different mortality tables which can be used for different populations or under differing assumptions. The common factor in all is that they are using actuarial tables and interest rates to determine the current amount required to fund an annuity stream of retirement payments.

- Converting to a benefit of $1,000 per month, the cost to the plan is $120,430. This represents the amount needed in the plan at age 65 to provide the employee with $1,000 per month after retirement until death, or for a minimum of 10 years, with the remaining benefits payable to the employee's estate if death occurs before the 10-year minimum.

- The amount required to fund the annuity will change if different interest rates or mortality tables are used. Higher interest rates will reduce the cost per benefit dollar, while lower interest rates will increase the cost per benefit dollar. Utilizing a mortality table with longer assumed lifetimes will increase the cost per benefit dollar, while tables with shorter assumed lifetimes will decrease the cost per benefit dollar.

- Mortality tables and annuity calculations generally assume retirement at a specific age (usually 65). If employees retire at an earlier age, the amount of funding needed will increase to reflect the longer expected lifetime and to cover payments made over a longer period of time.

2. Plan Funding: Once the actuarial analysis has established the amount needed in the fund for the employee at retirement, it is necessary to determine the amount to be contributed in the current period to provide funding.

- In large companies, a discount rate is developed based on various probabilities associated with the plan. These probabilities include:

  1. Probability of employees quitting or being fired prior to retirement

  2. Probability of employees dying or becoming disabled prior to retirement

  3. Amount employee salaries will increase prior to retirement

  4. Age at which employees will retire

  5. The income and appreciation experience of the fund

- Small plans usually use a conservative discount rate to adjust for fluctuations in the above factors. Laws of probability do not work well for small numbers, so the plan may not adjust for certain probabilities.

3. Accrued Benefits: The accrued benefit is the amount of benefits the employee has earned to date, determined by the employee's years of service with the company or years of plan participation.

- There are several methods for determining the accrued benefit.

  - One of the most important factors is whether the accrual is determined based on years of service or years of plan participation.

  - For some employees, the difference in these periods can have a significant impact on the amount and rate of the accrual.

D. Setting Investment Objectives and Asset Allocations

The process of setting the investment objectives and determining allocations for the plan's assets is critical and sometimes difficult, as it involves attempting to maximize return while minimizing risk. Generally, the objectives and allocations should be set to meet the plan's needs for future payments to the employees.

1. Investment Objectives: There is an important difference between setting investment objectives and setting portfolio guidelines. Guidelines are adopted to facilitate the attainment of the objectives and, thus, form the building blocks of policy and strategy. Investment objectives should be governed by these considerations:

1. Any objectives adopted should be in conformity with the plan's documents and with the fiduciary standards of ERISA and related regulations.

2. Funds should be available to make benefit payments in a timely manner. This requires developing a financial profile of the fund that projects the immediate, short-term and long-term cash flow requirements for potential benefit payments. These requirements will be affected by the type of plan (defined benefit or defined contribution) employee demographics, economic conditions and early retirements.

3. Given the cash flow requirements and the economic environment in which funds will be invested, the trade-off between risk and return must be considered. The desire for additional returns must be balanced with the increased risk required in order to achieve those returns. This portion of the objective-setting process involves the development of portfolio guidelines, constraints on investment managers, and projected asset allocations.

4. In light of the above, a method for evaluating investment and fund manager performance must be developed. This provides a means for measuring returns and comparing funds managers against a standard or goal. Most important, these performance objectives should be achievable, given the constraints and requirements of the fund. Some sample evaluation criteria are:

   ■ Comparing total return to a cost-of-living index

   ■ Comparing segments of the portfolio to relative benchmarks (i.e., measuring the growth stock component of a portfolio to an index of mutual funds investing in similar instruments)

   ■ Measuring both real and nominal components over different time frames

5. Finally, all of the investment objectives should be set down in writing and agreed to by the principals involved.

2. Asset Allocations: The decision-maker's task is to determine asset allocations, within the firm's tolerance for risk, to meet the investment objectives.

■ Remember that there is a tradeoff between risk and expected return. If the firm determines that a very high rate of return is needed, it must be willing to take on the level of risk necessary to achieve that return.

■ There are four general classes of assets which can be used in a firm's pension fund portfolio: (1) cash and near-cash assets (money market investments), (2) fixed income-securities (usually short- and long-term debt instruments and preferred stock), (3) common stock (for both dividend income and growth), and (4) real estate (for long-term price appreciation and inflation protection). In today's rapidly changing investment environment other securities may be suitable for inclusion in pension funds, such as guaranteed investment contracts, mortgages, venture capital, loan participations, etc.

■ Asset allocations should be set in accordance with the basic guidelines and constraints on the investment portfolio.

■ Some questions that will help guide the decision maker (fiduciary) are:

   1. What average annual rate of return on the plan's investments does the company realistically desire to achieve?

   2. How much portfolio risk is the company willing to take on its pension fund investments, and what devices are available to manage and limit this risk?

   3. What is the worst annual rate of return acceptable to the company?

   4. What probability of a negative rate of return will the company accept?

   5. What are the liquidity needs of the plan?

Answering these questions adequately, and documenting them so that there will be no misunderstandings at a later date, will help the fund manager determine the best investment allocations for plan assets.

E. Managing the Plan's Funds

1. Investment Management:

a. Internal Management: The company may decide that managing the investments of the fund internally is best in because the company will control the day-to-day investment decisions of the plan.

- With this decision, the firm will need to retain the services of a Registered Representative (RR) to make the market transactions for the plan.

- The RR must be licensed by the National Association of Securities Dealers (NASD) to sell individual securities or mutual funds. The RR is usually employed by either a stock brokerage firm or a broker-dealer.

- This relationship allows the RR to provide research and resources to the firm's decision maker, and to execute transactions that the firm wishes to make.

b. External Management: If the firm decides not to make the investment decisions itself, there are two options available for outside management of the funds.

1) Bank Trust Departments: Bank trust departments offer two types of services for qualified plans.

- First, smaller plans can enter into a commingling of funds with other small plans. This allows the bank to spread the overhead of funds management among the participating plans. It allows for greater diversification possibilities than could be achieved by a stand-alone fund. This is essentially a bank-sponsored mutual fund. The primary disadvantage is that the bank usually limits the number and timing of withdrawals from the fund. Also, there is usually little interaction between the investment decision makers of the bank and the firm. The firm has little or no say in the investments made by the bank.

- The second option available at the bank is generally reserved for large plans and is referred to as "stand-alone management of the fund." The plan's funds are not commingled with other plans, and the firm has much more contact with the bank and control over the investments of the funds. The size requirement for individually managed plans will vary among different bank trust departments. Also, the management costs are not shared in this type of plan.

2) Independent Investment Advisors and Managers: A money management firm works with companies to determine investment strategies for the plan.

- These management firms will even work with small plans to set objectives and aid in the determination of transactions for the pension fund.

- These firms often have unique investment strategies that allow a great deal of flexibility in the management of pension plans. The securities purchased by the plan are held in custodial accounts, usually at banks, brokerage firms or trust companies.

- In some firms this function is split, with the advisor helping in the selection of the portfolio managers, who are then responsible for managing the assets (or a portion of the assets) in the portfolio.

2. Measuring Performance: Whether the firm manages the funds internally, or hires outside managers, it must periodically measure the performance of the fund and determine that it is meeting or not meeting its established objectives.

- If the firm has hired an outside manager, the firm must verify that the outside manager is performing as expected.
- The firm should measure the performance over several different time frames: quarterly, annually, three years, five years, ten years, and over complete market cycles.
- The firm should take into account the investment objectives of the plan as well as the management style of the fund manager. Basic management styles include: (1) growth management (focus on price appreciation of stocks and other securities), (2) income management (focus on generation of stable income over time—dividends and bond coupons), and (3) value management (a mix of growth and income that attempts to maximize long-term value).
- Management should set clear portfolio performance objectives against which portfolio managers can be judged. Some examples of these objectives are:
  1. To achieve the rate of return of a published index, possibly with some additional premium of a stated percentage.
  2. To achieve the rate of return of a special benchmark index reflecting a chosen risk-reward preference.
  3. To achieve performance comparable to other accounts having similar objectives.
  4. To achieve total return sufficient to stabilize contributions at some specified percentage of payroll.
  5. To maintain a specified level of plan surplus.
- Performance can be measured against returns on the S&P 500 or other broad-based indexes, or against other pension funds or established mutual funds. There are also several measures used specifically for evaluating pension fund managers, such as the Shearson-Lehman Corporate/Government Index and the SEI Median Index. Fund managers are usually rated against funds or measures with similar strategies over various time periods. This comparison may be done on either a total return basis or on a portion of the fund.
- The fund management business has become very competitive over the last several years, so firms should be willing to change outside managers if performance is consistently below average, if the individual managers change frequently, or if there are large swings in the company's portfolio mix.

3. Types of Investments: There are many types of investments suitable for a pension plan, such as common stocks, bonds, real estate, money market instruments, etc. A portfolio of assets for the fund will need a mix of short-term and long-term investments as well as investments of differing risks and returns. A discussion of risk-return principles and portfolio management is provided in Chapter 4.

F. Insured Pension Plans

The plan can invest in guaranteed investment securities that are usually sold by insurance companies. These investments are usually referred to as guaranteed investment contracts (GIC) which guarantee the rate of interest to be credited to a deposit account for a limited period (generally 5–10 years). Most GICs guarantee that the full principal will be paid out with no surrender charge or adjustment at the end of that period. Two types of insured securities can be purchased: individual policy plans and group pension plans.

1. Individual Policy Plans:

- One type of individual policy plan is the retirement annuity contract, where each year the plan purchases an individual deferred annuity for each participant worth a predetermined amount in annuity benefits payable at retirement.

- The other type of individual policy plan is the retirement income policy, where the plan purchases life insurance with the face amount for each participant determined as a multiplier of the participant's eligible monthly annuity benefits.

- These plans are exempt from ERISA funding requirements for defined benefit plans. However, the advantage that these plans gain by the exemption can be more than offset by a number of disadvantages, including:

  1. High acquisition costs
  2. Low rates of return
  3. No choice of actuarial assumptions
  4. No advance discount for employee turnover (forfeited balances from employees terminating prior to vesting)
  5. No control over the insurance company's dividend formula
  6. Inflexible funding methods for older employees
  7. Inconsistency of policy dates with the employer's fiscal year end and the employees' retirement dates

- The company will have very little control over the plan's costs and design if it uses such fully insured plans. The quality of the underlying insurance company is a factor that must be taken into account when deciding whether to invest in this type of plan.

- There are some hybrid investment strategies whereby part of the plan is invested in insured contracts and part is administered as described in earlier sections.

2. Group Pension Plans: Group pension securities eliminate some of the disadvantages associated with the individual contracts.

- One type of group plan is the Group Deposit Administration Contract. All contributions into the plan accumulate in an unallocated pension fund invested in the insurance company's general account.

- This account is a pooled fund invested in fixed income securities such as bonds, mortgages and direct placement loans.
- Some of the disadvantages of this type of plan are:

   a. Hidden Operating Expenses: Operating expenses are hidden in the earnings credited to the fund. For example, if the fund earns 10%, it may only be credited with 8.5%, with the rest going to cover the administrative costs of the plan.

   b. Annuity Purchases: The plan may be required to purchase an annuity when an employee retires. This requirement could be costly to the plan if contract annuity rates exceed the plan's actuarial assumptions. For example, if the plan assumed a higher future earnings (investment) rate or the particular mortality table assumed a shorter life expectancy than the insurance company providing the actual annuity, the annuity expected, would be more expensive than planned (i.e., the life insurance company would want more money to provide the given benefit).

- Insurance companies offer other types of securities for plan investment. Some of these eliminate the disadvantages above, but their cost will usually be higher.
- It is important to evaluate the credit quality of the insurance company issuing the securities, that is: Will they be around in the future when the benefits are paid?

G. Deferred Compensation and Non-Qualified Plans

1. Tax-Qualified versus Non-Qualified Plans: Employees can obtain significant tax benefits by deferring part of their compensation until a later date when they will be taxed at a lower rate. The firm will recognize significant tax benefits if this is done in conjunction with a pension or profit-sharing plan. However, to qualify for these benefits, the plan must meet the requirements of section 401(a) of the Internal Revenue Code (IRC). This section requires broad-based employee participation, and sets limits on the amount of income that can be deferred. Also the IRC prevents qualified plans from discriminating in favor of officers, shareholders and highly paid employees. If a plan does not meet IRC requirements, the business expense deduction for all contributions to date could be disallowed, and employees could be taxed on the amounts of the contributions in the years in which they were made.

A non-qualified plan can be established to eliminate these requirements, but it loses the tax benefits. Such a plan can include only those employees a company wishes to include. The employee can still defer the taxability of the income until it is received, but the company cannot take the tax deduction associated with the compensation until the employee receives it. A chart comparing the features of qualified and non-qualified plans is included at the end of this chapter.

Other types of plans in this category include the 401(k) plan and the 403(b) or Tax Deferred Annuity (TDA).

2. 401(k) Plans: These plans are generally referred to as cash-deferred/salary reduction plans and are sanctioned by IRC Section 401(k). Essentially, the employee is given the choice of receiving an amount in the form of currently taxable compensation (for federal income tax purposes) or of deferring the amount to be taxed at a future time. More specifically, the employee has the choice of receiving an employer contribution in cash or having it deferred under the plan. Employees may have the choice of making additional contributions of their own into the plan on a before-tax basis, thus avoiding any federal income tax on this amount until it is received at retirement. This type of plan must meet the same strict guidelines concerning non-discrimination as the qualified deferred compensation plans outlined above.

3. 403(b) Plans or Tax-Deferred Annuities: Tax-Deferred Annuities (TDAs) are generally made available to employees of religious, charitable, educational, scientific, and literary organizations, which are chartered on a non-profit basis.

- In these plans, only the employee may make contributions, generally by a payroll deduction. The advantage to the employee is that such contributions may be made on a before-tax basis (thus eliminating current income taxes on the deferred amounts) and the funds in the TDA can accrue interest on a non-taxable basis until they are removed at retirement.

- There are limits to the amount that can be deferred based on the level of annual income and coverage by other types of tax-deferred plans. These limits are essentially the same as those for the 401(k) plans. These plans offer the employee the right to borrow money from the plan under certain conditions, or to withdraw all funds prior to retirement (age $59\frac{1}{2}$) under certain "emergencies" (medical, hardship, education, etc.).

H. Emerging Trends in Pension Plans

Several trends have been observed in the area of pension funds. These include:

1. Defined benefit plans are losing favor with firms, primarily due to their fixed nature, but including the difficulty in making changes over time and the high overall cost of the plans. Due to the threat of inflationary pressures, the potential costs to the firm are much higher under this type of plan. Also, an aging workforce and a more volatile earnings environment make this type of plan more difficult to administer and maintain, especially in a rapidly changing workplace.

2. Many firms are avoiding pension and benefits problems simply by paying employees higher wages and allowing the employees to make their own retirement plans.

3. 401(k) plans and other types of deferred compensation plans are becoming very popular due to the tax benefits to the firm and the employee, and to their portability.

4. Employee Stock Ownership Plans (ESOPs) are increasing in popularity, especially as a corporate financing vehicle due to the tax preferences granted to such plans. ESOPs allow management to get more shares into "friendly hands," causing employees to become more interested in the firm's stock price (ultimately benefiting all shareholders). If a firm's stock price is overvalued, the stock provides an inexpensive form of compensation. This may, however, cause employee dissatisfaction if the value of the stock subsequently falls. ESOPs provide a market for the shares of a closely held company or provide employees an opportunity to take over their corporation.

I. Group Health Plans and Benefits

1. Group Health Plans: Group health and other benefit plans are a growing part of company expense. In addition to the cost of the health care, the cost and problems associated with the management of claims on health plans has increased significantly in recent years. There are numerous options related to plan design and the financing and funding of these plans.

- In the past, companies simply bought insurance from insurance companies, without realizing that they could use the same risk evaluation that they had used with property/casualty insurance.

- Firms now evaluate actual needs and risks that their employees face and purchase the coverage needed. This means that many companies have self-insuring plans and are purchasing stop-loss insurance policies to cap their exposure, or, they are setting up their own private plans or health maintenance organizations (HMOs). In a self-insuring plan, the company becomes its own health insurance provider, paying claims directly. Stop-loss insurance is essentially an insurance policy that only kicks in at higher levels of claims.

- Some firms are allowing employees to choose the coverage that they need, which further reduces the cost of the plan to the company.

- Many large firms now "self-insure" their employee health benefits, contracting directly with hospitals and medical groups to provide health care coverage. These plans are usually combined with some type of umbrella or excess insurance coverage for large or catastrophic losses. Companies that are self-insured may either manage the claims processing themselves or outsource this operation to an insurer or other third-party provider. This topic is covered in more detail in Chapter 14.

2. Emerging Trends in Employee Benefits: Several trends are emerging in the employee benefit arena. Some of these are:

1. "Cafeteria plans," which allow the employee to "pick and choose" the benefits desired, are becoming more common.

    - These include health plans with different limits, deductibles and coverage, such as HMOs or preferred provider plans (lists of approved providers). In addition, the plan options may include dental care, eye care, disability insurance, life insurance, 401(k) plans, flexible spending accounts, or cash to the employee.

    - In addition, differing levels of life and disability insurance may be offered for different contributions by the employee. The versatility and lower costs are advantageous to both the employee and the firm.

    - Employer contributions to the plan may be uniform for all employees or may be based on salary, age, family status and length of service. Care should be taken, however, to provide a minimum level of benefits for even the lowest-level employee.

    - Employees in these plans can often choose to "purchase" additional benefits with their own before-tax dollars. In addition, many plans include flexible spending accounts which allow employees to allocate before-tax dollars to "reimbursement accounts" which can be used for payment of certain non-insured medical and child-care expenses.

- These plans have become more popular in recent years due to changes in the tax laws and the desire on the part of both employees and employers for a wider range of benefits at lower cost.

- Section 125 of the IRC (Revenue Act of 1978) provided favorable tax treatment for qualifying cafeteria plans. Under such plans, all participants are employees and all may choose among two or more benefits consisting of cash and other qualifying benefits. Certain benefits, such as scholarships, transportation benefits, educational assistance and employee discounts, may not be included in a qualifying plan. The plan may include a limited amount of life and disability insurance, but cannot include any retirement benefits except for a 401(k) plan. As long as these constraints are met, employer contributions to the plan are tax-deductible and employees have taxable income only if they elect taxable benefits such as excess life insurance (above IRS maximum) or cash.

- Some disadvantages of these plans are: (1) employees may need to be educated in the various benefits in order to make the best choices (or to not make bad choices); (2) there are non-discrimination tests that must be met in order to ensure that highly compensated employees are not receiving the bulk of benefits; (3) employees, unions and insurers may have objections to the program; and (4) administrative costs of the program may be high, especially if there are numerous options.

2. Benefit costs are becoming very costly to firms and, therefore, firms are allocating more resources to controlling them. Many health care plans now require second or third opinions prior to expensive surgery or treatments, or will pay reduced levels of benefits if such screening is not obtained.

3. Companies are marketing benefits to employees so they gain better understanding of the cost to the company and the value of the benefits. This is often exemplified by an individualized annual benefits statement for each employee. These statements list all contributions and benefits provided for the employee during the preceding benefit year. This statement can then be used by the employee in planning the next year's benefits. Employers may price benefit options in a cafeteria plan so as to "steer" employees to less costly options (from the employer's point of view).

4. More emphasis is being placed on the need for child day-care as an employee benefit. Many firms are either establishing day-care facilities on-site or are contracting with third parties to provide day care on a fully or partially subsidized basis.

5. More companies are providing flexible spending accounts, as provided for in recent legislation, to allow employees to set aside pre-tax contributions for use in paying health and child-care expenses. These plans generally allow the employee to set aside a regular amount from each paycheck in a special account. Upon

presentation of valid receipts, the employee can be reimbursed for non-covered medical expenses and child-care expenses. Any money remaining unclaimed in the account at the end of the benefit year is returned to the employer and is lost to the employee.

IV. Chapter Checklists

A. ERISA Guidelines[4]

ERISA retains the basic provisions for plan qualification established in the Revenue Act of 1942, but ERISA and subsequent legislation (especially the Tax Reform Act of 1986) have developed new standards that must be met by all employee benefit plans to qualify for favorable tax treatment and to avoid tough civil and criminal penalties. Failure to meet these standards can mean disqualification and, in some pension plan cases, an excise tax. Penalties on employees who receive benefits above certain limits range from additional taxes to loss of tax exclusion for the benefits.

ERISA has several major objectives:

- To ensure that workers and beneficiaries receive adequate information about their employee benefit plans.
- To set standards of conduct for those managing employee benefit plans and plan funds.
- To determine that adequate funds are being set aside to pay promised pension benefits.
- To ensure that workers receive pension benefits after they have satisfied certain minimum requirements.
- To safeguard pension benefits for workers whose pension plans are terminated.

A summary of ERISA's major provisions follows. Where these provisions have been amended by recent legislation, the current versions are given.

Title I: Protection of Employee Benefits

This section of ERISA contains labor provisions that provide protections for employee benefit rights. The following provisions are included:

Reporting and Disclosure

- Employees must be furnished with understandable and reasonably comprehensive summaries of employee benefit plans, updates when major changes are made, summaries of annual reports on the financing and operation of the plans, and advance notification if an employer intends to terminate a pension plan.
- At their request, employees must be given a report on the status of their vesting and accrued pension benefits. If they leave their employer on a temporary or permanent basis, they must be given such a report automatically.
- Employee benefit plans must report certain detailed financial and actuarial data annually to the Department of the Treasury and submit audited financial statements to federal agencies.

Participation

- Employees must be allowed to begin participation in a pension plan after they have reached age 21 and have completed one year of service (which includes at least 1,000 hours of work). The service requirement can be two years instead of one year if the employee is 100% vested after the two years.

- Employees cannot be excluded from a pension plan on the grounds that they are too old, even if they begin their employment with the plan sponsor within only a few years of the plan's normal retirement age (for defined benefit plans).

Vesting

- Employees acquire nonforfeitable, vested rights to pension benefits under one of two schedules: Employees must be either 100% vested after no more than five years of service (ten years for multi-employer collectively bargained plans), partially vested after no more than three years of service, and 100% vested after no more than seven years of service.

- Once 100% vested, employees cannot lose their pension benefits even if they leave their jobs before retirement. If they leave and return, their years of service before and after the break must be added together in determining the amount of their pensions.

- Pension plans must contain provisions for automatic survivor annuities and pre-retirement survivor benefits to married employees, with an option for employees to waive survivor benefits if they wish, but only with a spouse's written consent.

Funding

- Employers are required to fund annually all pension benefits earned that year by employees. They also must amortize over time the cost of benefit increases, investment losses or gains, and benefit credits for the past service of employees that were not previously funded.

- Employers who fail to meet the minimum funding standards must pay an excise tax penalty of 10% of the amount that should have been contributed. A 100% tax can be levied if an employer fails to correct a funding deficiency within a certain period of time.

- Plans that become underfunded because of benefit increases or other reasons must speed up the amortization schedule for covering certain liabilities.

- The Secretary of the Treasury can waive the funding requirement for companies that would suffer financial hardship by complying with the minimum standards, but may require security if the amount to be waived exceeds $1 million.

- A lien may be levied against an employer's assets if the employer fails to meet minimum funding standards. The employer must also notify plan participants and beneficiaries of any failure by the plan to meet the funding requirements.

- An employer who, by increasing benefits, causes the pension plan to be less than 60% funded in terms of what would be owed to the workers if the plan were terminated must post a security bond to keep the plan qualified for tax breaks.

- Employer deductions for contributions to a fully funded pension plan may not exceed 150% of current liabilities—the value of all vested and nonvested benefits that would be owed to plan participants if the plan terminated.

Fiduciary Standards

- The persons who control and manage employee benefit plans and plan funds (fiduciaries) must exercise their duties in a prudent manner, solely for the benefit of participants and beneficiaries.
- Fiduciaries are prohibited from engaging in certain transactions with parties having interests adverse to those of the participants of the plan, and from dealing with the income or assets of the employee benefit plan in their own interests.
- Fiduciaries are required to diversify pension fund investments to minimize the risk of large losses.

Enforcement and Administration

- Civil actions may be brought by employees or beneficiaries to recover benefits, clarify rights to benefits, or seek relief from violations of the fiduciary standards.
- Criminal penalties are provided for individuals or corporations violating the reporting and disclosure regulations.

Title II: IRS Rules

This section of ERISA covers tax provisions, which consist of amendments to the Internal Revenue Code (IRC), including amendments that mirror the participation, vesting and funding provisions of Title I. Some of the specific amendments to the IRC are listed below:

IRAs and Keogh Plans

Individual Retirement Accounts (IRAs) and Keogh plans for self-employed persons contain these provisions:

- If an individual, or his or her spouse, is not covered by an employer-sponsored pension plan, that person may make an annual tax-deductible contribution of up to $2,000 (or 100% of earnings, whichever is less) to an IRA.
- Persons who are covered by employer-sponsored plans may also make the maximum $2,000 IRA contribution if they are single with an annual income under $25,000 or married (and filing jointly) with an annual income under $40,000.
- Self-employed persons who establish pension plans for themselves (Keogh plans) can make annual tax-deductible contributions of up to $30,000 or 25% of income, whichever is less.

Contribution and Benefit Limits

- The limit on an annual benefit payable from a defined benefit pension plan is the lesser of 100% of average salary or $90,000, indexed for inflation beginning in 1988 (the limit was $112,221 in 1992).

- Annual additions (employer contributions plus employee after-tax contributions) under a defined contribution plan are limited to the lesser of 25% of compensation or $30,000, whichever is less.

- The $30,000 limit is frozen until the defined benefit dollar limit, indexed for inflation, reaches $120,000. Thereafter, a 4-to-1 ratio is maintained between the two limits.

- The ceiling on annual retirement benefits paid before Social Security retirement age is reduced to the actuarial equivalent of a $90,000 (inflation-adjusted) benefit beginning at the Social Security age. (The Social Security retirement age of 65 increases to age 66 in 2005 and to age 67 in 2022.)

Nondiscrimination Coverage Requirements

- Qualified employee benefit plans have to meet minimum nondiscrimination requirements designed to ensure that the plans are not providing disproportionate benefits to officers, shareholders or highly paid employees.

- Welfare benefit plans also must meet nondiscrimination coverage standards that differ by type of plan, either by covering a fair cross-section of workers or by satisfying various percentage tests.

Title III. Jurisdiction

This section of ERISA covers the responsibilities of the two federal agencies that administer and enforce ERISA.

- The Treasury Department has primary jurisdiction over participation, vesting and funding issues, and enforces compliance through tax exemption disqualification and through imposition of excise taxes.

- The Labor Department has primary jurisdiction over reporting, and disclosure and fiduciary matters and can, in certain circumstances, enforce employee benefit rights and reporting and disclosure through civil or criminal actions.

Title IV. Termination Insurance

- The Pension Benefit Guaranty Corporation (PBGC), created by ERISA, is responsible for insuring against loss of pension benefits when plans collapse or are terminated. Defined benefit plans are required to purchase termination insurance through the payment of annual premiums whose rates are based on the number of participants in the pension plan and on whether the plan covers the employees of one employer (a "single-employer plan") or is a plan maintained under a collective bargaining agreement to which more than one employer contributes (a "multi-employer plan").

- In the case of termination of a single-employer plan, PBGC insurance kicks in only if plan assets are insufficient to cover all benefits to which workers are entitled and the employer demonstrates financial distress.

- In a "distress termination," an employer is liable for a percentage of the company's net worth, plus a percentage of the employee benefits for which the plan has no funds.

- Employers who pull out of a multi-employer pension plan must still pay their share of the unfunded pension obligations of the plan.

Updates to ERISA

Since the original passage of ERISA, there have been numerous updates and changes, especially through tax legislation. These were covered earlier. A listing of the legislation impacting ERISA is provided below:

Tax Legislation from 1975 to 1978
Multi-employer Pension Plan Amendments Act (1980)
Economic Recovery Tax Act of 1981 (ERTA)
Tax Equity and Fiscal Responsibility Act of 1983 (TEFRA)
Deficit Reduction Act of 1984
Retirement Equity Act of 1984
Consolidated Omnibus Budget Reconciliation Act of 1985 (COBRA)
Tax Reform Act of 1986
Omnibus Budget Reconciliation Act of 1986
Omnibus Budget Reconciliation Act of 1987
The Technical and Miscellaneous Revenue Act of 1988
Retiree Benefits Bankruptcy Protection Act
Omnibus Budget Reconciliation Act of 1989
Debt Ceiling Increase of 1989 (Repeal of Section 89)
Americans with Disabilities Act of 1992 (ADA)
Omnibus Budget Reconciliation Act of 1990
Unemployment Compensation Extension of 1992 (Lump-Sum Distributions)

B. Factors to Consider in Selecting Defined Contribution versus Defined Benefit Pension Plans[5]

1. Most employers have specific income replacement objectives in mind when they establish a retirement plan. A defined benefit plan can be structured to achieve these objectives. The defined contribution approach will probably produce benefits that either fall short or exceed these objectives for individual employees.

2. By the same token, most employers want to take Social Security benefits into account so that the combined level of benefits from both sources will produce the desired results. Defined contribution plans can be integrated with Social Security benefits to some extent by adjusting contribution levels, but integration can be accomplished more efficiently under defined benefit plans.

3. The defined benefit plan requires an employer commitment to pay the cost of the promised benefits. Thus, the employer must assume any additional costs associated with inflation and adverse investment results. The defined contribution plan transfers these risks to the employee and allows the employer to fix its cost.

4. A deferred profit-sharing plan offers an employer the ultimate in contribution and funding flexibility. The money purchase pension plan, however, offers little flexibility

because contributions are fixed and must be made each year. Although the defined benefit plan involves an employer commitment as to ultimate cost, there can be significant funding flexibility on a year-to-year basis through the use of various actuarial methods and assumptions. (There is less flexibility with respect to establishing the annual charge to earnings for defined benefit plans, however, due to new accounting standards.)

5. The other side of the cost issue concerns benefits for employees. A defined benefit plan can protect the employee against the risk of pre-retirement inflation. In a defined contribution plan, this risk is assumed by the employee, who must rely primarily on investment results to increase the value of benefits during inflationary periods.

6. Employees also assume the risk of investment loss under a defined contribution plan. Many observers feel it is inappropriate for the average employee to assume such a risk with respect to a major component of his or her retirement security.

7. The typical defined contribution plan provides that the employee's account balance is payable in the event of death and, frequently, in the case of disability. This, of course, produces additional plan costs or, alternatively, lower retirement benefits if overall costs are held constant. An employer who is interested primarily in providing retirement benefits can use available funds more efficiently for this purpose under a defined benefit plan.

8. Many observers believe that a more equitable allocation of employer contributions occurs under a defined benefit plan because the employee's age, past service, and pay can all be taken into account; the typical defined contribution plan allocates contributions only on the basis of pay. On the other hand, it is in the very nature of a final pay-defined benefit plan that the value of total benefits accrued becomes progressively greater each year as the employee approaches retirement; under a defined contribution plan, a greater value will accrue during the earlier years of participation. As a result of the greater values accrued during the early years, defined contribution plans produce higher benefits and costs for terminating employees than do defined benefit plans.

9. Profit-sharing and savings plans offer two potential advantages that are not available under defined benefit and money purchase pension plans. Profit-sharing can create employee incentives. These plans can also invest in employer securities, giving the employees, as shareholders, the opportunity to identify with overall corporate interests.

10. Younger employees are likely to perceive a defined contribution plan, with its accumulating account values, as more valuable than a defined benefit plan. The reverse is true for older employees. Thus, the average age of the group to be covered is critical.

11. Defined benefit plans are subject to the plan termination provisions of ERISA, requiring the employer to pay annual Pension Benefit Guaranty Corporation (PBGC) premiums and exposing the employer's net worth to liability if the plan is terminated with ensured but unfunded benefit promises. Defined contribution plans do not have this exposure.

These factors will have different significance for different employers, and a choice that is appropriate for one organization may be inappropriate for another. Many employers will find that a combination of the two approaches is the right answer—a defined benefit plan that provides a basic layer of benefits, together with a defined contribution arrangement that is a source of supplemental benefits.

C. Sample Guidelines for Asset Allocations in Investment Portfolios

These guidelines are provided by the Treasury Management Association as a sample of balance asset allocations for a pension fund investment portfolio. They are for illustration purposes only, and not meant to be a recommendation or endorsement.

1. Pension fund investment objectives are threefold: first and foremost is the preservation of portfolio capital. Second is to realize a total return in excess of that generated by the major market averages, weighted by maturity characteristics and determined by security type, over a sustained period of time. The market benchmarks are the S&P 500 for the equity portion of the portfolio, and the Shearson-Lehman Government/Corporate for the fixed income portion of the portfolio. Third is to provide sufficient liquidity within the portfolio to accommodate plant closings and cash-outs. Estimated cashflow and liquidity requirements will be conveyed to the fund manager as needed.

2. The minimum quality rating for any equity or fixed income security held within the portfolio is Baa or BBB (Investment Grade). However, fixed income securities, other than cash equivalents, shall have a weighted average quality of at least "A" rating. Convertible securities must be rated "BBB/Baa" or better at the time of investment.

3. Short-term cash equivalent investments shall be rated either A1/P1 or, if with a bank, rated AA or better.

4. Investments other than cash equivalents will be limited to publicly traded, actively marketed securities for the following listings: New York Exchange, American Exchange, Pacific Exchange, Philadelphia Exchange, Frankfurt Exchange, London Exchange, Paris Exchange, Switzerland Exchange, and OTC and NASDAQ issues.

5. The investment manager shall have full discretion as to how to establish the maturity pattern of the fixed income security investments within the context of a maximum weighted average maturity of seven years, with a maximum average life of 10 years on any individual security.

6. Allowable equity investments cannot exceed a maximum of 70% of the total market value of the pension portfolio.

7. ADRs, overseas exchange equities, overseas fixed income securities, and/or overseas cash equivalents shall not exceed in the aggregate 15% of the total market value of the portfolio (Rule 8 applies to all classes of securities).

8. No investment will be acquired for the portfolio if the total securities (equities plus fixed) of a company would represent more than 10% of the total market value of the portfolio at the time of purchase, or if the total investments in a company represent 5% of that firm's securities outstanding or any class of securities outstanding. However, there is an individual 5%-per-company maximum investment limit for either equities, fixed income securities, or cash equivalents as a percentage of the total market value of the portfolio. The limits and maximums do not apply to U.S. Government or U.S. agency obligations backed by the full faith and credit of the U.S. Government.

9. The following investments are prohibited from being in the portfolio:
   - Puts, Calls, Index, and Future Options
   - Commodities
   - Letter-of-Credit Enhanced Securities
   - REITS (Real Estate Investment Trusts)
   - Real Estate Mutual Funds
   - Investments with firms who have business investments in certain countries
   - Investments in the fixed income or equity securities of major media companies.

10. Should the economic and market outlook indicate the need to depart from the above guidelines, investment committee approval must be obtained in writing.

11. If the guidelines are unclear to the fund manager, the manager should confer with the investment committee before proceeding.

D. Comparison of Non-Qualified and Qualified Deferred Compensation Plans[6]

Comparison of Non-Qualified and Qualified Deferred Compensation Plans		
Plan Provisions	**Non-Qualified Plan**	**Qualified Plan**
1. Participation	Can be selective	Cannot discriminate in favor of prohibited group
2a. Statutory Limitation on Annual Benefit	None	Lesser of $90,000 or 100% of compensation
2b. Statutory Limitation on Annual Allocation	None	Lesser of $30,000 or 25% of compensation
3. Funding Method	Not required	Required
4. Funding Vehicle	Usually reserve on balance sheet	Required
5. Earnings on Reserve	Taxable at ordinary rates	Tax-deferred while in trust
6. Deductibility to Company	When paid to participant	Immediately
7. Taxable to Employee	When received	When received
8. Tax Basis to Employee	Subject to ordinary income tax rates	May employ special 10-year forward averaging
9. Rollover	Not permitted	Permitted tax-free to another qualified plan or to IRA
10. Termination of Plan	Flexible	May need approval from Pension Benefit Guarantee Corporation and Internal Revenue Service

V. Endnotes

1. See: *The Handbook of Employee Benefits: Design, Funding, and Administration, Second Edition,* edited by Jerry S. Rosenbloom, Dow Jones-Irwin, Homewood, IL, 1988.

2. See: *The Handbook of Employee Benefits: Design, Funding, and Administration, Second Edition,* Chapter 3, edited by Jerry S. Rosenbloom, Dow Jones-Irwin, Homewood, IL, 1988.

3. Current limitations (1994) are a maximum $8,700 per year or 15% of annual salary, whichever is less. As these figures may change with updates to the IRC, the reader is urged to consult tax or retirement specialists to determine the most current limitations and restrictions.

4. This section is taken from: *Primer on Employee Retirement Income Security Act, Fourth Edition,* Barbara J. Coleman, The Bureau of National Affairs, Inc., Washington, DC, 1993, pp. 7–29.

5. See: *The Handbook of Employee Benefits, Second Edition,* Chapter 24, edited by Jerry S. Rosenbloom, Dow-Jones Irwin Publishers, 1988.

6. See: *The Handbook of Employee Benefits, Second Edition,* Chapter 18, edited by Jerry S. Rosenbloom, Dow Jones-Irwin, Publishers, 1988.

16 Tax, Legal, Audit, and Ethical Issues

I. Outline of the Chapter

A. Tax Issues Related to Treasury Management

   1. Types of Taxes

     a. Income Tax

     b. Property Tax

     c. Sales and Use Tax

     d. Payroll Tax

     e. Withholding Tax

   2. General Tax Principles

     a. After-Tax Cash Flow

     b. Capitalization and Depreciation

     c. Deductions versus Credits

     d. Timing of Losses

     e. Ordinary Income/Losses versus Capital Gains/Losses

     f. Current Status of Capital Gains/Losses versus Ordinary Income

     g. Improper Accumulation of Earnings

   3. Taxation and Investment Alternatives

     a. Fully Taxable Securities

     b. Municipal Securities (MUNIs)

     c. Federal Government Securities

     d. Corporate Dividends

   4. Tax Strategies for Investment Portfolios

     a. Tax Strategies for Capital Losses

     b. Diversification and Municipal Securities

        c.   Municipal Securities with Put Options

        d.   Tax Swap Strategies

   5.   International Accounting and Tax Issues

        a.   Translation of Foreign Currency Financial Statements

        b.   Differences in Accounting Standards

        c.   Other International Tax Issues

B.   Legal Issues Related to Treasury Management

   1.   Laws Related to Banking Services

        a.   McFadden Act (1927)

        b.   Glass-Steagall Act (1933)

        c.   Depository Institutions Deregulation and Monetary Control Act (DIDMCA) (1980)

        d.   Other Legislation

        e.   Federal Reserve Regulations

   2.   Antitrust Laws Related to Competition and Pricing

        a.   Sherman Antitrust Act (1890)

        b.   Clayton Act (1914)

        c.   Robinson-Patman Act (1936)

   3.   Laws Related to Payments

        a.   State Laws Requiring Local Payments

        b.   Uniform Commercial Code, Article 4A (UCC 4A)

        c.   Statute of Frauds

   4.   Laws Related to Bankruptcy

        a.   Chapter 7 Bankruptcy (Liquidation)

        b.   Chapter 11 Bankruptcy (Reorganization)

        c.   Chapter 13 Bankruptcy

   5.   Laws Related to Other Treasury Functions

        a.   Retirement Benefits (ERISA—Employee Retirement and Income Security Act) (1974)

        b.   Prudent Person Rules

        c.   SEC Security Registration Requirements

        d.   Insider Trading Rules

        e.   Environmental Law

C.   Audit, Control and Security Principles

   1.   Definition of Auditing

a. Written Agreements

b. Circular Cash Flows

c. Improper Incentive Programs

d. Bank Account Analysis Statements

4. Ethical Issues in Disbursement System Design

a. Questionable Disbursement Practices

b. Remote versus Controlled Disbursing

5. Investment Programs

a. Speculating on Interest Rate Movements

b. Speculating in Risky or Less Liquid Securities

c. Over-Leveraging

Chapter Checklist

A. Summary of International Tax Codes

B. Checklist of Laws/Dates in Treasury Management

C. TMA Code of Conduct

Suggestions for References and Additional Reading

A. Taxation

B. Legal Issues

C. Audit and Security

D. Ethics

II. Introduction

This chapter highlights basic issues impacting the treasurer in the areas of taxation, law, audit and ethics. While detailed discussion of any one of these issues would require an entire treatise, we focus here on issues that have major importance in the management of the treasury function. It is important to note that tax codes and laws change frequently and that treasurers must keep abreast of these changes.

The issues discussed in this chapter underlie all other functions performed by treasurers or their staffs. For example, a manager may utilize confidential information for personal gain, or may deliberately mislead banks in obtaining a loan or suppliers in obtaining goods. Such practices raise ethical questions and, in some cases, legal ones. Or, a Treasury Management System (TMS), may give the treasurer convenient access to wire transfer capabilities but may lack adequate controls. Similar examples could be given for almost every area of treasury management.

III. Coverage of the Chapter Material

A. Tax Issues Related to Treasury Management

Virtually all financial decisions made by the treasurer will have some tax consequences because they generally impact revenues, expenses and cash flows. The tax code of the U.S. is an extremely complex and constantly evolving document. The principles outlined here are generally applicable, but may require further in-depth research for each specific situation. In addition, tax codes are constantly changing through issuance of new laws, regulations, rulings and cases. Therefore, readers should consult with qualified tax experts as necessary.

1. Types of Taxes: There are many types of taxes that corporations are responsible for either paying or collecting. The major ones are:

a. Income Tax: This is a government (federal, state or local) levy on the net earnings of an individual, corporation or other taxable unit. The tax rate is usually graduated as earnings go from one tax bracket to another. Corporate income tax is generally estimated and paid on a quarterly basis, with a final accounting and settlement in the annual tax filing. Income tax may include an addition to the regular tax, such as a surtax, and certain business expense items may be deemed non-deductible (or only partially deductible) for tax purposes. The provision for income taxes (estimated) is shown as an expense on the income statement.

b. Property Tax: These are taxes paid on the assessed value of property such as real estate, plants and equipment. They are generally levied by state and local governments and vary widely by location, with some states and localities having no property tax.

c. Sales and Use Tax: Sales tax is a state or local tax based on a percentage of the selling price of the goods or services bought. It is not revenue to the seller, who simply collects it and passes it onto the state or local government. Use tax, a complement to sales tax, is imposed by state or local governments on the storage, use, or consumption of tangible personal property upon which sales tax has not been paid.

d. Payroll Tax: These are taxes levied on employees' salaries or net income of self-employed individuals. Social Security taxes are levied on employees, and employers are responsible for a matching amount. Unemployment taxes are also included in this category and are levied only on the employer, based on a past history of unemployment claims. Some states or local governments also impose a "head" tax or other employment taxes on firms in their jurisdictions.

e. Withholding Tax: This is a deduction by an employer from employee salaries for the payment of federal and state income taxes. It is paid in a prescribed manner to the taxing authority. For federal withholding tax, the employer must remit the payment to the IRS on a regular basis, usually by deposits into a designated bank.

2. General Tax Principles

a. After-Tax Cash Flow: Cash expenses are generally tax-deductible. This means that if a firm has a tax rate of 40% (combined state and federal income tax), a cash expense of $100 for computer maintenance will result in an after-tax cash outflow of only $60. This is because the $100 may be counted as a tax deduction, thereby, reducing the firm's tax liability by $40 (assuming the firm is profitable). In general, the relationship between after-tax cash flow and cash expense is:

$$\text{After-tax cash flow} = \text{Cash Expense} \times (1 - \text{Tax Rate})$$
$$= \$100 \times (1 - .40) = \$60$$

The tax rate used here is the firm's estimated effective combined tax rate for federal taxes and effective state tax rate after deducting them from federal taxes. This percentage can be found by dividing the total of income taxes paid (both state and federal) by the amount of taxable income.

The same relationship applies for cash revenues. If a firm has cash revenues of $100 from interest on a short-term investment, the after-tax cash flow is actually only $60. The other $40 is paid out for taxes.

$$\text{After-tax cash flow} = \text{Cash Revenue} \times (1 - \text{Tax Rate})$$
$$= \$100 \times (1 - .40) = \$60$$

b. Capitalization and Depreciation: Cash outflow for long-term assets such as buildings, machinery or computers may not necessarily be treated as expenses for tax purposes and may not be immediately deducted from the current period's taxable income. Such investments must be capitalized, i.e., entered into the firm's accounts as assets and then depreciated over multiple years. In other words, the "expense" is stored in an asset account and is gradually released over time for tax and book purposes. The number of years of depreciation and the allowable percentage per year for tax purposes is determined by IRS guidelines and may change from time to time. While several different methods are currently available, the most rapid schedule permitted is the IRS's Modified Accelerated Cost Recovery System (MACRS). As an example, for an asset with a five-year life (automobiles, light-duty trucks, some computer equipment and tools) the depreciation is defined by IRS regulations, as shown in the table below. The straight-line method is included for comparison purposes, and the standard IRS half-year convention is used in computing depreciation in the first year. The IRS code assumes that an asset is purchased mid-year, regardless of when it is actually purchased, and is therefore entitled to only half of the first year's calculated depreciation. Thus, a five-year-class asset is actually depreciated over six years as shown in the table.

Year	1	2	3	4	5	6	Total
MACRS	20%	32%	19%	12%	11%	6%	100%
Straight-Line	10%	20%	20%	20%	20%	10%	100%

To illustrate, if a computer system costs $10,000 and is determined for tax purposes to have a depreciable life of five years (assume a marginal tax rate of 40%), the after-tax cash flows for the initial purchase price are as follows:

In the first year, 20% of the $10,000 becomes tax deductible reducing the firm's tax liability by 40% of $2,000.

$$\text{After-tax cash flow} = \$10,000 + (.20 \times \$10,000 \times .40) = (\$9,200)$$
(Purchase price less depreciation, Year 1)

In the second year, the after-tax cash flow is computed by using the 32% from the schedule for Year 2:

$$\text{After-tax cash flow (Year 2)} = .32 \times \$10,000 \times .40 = \$1,280.$$

In remaining years, the after-tax cash flow is computed in the same way by applying the percentage permitted by the tax code.

Year	Dep. Rate × Amount × Tax %	After-Tax CF
1	$-\$10,000 + (.20 \times \$10,000 \times .40)$	($9,200)
2	$.32 \times \$10,000 \times .40$	1,280
3	$.19 \times \$10,000 \times .40$	760
4	$.12 \times \$10,000 \times .40$	480
5	$.11 \times \$10,000 \times .40$	440
6	$.06 \times \$10,000 \times .40$	240

The cumulative result is a cash outflow of $6,000 or (1–.40) times the initial capitalized amount of $10,000. This is the same as if the $10,000 were treated as a cash expense except that the cash inflow from deductions is spread out over multiple years. Therefore, depreciation can be thought of as a deferred expense for tax purposes. Note, this discussion does not take into account the time value of the cash flows.

c. Deductions versus Credits: Expenses and depreciation are treated as tax deductions. Some cash flows are treated as tax credits. For example, income taxes paid to foreign governments are treated as tax credits for the domestic parent of a foreign subsidiary. This means that the full amount of the credit can be used to reduce tax liability. While a tax deduction, in terms of cash flow, is worth only the tax rate times the deduction, a tax credit is worth 100% times the credit (i.e., a tax credit provides a dollar for dollar reduction of taxes).

d. Timing of Losses: If a corporation has net losses for tax purposes, it can carry the losses back three years to offset any taxable profits it had in those years. The firm may then claim a refund for taxes paid. Similarly, losses can be carried forward up to 15 years to offset future taxable profits.

e. Ordinary Income/Losses versus Capital Gains/Losses: Ordinary income or losses are related to operations and accounting profits or losses. Interest earned from financial investments is included in ordinary income for tax purposes. Capital gains and losses are derived from changes in the value of assets (real or financial) and are not related to operations. There are provisions in the tax code that make ordinary income or losses not equivalent to capital gains or losses. For example, if a corporation has ordinary income and capital losses in one year, the losses cannot offset the ordinary income in that year. Net capital losses can only offset capital gains in the present or subsequent year(s) through the tax loss carry-over provisions of the code.

f. Current Status of Capital Gains/Losses versus Ordinary Income: In times past, the U.S. Government taxed realized capital gains and losses at a rate lower than that for ordinary income.

- For example, a security is purchased at $500 and held for over a year. The security is then sold for $600. At a tax rate of 40%, the gain on the security transaction would result in taxes of .40 times the $100 gain or $40. With a lower capital gains tax in place (20% for example), the taxes would be half that of the normal 40% rate or $20.

- There is currently no differential between the rate on ordinary income and capital gains for corporations (except that in some cases corporations may exclude a portion of dividend income from taxation). In the case of individuals, there are slight differences due to minimal exclusion of dividends and other allowable adjustments. This is another area where the tax code can change rapidly.

g. Improper Accumulation of Earnings: The tax code imposes special penalties and taxes on earnings of the corporation accumulated for the sole purpose of avoiding the payment of dividends, thereby lowering shareholders' taxes. If a firm has excessive accumulations, it may have to justify that the funds are needed for business operations. This usually applies only to privately held corporations where owner-managers may improperly accumulate earnings in an attempt to avoid taxes.

2. Taxation and Investment Alternatives

a. Fully Taxable Securities: In comparing the yields of various investment alternatives, the treasurer must be aware of the tax status of the investments. Since interest and gains are treated as revenue by the tax code, only the after-tax yield should be used for the comparisons. Individual classes of short-term and long-term investments vary as to their tax status. Many short-term securities, such as commercial paper and certificates of deposit, are fully taxable. Their after-tax yield is related to their before-tax yield by the following equation:

After-tax yield for Fully Taxable Securities

$$= \text{Before--tax yield} \times \left[1 - \left[Tf + [Ts \times (1 - Tf)] \right] \right]$$

Where: Tf = the marginal federal tax rate.
         Ts = the marginal state tax rate.

For example, if a certificate of deposit offers a before-tax rate of 10.0% and the federal tax rate is 34% and the state tax rate is 5%, then the after-tax yield is:

$$\text{After–tax yield} = 10.0\% \times \left[1 - \left[.34 + [.05 \times (1 - .34)]\right]\right]$$
$$= 6.3\%$$

Over the years, primarily to encourage investment in selected activities, governments have granted various tax concessions to certain types of securities. These securities are called "tax preferred" securities because they are exempt from some portion of usual taxes.

b. Municipal Securities (MUNIs): MUNIs are issued by state and local governments to fund various activities related to government. Section 103 of the U.S. tax code exempts the interest on such securities from federal taxes. Many states exempt such interest from state taxes as long as the securities are issued by a governmental body in that state. For example, suppose a security is issued in a state which allows this kind of exemption. If the before-tax yield on the security is 7.0% the after-tax yield is:

$$\text{After–tax yield} = \text{Before–tax yield} \times \left[1 - \left[T_f + [T_s \times (1 - T_f)]\right]\right]$$

$$\text{After–tax yield} = 7.0\% \times \left[1 - \left[0 + [0 \times (1 - 0)]\right]\right] = 7.0\%$$

(Completely exempt security)

If the purchasing firm were in a state that did not exempt the security from state taxation, then only federal taxes would be zero. If state taxes were 5%, then the after-tax yield becomes:

$$\text{After–tax yield} = 7.0\% \times \left[1 - \left[0 + [.05 \times (1-0)]\right]\right] = 6.65\%$$

(Security exempt from federal tax)

Note of caution: The tax code prohibits the deduction of interest on loans incurred to invest in tax-exempt securities. Therefore, firms that have used such loans may not be able to take advantage of the tax-preferred status of such investments. Tax counsel should be sought on this and other tax-related matters.

c. Federal Government Securities: Securities such as Treasury bills, notes and bonds are subject to federal income taxes but are exempt from state and local taxes. For a T-bill yielding 8.0% interest with a federal tax rate of 34%, the after-tax yield is

$$\text{After–tax yield} = 8.0\% \times \left[1 - \left[.34 + [0 \times (1 - .34)]\right]\right] = 5.28\%$$

(Securities exempt from state tax)

d. Corporate Dividends: Dividends paid are an after-tax disbursement by the paying corporation. To help reduce the impact of double taxation to corporations, current federal tax regulations (1990) allow a partial exemption on dividends received from domestic corporations by another corporation.

- A corporation may deduct, subject to certain limitations, 70% of the dividends received if it owns less than 20% of the distributing corporation. A corporation can take a deduction of 80% of dividends received if it owns 20% or more of the paying domestic corporation. The latter is referred to as a 20%-owned corporation. The security must be held for at least 45 days to qualify for the exemption. Special rules limit the exemption in the case of debt-financed portfolio stock.

- Normally, common and preferred stock does not qualify as an acceptable short-term corporate investment because of price volatility. However, in the last several years, the creation of variable-rate preferred stock has eliminated much of the price risk. For a corporation with a combined (federal and state) corporate tax rate of 40% investing in a variable-rate preferred stock yielding 8.0%, the after-tax yield is:

After-tax yield = $8.0 \times (1 - [1 - .7] \times .40) = 7.04\%$

(Assuming 70% dividend exclusion)

Without the exclusion, the after-tax yield would have been:

$8.0 \times (1 - .40) = 4.8\%.$

3. Tax Strategies for Investment Portfolios: Because the tax codes are so complex and change over time, tax strategies can become very complex. We list here only a small sample of possible strategies to increase the firm's overall after-tax return from treasury activities. It is strongly recommended that treasurers obtain the advice of tax attorneys or accountants in this area.

a. Tax Strategies for Capital Losses: If a firm expects capital losses in one year and is unwilling or unable to carry the losses forward or backward, it may want to generate capital gains to offset the losses. The problem is that the firm may not want to invest in long-term securities to generate the gains because of the price uncertainty in such investments. It may be possible to handle this situation by purchasing a commodity (such as silver, gold or securities in a mutual fund) and then sell futures contracts in the same amount. This process locks in a capital gain and the commodity can be sold in the future with price certainty. This is called a cash-and- carry strategy.

b. Diversification and Municipal Securities: Many municipal securities are not widely traded and, therefore, may be difficult to sell quickly if that becomes necessary. To protect against this liquidity risk, firms usually keep the municipal securities component of the investment portfolio below a stated percentage. When diversified with other, more liquid securities, municipal securities can boost after-tax yields without appreciably increasing overall liquidity risk.

c. Municipal Securities with Put Options: Another way to reduce the risk of municipal securities and avoid the liquidity problems of long-term securities is to invest in municipal securities in conjunction with a put option. A put option gives the owner of the security the right to sell it to a specific buyer at a given price within a fixed time period. Some securities firms offer this kind of pre-packaged investment.

d. Tax Swap Strategies: Firms may sometimes hold part of their portfolios in medium- or long-term bonds. A strategy used by banks and some corporations is the tax swap involving municipal bonds.

- Assume a five-year municipal bond was purchased two years ago for $1,000. Market conditions have changed in the last two years, so the bond now has a market price of $950.

- The firm sells the bond incurring a long-term capital loss of $50 which is deductible from income taxes (assuming the firm has offsetting capital gains). At a tax rate of 40%, the firm saves $20 in taxes.

- After the bond is sold, another bond with similar (but not exactly the same) characteristics (such as three years remaining to maturity) is purchased for $950 and held for three years. At that time the bond has a value of $1,000 and a taxable gain of $50. At a 40% tax rate, the firm pays taxes of $20.

- The net effect of these transactions is to receive an interest-free loan of $20 for three years. Caution must be taken not to purchase substantially the same security within 30 days of sale since the IRS disallows losses on a "wash sale" in which a security is sold primarily to claim the loss.

4. International Accounting and Tax Issues:[1] International accounting and tax issues can be very difficult and complex, and experts in this area should be consulted wherever possible. For the treasurer of a multinational firm, several areas relating to these issues must be addressed.

a. Translation of Foreign Currency Financial Statements: The translation of foreign currency financial statements will have an impact of a firm's overall financial performance. The accounting procedures for handling both foreign currency transactions and financial statement translation are described in FASB Statement 52.[2] Four basic issues need to be resolved in accounting for foreign currency transactions:

1. The initial recording of the transaction
2. The recording of the foreign currency balances at subsequent balance sheet dates
3. The treatment of any foreign exchange gains and losses
4. The recording of the settlement of foreign currency receivables and payables when they come due

Some of the more important points of FASB Statement 52 are:[3]

- The functional currency of an entity is the currency of the primary economic environment in which the entity operates.

- The current exchange rate as of the reporting date is used to translate the balance sheet of a foreign entity from its functional currency into its reporting currency.

- The weighted average exchange rate (over the accounting period represented in the income statement) is used to translate revenue, expenses, and gains and losses of a foreign entity from its functional currency into the reporting currency.

- Translated income gains or losses due to change in foreign currency values are not recognized in current net income, but are reported as a second component of stockholders' equity (cumulative translation adjustment account). An exception to this rule is a foreign entity located in a country with high inflation.

- Realized income gains or losses due to foreign currency transactions are included in the current period's net income, although there are some exceptions.

b. Differences in Accounting Standards: When dealing in foreign countries there are many differences in both accounting standards and disclosure requirements. In many cases, a multinational firm (MNF) is required to maintain several different sets of accounting records based on the different standards and regulations. The primary areas of difference are generally related to the following: consolidation practices, accounting for goodwill, deferred taxes, long-term leases, discretionary reserves, inflation, pension liabilities and assets, and foreign currency translation. In some cases, tax laws or accounting practices in foreign countries require maintaining accounting books that conform to local conventions.

c. Other International Tax Issues:[4] Tax laws vary in many ways among countries, but any type of tax causes before-tax cash flows to vary from after-tax cash flows. Since the MNF is most concerned with after-tax cash flows, anticipated taxes must be accounted for.

- Each country varies in the way it generates tax revenues.

- The United States relies on corporate and individual income taxes for federal revenues. Other countries may depend more on the value-added taxes (VAT) or excise taxes. Since each country has its own philosophy about whom to tax and how much, it is not surprising that from country to country corporations may be subject to unequal tax treatment.

- Because systems and tax rates are unique to each country, corporations need to compare their varying provisions. The important characteristics to consider in international taxation are:

  1) Corporate Income Taxes: Each country has its unique corporate income tax laws. A corporation with operations in a foreign country will have to abide by that country's tax laws, plus those of its home country. In addition, foreign firms may be treated differently from local firms, or there may be significant differences in corporate income tax laws by industry. A listing of some of the major features of international tax codes is provided at the end of this chapter.

  2) Withholding Taxes: Again, these taxes can vary substantially from country to country. They are often applied to dividends, interest payments, and royalty fees paid by foreign subsidiaries to the parent corporation.

  3) Provision for Carrybacks and Carryforwards: Negative earnings (losses) from operations often can be carried back or forward to offset earnings in other years. The laws governing the use of these losses vary significantly from country to country.

4) Tax Treaties: In order to prevent double taxation of corporate earnings, most countries establish tax treaties with their trading partners. Such treaties between nations entail the granting of credits by one nation for taxes paid by corporations operating in another nation's jurisdiction.

5) Tax Credits: Even without income tax treaties, an MNF may be allowed to credit income and withholding taxes paid in one country against taxes owed by the parent if certain requirements are met. Like income tax treaties, tax credits help to avoid double taxation and help to stimulate direct foreign investment.

6) Value-Added Tax (VAT): This is an indirect percentage tax levied on products or services at various stages of production and distribution. The actual value added to the product, including raw materials, labor, and profit, is determined at each stage or state of production and the tax is computed on the increase in value. It is basically a tax allocated among the economic units responsible for the production and distribution of goods and services. Because collection of VAT takes place at the product's ultimate destination, VAT is not charged on export sales. VAT is charged on all domestically sold products regardless of the country of origin. Thus VAT is designed to provide an incentive to export and a disincentive to import.

7) Other Types of International Taxes: The firm must consider other taxes levied by foreign governments. These would include sales and use taxes, property taxes, and others.

B. Legal Issues Related to Treasury Management

Treasury management is highly influenced by laws. Many of these laws directly impact the banking system and indirectly affect treasury management by defining the kinds of products banks can offer. Other laws relate to securities issued and purchased by treasurers.

1. Laws Related to Banking Services

a. McFadden Act (1927):

- This act prohibits a bank from taking deposits and engaging in banking business outside the state in which the bank is chartered. The act inhibits nationwide branching that is available in many other countries, such as Canada and Germany.

- It requires the treasurer to monitor collection and disbursement systems that involve multiple banks, rather than permitting a single bank to administer the systems for the treasurer in a multi-state environment.

- In spite of the McFadden Act, some banks operate in multiple states through holding companies and/or through the acquisition of troubled banks under the auspices of the Federal Deposit Insurance Corporation. This type of interstate acquisition was sanctioned by the 1982 Garn-St. Germain Act.

- The Douglas Amendment (1956) and recent court rulings have cleared the way for banks to operate on a multi-state, regional basis as long as approval is received from the states involved.

- At the time of printing this text, Congress was considering approval of interstate banking.

b. Glass-Steagall Act (1933): This act prohibits commercial banks from securities underwriting except for government issues.

- Banks can only offer services closely related to their banking activities which are defined as taking demand deposits and making commercial loans. Recently, banks have been permitted to engage in some types of security transactions for customers provided that they do not provide investment advice.

- This law prohibits securities firms from engaging in bank-like activities. Nevertheless, many offer interest-bearing accounts that have check-writing privileges. Commercial banks have been lobbying to have these legal restrictions removed so that they (the banks) will be able to compete on a more level playing field with securities firms (investment banks).

c. Depository Institutions Deregulation and Monetary Control Act (DID-MCA) (1980): This act mandated six major changes in bank practices and in the banking system:

1. Required all depository-taking institutions to maintain cash balances (reserves) at their Federal Reserve Bank.

2. Made Fed services (i.e., discount window borrowing and check clearing) available to all deposit-taking institutions, not just Federal Reserve members.

3. Mandated the Fed reduce and/or price float in the system, rather than allowing it to remain a "free" benefit to depository banks.

4. Priced previously free Fed services on a scale equal to that of a tax-paying competitor.

5. Provided for phasing out of Regulation Q (defined below) interest rate ceilings over a five-year period through 1986.

6. Permitted banks to offer Negotiable Orders of Withdrawal (NOW) accounts, which are check-writing accounts with an unregulated interest rate for individuals and not-for-profit organizations.

d. Other Legislation: Several other regulations or laws relating to banking and finance must be considered:

1) Electronic Funds Transfer Act (EFTA) (1978): This act defined the rights and responsibilities of individuals using EFT services other than wire transfers. It limits customer liability for unauthorized banking transactions involving Automated Teller Machines (ATMs) and Point-of-Sale (POS) terminals provided the customer notifies the issuing bank or other issuing institution of the loss of the ATM or debit card.

2) Garn-St. Germain Depository Institutions Act (1982): This act extended the deregulation of the banking industry. Its major points included the extension of bank legal lending limits (amount it can lend to any one borrower) up to 15% of the bank's capital base for unsecured loans (it was previously 10%) and up to 25% for secured loans. Allowed the FDIC to arrange mergers of banks across state lines when suitable intrastate partners could not be found. Allowed banks to offer accounts fully competitive with money market mutual funds.

3) Expedited Funds Availability Act (EFAA) (1988): This act defined check availability time periods, payable through draft and check return procedures. Provisions of this act are incorporated in Federal Reserve Regulation CC.

4) Financial Institutions Reform, Recovery and Enforcement Act (FIR-REA) (1989): This act was passed to deal with the savings and loan problems that surfaced during the 1980s. It merged the FSLIC (Federal Savings and Loan Insurance Corporation) into the FDIC and gave it increased flexibility to raise insurance premiums paid by member institutions. It also dismantled the Federal Home Loan Bank Board (FHLBB) and established the Office of Thrift Supervisors (OTS) to assume the FHLBB's supervisory role. Finally, this act created the Resolution Trust Corporation (RTC) to make timely disposal of failed S&Ls and their assets.

e. Federal Reserve Regulations: The Federal Reserve System (the Fed) is responsible, with other agencies, for regulating banks. The Fed accomplishes this through a series of lettered regulations.

- **Regulation E:** This regulation defines a consumer's rights and obligations with respect to electronic payments.

- **Regulation D:** This regulation specifies the percentage of various types and amounts of deposits that the bank must keep in Federal Reserve balances.

- **Regulation J:** This regulation establishes procedures, duties, and responsibilities for check collection and settlement through the Federal Reserve System.

- **Regulation Q:** This regulation prohibits depository institutions from paying interest on corporate demand deposit accounts. Sections of Regulation Q that imposed ceilings on interest rates paid on retail savings accounts are no longer in effect.

- **Regulation CC:** This regulation sets policies on holding funds (as provided in the Expedited Funds Availability Act), and requires banks to disclose their availability policies to their customers. It also established rules regarding the handling of returned checks and the endorsement standard to be used by both companies and banks in depositing and clearing checks.

2. Antitrust Laws Related to Competition and Pricing: The U.S. system of free enterprise is based on the premise of free and open competition between economic units. Business activities that reduce competition may fall afoul of antitrust laws. Examples are mergers between firms that produce competing products. With less competition, the merged firm may be able to charge higher prices for its products than would be possible under more open competition. The Federal Trade Commission (FTC) was set up in 1914 to promote free and fair competition and protect against antitrust activities. Major antitrust laws are:

a. Sherman Antitrust Act (1890): This act prohibits competing firms from cooperatively setting prices.

b. Clayton Act (1914): This act extends the Sherman Antitrust Act by prohibiting any form of price discrimination, exclusive contracts, mergers and interlocking directorates that serve to lessen competition.

c. Robinson-Patman Act (1936): This act is an amendment to the Clayton Act.

- It prohibits firms from charging different prices for the sale of products and services of like grade and quality where the result would be to lessen competition among firms.

- Exceptions are permitted for justifiable economic reasons, such as differences in transportation costs, bulk purchases, special manufacturing or delivery requirements. Provisions of the act imply that credit terms, often under the influence of the treasurer, should be the same for the same products within a class of customers.

3. Laws Related to Payments

a. State Laws Requiring Local Payments: Some states have laws governing the drawee bank for consumer/employee payments. Specifically, for some kinds of payments, such as payroll checks, insurance reimbursements or dividends, the drawee bank must be located within the state. This has a bearing on how the treasurer designs a disbursement system.

b. Uniform Commercial Code, Article 4A (UCC 4A): This is a 1992 regulation that applies primarily to wire transfers, as well as some other electronic credit transactions. It defines the responsibilities of payors, payees and financial institutions with respect to security, and spells out liabilities of parties to a wire transfer. In general, banks bear liability only for lost interest incurred in a misdirected wire, but they do not bear liability for consequential damages, which may be substantial.

UCC 4A provides a legal framework that outlines the risks, rights and obligations of parties in connection with an electronic payment.

1) Transactions Covered: The new article governs wire transfers through Fedwire, CHIPS (Clearing House for Interbank Payments System), as well as SWIFT (Society for Worldwide Interbank Financial Telecommunications), and book transfers and wholesale credit transfers through ACH and SWIFT transfers. It is not clear to what extent UCC 4A may apply to SWIFT, because it is primarily an international information system, rather than a value transfer system. However, due to the fact that many SWIFT messages are legally binding on the banks involved, UCC 4A may apply to those transaction segments which occur in the U.S. prior to transmission overseas or after receipt in the U.S. via SWIFT facilities.

2) Security Procedures: UCC 4A uses the concepts of commercially reasonable security procedures and verified payment orders to determine when the purported sender of an unauthorized payment instruction will be obligated to make payment. The bank must make security procedures for verifying payment orders available to the customer, and the bank and the customer must agree that those procedures are commercially reasonable. Some common security measures include the use of Personal Identification Numbers (PINs), callbacks, encryption and message authentication.

3) Consequential Damages: Banks are not responsible for consequential damages, which are losses resulting from the action or error made by the bank beyond the simple loss of funds. A bank incorrectly executing a payment order remains liable for interest losses or incidental expenses. The bank is liable for consequential damages, such as lost revenues or profits, only if it agrees to assume this liability in a written agreement with the customer.

c. Statute of Frauds: This is part of the Uniform Commercial Code. It requires that all contracts for $500 or more must be evidenced by a written record and signatures. Care must be taken to ensure that electronic communications comply with the intent of this statute.

4. Laws Related to Bankruptcy: By filing for bankruptcy, a firm receives protection from the courts against certain actions that could otherwise be taken by creditors. A creditor, for example, may not attempt to regain secured property or make liens against other property during bankruptcy protection. On the other hand, the court may reverse some actions that the firm may have taken before bankruptcy, such as selling assets. There are several different forms of bankruptcy defined in the bankruptcy codes. The appropriate form depends on the size of the firm and the court's assessment of the firm's viability as a going concern. The topic of bankruptcy is covered in greater detail in Chapter 3.

Three of the most important forms of bankruptcy for corporations are:

a. Chapter 7 Bankruptcy (Liquidation): This involves the appointment of a trustee who conducts an orderly liquidation of the firm's assets, paying off as many creditors as can be accommodated. More than 70% of bankruptcy filings are for Chapter 7. It is the least complex form of bankruptcy and legally the least costly.

b. Chapter 11 Bankruptcy (Reorganization): This seeks to reorganize the corporation as a going concern while shielding it from creditors until new financing plans can be worked out. Such protection requires a court-approved plan that may involve a renegotiation of debt with reduced principal amounts and/or interest payments. Sometimes debt is converted into equity. Chapter 11 protection continues until the firm either returns to profitability and emerges from bankruptcy or the court decides to liquidate its assets. The different types of reorganization are covered in Chapter 3.

c. Chapter 13 Bankruptcy: This is similar to Chapter 11 but is for individuals and small business owners rather than corporations. It allows the debtor to restructure debts under court protection.

5. Laws Related to Other Treasury Functions

a. Retirement Benefits (ERISA—Employee Retirement and Income Security Act) (1974): This Act was designed to protect employee pension plans. It defines how such pension plans are to be funded, conditions of participation, vesting of benefits and employee pension rights. An important aspect of the law relating to treasury management is that organizations must make actual cash contributions to pension plans in accordance with actuarial estimates of future cash flow needs of the plan. More details on this topic are provided in Chapter 15.

b. Prudent Person Rules: This is a standard applied to fiduciaries and corporate managers who invest funds for others. The standard may differ by state. A prudent person standard in ERISA governs investment of retirement funds. The standard generally requires those who invest money on behalf of others to invest only in securities that would be purchased by a prudent person of discretion and intelligence who seeks a reasonable income and preservation of capital.

c. SEC Security Registration Requirements: To ensure full and open disclosure of information, the Securities and Exchange Act of 1933 requires the registration of many corporate security offerings. This topic is covered in detail in Chapter 2.

- Exemptions are possible for certain securities such as commercial paper (less than 270-day maturity), intra-state offerings, some exchange offerings, small issues involving a limited number of shareholders (private placements) and issues by nonprofit institutions.

- The filing consists of any information the SEC believes will be material to informing potential investors in the registered securities. Such information includes, but is not limited to, current and historical financial statements, detailed business information, risks facing the company, unresolved legal issues, projections, accountant's letter, ownership and management data. Considerable time is often required to satisfy the SEC that all relevant information has been disclosed.

d. Insider Trading Rules: SEC and state laws on insider trading impact firms that issue publicly traded securities. These laws require a firm's officers, directors and major shareholders (i.e., those who own more than 10% of the stock of the firm) to report monthly their sale and purchase of the firm's shares. The intent is to prevent such individuals from benefiting from insider information, which is material data not available to the general public. Since the treasurer often has access to such information, it is crucial to be aware of the very strict disclosure requirements of SEC Rule 10b-5. Trading on, or disclosure of, inside information, or communicating misinformation of a material nature, can lead to serious civil and/or criminal penalties.

e. Environmental Law: The treasurer needs to be aware of applicable federal, state and local environmental laws due to the potential financial impact on the company from adhering to or violating such laws. A firm may need to account for the future cleanup of hazardous materials, or to factor the cost of environmental regulations into the financial analysis for a new plant or the closing of an existing facility.

C. Audit, Control and Security Principles

Much of what a treasurer does is recorded as accounting information. This information may then be audited by several parties: internal and external auditors, public accounting firm, government agency auditors, etc. Therefore, an understanding of auditing and internal controls by the treasurer is essential.

1. Definition of Auditing: Auditing is the process by which a competent, independent person accumulates and evaluates evidence about quantifiable information related to a specific economic entity for the purpose of determining and reporting on the degree of correspondence between the quantifiable information and established criteria. For the treasurer, the primary areas of concern with respect to auditing are accounts payable, accounts receivable, foreign exchange, investment and cash management operations. Auditors (usually CPA firms) may provide varying opinions relating to a firm's financial statements depending on how they evaluated its statements and its ongoing operations.

a. Unqualified Opinion: This type of opinion means that the auditing firm has no reservations about fairness in the representation of a company's financial statements, and their conformity with generally accepted accounting principles (GAAP).

b. Qualified Opinion: This type of opinion means that the auditing firm has some limited reservations as to the fairness of the representation. The limitation generally results from the auditor's failure to obtain sufficient objective and verifiable evidence in support of certain of the business transactions being audited.

c. Adverse Opinion: This is the term used when an auditor reports that the company's financial statements do not present fairly the financial position, results of operations or changes in financial position, or are not in conformity with GAAP. The auditor must provide the reasons for the adverse opinion in the audit report. An adverse opinion is rare and usually results when the auditor has been unable to convince the client to amend the financial statements so that they reflect the auditor's estimate about the outcome of future events or so that they adhere to GAAP.

d. Disclaimer: This is actually a form of "non-opinion" rendered by an auditor when insufficient competent evidential matter exists to form an audit opinion. This can occur when audit scope limitations exist, or uncertainties (e.g., lawsuits) are such that the auditor cannot reasonably predict their ultimate outcome, which may have significantly adverse effects on the firm.

e. Going Concern: In this case, the auditor is actually commenting on the future prospects of the firm, rather than the accuracy of the financial statements. The question being answered in this opinion is whether or not the firm will be around in the future (i.e., is the firm a going concern or a candidate for bankruptcy?).

2. Auditing Standards

a. Fundamental Auditing Standards: These standards were codified in 1947 by the Auditing Standards Board of the American Institute of Certified Public Accountants (AICPA) and still guide auditors today. They require that the auditor: (1) be independent, (2) understand the organization's control structure sufficiently to perform the audit, (3) state whether the organization's financial statements are presented in accordance with GAAP and (4) state whether the information disclosed is reasonably adequate.

b. Statements on Auditing Standards (SAS): In 1972 the AICPA began issuing authoritative statements based on the fundamental auditing standards. These SASs guide auditors in specific applications of the more general principles. More than 65 SASs have been issued to date.

3. Audit Trail: An audit trail is a sequence of recorded data that permits tracing a transaction through the various steps taken to complete it.

- The purpose of an audit trail, or transaction trail, is to allow the transaction to be traced to its source. This is valuable to establish if and/or where errors occurred and to determine responsibility for the errors, as well as for the task of reconciling deposit, concentration and disbursement accounts.

- For example, if a treasury department sends a wire transfer from one of its accounts to a supplier, sufficient documentation should be maintained to determine at least the following: who requested the payment, who authorized the payment, when the payment was made, which accounts were involved and when posting was made to the supplier's record.

4. Internal Control Issues: Internal control primarily involves checks and balances and the monitoring of transactions, cash flows and other financial information within the firm. It helps to protect the firm from employee error and fraud.

a. Matching: When an invoice arrives, it is matched to the original purchase order to determine if a purchase order was in fact sent and/or if the invoice is in compliance with the terms of a contract covering the transaction. A further match is usually done to determine if the order was actually filled. The matching process looks for possible errors in amounts, prices, etc.

b. Verification: This process determines if a purchase order, for example, should be sent from the firm. By examining the signatures or the authorization codes, one can determine if the person placing the order has the authority to do so. Also important to determine are: (1) does the order comply with company policies and contracts? (2) is the "ship to" address valid?, and (3) is this a properly authorized transaction?

c. Separation of Duties: To protect the firm from possible fraud, internal control guidelines call for a separation of responsibilities in handling different aspects of a transaction.

- Each transaction goes through at least five steps: (1) authorization, (2) initiation, (3) approval, (4) execution and (5) recording.

- For example, a manager may authorize the purchase of a microcomputer. A subordinate is asked to initiate the paperwork. A computer committee approves the purchase, and the purchasing department is given permission to execute the transaction. The accounting department records data about the order and the payable created.

- It is desirable to have different individuals perform each of the five steps to reduce the possibility of mistakes and unauthorized transactions. As another example, the person preparing and sending checks should not be the person reconciling the firm's corporate checkbook. Both separations make it harder for someone to misuse the firm's assets.
- Care must be taken in using computer programmers to write systems that should be separated. A programmer who helps design and program the check-writing system should not also help design and program the reconciliation system.

d. Audit Tests: One role of the auditor is to substantiate the details of account balances to ensure they are fairly stated.

- For example, if accounts receivable are reported to total $3 million, the auditor must determine if that is materially correct. To do an audit test of the receivables balance, the auditor would: (1) determine a sample size required to give a good statistical representation of total receivables, (2) select the sample of documents to examine, (3) evaluate the sample documents compared to the accounting ledger, and (4) verify balances on loans, investments and amounts of credit.
- This evaluation will allow the auditor to make an estimate of any misstatement of receivables. If the error is large, further sampling may be required. If small, the error may be immaterial to the financial reports to which the auditor must attest.

5. Security of Treasury Systems: Part of the auditor's concern is to observe and comment on security measures. There are many levels and forms of security designed to protect the firm's assets and protect the integrity of data. In most cases, the items discussed below are technical methods for reducing the riskiness in managing a firm's treasury management system. Overall, risk can be reduced because people are being "taken out of the loop," and the accounting and auditing processes are being automated.

a. Physical Restrictions: Restrictions are placed on paper documents or computer equipment.

- The first level of defense against unauthorized access to treasury systems is physical restriction. For example, check stock should be kept in securely locked areas with only limited access permitted.
- Computer hardware that allows access to sensitive information should be kept in secure areas. Disk drives and other magnetic or optical storage devices with sensitive data should be kept secure.
- Computer hardware that can access a bank should be kept locked when not in use.

b. Password and Other Personal Restrictions: The second line of defense for computer systems is software control programs.

- Control programs may be equipped with password protection to prevent persons from entering programs (or parts of programs) for which they lack authorization.

- Password protection is common in treasury management systems, particularly in modules that permit the user to initiate wire transfers or other payments.

- Other ways of verifying user identities have been developed, such as magnetic cards, biological sensing devices, fingerprint or voice recognition, and personal information other than passwords (e.g., birth dates, maiden names, etc.).

c. **Communications Restrictions:** Many banks and other information processors have call-back systems that prevent acceptance of communications from unauthorized sources.

- For example, a firm calls the bank with wire transfer instructions. The bank receives the call, records the firm's identifying numbers and hangs up. Then the bank computer calls the firm back at a pre-arranged number and, once the call has been acknowledged, proceeds to accept wire transfer instructions from authorized personnel.

- An unauthorized computer user attempting to enter the wire transfer system probably would not be equipped to receive the call-back from the bank, so the communication would be voided.

d. **Pre-Formatting Payment and Order Instructions:** A pre-formatted wire transfer agreement with a bank means that only wire transfer instructions of a certain type are acceptable from the sender.

- For example, the bank may be given a list of eight accounts to which wire transfers may be sent. If someone from the firm attempts to send a wire to an account that is not on the list, the bank refuses unless the instructions are validated in advance. When a firm makes frequent wire transfers to a particular payee, a repetitive or semi-repetitive wire may be used. The repetitive wire allows only the date and the dollar amount of the transfer to be changed, with the payee and description of transfer remaining constant. A semi-repetitive wire allows the description to be changed as well as the date and the dollar amount.

- The same concept applies to purchase orders. A firm may program its purchasing system to send orders only to a certain approved list of suppliers or certain "ship-to" addresses. This reduces the possibility of unauthorized orders. Such measures may be taken whether or not the firm uses a computer system.

e. **Encryption and Authentication:**

- An encryption process converts data into a scrambled form that can be read only by a party having the encryption key. Encryption is most widely used for scrambling transmitted data, but may also be used for scrambling stored data.

- Authentication uses some of the same algorithms as encryption to form a message authentication code unique to a particular message. When the message in plain form is sent, the authentication code is sent along with it. The receiving party, using an encryption key, can generate a second authentication code. If the sender's and receiver's authentication codes are identical, the receiver knows that the message has been received without modification.

- The purpose of encryption is to hide data from unauthorized parties while the purpose of authentication is to provide the receiver with a way to independently verify that the data have been received without alteration.

- Some treasurers use encryption and/or authentication in sending payment instructions to a financial institution or in sending sensitive business plans.

f. Virus Protection: A virus is an executable computer code that causes unwanted and sometimes destructive effects in a computer system, and that may replicate itself for transmission to other computers. The effects might be, for example, filling all available space in the computer's memory or erasing data on a hard disk. Viruses are transferred from one machine to another via the importation of contaminated programs, from contaminated disks or from direct connections with other computers. Protective measures against viruses include:

1. Avoid bulletin boards and "free" or pirated software.

2. Use a virus protection program that detects viruses.

3. Isolate new software programs before bringing them up on a distributed system.

g. Electronic Data Interchange (EDI): EDI is the electronic exchange of data in a structured format that does not require the intervention of manual processes. Many business documents, such as purchase orders, invoices, transportation documents and payments have been standardized by national and international user committees. The use of EDI promises to reduce error rates, improve auditing procedures, increase management control of vital information and lower the cost of exchanging data. This topic is covered in detail in Chapter 13.

h. Bar Coding: Bar coding helps in the capture of information in automated processes. Because bar coding does not rely on manually keyed data, error rates in data processing can be significantly reduced. Bar coding and EDI are often combined. For example, a shipper captures bar-coded shipping data on a packing carton and incorporates the data in an EDI message to the intended recipient of the package. Upon receipt of the shipment, the recipient scans the bar code data and matches its data against the EDI shipping information and original purchase order.

D. Ethical Issues in Treasury Management

1. Areas of Ethical Concern for Treasurers: Treasurers have ethical obligations to a number of constituencies:

a. Employers: who employ them and depend upon them for vital information, sound decision-making and diligent effort.

b. Shareholders: who depend on them for accurate information, conservation of scarce resources and financial rewards.

c. Bondholders and Creditors: who depend on them for accurate information, adherence to covenants, and timely interest payment and debt retirement.

d. Banks: that provide financial services and loans.

e. Suppliers: who provide goods and services and expect payment and information.

f. Government Agencies: that receive information and tax revenues from them and regulate some of their activities.

g. Employees: who receive direction, compensation and career guidance and training from them.

h. Communities: in which the treasurer and the firm reside.

2. Codes of Conduct: To guide the actions of employees toward these constituencies, many firms have codes of ethics or codes of conduct. Some even have a code specifically for treasurers. The Code of Conduct adopted by the Treasury Management Association (TMA) is an example, and a copy is provided at the end of this chapter.

3. Fair Compensation for Banking Services: In the early 1980s, many companies used highly aggressive cash management practices that placed some of the smaller banks they dealt with at a disadvantage. Those companies had excellent reporting systems that provided accurate and timely information on check-clearing times. These systems were frequently superior to those at many of the smaller collection banks where funds were deposited for later concentration into a single account. The collection banks often granted availability for deposited funds earlier than the clearing times that they and the Federal Reserve actually experienced. By channeling check deposits through unsophisticated banks that treated ledger balances as if they were available balances, a firm could effectively borrow interest free from the banks by withdrawing funds before they were collected. This is often referred to as creating circular cash flows. Firms may want to consider the following guidelines concerning this problem area:

a. Written Agreements: Agreements with banks concerning deposit and transfer practices should spell out how overdrafts (ledger and available) will be treated.

b. Circular Cash Flows: Firms should avoid deposits and other account transactions that are not directly connected to business activity. In other words, avoid circular cash flows (described in the above example) that could lead to uncompensated, available balance overdrafts.

c. Improper Incentive Programs: These are programs that give benefits indirectly to those who engage in questionable cash management practices. Firms should review incentive programs to ensure that they are devoid of all such illegal practices.

d. Bank Account Analysis Statements: Firms should demand regular account analysis statements from banks that provide cash management services. If such statements are impossible to obtain, the firm may want to make its own account analysis. The analysis should detail the costs for each line item charge on a per-item-detail basis.

4. Ethical Issues in Disbursement System Design: In attempting to accelerate cash inflows, almost any practice is considered ethical. On the other hand, some methods of slowing cash outflows may raise serious issues of ethical and even illegal conduct.

a. Questionable Disbursement Practices: These may include:

- Physically or magnetically damaging a check so it cannot be easily processed by automated equipment.

- Writing the check for an amount different from the invoiced amount solely to extend processing time.

- Creating intentional errors on checks (post-dated, no signature, non-matching dollar and written amounts, etc.).

b. Remote versus Controlled Disbursing: Remote disbursing involves utilizing geographically remote, smaller banks for the disbursement of checks in order to gain additional clearing float time on the check. This is considered an overly aggressive cash management practice because the intent is to maximize disbursement float at the expense of either the payee or the clearing system. The Federal Reserve has made significant improvements in the clearing system over the last 10 years that eliminate much of the potential benefit from this practice.

Controlled disbursing, on the other hand, is primarily designed to consolidate disbursement at a few key bank locations, providing better information for the company and greater certainty in funding disbursement accounts. Generally, controlled disbursement systems use zero-balance accounts (ZBAs), which are not funded until the checks are presented. The bank provides the firm with check-clearing information at each presentment so that the firm can determine the amount of funding required.

5. Investment Programs: Some investment practices may call into question the treasurer's ethical responsibilities to employers and investors. The treasurer is responsible for protecting the principal of the firm's short-term portfolio and, at the same time, is rewarded for producing high returns. These objectives conflict, and ethical conduct demands a careful balancing of the two dimensions: risk and return.

a. Speculating on Interest Rate Movements:

- The key issue in any type of speculative investment is whether or not it is approved practice in accordance with the firm's investment guidelines. Due to the potential for significant losses, a treasurer should be sure to get this authority in writing or as part of an approved written investment policy, usually approved by the board of directors.

- To gain extra returns on the short-term portfolio, a treasurer may be tempted to invest more funds than is wise in longer-term securities. This is because the yield curve is usually upward-sloping. A higher return rewards longer-term investments. If the yield curve remains upward-sloping, and the level remains the same from the time of purchase to the time of sale, a higher return will be realized than had the treasurer invested in a short-term security.

- This practice is sometimes called "riding the yield curve." The danger is, of course, that the yield curve will shift in level or slope, causing the security to lose value at the time it must be sold. This may cause the realized yield to be far below that expected.

- It is possible to have negative yields if rates rise enough. Because of these dangers, some treasury codes of conduct and investment policies prohibit a firm from speculating on interest rate movements. Instead, they stipulate that the treasurer must invest in securities that mature when cash outflows are expected to occur.

- This is a valid strategy as long as it is permitted by investment guidelines and is in line with the risk profile the firm has set for its investment portfolio. This topic is covered in detail in Chapter 8.

b. Speculating in Risky or Less Liquid Securities:

- Higher returns are possible when securities are viewed by the market as more risky or less liquid. Therefore, treasurers are tempted to invest in such securities to bolster returns on the short-term portfolio.

- To prevent such investments, some firms produce an "acceptable" list of securities that are relatively safe and liquid, and audit the portfolio on a regular basis to ensure that proper guidelines are being followed and only securities on the acceptable list are being purchased. The firm may place constraints on the make-up of the short-term investment portfolio that permit only a certain percentage of higher risk or less liquid security investments.

c. Over-Leveraging: With modern financial instruments, such as futures contracts or options, it is possible to take a highly leveraged position that exposes the firm to extreme profit or loss.

- For example, a treasurer may sell or buy futures contracts on Treasury bills. An investment of only about $1,500 controls a Treasury bill worth $1 million. If the market moves in the wrong direction, the firm could lose much more than the $1,500 in only a few days.

- To protect against taking such high-risk positions, the firm's investment policy may prohibit investment in futures contracts or in options, or may require that such contracts or options be used only for hedging and not for speculation. If the firm owns a Treasury bill, then selling or buying a futures contract against it may not create excessive risk.

IV. Chapter Checklist

A. Summary of International Tax Codes

IRS Publication 515 is represented on the next two pages.[5]

B. Checklist of Laws/Dates in Treasury Management

Federal Legislation

1. *Federal Reserve Act (1913)*—This legislative act is the foundation for the current banking system, giving the Federal Reserve supervisory power over banks and empowering the Fed to create a check collection and settlement system through member banks.

Table 1
Withholding Tax Rates on Income Other Than Personal Service Income under Chapter 3, Internal Revenue Code, and Income Tax Treaties—For Withholding in 1994

| Income code number | | 1 | 2 | 3 | Dividends paid by | | 9 | 10 | Copyright royalties | | 13 | 14 |
| Country of residence of payee | | Interest paid by U.S. obligors General | Interest on real property mortgages | Interest paid to controlling foreign corporations | 6 U.S. Corporations General | 7 U.S. subsidiaries to foreign parent corporations | Capital Gains | Industrial Royalties | 11 Motion Pictures and Television | 12 Other | Real Property Income and Natural Resources Royalties | Pensions and Annuities |
Name	Code											
Australia	AS	10	10	10	15	15	30	10	10	10	30	0
Austria	AU	0	30	0	15	5	30	0	10	0	30	0
Barbados	BB	12½	12½	12½	15	5	0	12½	12½	12½	30	0
Belgium	BE	15	15	15	15	5	0	0	0	0	30	0
Canada	CA	15	15	15	15	10	30	10	10	0	30	15
China, People's Republic of	CH	10	10	10	10	10	30	10	10	10	30	0
Commonwealth of Independent States and Georgia		0	30	30	30	30	0	0	0	0	30	30
Cyprus	CY	10	10	10	15	5	0	0	0	0	30	0
Denmark	DA	0	0	0	15	5	30	0	0	0	30	0
Egypt	EG	15	30	15	15	5	0	0	0	15	30	0
Finland	FI	0	0	0	15	5	0	5	0	0	30	0
France	FR	0	0	0	15	5	0	5	0	0	30	0
Germany	GM	0	0	0	15	5	0	0	0	0	30	0
Greece	GR	0	0	30	30	30	30	0	30	0	30	0
Hungary	HU	0	0	0	15	5	0	0	0	0	30	0
Iceland	IC	0	0	0	15	5	0	0	30	0	30	0
India	IN	15	15	15	25	15	30	10	20	20	30	0
Indonesia	ID	15	15	15	15	15	0	10	15	15	30	15
Ireland	EI	0	0	30	15	5	30	0	0	0	15	0
Italy	IT	15	15	15	15	5	0	10	8	5	30	0
Jamaica	JM	12½	12½	12½	15	10	0	10	10	10	30	0
Japan	JA	10	10	10	15	10	0	10	10	10	30	0
Korea, Republic of	KS	12	12	12	15	10	0	15	10	10	15	0
Luxembourg	LU	0	30	0	15	5	30	0	0	0	30	0
Malta	MT	12½	12½	12½	15	5	0	12½	12½	0	30	0

Table 1 (Continued)

Income code number		1	2	3	6	7	9	10	11	12	13	14
Country of residence of payee					Dividends paid by				Copyright royalties			
Name	Code	Interest paid by U.S. obligors General	Interest on real property mortgages	Interest paid to controlling foreign corporations	U.S. Corporations General	U.S. subsidiaries to foreign parent corporations	Capital Gains	Industrial Royalties	Motion Pictures and Television	Other	Real Property Income and Natural Resources Royalties	Pensions and Annuities
Morocco	MO	15	15	15	15	10	10	10	10	10	30	0
Netherlands	NL	0	0	0	15	5	10	0	0	0	30	0
Netherlands Antilles, Aruba	NA, AA	0	30	30	30	30	30	30	30	30	30	30
New Zealand	NZ	10	10	10	15	15	10	10	10	10	30	0
Norway	NO	0	0	0	15	15	10	0	0	0	30	0
Pakistan	PK	30	30	30	30	15	30	0	30	0	30	0
Philippines	RP	15	15	15	25	20	0	15	15	15	30	30
Poland	PL	0	0	0	15	5	0	10	10	10	30	30
Romania	RO	10	10	10	10	10	0	15	10	10	30	0
Spain	SP	10	10	10	15	10	0	8	10	5	30	0
Sweden	SW	0	0	0	15	5	0	0	0	0	30	0
Switzerland	SZ	5	5	5	15	5	30	0	0	0	30	0
Trinidad & Tobago	TD	30	30	30	30	30	30	15	30	0	30	0
Tunisia	TS	15	15	15	20	14	0	10	15	15	30	0
United Kingdom	UK	0	0	0	15	5	30	0	0	0	30	0
Other countries		30	30	30	30	30	30	30	30	30	30	30

NOTE: All figures are percentages.

2. *Edge Act (1918)*—This legislative act permitted U.S. banks to invest in corporations that engage in international banking and finance. Subsidiaries could be established to conduct international banking business such as import and export financing, foreign exchange, letters of credit and documentary collections in other cities as well as overseas.

3. *McFadden Act (1927)*—This legislative act prohibited banks from accepting deposits across state lines, and prohibited branching across state lines unless approved by state governments.

4. *Glass-Steagall Act (Banking Act of 1933)*—This legislative act defines the legal barriers that separate investment and commercial banking. It: (1) required the Fed to establish interest-rate ceilings on all types of accounts, (2) prohibited the payment of interest on demand deposits, and (3) created the FDIC.

5. *Electronic Funds Transfer Act (EFTA/1978)*—This legislative act outlines the rights and responsibilities of individuals using EFT services (Reg E).

6. *Depository Institutions Deregulation and Monetary Control Act (DID-MCA/1980)*—This legislative act: (1) allows banks to offer unregulated interest-bearing accounts, (2) makes Federal Reserve services available to all deposit-taking institutions, (3) requires all deposit-taking institutions to keep reserves at the Fed, and (4) mandates that the Fed reduce and/or price float.

7. *Garn-St. Germain Depository Institutions Act (1982)*—This legislative act: (1) allows banks to offer accounts that are competitive with mutual funds, (2) allows increased bank lending limits to any one individual borrower, and (3) allows banks to merge with out-of-state partners.

8. *Expedited Funds Availability Act (EFAA/1988)*—This legislative act governs payable through-draft and check return policies, as well as check availability time periods (Reg CC).

9. *Financial Institutions Reform, Recovery, and Enforcement Act (FIR-REA/1989)*—This legislative act: (1) consolidated and dismantled several government regulatory bodies, (2) requires the Resolution Trust Corporation (RTC) to dispose of assets of failed S&Ls in a timely fashion, and (3) gives the FDIC the authority to raise deposit insurance premiums on a risk-adjusted basis.

Federal Reserve Regulations

1. *Regulation D*—This regulation governs reserve requirements by type of account.

2. *Regulation E*—This regulation provides records of EFT transactions, protects consumers using EFT systems, and outlines the rights and obligations of all parties in an EFT transaction.

3. *Regulation J*—This regulation governs check collection and settlement through the Federal Reserve System.

4. *Regulation Q*—This regulation prevents banks from paying interest on the demand deposit accounts of corporations.

5. **Regulation CC**—This regulation requires banks to provide customers with information pertaining to funds availability, to return checks drawn on insufficient funds on a timely basis, and created new endorsement requirements and procedures.

C. TMA Code of Conduct

The conduct of treasury professionals has a direct effect on the reputation of the treasury management profession. A good reputation is earned on a continuing basis by conducting one's business with competence, appropriate confidentiality, integrity, and by complying with applicable laws and regulations. Treasury professionals, therefore, have an obligation to their employers, colleagues, customers, profession and themselves to maintain the highest standards of conduct and to encourage their peers to do likewise.

In recognition of this obligation, the Treasury Management Association (TMA) has adopted the following Standards of Ethical Conduct and recommends that members and Certified Cash Managers (CCMs) acknowledge and maintain the following Standards:

Competence

1. Continue to acquire an appropriate level of professional knowledge and skill in the treasury management field.

2. Perform professional duties in accordance with technical, legal, and regulatory practices in the field of treasury management.

Confidentiality

3. Refrain from disclosing confidential information acquired in the course of professional activities unless legally obligated to do so.

4. Refrain from using or appearing to use confidential information for unethical or illegal advantage either personally or through third parties.

Integrity

5. Refrain from participating in any activity that would prejudice the ability to carry out professional responsibilities competently, honestly, and fairly while avoiding conflicts of interest or the appearance thereof.

6. Refrain from the intentional abuses of financial systems and markets.

7. Disclose fully all relevant information that could reasonably be expected to influence business dealings.

8. Refrain from using the Certified Cash Manager (CCM) designation unless the certificate is active.

V. Suggestions for References and Additional Reading

Due to the wide variety and topicality of the subjects covered in this chapter, we list below some additional reference materials for each major category.

A. Taxation: A widely used text covering managerial implications of federal taxes is found in *Federal Taxes and Management Decisions,* 1988–1990 Edition, by Ray M.

Sommerfeld, Irwin, Homewood, IL, 1989. Another comprehensive treatment of corporate tax issues is found in *Corporate Taxation, 3rd Edition,* by D.A. Kahn and P.B. Gann, West Publishing, St. Paul, MN, 1989. Tax-exempt securities are outlined in "Finding the Fattest After-Tax Sandwich," by Paul Sandford, *Corporate Cashflow,* March 1990, pp. 29–31.

B. Legal Issues: Legal terminology is explained in *Black's Law Dictionary, 5th Edition,* by Henry Campbell Black, West Publishing, St. Paul, MN, 1979. Another helpful reference particularly useful in treasury management is *Prentice-Hall Dictionary of Business, Finance and Law* by Michael Downey Rice, Prentice-Hall, Englewood Cliffs, NJ, 1983. There are many excellent textbooks covering business law. One widely used text is *West's Business Law: Text, Cases and Legal Environment* by Kenneth W. Clarkson, Roger L. Miller, Gaylord A. Jentz, and Frank B. Cross, West Publishing, St. Paul, 1989. A compact treatment of elementary business law for smaller corporations can be found in *Business Law* by Christopher Dungan and Donald Ridings, Barron's, New York, 1990.

C. Audit and Security: An excellent overview of the auditing function is found in *Auditing: An Integrated Approach, 4th Edition,* by Alvin A. Arens and James K. Loebbecke, Prentice-Hall, Englewood Cliffs, NJ, 1988. Treasury security issues are discussed in three articles in the *Journal of Cash Management,* (1) "Security in Treasury Management: The Forgotten Exposure," Paul J. Beehler, March/April 1985, pp. 28–32; (2) "Treasury Controls," by Andrea H. Bierce and Diane H. McDevitt, November/December 1986, pp. 26–28; and (3) "What You Should Know About Treasury System Security," by John Van den Bergh and Kenneth J. Frier, November/December 1987, pp. 69–72.

D. Ethics: The primary reference here is the TMA Code of Ethics, reprinted in the chapter checklist section of this chapter.

VI. Endnotes

1. See: *Handbook of Modern Finance,* Chapter 45, International Accounting, edited by Dennis Logue, Warren, Gorham & Lamont, publishers.

2. The Financial Accounting Standards Board (FASB) issued *Statement of Financial Accounting Standards No. 52—Foreign Currency Translation* in December 1981. This Standard deals with two major issues: accounting for foreign currency transactions and the translation of foreign currency financial statements.

3. See: Chapter 9, *International Financial Management,* Jeff Madura, West Publishers, 1989.

4 See: Chapter 19, *International Financial Management,* Jeff Madura, West Publishers, 1989.

5. The table is copied from IRS Publication 515, "Withholding of Tax on Nonresident Aliens and Foreign Corporations (For Withholding in 1994)."

Index

investment banker and, 64-65
registration of issue, 65-66, 67
selling/issuing stock, 66-67
insider trading. *See* legal issues.
insurance, 1, 2, 4, 371-372, 377-378. *See also* risk management.
brokers and, 379, 385-386
business interruption, 370
captives and, 377, 381-382
cash flow casualty retro programs, 378
deductibles, 380
difference in conditions (DIC), 370
directors and officers, 370
as employee benefit, 371
excess and umbrella, 369
exclusions policies, 371
fidelity and crime, 370-371
group captives and, 378
insurers, 379-380
liability, 369, 384
liability limits, 380-381
negotiating programs, 379-381, 384-385
non-insurance, 376
ocean/marine policies, 371
property and casualty, 369-370
self-insurance, 376-377
special multiperil, 371
workers' compensation, 371
insurance brokers, 5
insurance companies, 10
insurance underwriters, 5
interest, 11, 12, 17
interest rates, 5, 13, 14, 17, 19, 20, 22, 126, 201, 218, 441-442. *See also* London Interbank Offered Rate; prime rate.
caps on, 34
collars on, 34
floors on, 34
forward rate agreements (FRAs), 35
inventories, 1, 2, 274
borrowing on, 193
conversion period, 177-178
cost/benefit tradeoffs and, 243
economic order quantity (EOQ) models, 243-244
financing, 3, 246-248
just-in-time method, 244-246
managing, 3, 240-246
transaction costs and, 245-246
types of, 241
use of, 240
inventory accounting, 257, 284-285
IRS, 144, 145, 332, 392

J–K–L

just-in-time (JIT) models, 3, 244-246

leases and leasing, 2, 3, 274, 339-342
combination, 332
components of, 336-337
computer model, 335
depreciation tax savings, 335
estimated residual value and, 335
evaluation by lessee, 333-334
evaluation by lessor, 334
financial (capital), 331
financial statement effects and, 333
leveraged lease analysis, 334-335
1986 Tax Act and, 335-336
operating, 330-331
sale and leaseback, 330
tax considerations and, 332
legal issues, 1, 2, 4
antitrust laws, 431-432
banking services laws, 429-431
bankruptcy, 433
environmental law, 434
insider trading rules, 434
laws relating to payments, 432-433
letters of credit, 14, 15, 193, 210-211
leveraged buyouts (LBOs), 17, 69-70, 163
liabilities
maturities of, 12
liens, 20
lines of credit, 11, 14, 193, 209, 216-217, 235
liquidity, 199-200, 227, 260
liquidity preference theory, 201-202
liquidity ratios, 260-261, 275
loan agreements, 212
loans. *See also* borrowing, short-term.
asset based, 211-212, 218, 247-248
bank, 14, 186, 193
collateralized, 211, 247
equipment, 14, 17
fixed-rate, 215
secured, 211
single-payment, 209
term, 15, 193, 210
term sheet, 231-233
troubled, 213
unsecured, 211
variable rate, 215
London Interbank Offered Rate (LIBOR), 14, 18

M

McFadden Act, 429, 445